## DATE DUE

# CURRICULUM AND TEACHING STRATEGIES
## FOR STUDENTS WITH BEHAVIORAL DISORDERS

# CURRICULUM AND TEACHING STRATEGIES
## FOR STUDENTS
## WITH BEHAVIORAL
## DISORDERS

DAVID B. CENTER
*Georgia State University*

PRENTICE HALL, Englewood Cliffs, New Jersey 07632

Library of Congress Cataloging-in-Publication Data

Center, David B.
    Curriculum and teaching strategies for students with behavioral
disorders / David B. Center.
        p.    cm.
    Bibliography: p.
    Includes index.
    ISBN 0-13-195504-7
    1. Problem children--Education--United States.  2. Behavior
disorders in children--United States.  3. Special education--United
States.    I. Title.
LC4802.C46 1989
371.93'0973--dc19                                      88-29264
                                                          CIP

Editorial/production supervision
  and interior design:  Virginia L. McCarthy
Cover design:  Lundgren Graphics, Ltd.
Manufacturing buyer:  Peter Havens

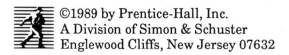 ©1989 by Prentice-Hall, Inc.
A Division of Simon & Schuster
Englewood Cliffs, New Jersey 07632

Printed in the United States of America

10  9  8  7  6  5  4  3  2  1

ISBN 0-13-195504-7

Prentice-Hall International (UK) Limited, *London*
Prentice-Hall of Australia Pty. Limited, *Sydney*
Prentice-Hall Canada Inc., *Toronto*
Prentice-Hall Hispanoamericana, S.A., *Mexico*
Prentice-Hall of India Private Limited, *New Delhi*
Prentice-Hall of Japan, Inc., *Tokyo*
Simon & Schuster Asia Pte. Ltd., *Singapore*
Editora Prentice-Hall do Brasil, Ltda., *Rio de Janeiro*

This book is dedicated to my parents, Dr. and Mrs. William R. Center; my wife and children, Shirley, Brian, and Daniel; and to the many students and colleagues who have influenced me over the course of my professional career.

# CONTENTS

# PREFACE

This is a methods book intended for teachers of students with behavioral disorders (BD). A methods book, in my opinion, should be limited to considerations appropriate after a student has been identified and placed in a BD program. The book is based on 15 years' experience teaching BD students and teaching BD methods to teachers in university courses. During the 10 years that I have been teaching this course, I have not found a text that met my conception of what should be in such a course and have usually taught the course without an official textbook.

My major objections to existing texts have been twofold. First, most of the texts I have examined have been of the smorgasbord variety. These texts attempt to cover every possible approach and in doing so cover none in sufficient depth to be useful. Second, the texts that do go into some detail often do not cover all of the major programming areas that I think teachers need to be prepared to address in their classes. In addition, many of these texts do not provide a balance between different approaches to BD programming.

In this text, I have tried to address the major programming areas that need to be addressed based on the definition of "seriously emotionally disturbed" in P.L. 94-142. I have also provided a chapter-length discussion of each approach covered, including numerous references for additional reading. In doing so, I think I have provided enough detail on each approach to be useful. In those chapters where it is appropriate, I have tried to cover developmental considerations in using the approach and to suggest materials appropriate for elementary- and for secondary-level students. Finally, I have attempted to strike a balance between behavioral and cognitive approaches to programming for behavior-disordered students.

A teacher who has mastered the material in this text should, in my opinion, be prepared to provide programming for most problems encountered in BD students and be able to do so with either or both behavioral and cognitive strategies. While some may differ with me in my selection of approaches and may have their own idea of what are the best approaches, I have attempted to base my selections on several criteria. First, I tried to select approaches essentially "educational," using that term in a broad sense. Second, I tried to select approaches with a body of educational resources and materials available or for which materials could be developed by a classroom teacher. Third, I tried to select approaches that appeared to have sufficient research support to lend them some credibility. Finally, I tried to select approaches that provided a balance between behavioral and cognitive strategies.

I sincerely hope that the resulting text will be useful to both university and classroom teachers. I would appreciate hearing from anyone using the book who has constructive suggestions about how the text might be improved or who has discovered errors in the book. If I can be of any assistance to anyone using the text, I will be happy to lend whatever assistance I can.

D.B.C.

# CURRICULUM AND TEACHING STRATEGIES
## FOR STUDENTS WITH BEHAVIORAL DISORDERS

# 1

# CHILDREN AND YOUTH WITH BEHAVIORAL DISORDERS

## INTRODUCTION

George Albee (1968), in an address before the National Association for Mental Health, discussed the mental health needs of Americans. Albee argued that mental health demands and the supply of manpower to meet them would probably never reach a balance. He argued that need would probably always outstrip supply. In particular, Albee felt that the mental health needs of children and adolescents are neglected.

The cause of the problem, according to Albee, is two widely accepted myths. The first myth is that people who exhibit disturbed and disturbing behavior are sick. The second myth is that the mental health manpower picture is improving. Closely associated with the supply and demand problem is the conceptual model adopted by the mental health field, i.e., the medical model. Albee argued that the first myth is a direct product of the adoption of the medical model. In Albee's opinion, the medical model isn't supported by the research evidence. He believes that the type of professional, level of training, and treatment implied by the medical model make shortages of mental health professionals unavoidable.

The solution, in Albee's opinion, is to adopt a new model. The model favored by Albee is an educational model. An educational model suggests a three-part solution to the service problem: first, a new class of professionals who are more like school teachers than like psychiatrists and psychologists; second, a new type of service delivery facility more like a school than like a hospital or clinic; and finally, an approach to intervention more like reeducation and rehabilitation than like psychotherapy.

A mechanism for delivering services to children and adolescents similiar to what Albee suggested is special education. We special educators are comfortable with an educational approach to problems. Special educators trained to work with behavior disordered students are a class of professionals similar to that proposed by Albee. Special education classes for behavior-disordered students approximate the service facility proposed by Albee. Finally, special education programming for academic, social, and emotional problems is a reeducation approach to treatment. Not only does special education have service delivery personnel, facilities, and approaches similar to the solution proposed by Albee, but we also have a legal mandate in P.L. 94-142 to implement it.

### Definition

The population that we are charged with serving under the provisions of P.L. 94-142 is defined below.

34 C.F.R. 300.5(b)(8) provides:
*seriously emotionally disturbed* is defined as follows.

(i) The term means a condition exhibiting one or more of the following characteristics over a long period of time and to a marked degree, which adversely affects educational performance.

A. An inability to learn which cannot be explained by intellectual, sensory, or other health factors.

B. An inability to build or maintain satisfactory interpersonal relationships with peers and teachers.

C. Inappropriate types of behavior or feelings under normal circumstances.

D. A general pervasive mood of unhappiness or depression.

E. A tendency to develop physical symptoms or fears associated with personal or school problems.

(ii) The term includes children who are schizophrenic. The term does not include children who are socially maladjusted unless it is determined that they are seriously emotionally disturbed.

In my opinion, a reasonable interpretation of this definition implies the following.

1. The problem is present over a long period of time, that is, for a minimum of six months to one year (part i).

2. The problem is exhibited in a significant way. It must be overt and observable to the untrained "eye," not just indicated by an assessment device such as a personality test (part i).

3. The problem must adversely affect educational performance. Performance should be at least one standard deviation below expectations for the student, taking into consideration years in school, intellectual potential, and opportunity to learn (part i).

4. In addition, a student must meet one or more of the following characteristics.

    a. An inability to learn that cannot be explained by other conditions. The problem adversely affects academic performance. This clause would exclude students whose academic deficits can be explained by other handicaps.

    b. An inability to build or maintain satisfactory relationships. A student lacks the social skills necessary for satisfactory interpersonal relations.

    c. (1) Inappropriate types of behavior...under normal conditions. A student exhibits inappropriate social behavior under normal conditions.

       (2) Inappropriate types of...feelings under normal conditions. A student exhibits inappropriate emotional behavior under normal conditions.

    d. A general pervasive mood of unhappiness or depression. A student exhibits a uniform and excessive state of depressed affect. Some authorities would include as depression a condition called *masked depression*. Masked depression, particularly in children and youth, is suggested by such problems as delinquent behavior, rebelliousness, psychopathic behavior, hyperactivity, and school failure (Malmquist, 1972).

    e. A tendency to develop physical symptoms or fears. A student exhibits an excessive state of anxiety, with such symptoms as abdominal complaints, migraine headaches, anorexia, and phobias.

5. Finally, the definition includes children or youth diagnosed as schizophrenic. These students' behavior appears to have no logical connection with environmental events going on around them. They often engage in excessive amounts of inappropriate and bizarre behavior, e.g., ritualistic behaviors and self-injurious behavior. These students also have significant behavioral deficits, e.g., lack of functional language and deficit self-help skills (part ii).

6. The definition does not include children diagnosed as infantile autistic. These are children who exhibit severe impairments, with characteristics similar to those described in (5) above. The autistic usually exhibit those characteristics prior to 30 months of age (part ii, as amended).

7. The definition does not include children who are socially maladjusted. This definition was written during the period when DSM-II was the accepted classification system. I assume that the term refers to social maladjustment as defined in that manual. That is to an individual "...thrown into an unfamiliar

culture or [with]...divided loyalties to two cultures..." (Ullmann & Krasner, 1975, p. 27). A socially maladjusted student can be classified as emotionally disturbed. The classification must, however, be made for some problem other than social maladjustment (part ii).

### Terminology

There has been a debate in progress since the passage of P.L. 94-142 about the label used for this population. The law uses the label "seriously emotionally disturbed" (SED). The Council for Children with Behavioral Disorders (CCBD), the professional organization concerned with the population, uses the label "behavior disordered" (BD). The CCBD (Huntze, 1985), in a position paper on the issue, discusses the rationale for the use of the label "behavior disordered." Briefly, the argument is as follows:

1. The label has greater utility for education.

2. The label isn't associated with any particular theory of causation.

3. The label promotes a more comprehensive approach to assessment.

4. The label is less stigmatizing.

5. The label is preferred by most professionals in the field.

6. The label is more descriptive of the population served.

The label used in P.L. 94-142 has important implications for interpretation of the definition. Slenkovich (1983) wrote a book-length analysis of the P.L. 94-142 definition keyed to the American Psychiatric Association's *Diagnostic and Statistical Manual*, third edition (DSM III). The book illustrates the interpretive debate. Center (1985), in a review of the book, shows how Slenkovich used the label "seriously emotionally disturbed" to interpret a phrase in the definition. The phrase reads, "The term means a condition...." The phrase is interpreted to read, "the term means an emotional condition...." As the analysis proceeds from this interpretation, the implications become clear. Slenkovich's interpretation allows, with a few exceptions, only those DSM III diagnoses involving disturbed thoughts and feelings, especially those disorders involving anxiety.

This is an unacceptable interpretation to many professionals. First, it is contrary to the intent of the author of the definition (Bower, 1982). Second, it is not consistent with the characteristics of the population served (Huntze, 1985). Third, it excludes most students whose classroom behavior is associated with their educational deficits (Swift & Spivack, 1969). Finally, it excludes most students that follow-up research suggests are in greatest need of service (Robins, 1979).

The term "behavioral disordered" is a generic term and includes all types of psychopathology (Anthony, 1970). In Table 1–1, the inclusiveness of the BD label is illustrated. As you can see, the BD label, used generically, applies to most types of disorders. Students would still have to meet the P.L. 94-142 definition before they would be eligible for special education services.

**Table 1-1**    A taxonomy of childhood behavior disorders

| CLASS | SUBCLASS | ITEMS OF DISORDERRED BEHAVIOR |
|---|---|---|
| I. Functional behavior | A. Eating | Anorexia, bulimia, food fads, pica, rumination |
| | B. Eliminating | Enuresis, encopresis, constipation, diarrhea, vomiting |
| | C. Sleeping | Nightmares, night terrors, sleepwalking, insomnia |
| | D. Moving | Hyperkinesis, tics, rocking, head banging, incoordination |
| | E. Speaking | Retarded speech, mutism, lisping, stammering |
| II. Cognitive behavior | A. Thinking | Prelogical, magical, concrete, amorphous, confused |
| | B. Remembering | Amnesia, forgetful, reduced memory span |
| | C. Learning | General and specific learning disability, pseudo-retardation |
| | D. Orienting | Disorientation in space, time, and identity |
| | E. Reality testing | Confusion of internal-external, subjective-objective |
| III. Affective behavior | A. Fearfulness | Single and multiple fears, cowardice, flight reactions |
| | B. Anxiety | Agitation, apprehension, panic, separation anxiety, tension habits |
| | C. Depression-elation | Sadness, grief, euphoria, clowning, nostalgia, despair |
| | D. Shame-guilt | Inferiority, inadequacy feelings, retribution, restitution |
| | E. Disgust | Anticontamination behavior |
| IV. Social behavior | A. Attacking | Aggressive, homicidal, suicidal, destructive |
| | B. Avoiding | Withdrawal, self-isolation, autism, daydreaming |

**Table 1-1**   Continued

| CLASS | SUBCLASS | ITEMS OF DISORDERRED BEHAVIOR |
|---|---|---|
| | C. Oppositional | Negativism, noncooperation, wilfulness, contrariness |
| | D. Dominance-submission | Bossy, controlling, egocentric-dependent, clinging |
| | E. Abnormal sexual | Masturbation, homosexuality, promiscuity, transvestitism |
| V. Integrative behavior | A. Poor impulse control | Hyperkinetic, undisciplined, incorrigible, impulsive |
| | B. Low frustration tolerance | Demands for immediate gratification |
| | C. Rigid-stereo-typed | Perseverative, repetitious, compulsive, stimulus-bound, inhibited |
| | D. Inadequate coping | Sense of helplessness |
| | E. Disorganized | Chaotic, aimless, disorderly, unplanful |

SOURCE: Anthony, 1970.

### Prevalence

The estimated prevalence of children with behavioral disorders is 2% of the school-age population (National Center for Educational Statistics, 1979). Recently, the school-age population of the United States and its territories was 42,540,000. Based on the prevalence figure above, there are potentially 850,800 behaviorally disordered students. Recently, the service level for BD students was .91%, which represents approximately 387,114 students served. These figures suggest that BD students are underidentified and underserved. A discussion of some reasons that this situation exists can be found in Long (1983). The rate of service is improving. During a recent seven-year period, the service level went from .64% to .91%. That is a 40% increase over the seven-year period, or a growth rate averaging 5.7% per year.

Many professionals believe that the 2% prevalence figure is conservative (Kauffman, 1985). Opinion about the true prevalence of behavioral disorders ranges as high as 10%. For example, Bower (1981) estimated that 10% of the school-age population would meet his definition. In a study by Rubin and Balow (1978), over a three-year period, 7.4% of the children studied were judged by all their teachers to have a behavior problem. The male-to-female ratio in this group was 3.23:1. Kauffman (1985) believes that most of the children identified by Rubin and Balow would meet the P.L. 94-142 definition.

## CLASSIFICATION

Quay (1979) discusses two major types of classification systems, qualitative and quantitative. The qualitative approach bases categories on observations of clinicians in field settings. Most qualitative classification systems suffer from a lack of demonstrated reliability and validity. The quantitative approach bases categories on statistical procedures. These procedures allow identification of related behaviors that occur together and form a distinct pattern. Since the quantitative approach is research based, it usually addresses reliability and validity better than does the qualitative approach.

### DSM III

DSM III is a qualitative approach to classification and represents the most widely used system. Rapoport and Ismond (1984) discuss in detail the application of this system to children. DSM III uses a five-axial approach to classification. The first two axes include all the diagnostic categories. A multiple diagnosis with components from both axes I and II is possible. Axis III includes factors important in understanding or treating a diagnosed condition. Axes IV and V are optional. Axis IV includes possible contributing factors in the diagnosed problem. Axis V covers factors important for determining the likely outcome of treatment. A brief outline of the five axes follows.

AXIS I:    Clinical syndromes, e.g., schizophrenic disorder

AXIS II:    Personality and developmental disorders, e.g., compulsive personality disorder

AXIS III:    Physical disorders, e.g., diabetes

AXIS IV:    Psychosocial stressors, e.g., rape

AXIS V:    Previous level of adaptive functioning, e.g., social skills

Each classification on axes I and II has a numerical code. The first three digits indicate the diagnostic category, e.g., 302 (conduct disorder). This three-digit code is followed by a decimal point and up to two additional digits. These digits show additional features of the diagnosis, e.g., 302.23 (conduct disorder, socialized, aggressive) or 301.20 (personality disorder, schizoid). Axis III is coded with a word or phrase for any associated physical condition, e.g., possible seizure disorder. Axis IV is coded using a scale of 0 to 7. Points on the scale estimate severity. Zero on the scale means unspecified, 1 means none, and 7 means catastrophic. Axis V is also coded using a scale of 0 to 7. Points on this scale estimate the level of adaptive functioning. Zero on the scale means unspecified, 1 means superior, and 7 means grossly impaired. Table 1–2 is a list of DSM III diagnoses for behavior-disordered children and youth. "Behavior-disordered" is used here as a generic label. A child or youth with one of these diagnoses would

**Table 1-2**  A list of most of the DSM III diagnoses that a child labeled "behavior-disordered" might have (example of a qualitative system)

| | |
|---|---|
| 295.xx | Schizophrenic disorders (five types that might apply) |
| 295.40 | Schizophreniform disorder |
| 296.xx | Major affective disorders (eight types that might apply) |
| 299.80 | Atypical pervasive developmental disorder: full syndrome present |
| 299.81 | Atypical pervasive developmental disorder: residual state |
| 299.90 | Childhood onset pervasive developmental disorder: full syndrome present |
| 299.91 | Pervasive developmental disorder: residual state |
| 300.xx | Anxiety disorders (eight types that might apply) |
| 300.11 | Conversion disorder |
| 301.20 | Schizoid personality disorder |
| 301.22 | Schizotypal personality disorder |
| 301.60 | Dependent personality disorder |
| 301.70 | Antisocial personality disorder |
| 301.82 | Avoidant personality disorder |
| 301.83 | Borderline personality disorder |
| 301.84 | Passive-aggressive personality disorder |
| 302.60 | Gender-identity disorder of childhood |
| 307.10 | Anorexia nervosa |
| 309.xx | Adjustment disorders (eight types that might apply) |
| 309.21 | Separation anxiety disorder |
| 312.00 | Conduct disorder, undersocialized, aggressive |
| 312.10 | Conduct disorder, undersocialized, nonaggressive |
| 312.23 | Conduct disorder, socialized, aggressive[a] |
| 312.21 | Conduct disorder, socialized, nonaggressive[a] |
| 313.00 | Overanxious disorder |
| 313.21 | Avoidant disorder of childhood or adolescence |
| 313.22 | Schizoid disorder of childhood or adolescence |
| 313.23 | Elective mutism |
| 313.81 | Oppositional disorder |
| 313.82 | Identity disorder |
| 314.01 | Attention deficit disorder with hyperactivity |

[a]This category would probably be excluded from special education because of the social maladjustment exception in P.L. 94-142.

still need to meet the criteria in the P.L. 94-142 definition. In other words, a DSM III diagnosis alone isn't sufficient grounds for special education services.

### Dimensional Classification

An example of a quantitative approach to classification is Quay's (1983) dimensional system. This classification system is based on behavior problems in children seen in hospitals, clinics, and schools. The data on these problems were analyzed using a statistical technique called *factor analysis*. This technique identifies behaviors that vary together and form patterns. Each pattern (factor) is given a name descriptive of the behavior problems in it. Quay (1983), in a revision of earlier work, identified six patterns or dimensions in children with behavior problems (see Table 1–3).

**Table 1–3**   A list of the problem behavior dimensions identified by Quay (1983) (example of a quantitative system)

I. Conduct disorder (CD)
II. Socialized aggression (SA)
III. Attention problems-immaturity (AP)
III. Anxiety-withdrawal (AW)
IV. Psychotic behavior (PB)
V. Motor excess (ME)

     Quay's six patterns represent a much briefer classification system than DSM III. Most DSM III diagnostic categories for children and youth will fit into Quay's six categories. Why is there such a difference in the number of categories between these two systems? Quay would say that his system has only six categories or dimensions because that is all that could be distinguished accurately. Conversely, he might argue that DSM III has a large number of categories and it is difficult to discriminate among them reliably. In other words, three clinicians giving a child a DSM III diagnosis might each assign a different diagnostic label.

     In this book, we will use a modified form of Quay's system to discuss the relationship between classification and methods. The modified system is presented in Table 1–4. The rationale for this modification is based on Anthony's (1970) taxonomy discussed earlier. In the modification, three of Quay's dimensions are reorganized. "Unsocialized aggressive" replaces Quay's "conduct disorder." "Conduct disorder" is used more broadly to cover unsocialized aggressive, socialized aggressive, and motor excess. All three of these subgroups fit Anthony's behavior classes for social and integrative behavior. Quay's dimension "anxiety-withdrawal" is changed to "emotional disorder" and fits Anthony's behavior classes for affective and social behavior. Quay's dimension "psychotic behavior" is changed to "psychotic disorder" and is related to all five classes of behavior in Anthony's taxonomy. Quay's dimension "attention problem-immaturity" is similar to the special education category "learning disabilities." It best fits Anthony's behavior classes for cognitive and integrative behavior. This dimension isn't included in our modified classification. "Learning disabilities" is a separate category in special education. Underachievement and learning problems are present, by definition, in all children and youth classified as be-

**Table 1–4**   A classification system based on a modification of Quay (1983)

I. Conduct disorder
  1. Unsocialized aggressive
  2. Socialized aggressive
  3. Motor excess
II. Emotional disorder
III. Psychotic disorder

havior disordered. However, these academic problems are not usually classified as learning disabilities under current practice.

### Conduct Disorder

*Unsocialized Aggressive.*   Members of this group are characterized by antisocial and acting-out behaviors. Usually, a lack of or insufficient socialization is the best way to account for the problems of this group. Some of the problems typically seen include fighting, disruption, argumentativeness, destructiveness, selfishness, and defiance.

*Socialized Aggressive.*   Members of this group are sometimes called *socialized delinquents*. Again, the most common problem is antisocial behavior. The behaviors are believed to be due, not to a failure in socialization, but to an atypical socialization. Socialization occurred but in a subculture with values and expectations different from the mainstream culture. The behaviors exhibited are not deviant in the subculture in which socialization occurred. The problems typically seen in this group are similar to those given for the unsocialized aggressive. What distinguishes this group from the unsocialized aggressive is the fact that problem behaviors occur in a gang or group. Much of the deviant socialization may take place in the deviant peer group through "differential association" (Sutherland & Cressey, 1970). This group is considered socially maladjusted by some educators. The socially maladjusted do not qualify for special education services under P.L. 94-142, unless other problems are also present.

*Motor Excess.*   Members of this group are sometimes called *hyperactive*. The group's problems are associated with excessive motor behavior. There are many possible explanations for their problems (Ross & Ross, 1982). Some of the problems typically seen include: restlessness, extraneous nonpurposeful motor activity, and impulsiveness.

### Emotional Disorder

Members of this group are characterized by anxiety and avoidance behavior. These behaviors are believed to be due mostly to respondent learning. Maladaptive emotional behaviors are learned directly (experientially), indirectly (cognitively), or by a combination of both. There is some evidence for a biological predisposition for some problems in this group. Problems typically seen include: fearfulness, withdrawal, depression, hypersensitivity, self-consciousness, and secretiveness.

### Psychotic disorder

Members of this group are characterized by extreme deviation from normal patterns of thinking, feeling, and acting. These behaviors are believed to be due to a combination of biological and experiential factors. Children with psychotic disorder are often divided into two groups, labeled infantile autism and childhood schizophrenia. *Infantile autism* is the label applied to psychotic children diagnosed prior to 30 months of age. *Childhood schizophrenia* is the label applied to psychotic children diagnosed after 30 months of age. With older children and youth, particularly adolescents, the label for one of the adult psychotic diagnoses may be used. The younger the child, at the time of diagnosis, the more severe the symptoms appear to be. Likewise, the more severe the symptoms, the worse the outcome. The P.L. 94-142 definition of emotional disturbance originally included both infantile autism and schizophrenia. Subsequently, infantile autism was dropped from the category and included under "health impaired." The rationale for this was the evidence suggesting that autism is a biological disorder. Problems typically seen in psychotic disorder include impaired affect, loss of or failure to develop speech, bizarre or stereotyped behavior, panic, self-injurious behavior, and fragmented intellectual development.

## SOURCES OF BEHAVIOR

One important question about the child or youth with a behavioral disorder is: Where does this behavior come from? There are two major sources of all behavior. These two sources are constitutional or biological influences and environmental influences. The following is a brief description of these two influences.

### Constitutional

*Prenatal.*    Biological influences occurring before birth include genetically transmitted problems and predispositions. In extreme deviation, such as psychotic disorders, there is a growing body of research suggesting that biological factors may be the primary influence (Rutter, 1972). In less severe disorders, there is evidence that biological predisposition, such as temperament (Thomas, Chess, & Birch, 1968), may be a contributing factor.

*Perinatal and Postnatal.*    Biological influences occurring during or after birth are often due to disease or physical traumas that cause neurological impairment (Werry, 1979). These problems may result from brain damage caused by birth complications, e.g., anoxia, or from accidents, e.g., automobile wrecks. Brain damage may also be caused by various diseases, e.g., encephalitis, or exposure to toxic substances, e.g., lead. These influences are often thought to contribute to the development of behavioral disorders but not to cause them.

### Environmental

*Cultural.*    The culture in which we are born, reared, and live plays a powerful role in shaping how we perceive and respond to the world around us

(Barnouw, 1979). In addition to the broad influence that culture has on us, society is fragmented into various ethnic groups (Eisner & Tsuyemura, 1965) and social classes (Dunham, 1976) that influence behavior. Finally, society defines deviance, the role of the deviant, and sets expectations for behavior in the deviant (Scheff, 1966).

*Home.* The home and, in particular, parents have considerable influence on the development of behavior. Baumrind (1967) studied the parenting styles of parents of young children. She found noteworthy differences in the styles of parents of aggressive, conflicted, and healthy children. Rutter (1971) found that family discord contributes to behavioral disorders in children. Different discipline patterns have been found in families of normal and antisocial adolescents (Singer, 1974). Patterson (1976) studied home influences on the development of aggressive behavior in boys and identified several home factors believed to contribute to aggressiveness. Communication patterns in families of schizophrenic children were found to be deviant (Wynne, 1968) and may have contributed to the children's problems. The research findings on family influences are very complex. It is difficult to draw any firm conclusions about family influences. However, there is little doubt that family factors are important (Hetherington & Martin, 1979).

*School.* The school and, in particular, teachers can influence the development of behavior problems. Teachers are largely from middle-class backgrounds, and students are from all social classes. Teachers and students may become involved in values conflicts. These conflicts can contribute to behavior problems. It is known that teachers respond differently to children based on their expectations for the child (Brophy & Good, 1970). There is little doubt that differences in teacher behavior toward students can influence student behavior. Kounin and Obradovic (1968) identified specific teacher behaviors that contribute to deviant behavior in the classroom. Different educational models also appear to have different implications for behavior (Haring & Phillips, 1962). Swift and Spivak (1969) established a clear association between academic problems and behavior problems. This association suggests that curriculum factors may influence classroom behavior. Center, Deitz, and Kauffman (1982) demonstrated that curriculum adjustment, by careful individualization of instruction, resulted in decreased inappropriate behavior. Conversely, failure to individualize properly resulted in increased inappropriate behavior. Long and Duffner (1976) discussed the role of stress in both home and school on the problems of children. Finally, Preiser and Taylor (1983) discussed the possible influence of the school's physical environment on behavior.

*Peers.* The peer group is a source of behavior and is second only to parents as an agent of socialization. Segal and Yahraes (1979) point out that the peer group is a significant influence on sexual attitudes, sexual behavior, management of aggression, moral standards, and emotional security. Boocock (1966) discussed the role of the peer group on attitudes and behaviors affecting school performance. Finally, Sutherland and Cressey (1970) discussed the concept of "differential association" as a possible mechanism for the socialization of deviant behavior in children and youth.

## SERVICE NEEDS

Considering the definition and the characteristics of behavior-disordered children and youth, we can specify the areas that a special education program should be prepared to address. First, the program must address academic behavior (part i and criterion A). Second, the program must address social behavior (criteria B and C). Third, the program must address emotional behavior (criteria C, D, and E). Finally, some programs should also be prepared to address the special problems of the schizophrenic child or youth (part ii). Although not covered in the definition, the program should also address career education. This is a curriculum area important for all students, particularly handicapped students.

In the following text, Chapters 2 and 3 deal with academic needs and cover basic skills instruction and generic learning skills. Chapters 4, 5, and 6 address the area of social behavior and cover reducing inappropriate social behavior, teaching prosocial behavior, and teaching social reasoning. Chapters 7 and 8 deal with emotional behavior and cover behavioral and cognitive strategies for reducing inappropriate emotional behavior. Chapter 9 addresses programming and techniques for the psychotic student. Chapter 10 deals with the important area of career education. Chapter 11 addresses the development of individualized education programs (IEP) and the development of lesson plans based on an IEP, and examines various service delivery models used in programs for children and youth with behavioral disorders. Finally, Chapter 12 looks at some legal considerations related to serving BD students.

Table 1–5 is a summary of the relationship between the classification of behavior-disordered students and the content of this textbook. The relationships illustrated are those that are most probable. It is possible in individual cases that there will be variations on what is presented in Table 1–5. Table 1–5 shows that the material in Chapters 1 (basic skills), 2 (learning skills), 10 (career education), 11 (IEP development, lesson plan development, and service delivery), and 12 (legal considerations) is potentially applicable to all classification categories. In addition, the material in Chapters 4 (reduction of inappropriate social behavior), 5 (social skills), and 6 (social reasoning) is potentially applicable to all three subcategories of conduct disorder. The material in Chapters 5 (social skills), 7 (reduction of emotional behavior—behavioral approach), and 8 (reduction of emotional behavior—cognitive approach) is potentially applicable to the emotional disorder category. Finally, the material in Chapter 9 (programming for childhood psychosis) is specifically directed at the category "psychotic disorder." Due to the pervasiveness of the problems in children and youth with psychotic disorders, the material indicated for both conduct disorder and emotional disorder is also potentially applicable to this population.

**Table 1–5**    The relationship of a classification system for children and youth with behavioral disorders to the content of this book

I. Conduct Disorder
   1. Unsolcialized aggressive: Chapters 2, 3, 4, 5, 6, 10, 11, and 12
   2. Socialized aggressive: Chapters 2, 3, 4, 5, 6, 10, 11, and 12
   3. Motor excess: Chapters 2, 3, 4, 5, 6, 10, 11, and 12
II. Emotional disorder: Chapters 2, 3, 5, 7, 8, 10, 11, and 12
III. Psychotic disorder: Chapters 2, 3, 4, 5, 6, 7, 8, 9, 10, 11, and 12

## REFERENCES

ALBEE, B. (1968). Models, myths, and manpower. *Mental Hygiene, 52*, 168–180.

ANTHONY, E. (1970). The behavior disorders of childhood. In P. Mussen (Ed.), *Carmichael's Manual Of Child Psychology*, (Vol. 2, 3rd ed.). New York: Wiley.

BARNOUW, V. (1979). *Culture and Personality* (3rd ed.). Homewood, IL: Dorsey Press.

BAUMRIND, D. (1967). Child care practices anteceding three patterns of preschool behavior. *Genetic Psychology Monographs, 75*, 43–88.

BOOCOCK, S. (1966). Toward a sociology of learning: Peer group effects on student performance. *Sociology of Education, 39*, 26–32.

BOWER, E. (1981). *Early Identification of Emotionally Disturbed Children in School* (3rd ed.). Springfield, IL: Charles C. Thomas.

BOWER, E. (1982). Defining emotional disturbance: Public policy and research. *Psychology in the Schools, 19*(1), 55–60.

BROPHY, J., & GOOD, T. (1970). Teachers' communication of differential expectations for children's classroom performance: Some behavioral data. *Journal of Educational Psychology, 61*(5), 365–374.

CENTER, D. (1985). P.L. 94-142 as applied to DSM III diagnoses: A book review. *Behavioral Disorders, 10* (4), 305–306.

CENTER, D., DEITZ, S., & KAUFMAN, M. (1982). Student ability, task difficulty, and inappropriate behavior in children with behavior disorders. *Behavior Modification, 6*(3), 355–374.

DUNHAM, H. (1976). Society, culture, and mental disorder. *Archives of General Psychiatry, 33*, 147–156.

EISNER, V., & TSUYEMURA, H. (1965). Interaction of juveniles with the law. *Public Health Report, 80*, 689–691.

HARING, N., & PHILLIPS, E. (1962). *Educating Emotionally Disturbed Children*. New York: McGraw-Hill.

HETHERINGTON, E., & MARTIN, B. (1979). Family interaction. In H. Quay & J. Werry (Eds.), *Psychopathological Disorders of Childhood* (2nd ed.). New York: Wiley.

HUNTZE, S. (1985). A position paper of the Council for Children with Behavioral Disorders. *Behavioral Disorders, 10*(3), 167–174.

KAUFFMAN, J. (1985). *Characteristics of Children's Behavior Disorders* (3rd ed.). Columbus, OH: Merrill.

KOUNIN, J., & OBRADOVIC, S. (1968). Managing emotionally disturbed children in regular classrooms: A replication and extension. *Journal of Special Education, 2*, 129–135.

LONG, K. (1983). Emotionally disturbed children as the underdetected and underserved public school population. *Behavioral Disorders, 9*(1), 46–54.

LONG, N., & DUFFNER, B. (1976). The stress cycle or the coping cycle? The impact of home and school stresses on pupils' classroom behavior. In N. Long, W. Morse, & R. Newman (Eds.), *Conflict in the Classroom* (4th ed.). Belmont, CA: Wadsworth.

MALMQUIST, C. (1972). Depressive phenomena in children. In B. Wolman (Ed.), *Manual of Child Psychopathology*. New York: McGraw-Hill.

NATIONAL CENTER FOR EDUCATIONAL STATISTICS (1979). *Statistics of Public Elementary and Secondary Day Schools*. Washington, DC: Author.

PATTERSON, G. (1976). The aggressive child: Victim and architect of a coercive system. In E. Marsh, L. Hamerlynck, & L. Handy (Eds.), *Behavior Modification and Families*. New York: Brunner/Mazel.

PREISER, W., & TAYLOR, A. (1983). The habitability framework: Linking human behavior and physical environment in special education. *Exceptional Educational Quarterly, 4*(2), 1–15.

QUAY, H. (1979). Classification. In H. Quay & J. Werry (eds.), *Psychopathological Disorders of Childhood* (2nd ed.). New York: Wiley.

QUAY, H. (1983). A dimensional approach to behavior disorder: The revised behavior problem checklist. *School Psychology Review*, 12(3), 244–249.

RAPOPORT, J., & ISMOND, D. (1984). *DSM III Training Guide for Diagnosis of Childhood Disorders.* New York: Brunner/Mazel.

ROBINS, L. (1979). Follow-up studies. In H. Quay & J. Werry (Eds.), *Psychopathological Disorders of Childhood* (2nd ed.). New York: Wiley.

ROSS, D., & ROSS, S. (1982). *Hyperactivity: Current Issues, Research, and Theory* (2nd ed.). New York: Wiley.

RUBIN, R., & BALOW, B. (1978). Prevalence of teacher identified behavior problems: A longitudinal study. *Exceptional Children, 45*, 102–111.

RUTTER, M. (1971). Parent-child separation: Psychological effects on children. *Journal of Child Psychology and Psychiatry and Allied Disciplines*, 12, 233–260.

RUTTER, M. (1972). Childhood schizophrenia reconsidered. Journal of Autism and Childhood Schizophrenia, 2, 315–337.

SCHEFF, T. (1966). *Being Mentally Ill.* Chicago: Aldine.

SEGAL, J., & YAHRAES, H. (1979). *A Child's Journey: Forces That Shape the Lives of Our Young.* New York: McGraw-Hill.

SINGER, M. (1974). Delinquency and family disciplinary configurations. *Archives of General Psychiatry*, 31, 795–798.

SLENKOVICH, J. (1983). *P. L. 94-142 As Applied to DSM III Diagnoses: An Analysis of DSM III Diagnoses vis-a-vis Special Education Law.* Cupertino, CA: Kinghorn Press.

SUTHERLAND, E., & CRESSEY, D. (1970). *Criminology.* Philadelphia: Lippincott.

SWIFT, M. & SPIVACK, G. (1969). Clarifying the relationship between academic success and overt classroom behavior. *Exceptional Children, 36*, 99–104.

THOMAS, A., CHESS, S., & BIRCH, H. (1968). *Temperament and Behavior Disorders in Children.* New York: New York University Press.

ULLMANN, L., & KRASNER, L. (1975). *A Psychological Approach to Abnormal Behavior* (2nd ed.). Englewood Cliffs, NJ: Prentice-Hall.

WERRY, J. (1979). Organic factors. In H. Quay & J. Werry (Eds.), *Psychopathological Disorders of Childhood* (2nd ed.). New York: Wiley.

WYNNE, L. (1968). Methodologic and conceptual issues in the study of schizophrenics and their families. *Journal of Psychiatric Research, 6* (Suppl. 1), 185–199.

# 2

# TEACHING ACADEMICS

## Basic Skills

**INTRODUCTION**

The direct approach to teaching basic skills has a variety of names. These names include precision teaching, directive teaching, direct instruction, and mastery learning. Regardless of the name used, all are based on the operant model of learning. One of the earliest discussions on applying operant learning to classroom instruction was by B. F. Skinner in 1954. This paper and related material (Skinner, 1968) are available to anyone interested in the early development of direct instruction. More recent discussions of the operant approach include those by Lindsley (1972), Stephens (1976), Becker and Engelmann (1978), and Becker and Carnine (1981).

### Operant Model

The operant model will be discussed more fully in Chapter 4. For our present purpose, we need only a brief discussion of the model. Operant learning is represented by a three-term model (see Figure 2–1). In Figure 2–1, the first term is a *discriminative stimulus* ($S^D$). The second term is a *response* (R) made to the $S^D$. The last term is a *reinforcing stimulus* ($S^R$), which follows the R. The systematic relationship of these three factors to one another is called a *contingency*.

Let's look at this model again and use a familiar set of elements in a simple example. You say to a student, "Spell the word 'kitten' for me." This is a $S^D$ for the response you want from the student. The student responds, "Kitten, k-i-t-t-e-n." This is a correct R to the $S^D$ you presented. You follow the student's

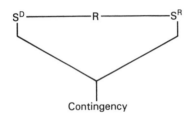

**Figure 2–1**
An illustration of the three-factor model of operant learning. From left to right, the components are discriminative stimulus, response, and reinforcing stimulus. The relationship of the three components to one another is called a contingency.

R with, "That is correct, very good spelling." This is a $S^R$ to the student's R. This $S^R$ provides both feedback on correctness and verbal praise. This simple example concretely illustrates the three basic elements in the operant model. Teaching complex tasks and concepts can also be represented, analyzed, and understood with this model.

### Research

There is an extensive body of literature on the operant-based instruction model (Bloom, 1976; Haring, Lovitt, Eaton, & Hansen, 1978; Bijou & Ruiz, 1981). In addition, there are two collections of readings (Holland, Soloman, Doran, & Frezza, 1976; Ulrich, Stachnik, & Mabry, 1974) on the application of the operant model to education. Research shows that this approach significantly increases achievement in students. In fact, operant-based instruction is superior to a variety of alternative approaches (Becker & Carnine, 1981). Superiority was found for both academic achievement and affective development.

## ASSESSMENT

Assessment in the operant model requires that instructional tasks be stated as measurable outcomes. When your goal is only to teach reading, you have a very broad and vague goal. Many standardized reading tests give you a reading-grade level. These tests may give you some clues about what needs to be taught. They usually do not pinpoint for you the specific skills that need to be taught. Most standardized tests do not give the kind of assessment data needed for direct skill instruction.

Direct skill instruction requires assessment based on discrete, sequenced skills. Each of these skills must, in turn, be assessed against a specific criterion. The criterion must set a standard for a functional level of skill. You must then have a set of discrete, sequenced skills with measurable outcomes before doing an assessment. The process of analyzing a subject area, such as reading, into a discrete skills sequence is called *content analysis* or *task analysis*. Some educators use these two terms interchangeably. Others use the two terms to refer to different levels of the same process. We will follow the latter usage.

### Content Analysis

Content analysis refers to the process of breaking down a subject area, e.g., reading. This process usually begins with a long-term goal such as, "The student will master functional reading skills." The next step is to work backward from this goal. At each step in the analysis, subgoals or objectives needed to achieve the long-term goal are identified. The number of steps or levels in the analysis depends on the complexity of the subject matter and student characteristics. Figure 2–2 is an illustration of a content analysis and is sometimes called a *pyramid*.

Let's follow the analysis down through one of the paths illustrated. The goal (I): The student will master functional reading skills. Level One, A: The student will master essential phonics skills. Level two, 1: The student will master vowel sounds. Level three, a: the student will master the *a* sounds. Thus, the last objective would carry the notation IA1a. To master objective IA1, a student must master 1a, 1b, and 1c. To master objective IA, a student must master A1, A2, and A3. To master objective I, a student must master IA, IB, and IC.

Of course, our illustration in Figure 2–2 is somewhat idealized. In practice, the analysis may not result in a *pyramid* as symmetrical as our illustration. You will not always get a consistent number of parallel objectives at each level of the analysis. Also, there is no fixed number of levels through which the analysis must proceed. The extent of the analysis and the numbers of objectives generated is determined by subject content and the purpose of the analysis. Content analysis can be applied to cognitive goals, affective goals, and psychomotor goals (Moyer & Dardig, 1978).

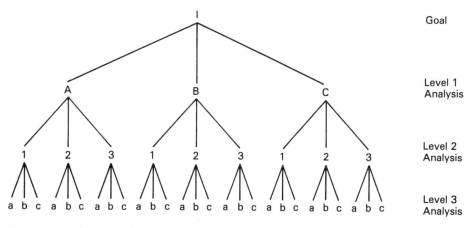

**Figure 2–2**    An illustration of the pyramid produced by the content analysis process. The analysis of the goal (I) has been taken through three levels of analysis.

### Task Analysis

Task analysis refers to breaking down a specific instructional task into small, teachable steps. This process usually begins with a short-term objective such as, "The student will master the $a$ sounds." The ability level and learning rate of the student will determine whether the task analysis is needed and how small the steps must be. Figure 2–3 is an illustration of the process. At this level of the analysis, we are generating instructional objectives for individualized lesson plans for teaching a particular student.

Let's follow the analysis down through one of the paths illustrated. The objective (IA1a): The student will master the $a$ sounds. Level four, (1): The student will master the short $a$ sound. Level five, (a): The student will master identification of the short $a$ sound presented auditorily and in isolation with two foils. To master IA1a(1)(a), a student must master both (a)1, sound in isolation, and (a)2, sound in words. To master IA1a(1), a student must master both (1)(a), auditory recognition of the sound, and (1)(b), visual recognition of the sound. To master IA1a, a student must master both (1), short $a$ sound, and (2), long $a$ sound.

It is not difficult to find content analyses already done for various subject areas. Content analyses can be found in commercial materials or in curriculum guides developed by state departments of education or local school systems. Most content analyses are done for a broadly defined student population. Hence, they may not carry the analysis far enough for a given teacher or for a particular student. You should obtain a good content analysis for each subject area you teach. If you do this, your analyses will be limited to task analysis. You will only need to extend the content analysis enough to tailor it individually for your students.

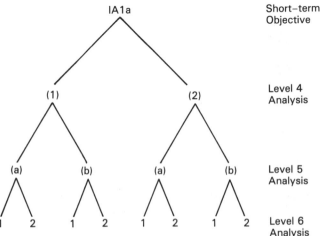

IA1a — Short-term Objective

(1)   (2) — Level 4 Analysis

(a)   (b)   (a)   (b) — Level 5 Analysis

1  2   1  2   1  2   1  2 — Level 6 Analysis

**Figure 2–3**
A fine-grained task analysis of a short-term objective to generate instructional objectives for a specific student.

### Criterion-Referenced Assessment

Criterion-referenced assessment is derived from the curriculum analysis process just described. Curriculum analysis, or content analysis, breaks down a subject area into a set of sequenced instructional steps. Criterion-referenced assessment complements content analysis. This approach to assessment focuses on specific skills. It evaluates those skills, not against a normative standard but against a functional criterion. Remember, meeting a functional criterion shows that a student can perform a skill at a meaningful level. Functional, or mastery, criteria are of two types, performance and consistency criteria.

A *performance criterion* is set at an accuracy level high enough to guarantee a useful level of skill. Setting the performance criterion is often left to teacher judgment. This is because the appropriate level depends on why the skill is being taught, and the characteristics of the student. There are two general rules useful when setting a performance criterion. First, the more basic and widely used the skill, the more accuracy required. For example, a very basic skill such as numeral recognition would require a high accuracy criterion. It is a very basic skill and many advanced skills depend on it, e.g., computation. It is also a widely used skill for coding information, e.g., addresses, phone numbers, price values, and temperature. On the other hand, an advanced skill such as dividing fractions doesn't require as high an accuracy criterion as that for numeral recognition. There are not nearly as many advanced skills requiring division of fractions as those requiring numeral recognition. Second, an accuracy criterion should allow margin for error. We all make errors even in very basic skills. Accuracy criteria between 70% and 98% should be appropriate for most objectives.

*Consistency criteria* complement performance criteria. To show a functional level of skill, a student must be able to perform a skill with accuracy. A student must also be able to produce that level of performance repeatedly. When any event occurs only one time, it is hard to say with confidence that the occurrence was not an "accident," i.e., a random event. We must be concerned with performance level and performance trends. It takes at least three consecutive occurrences of an event to establish a trend. Three consecutive occurrences is a minimum consistency criterion. To say that a student has mastered a skill, performance must meet a preset level of accuracy and consistency.

After you select a skill and set mastery criteria, there are two more steps before you can test. First, you must identify a task that requires the use of the skill. You must be careful to select a task that includes the skill but doesn't go beyond it. In other words, be sure your task doesn't depend on a skill the student hasn't mastered. For example, writing sentences with new sight words depends on knowledge of sight words and sentence structure, among other things. Second, you must develop an activity for the task selected. To assess the skill, give a student the activity and judge performance against your mastery criteria. Box 2–1 is an example of a criterion-referenced assessment plan.

**Box 2-1**    A criterion-referenced assessment plan for the short *a* sound presented vocally, in isolation, and with two foils

---

*Objective:* IA1a(1)(a)1, The student will master the short *a* sound when presented auditorily and in isolation with two foils.

*Performance criterion:* 80% accuracy.

*Consistency criterion:* Five consecutive sessions.

*Task:* Vocal presentation of five sets of three letter sounds. One presentation in each set of three will be the short *a* sound. The position of the short *a* in each set will be varied randomly to avoid discrimination by position.

*Student response:* The student will be given a response sheet using the following directions and format:

For each set (1, 2, 3, 4, or 5), mark the position of the short *a* sound by placing a check (✓) beside a, b, or c. For example, if the short *a* sound is the second sound presented in the first set, place a check (✓) beside b, under number 1.

| 1. | 2. | 3. | 4. | 5. |
|---|---|---|---|---|
| a.____ | a.____ | a.____ | a.____ | a.____ |
| b.____ | b.____ | b.____ | b.____ | b.____ |
| c.____ | c.____ | c.____ | c.____ | c.____ |

*Materials:* Five 3 x 5 cards with three letter sounds on each card. One sound in each set of three will be a short *a* sound.

---

The criterion-referenced assessment plan in Box 2–1 has several components. The components are an objective, performance criterion, consistency criterion, task statement, student response, and materials needed for the assessment activity. Criterion-referenced assessment can be used to pretest students to identify deficit skills (see Chapter 11). Once you have a curriculum sequence, a set of assessment tasks can be selected to use on a pretest. Begin testing in the curriculum sequence where you judge that the student is now functioning. If the student demonstrates mastery, move up in the sequence. If the student fails, move down in the sequence until mastery level is reached. After pretesting, identify the skill deficits immediately above the mastery level in the sequence and begin teaching those skills. Continue moving up through the sequence as new skills are mastered. As a skill is taught, continuously measure student performance to evaluate the instruction and to determine when mastery is achieved. Information on charting assessment data and record keeping is presented in Chapter 11.

## CURRICULUM

Common academic subjects taught in programs for behaviorally disordered children and youth include reading, arithmetic, handwriting, and language arts.

Some programs may address other curriculum areas, such as social studies and science. We will not address those here. Problems in those two areas are usually caused by skill deficits in one or more of the basic skill areas mentioned above.

**Reading Skills**

Reading is a very complex skill. A complete skills-based curriculum sequence would be too long to present in this chapter. Table 2–1 is an abbreviated sequence. The sequence covers kindergarten through sixth grade and includes the skills needed for functional reading. It could be expanded by further analysis. Table 2–1 includes the following:

1. Readiness skills, e.g., oral language skills

2. Beginning phonics skills, e.g., long vowel sounds

3. Advanced phonics skills, e.g., consonant digraphs

4. Other word attack skills, e.g., structural analysis

5. Comprehension skills, e.g., paraphrasing main ideas

6. Advanced comprehension skills, e.g., critical analysis

**Table 2-1**    A general curriculum sequence for reading for kindergarten through the sixth grade

| GRADE | SKILLS ACQUIRED |
|---|---|
| Kindergarten | Identify sounds and pictures<br>Express ideas in complete verbal sentences<br>Understand meaning of words such as *above* and *far*<br>Understand concepts of size, small, etc.<br>Recognize and identify colors<br>Organize objects into groups<br>Match forms<br>Understands beginning concepts of number |
| Grade 1 | Recognize letters of alphabet; can write and give sound<br>Auditory and visual perception and discrimination of initial and final consonants<br>Observe left-to-right progression<br>Recall what has been read<br>Aware of medial consonants, consonant blends, digraphs<br>Recognize long sound of vowels; root words; plural forms; verb endings, *-s, -ed, -d, -ing*; opposites; pronouns *he, she*<br>Understand concept of synonyms, homonyms, antonyms<br>Understand simple compound words<br>Copy simple sentences, fill-ins |

**Table 2-1**    Continued

| GRADE | SKILLS ACQUIRED |
|---|---|
| Grade 2 | Comprehension and analysis of what has been read<br>Identify vowel digraphs<br>Understand variant sounds of *y*<br>Identify medial vowels<br>Identify diphthongs<br>Understand influence of *r* on preceding vowel<br>Identify three-letter blends<br>Understand use of suffix *-er*<br>Understand verb endings (e.g., *stop, stopped*) |
| Grade 3 | Recognize multiple sounds of long *a* as in *ei,*<br>    *ay, ey*<br>Understand silent *e* in *-le* endings<br>Understand use of suffix *-est*<br>Know how to change *y* to *i* before adding *-er, -est*<br>Understand comparative and superlative forms of<br>    adjectives<br>Understand possessive form using s<br>Use contractions<br>Identify syllabic breaks |
| Grade 4 | Recognize main and subordinate parts<br>Recognize unknown words using configuration and<br>    other word attack skills<br>Identify various sounds of *ch*<br>Recognize various phonetic values of *gh*<br>Identify rounded *o* sound formed by *au, aw, al*<br>Use and interpret diacritical markings<br>Discriminate among multiple meanings of words |
| Grade 5 | Read critically to evaluate<br>Identify diagraphs *gn, mb, bt*<br>Recognize that *augh* and *ough* may have round *o* sound<br>Recognize and pronounce muted vowels in *el, al, le*<br>Recognize secondary and primary accents<br>Use of apostrophe<br>Understand suffixes *-al, -hand, -ship, -ist, -ling,*<br>    *-an, -ian, -dom, -ern*<br>Understand use of figures of speech: metaphor,<br>    simile<br>Ability to paraphrase main idea<br>Know ways paragraphs are developed<br>Outline using two or three main heads and<br>    subheadings<br>Use graphic material |
| Grade 6 | Develop ability for critical analysis<br>Recognize and use Latin and Greek roots, such as<br>    *photo, tele, graph, geo, auto*<br>Develop generalization that some suffixes can change<br>    part of speech, such as *ure* changing an adjective to<br>    noun (*moist-moisture*)<br>Understand meaning and pronunciation of homographs<br>Develop awareness of shifting accents |

SOURCE: Guerin and Maier, 1983.

**Arithmetic Skills**

Table 2–2 is an abbreviated sequence for basic arithmetic skills. The sequence covers kindergarten through sixth grade. The sequence includes the skills needed for functional math and for developing advanced math skills. The sequence could be expanded by additional analysis. Table 2–2 includes the following:

1. Readiness skills, e.g., one-to-one correspondence

2. Basic computational skills, e.g., addition

3. Advanced computational skills, e.g., division

4. Advanced concepts, e.g., fractions and decimals

5. Math reasoning skills, e.g., relating percent to ratio, fractions, and decimals.

**Table 2-2**   A general curriculum sequence for arithmetic for kindergarten through the sixth grade

| GRADE | SKILLS ACQUIRED |
|---|---|
| Kindergarten | Rote counting to 10<br>Use whole numbers in serial order<br>Begin cardinal numbers, ordinal numbers<br>Begin reading numerals<br>One-to-one matching<br>Addition as joining of sets |
| Grade 1:<br>first<br>half | Rote counting to 100<br>Read and write whole numbers through 50<br>Place value at tens place<br>Equivalent/nonequivalent sets<br>Know meaning of signs, −,+, and =<br>Addition and subtraction as inverse functions<br>Solving missing addend problems<br>Using 0 in subtraction |
| Grade 1:<br>second<br>half | Rote counting beyond 100<br>Counting by fives, twos, tens<br>Odd and even numbers<br>Signs (&)<br>Read and write to 99<br>Begin fractions 1/2, 1/3, 1/4<br>Addition combinations through 19<br>Addition of two-digit numbers with two or three addends<br>    through 99 (no carrying)<br>Subtract two-digit numbers to minuends of 19 or less<br>Multiples of 10 (2 tens = 20, 3 tens = 30) |
| Grade 2:<br>first half | Place value to hundredth place<br>Add two-digit numerals with three or four addends with<br>    sums less than 100 (no carrying)<br>Subtract two-digit numerals (no borrowing)<br>Understand division as separation of set into<br>    equivalent sets |

**Table 2-2**    Continued

| GRADE | SKILLS |
|---|---|
| Grade 2<br>second<br>half | Count by ones, twos, fives, tens, hundreds, through 999<br>Write numerals in expanded notation<br>Introduce carrying (regrouping)<br>Subtraction involving borrowing at the tens and hundreds places with numerals including 0<br>Begin combination of multiples of 2, 3, 4, and 5 with products of 0 to 25<br>Know meaning of $x$ and $y$<br>Begin division problem with same facts as above |
| Grade 3:<br>first<br>half | Count and write to 1,000<br>Place value for thousands<br>Equivalent fractions for 1/2, 1/4, 1/3<br>Roman numerals to XII<br>Addition of three-digit numerals with carrying<br>Subtraction facts with combinations of 0 to 19<br>Introduce $\sqrt{\phantom{x}}$ for division |
| Grade 3:<br>second<br>half | Read and write numerals with dollars and cents<br>Rounding of numbers<br>Fractions 1/6, 1/8<br>Roman numerals through XXX<br>Addition up to seven digits<br>Begin addition of fractions with like denominators, with sums less than 1<br>Subtraction of four to seven digits with borrowing<br>Multiplication through 9 x 9<br>Multiplication of two- or three-digit factors by one factor with or without carrying<br>Division with combination through 9 x 9 |
| Grade 4:<br>first<br>half | Read and write whole numbers to 9,999<br>Roman numerals through C<br>Understand concepts of 1/2, 1/4, 1/3 as equivalent sets of groups of objects, as well as congruent parts of a whole |
| Grade 4:<br>second<br>half | Read and write numerals to million<br>Place value for million<br>Learn names *numerator* and *denominator*<br>Multiplication of two-digit numeral by two-digit multipliers<br>Division with two-digit divisor<br>Fractional parts, fifths, sevenths, ninths |
| Grade 5:<br>first<br>half | Relationship between improper fractions and mixed fractions<br>Write improper and mixed fractions<br>Add three- and four-digit numbers of two to six addends<br>Add fractions with like denominators<br>Subtract like and mixed fractions with like denominators<br>Multiply three-digit numbers by two-digit multipliers<br>Two-digit divisors with 5 to 9 in one's place |

**Table 2-2**   Continued

| GRADE | SKILLS |
|---|---|
| Grade 5: second half | Decimals and place value<br>Add decimal fractions<br>Add fractions with unlike denominators<br>Subtract five-digit numerals, fractional numbers,<br>    mixed numbers from whole numbers<br>Multiplication with multiples of 100 |
| Grade 6: first half | Learn to express numbers by using exponents<br>Vocabulary: *power, squared, cubed*<br>Add and subtract fractions with unlike denominators<br>Multiplication with three-digit multipliers<br>Multiplication of fractional numbers with proper<br>    fractions, whole numbers, and improper fractions<br>Division of fractional numbers |
| Grade 6: second half | Relate percent to ratio, fractions, and decimals<br>Add positive and negative numbers<br>Multiplication with decimals and decimal fractions<br>Division of decimal fractions |

SOURCE: Guerin and Maier, 1983.

### Handwriting

Table 2–3 is a sequence for handwriting skills. The sequence covers basic handwriting skills taught in the elementary grades. Task analysis can be used to expand the sequence. Table 2–3 includes the following.

1. Readiness skills, e.g., forming circles

2. Manuscript letters, e.g., *E, e*

3. Cursive letters, e.g., $\mathcal{E}$ , $\mathcal{l}$

4. Height of letters, e.g., *t, a*

5. Spacing

6. Alignment

7. Punctuation marks, e.g., ?

**Table 2-3**   A curriculum sequence of skills for instruction in handwriting

| Readiness Skills | Vertical line drawn from top to bottom<br>Vertical line drawn from bottom to top<br>Horizontal line drawn from left to right<br>Forming circles<br>Forming Curves<br>Slanting lines vertically<br>Naming letters |
|---|---|

**Table 2-3**    Continued

| | |
|---|---|
| *Manuscript Letters* | Straight line letters: *l, L, i, I, t, T*<br>Circle letters: *o, c, a, e*<br>Curve letters: *m, n, r, R, s, S, u, U*<br>Tall letters: *d, D, f, F, h, H, b, B*<br>Slant letters: *w, W, v, V, k, K, x, X, z, Z*<br>Tail letters: *M, N, g, G, y, Y, p, P, j, J, q, Q*<br>Straight line numerals: *1, 4, 7*<br>Circle numerals: *0, 6, 8, 9*<br>Curve numerals: *2, 3, 5* |
| *Cursive Letters* | Letters beginning with an undercurve:<br>*i, t, e, l, u, w, r, s,*<br>*b, h, k, f, j, p*<br>Letters beginning with a down curve:<br>*a, d, o, c, q, g*<br><br>Letters beginning with an overcurve:<br>*n, m, v, x, y, z*<br><br>All uppercase cursive letters |
| *Height of Letters* | All similar letters should be of uniform height: *t, l*<br><br>Short letters should be about one-third the height<br>    of capitals: *a, u* |
| *Spacing* | Uniform spacing between letters in a word<br>Uniform spacing between words<br>Spacing between lines should be uniform on unlined<br>    paper |
| *Alignment* | All written lines should be straight on lined and<br>    unlined paper |
| *Punctuation* | Statements and commands (.)<br>Questions (?)<br>Exclamations (!)<br>Dividing sentences (, : ;)<br>Beginning sentences, proper names, and titles (capital letters)<br>Quotations ("    ")<br>Abbreviations (Pa.)<br>Contractions (can't) |

SOURCE: Stephens, 1977.

### Language Arts

Language arts is a broad content area and may include or exclude several components. For example, it could include handwriting or reading. We will include under language arts the following topics: oral language, spelling, grammar, and composition.

*Oral Language.*   Oral Language is an essential skill. It contributes to social skills, thinking skills, reading, and writing, among others. Table 2–4 is a sequence for expressive language development. The sequence covers phonology, syntax, description, vocabulary development, morphology, sentence development, voice control, and social communication. A more detailed sequence could be developed using task analysis.

**Table 2-4**   A curriculum sequence for expressive language development

1. Expressive phonology
   Using alliteration

2. Developing appropriate syntax
   Developing complete kernel sentences
   Developing correct word order
   Using word classes

3. Recalling details and describing objects and events
   Describing visual stimuli
   Describing events
   Giving verbal directions
   Reporting factual information
   Determining cause and effect

4. Developing expressive vocabulary
   Persons and objects (nouns)
   Action words (verbs)
   Descriptive words (adjectives and adverbs)
   New words
   Compound words
   Synonyms
   Antonyms
   Palindromes

5. Morphology
   Plurals
   Suffixes
   Verb tenses
   Pronouns

6. Making changes in the basic sentence
   Forming questions
   Combining sentences
   Expanding sentences

7. Voice control
   Stress
   Intonation
   Pitch and volume

8. Social communication
   Using appropriate phrases in conversation
   Communicating feelings
   Reaching group consensus

SOURCE:   J. Cole and M. Cole, *Language Lessons for the Special Education Classroom*, 1983. Reprinted with permission of Aspen Publishers, Inc.

*Spelling.* Table 2–5 is a sequence for teaching spelling skills. The sequence covers auditory discrimination, consonants, phonograms, plurals, syllabication, structural elements, ending changes, vowel digraphs and diphthongs, and silent *e*. As you can see in the sequence, spelling skills have a close relationship to word attack skills. To this sequence, some authorities would add such skills as visual discrimination, visual sequential memory, and revisualization.

**Table 2-5**  A curriculum sequence for teaching spelling skills

---

1.0  Auditory discrimination
   .1 Consonant sounds
   .2 Vowel sounds
   .3 Word pronunciation

2.0  Consonants
   .1 Initial
   .2 Final
   .3 Medial
   .4 Blends

3.0  Phonograms
   .1 Initial
   .2 Medial
   .3 Final
   .4 Word

4.0  Plurals
   .1 *s*
   .2 *es*
   .3 *f* to *v*
   .4 Medial changes
   .5 Exceptions

5.0  Syllabication
   .1 Word division

6.0  Structural elements
   .1 Roots
   .2 Prefixes
   .3 Suffixes

7.0  Ending changes
   .1 Final *e*
   .2 Final *y*
   .3 Final consonants

8.0  Vowel digraphs and diphthongs
   .1 One sound (*ai, ea, ay, ei, ie*)
   .2 Blends (*oi, ou, ow*)

9.0  Silent *e*
   .1 Single-syllable words ending in *e*

---

Source: Stephens, 1977.

***Grammar.***    Table 2–6 is a sequence of basic grammar and punctuation skills needed by most handicapped students. The sequence includes nouns, verbs, adjectives, adverbs, pronouns, sentence structures, capitalization, end punctuation, and the comma. This brief sequence could be greatly expanded using task analysis.

**Table 2-6**    A set of minimum requirements for basic grammar and punctuation

1. Use nouns in sentences.
2. Use verbs in sentences.
3. Use adjectives in sentences.
4. Correctly use the period and question mark at the end of sentences.
5. Use complete sentences.
6. Use subject and predicate in sentences.
7. Correctly use capital letters.
8. Use the four types of sentences.
9. Use singular and plural nouns in sentences.
10. Use noun determiners in sentences.
11. Use personal pronouns in sentences.
12. Use common and proper nouns.
13. Correctly use verb forms.
14. Use possessive form of nouns in sentences.
15. Correctly use present or past tense form of verb in complete sentences.
16. Use past tense form of irregular verb in complete sentences.
17. Use present or past tense form of *be* in complete sentences.
18. Use singular or plural noun as the subject of sentences.
19. Use personal pronoun as a noun phrase in the subject of sentences.
20. Use indefinite pronoun as a noun phrase in the subject of sentences.
21. Identify tense and time element of verbs.
22. Use pronouns as direct objects.
23. Use a verb phrase using a form of *be* with a noun phrase.
24. Use adverbs indicating time, place, or manner.
25. Expand verb phrase by supplying prepositional phrase.
26. Use the subordinator that combines two sentences.
27. Use noun phrase used as the subject of sentences.
28. Use verb phrase as the predicate of sentences.
29. Use the correct form of the auxiliary *have* in sentences.
30. Use sentence parts connected by a conjunction.
31. Correctly use comma to set off introductory expressions, interruptions, nouns in direct address, and items in a series.

***Composition.*** Table 2–7 is a functional set of basic composition skills for handicapped students. The set focuses on sentence writing, paragraph development, letter writing, brief descriptive narratives, outlining, bibliography writing, notetaking, and self-monitoring. The skills covered in Table 2–7 are minimal and could be expanded. For instructional purposes, most of these skills need to be broken down further using task analysis.

**Table 2-7**  A functional set of basic writing skills

1. Copies sentences
2. Organizes parts of sentences in sequential order
3. Uses a variety of words to build sentences
4. Writes simple sentences
5. Writes sentences
6. Writes sentences using connectives
7. Writes a paragraph containing sentences that are related
8. Writes a friendly letter
9. Writes a simple business letter
10. Writes sentences to compare and contrast ideas
11. Develops a simple outline
12. Writes brief experience stories
13. Writes sentences that show cause-and-effect relationship
14. Makes a simple bibliography
15. Writes a paragraph with a topic sentence
16. Takes brief notes
17. Proofs own work

## INSTRUCTION

Bloom (1976) identified three influences affecting instructional outcomes. The first is called *cognitive entry behaviors* (CEB). CEB refers to what the student brings to the instruction. The critical question is: Does the student have the necessary prerequisite skills to benefit from the instruction? The second influence is called *affective entry characteristics* (AEC). AEC refers to what is called an *attitudinal set*. Concepts closely related to this attitudinal set include locus of control (Crandall, Katkovsky, & Crandall, 1965) and self-efficacy (Bandura, 1977). Attitudinal set is a product of the student's previous experiences in learning situations. AEC affects interest in the learning task, willingness to engage the task, and persistence at the task. The third influence is called *quality of instruction* (QOI). QOI means something very similar to what we discussed earlier and called direct instruction. Bloom (1976) believes that QOI is the most important influence of the three. Bloom argues that QOI is the most important because it is the key to making positive changes in both CEB and AEC.

**Model**

Figure 2–4 is a QOI-type model. The model shows, in outline, a process for instruction. The model covers six major steps.

***1. Pretest.***    The first step is to conduct a preassessment of the student. The preassessment should be criterion referenced. This assessment will identify specific skills in the curriculum sequence that a student needs to be taught.

***2. Set Instructional Objective(s).***    From the skill deficits identified, you select a skill for instruction. You should begin with the deficit skill lowest in the curriculum sequence. An instructional objective is written for this skill.

***3. Plan Instruction.***    There are three basic steps in planning instruction: arranging antecedents, selecting responses, and arranging consequences.

a. ARRANGING ANTECEDENTS.    The first task is to plan an arrangement of environmental antecedents that make probable the desired behavior. There are several things that might be manipulated to increase the likelihood of the desired student response. These can be placed into two categories. The first category covers general environmental influences. The physical environment is one general influence that can help or hinder learning (Preiser & Taylor, 1983). In a classroom this would include lighting, spacing, temperature, potential intrusive stimuli, and seating arrangements. The size of an instructional group is another general influence on learning (Glass, Cahen, Smith, & Filby, 1979; Jenkins, Mayhall, Peschka, & Jenkins, 1974). Research suggests, all other

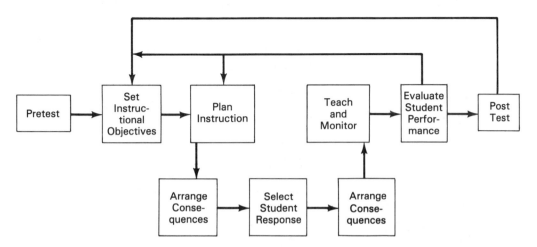

**Figure 2–4**    A diagram of the instructional model to be used for direct instruction of basic skills.

things being equal, that the smaller the instructional group, the more students learn. The highest achievement occurs in a one-on-one or tutorial condition. This is one rationale for emphasizing individualization and low teacher-to-student ratios in special education.

The second category addresses influences more specific to instruction. An initial influence to consider is the demand level for the instruction. Haring et al. (1978) developed a hierarchy related to the demand level of instruction. The hierarchy (from basic to advanced) is acquisition, proficiency, generalization, and adaptation. Thus, we must know what the appropriate demand level is before we begin to design instruction. Different demand levels require different response emphases and different instructional strategies. Corresponding response emphases for the demand levels given above are accuracy, speed, use in a new context, and use in a new application. Corresponding instructional strategies are direct instruction, varied drill, practice, and problem solving. Our focus, due to space limitations, is limited to response acquisition, with accuracy, using direct instruction.

There are two basic approaches to assisting response acquisition. The most efficient is modeling and the most effective is shaping. Modeling is the preferred approach and is the approach we will discuss in this chapter. Shaping is usually required only by students with severe learning handicaps. Shaping will be discussed in Chapter 9.

*Modeling* can be done live, e.g., by the teacher, representationally, e.g., on a videotape, or textually, e.g., in a book. Modeling may be done entirely by visual demonstration or illustration, by verbal explanation or print, or by a combination of these. Research shows that modeling should include both positive and negative examples. This aids rapid discrimination of the relevant characteristics of a correct response. Discrimination can also be aided, if necessary, by *prompting*. The teacher can supply prompts directly, e.g., a verbal cue or pointing a finger. Prompts can be incorporated into instructional drill materials, e.g., underlining or enlarging. The purpose of prompts is to direct attention to the relevant characteristics of an appropriate stimulus. Prompts allow a correct stimulus to be easily and accurately discriminated from other possible stimuli. In other words, you highlight what characteristic(s) of the positive example make it correct in contrast to the negative example. Prompts cannot remain a permanent feature of instruction. Prompts are eliminated through *fading*. Fading can be accomplished by reducing the frequency, intensity, or size of a prompt gradually and systematically over a series of trials.

Let's work through an example. Suppose that your objective is to teach a student to discriminate, auditorily, the short *a* sound within words. Your basic teaching strategy will be modeling. You will demonstrate to the student the sound of the short *a* in words. This could be done live (in person) or representationally (on tape). You first need to select both positive and negative examples (a list of words with the short *a* sound and a list without the short *a* sound, e.g., long *a* words). Next, you need to put the words into sets of two or three words. Only one word in each set will be a short *a* word. You also need to randomize the position of the short *a* word in each set. This is important because you want the student to recognize the short *a* by the sound it makes, not by position within a set.

Let's assume that a prompt will be needed. Since the words will be presented vocally, pointing, underlining, color coding, and similar prompts cannot be used. An easy prompt to use in vocally presented material is voice. In this example, let's use loudness as the prompt. Let's say that you double the volume of the short *a* sound above the long *a* sound. Your voice directs attention to the important characteristic distinguishing the short *a* sound. Thus, your prompt is the exaggeration of a relevant characteristic (phonetic sound) of the stimulus. As you present the word sets, you will vocalize the short *a* sound more loudly than other sounds in the words in the set. Now we have a prompt, we must have a way to get rid of it. After all, if the student isn't weaned away from the prompt, you haven't taught a functional skill. In other words, the student won't be able to use it independently of you. The way we get rid of a prompt is by fading. Our prompt is volume or loudness of vocalization. The obvious way to fade this prompt is to reduce the volume. Earlier we said that fading is done gradually and systematically. Gradually means in steps. You would not decrease the volume from double to normal in one step. We would use one or more intermediate steps. For illustration, let's limit ourselves to one intermediate step. During instruction, we will go through three levels of the prompt. There will be an initial level, intermediate level, and final level. These levels will correspond to double volume, one and one-half volume, and normal volume. Systematically means in a controlled manner. To do this, we must have a rule or criterion to tell us when to move from one prompt level to the next. Let's set the criterion at 95% correct responding in three consecutive practice sessions. If we practice daily, we can shift to the intermediate level of the prompt after three consecutive 95% days. When the same criterion is reached with the intermediate-level prompt, we can shift to the normal condition. When the criterion is obtained under the normal or prompt-free condition, we can say that the skill or objective has been mastered. There may be a large drop in response accuracy when you shift from one prompt level to another. This suggests a need for more intermediate levels of the prompt, a stricter criterion for changing prompt levels, or both. How much is too much loss in accuracy during fading depends on the characteristics of the student. However, accuracy should not drop more than 40%. This is about as low as you can go and still have most of the responses be correct. Thus, you should set a criterion to judge your fading procedure against.

When complex responses are taught, handicapped learners need instruction broken down into small steps. Those smaller instructional steps are generated with task analysis, taught by direct instruction, and formed into complex responses by *chaining*. Briefly, chaining is a process where a complex response, e.g., decoding words containing long and short *a* sounds, is developed by a linking procedure. As each subskill making up a complex response is taught, it is integrated with other subskills already taught. This process continues until all necessary subskills have been taught, mastered, and chained together to form an integrated whole.

b. SELECTING STUDENT RESPONSE.    This component has two aspects. First, it requires that you select an appropriate response to evaluate. Thus, the response emphasis must be directly related to the demand level of the instruction. Since we have limited ourselves here to the acquisition level, the corresponding response level is accuracy. This means that you must not use tasks which require responses that emphasize speed, use in a new context, or new applications. Second, it requires that you select an appropriate response mode. This will depend on the nature of the task used and on student characteristics, e.g., preference. Usually the response mode will be either vocal or motoric. These modes can each range from simple to complex. For example, vocal responses can range from vocalized sound signals to complex verbal descriptions. Motoric responses can range from mere physical movement to complex writing or drawing responses. The complexity of the response mode selected will, in part, be determined by the demand level of the instruction.    That is, as demand level goes up, complexity of response also tends to go up.

c. ARRANGING CONSEQUENCES.    The consequences that follow a response in an instructional situation should be one of two types. Incorrect responses should be put on extinction. This means that all consequences (positive or negative) are withheld. Correct responses should be reinforced. This means that they should be followed by a positive stimulus.

Positive stimuli can range from something as natural as verbal feedback, e.g., "That's correct!," to something as contrived as a piece of candy. There are several types of positive stimuli. First, there is feedback on response accuracy. This is the minimum consequation. Feedback may be provided verbally, by notation, or by graphing (see Figure 2–5). Feedback is sometimes sufficient by itself but is often combined with other stimuli. Second, there is social consequation for correct responses. Social stimuli can be verbal, e.g., "Very good!," nonverbal, e.g., a smile or nod, or physical, e.g., a hug or handshake. Third, material consequences are used to reinforce correct responses. Material consequences can include any type of tangible object, e.g., a smelly sticker or a record. Fourth, consumable consequences are provided for correct responses. Consumable stimuli include things eaten or drunk, e.g., raisin or juice. The categories above represent a sequence from natural to contrived. A "rule of thumb" is that the lower the developmental level, or the more severe the student's problems, the more contrived the consequences will have to be. You should always use the least contrived consequence that is effective. If you have to use a contrived consequence, one of your objectives should be to move to less contrived consequences as soon as possible.

Positive consequences should be delivered on a schedule. There are two basic types of schedules, continuous and intermittent. A *continuous schedule* is one consequence for each correct response. This schedule is best for teaching new responses or strengthening weak responses. Once a response has been established at an acceptable level (you must set a criterion for this), you should gradually and systematically shift to an intermittent schedule. The most common *intermittent schedule* used with academic tasks is a *fixed ratio schedule*.

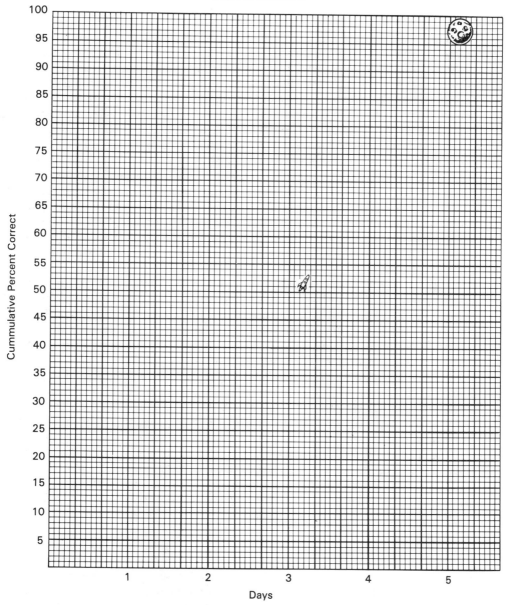

Flight to the Moon

**Figure 2–5** A feedback chart showing a student's progress, represented by a movable "spaceship," toward a weekly goal, represented by the moon, of a performance average of 95% correct over a week's work in a given subject. One hundred percent correct or 100 points is assumed to be possible each day. Thus, a 500-point week is the basis for the chart. Eighty-five percent correct on the first day translates into 17% of the weekly total (85/500). Each day, the "spaceship" would be repositioned according to the cumulative, mean percent correct up to that day relative to the total. For example, 85% on day 1, 90% on day 2, and 90% on day 3 would result in the "spaceship's nose" being placed on the intersection of the 53% (265/500) line (horizontal) and the day 3 line (vertical).

This is the delivery of a positive consequence on a ratio of one consequence to some number of correct responses, e.g., 1:3 or 1:10. When shifting or stretching the schedule, you should move in small steps, e.g., 1:5, then 1:10, then 1:15, etc. Each change in the schedule should occur only after a predetermined criterion has been met. This criterion is the mastery criterion previously discussed. You must also be concerned with what is called *schedule strain* when stretching a schedule. Schedule strain occurs when your change isn't gradual enough (you stretch too much at one time) or your criterion is too short (you stretch too quickly), or both. Schedule strain occurs after a shift in the schedule. It is present if there is too much decline in performance or very variable performance, i.e., up and down performance that doesn't soon begin to smooth out. You need to set a criterion to help you monitor your schedule stretching. This criterion should alert you that you are moving too much, too quickly, or both. The criterion can vary depending on the student. However, the criterion should never allow more than a 40% reduction in accuracy level. Variability above this minimum will usually smooth out in a short time.

Another problem you may have to deal with is logistical in nature. If you use a reinforcer difficult to handle, e.g., ice cream, or one difficult to parcel out, e.g., a model airplane, you may need to use a *reinforcement mediator*. A reinforcement mediator is something like points or tokens. A mediatior should be easy to handle and have exchange value for desirable reinforcers. There are two cautions about mediators. First, you must clearly establish the connection between the mediator and rewards before using it. Second, you should not have too much delay between collection of the mediator and exchange for the reward. It is desirable for the student to be able to tolerate delays between these two events. The delay period should, however, be lengthened in a gradual and systematic way.

The end objective for consequation should be to move the student to the most natural consequences, e.g., feedback on correctness, and the most natural schedule, e.g., at the end of a complete class period, assignment, or other logical division of instruction. These are the conditions of consequation that most nonhandicapped students work under in the regular classroom.

*4. Teach and Monitor Progress.* The next step is to teach the lesson and monitor student progress. To monitor the student when using direct instruction, you need to utilize continual measurement. That is, measurement is done each time the student responds. The two most common measures are event and permanent product recording. *Event recording* is usually used for vocal responses, e.g., oral responses to flashcards, or motor responses other than writing, e.g., pointing. *Permanent product recording* is usually used for written responses. The written response can be simple, e.g., a math computation, or complex, e.g., an essay. The important thing is that there is some lasting result of the student's response that can be used as a measure. Two other measures, less frequently used, are duration and latency recording. Both of these are related to time. Duration recording is used when it is important to know how long a response lasts. Latency recording is used when it is important to know how long it takes for a response to occur after its immediate antecedent occurs.

To have a reference point for monitoring the effect of instruction, measurement needs to be taken several times before instruction begins to get a baseline response level. After the baseline is established, instruction can begin. Measurement will continue during instruction. Usually measurements are graphed to make monitoring easier. With a visual representation of performance, it is much easier to tell how instruction is progressing and when preset criterion points are reached. Graphs will also make it easier to discuss with someone else how a student is doing. Figure 2–6 is an example of a performance graph. Looking at the graph, you see that it has four phases. Each phase is separated from the adjacent phase by a phase-change line. The phase-change lines are the vertical dashed lines. Let's assume that this is a graph of the instruction on short *a* sounds in words discussed earlier.

The first phase on the graph is the baseline. During this phase, the student was given no explanations or demonstrations concerning short *a* sound. The student was simply told to raise a hand when a short *a* word was heard. Ten sets of three words, where each set contained a short *a* word, were presented on three different occasions. Event recording was used to measure correct responses. That is, a tally of correct and incorrect responses was kept. The

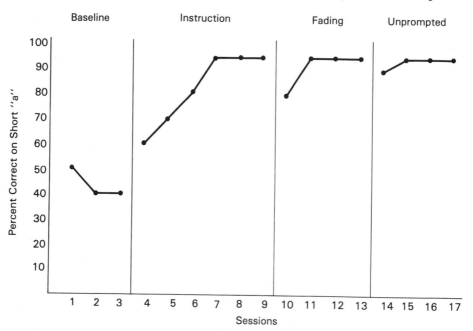

**Figure 2–6**    A graph to monitor student performance on mastering short *a* sound. The first phase is labeled "baseline" and runs for three sessions. The second phase, labled "instruction," runs six sessions and ends with three consecutive sessions at 95% correct. The third phase, labeled "fading," represents the intermediate level of the prompt and runs for four sessions. This phase also ends with three consecutive 95% sessions. The fourth phase, labeled "unprompted," represents complete elimination of the prompt. This phase also runs for four sessions and ends with three consecutive 95% sessions.

recording procedure did not provide the student with any feedback concerning correctness. In the second phase, the student was given an explanation and demonstration of the short *a* before presenting ten sets of words. In addition, the short *a* sound was prompted by increased volume. Finally, the student was given praise (social reinforcement) following each correct response. This phase continued until the mastery criterion was reached. The third phase was then entered. In this phase, everything continued as in the second phase except that the prompt was faded to the intermediate level. The procedure continued in the same way through the third phase and into the fourth. At the end of the fourth, we could start stretching the reinforcement schedule by adding a fifth phase.

*5. Evaluate Performance.*    The student's response to instruction is evaluated using the various criteria discussed previously. The evaluation can result in several possible outcomes. First, the evaluation may show that instruction is not succeeding or is producing results at too slow a pace. In this event, the model would send you back to the "plan instruction" component to modify the instructional plan. If the evaluation of the modified plan should be negative, the model sends you back to the "instructional objective" component. Once back at this component, you consider a modification of the objective or a different objective. Second, the evaluation may show success. In that event, the model sends you back to the "instructional objective" component for a new objective, i.e., assuming that more than one deficit skill was identified. Third, when the last objective for the identified deficits is mastered, the model sends you to the "post-test" component.

*6. Post-test.*    The post-test is a terminal assessment of the curriculum domain being addressed. Finally, if any deficits appear in the post-test, the model sends you back to the "instructional objective" component. If no deficits appear in the post-test, the student's remediation in this curriculum domain is complete.

## RESOURCES

There are several useful resources for direct instruction of academic skills. One excellent resource is a four-volume set of books under the general title, *A Technology of Reading and Writing*. Volumes in this set include a detailed task analysis (D. Smith, 1976), criterion-referenced tests (D. Smith, J. Smith, & Brink, 1977), classroom adaptations (D. Smith, 1977), and instructional design (J. Smith, 1978). Another useful resource is a curriculum handbook (Stephens, Hartman, & Lucas, 1982) which includes task analyses for reading, arithmetic, spelling, handwriting, and language arts for kindergarten through the eighth grade. Scope and sequence charts are provided for the objectives derived from the task analyses. This handbook also includes criterion-referenced tests for many of the curriculum objectives. Instructions are given on how to develop your own tests for the other objectives. Finally, the handbook provides sample lesson plans and instructional strategies. Another useful handbook (Howell & Kaplan, 1980) provides extensive coverage of criterion-referenced assessment of basic skills.

There are many materials compatible with the direct instruction approach. The *Criterion Referenced Curriculum* (Stephens, 1984) is a complete curriculum for math and reading for kindergarten through sixth grade. The program includes criterion-referenced tests and instructional strategies for all of the objectives covered in the curriculum. Another excellent source of materials is Science Research Associates. This publisher has several carefully developed kits for direct instruction covering reading, arithmetic, and language.

## REFERENCES

BANDURA, A. (1977). Self-efficacy: Toward a unifying theory of behavioral change. *Psychological Review, 84*, 191-215.

BECKER, W., & CARNINE, D. (1981). Direct instruction: A behavior theory model for comprehensive educational intervention with the disadvantaged. In S. Bijou & R. Ruiz (Eds.), *Behavior Modification: Contributions to Education*. Hillsdale, NJ: Lawrence Erlbaum.

BECKER, W., & ENGELMANN, S. (1978). Systems for basic instruction: Theory and applications. In A. Cantania & T. Brigham (Eds.), *Handbook of Applied Behavior Analysis: Social and Instructional Processes*. New York: Irvington.

BIJOU, S., & RUIZ, R. (1981). Behavior Modification: Contributions to Education. Hillsdale, NJ: Lawrence Erlbaum.

BLOOM, B. (1976). *Human Characteristics and School Learning*. New York: McGraw-Hill.

COLE, J., & COLE, M. (1983). *Language Lessons for the Special Education Classroom*. Rockville, MD: Aspen.

CRANDALL, V. C., KATKOVSKY, N., & CRANDALL, V. J. (1965). Children's beliefs in their own control of reinforcements in intellectual-academic achievement situations. *Child Development, 36*, 91-109.

GLASS, G., CAHEN, L., SMITH, M., & FILBY, N. (1979, April-May). Class size and learning: New interpretation of the research literature. *Today's Education*, pp. 42-44.

GUERIN, G., & MAIER, A. (1983). Informal Assessment in Education. Mountain View, CA: Mayfield.

HARING, N., LOVITT, T., EATON, M., & HANSEN, C. (1978). *The Fourth R: Research in the Classroom*. Columbus, OH: Merrill.

HOLLAND, J., SOLOMAN, C., DORAN, J., & FREZZA, D. (1976). *The Analysis of Behavior in Planning Instruction*. Reading, MA: Addison-Wesley.

HOWELL, K., & KAPLAN, J. (1980). *Diagnosing Basic Skills: A Handbook for Deciding What to Teach*. Columbus, OH: Merrill.

JENKINS, J., MAYHALL, W., PESCHKA, C., & JENKINS, L. (1974). Comparing small group and tutorial instruction in resource rooms. *Exceptional Children, 40*(4), 245-250.

LINDSLEY, O. (1972). From Skinner to precision teaching: The child knows best. In J. Jordan & L. Robbins (Eds.), *Let's Try Doing Something Else Kind of Thing*. Reston, VA: Council for Exceptional Children.

MOYER, R., & DARDIG, J. (1978). Practical task analysis for special educators. *Teaching Exceptional Children, 11*(1), 16-18.

PREISER, W., & TAYLOR, A. (1983). The habitability framework: Linking human behavior and physical environment in special education. *Exceptional Education Quarterly, 4*(2), 1-15.

SKINNER, B. (1954). The science of learning and the art of teaching. *Harvard Educational Review, 29*, 86-97.

SKINNER, B. (1968). *The Technology of Teaching*. New York: Appleton-Century-Crofts.

SMITH, D. (1976). *Learning to Read and Write: A Task Analysis*. New York: Academic Press.

SMITH, D. (1977). *The Adaptive Classroom*. New York: Academic Press.

SMITH, J. (1978). *Designing Instructional Tasks*. New York: Academic Press.

SMITH, J., SMITH, D., & BRINK, J. (1977). *Criterion Referenced Tests for Reading and Writing*. New York: Academic Press.

STEPHENS, T. (1976). *Directive Teaching of Children With Learning and Behavior Handicaps* (2nd ed.). Columbus, OH: Merrill.

STEPHENS, T. (1977). *Teaching Skills to Children with Learning and Behavior Disorders*. Columbus, OH: Merrill.

STEPHENS, T. (1977). *Teaching Skills to Children with Learning and Behavior Disorder*. Columbus, OH: Merrill.

STEPHENS, T. (1984). *Criterion Referenced Curriculum*. Columbus, OH: Merrill.

STEPHENS, T., HARTMAN, A., & LUCAS, V. (1982). *Teaching Children Basic Skills: A Curriculum Handbook* (2nd ed.). Columbus, OH: Merrill.

ULRICH, R., STACHNIK, T., & MABRY, J. (1974). *Control of Human Behavior: Behavior Modification in Education*. Glenview, IL: Scott, Foresman.

# 3

# TEACHING ACADEMICS

## Learning Skills

**INTRODUCTION**

The approach for assessing and teaching learning skills is the same as that suggested for teaching basic academic skills. The direct instruction model and criterion-referenced assessment can be applied to both learning skills and basic skills. There will be no additional discussion in this chapter of the instructional model. The student is referred to Chapter 2.

There are several reasons for including learning skills in the curriculum. First, generic learning skills are needed by all students (Bloom, 1979). Bloom suggests that besides the need to stress various academic skills, attention should also be given to more general skills. These include skills such as problem solving, library skills, and organization skills. Second, learning skills are especially needed by handicapped students (Alley & Deshler, 1979). Alley and Deshler point out that teachers usually assume that general learning skills are acquired incidentally while learning subject matter. This appears to be an unwarranted assumption for many nonhandicapped students and particularly for handicapped learners. Third, these skills improve learning efficiency because they are transferable across subject areas. Learning skills are needed not only to succeed in school but also for independent life-long learning.

## GENERAL SKILLS

### Following Directions

Burmeister (1978) suggested several explanations for why students fail to follow directions. One possibility is that they are simply careless about directions. There are several possible explanations for this carelessness. First, a student may not recognize the importance, or value, of directions. Directions will not command a student's attention if they are not believed to be important. Second, a student may recognize the importance of directions but has learned that they will be repeated as often as desired. A third possibility is that a student may simply decide not to follow the directions. This may be the fault of the directions. For example, a student may find the directions confusing or inadequate and decide to ignore them. Fourth, directions may be ignored as a way to avoid tasks. A fifth possibility is that a student does not know how to follow directions. There has either not been an opportunity to learn this skill or previous learning experiences have been faulty. If a student fails to follow directions for one of the reasons outlined above, there are several possible solutions.

A teacher must be careful when preparing directions or evaluating and possibly modifying directions provided in materials such as workbooks. Particular attention needs to be given to matching the difficulty level of the directions with student ability level. You must also be careful that failure to follow directions doesn't result in successfully avoiding task demands. Burmeister (1978) believes it is important to set the expectation in students that directions will be given only once. When this is done students are impressed with the necessity of giving directions their attention the first time they are presented. A procedure that represents a workable compromise with the one-time-only rule is to put a charge on repeated directions. This is easily done in classrooms with a systematic classroom management plan such as the token economy described in Chapter 4. If there is a classroom token economy, you can charge a student a fee for an unnecessary repetition of directions. In short, repeat the directions as often as requested but place a charge on repetitions. Another procedure, if there is a classroom token economy, is to place a reinforcement contingency on appropriate direction following. This is done by placing a value, in tokens, on direction following and paying students for following directions.

It is important to convey to students the importance of directions for success. Burns (1980) described a process that can be used to do this. Burns emphasizes the importance of establishing the importance of directions as concretely as possible. With a group of elementary-age students, she used making a peanut butter sandwich for a concrete demonstration. She asked students to give her directions on how to make a peanut butter sandwich and wrote them down. The next day she brought in the necessary ingredients for making a sandwich. She got the students to read her the directions and made a sandwich according to their directions. The students were not allowed to add anything new to the set of directions they had developed. She also took every opportunity to misunderstand the directions. The result was, as she had anticipated, a disaster. After the activity, she gave the students an opportunity to revise their directions, and the process was repeated. When the activity was completed successfully, they ate the properly constructed products. Thomas and Robinson (1977) described a method for concretely demonstrating the importance of directions with older students. They used directions in a lab course to make their point. They first gave the students a complex set of directions for conducting a lab experiment. They allowed the students to read the directions in their customary and cursory manner and then attempt to conduct the experiment. After the students botched up the experiment, they taught them the proper way of approaching a complex set of directions. The method taught was the "three-times-over" procedure. In this procedure students are first required to read the directions over lightly for a general overview. Next, students are taught to read the directions carefully and to rehearse each step cognitively before going on to the next step. Students are taught to review the entire set of directions again to get the full sequence firmly in mind. Finally, students are taught the importance of constantly referring to the directions as the experiment proceeds. Students are then asked to repeat the experiment. The results are usually much better on the repetition and clearly show the importance of giving the directions careful attention.

If instruction is necessary on following directions, attention should be given to both oral and written directions. When you teach direction following, you should always begin with simple directions and move progressively to more complex directions. You should also use emphasis cues, at least initially, when teaching direction following. With oral directions this can be done using the voice to give emphasis to key words in the directions. One approach to teaching oral directions is to use various games that involve direction following. Russell and Russell (1959) describe several games that can be used. One of the games suggested is You Must. In this game, a variation on Simon Says, children are put into a group and a leader is designated. The leader gives the group directions to do various things, e.g., to hop on one foot. Each direction must be prefaced by the words "You must." If these words are omitted, the directions must be ignored. If the words are omitted and any child follows the direction, the child is out of the game. Another approach to teaching oral direction following is to use various activities. Burns (1980) suggests several activities that depend on oral directions. One of these activities is building a structure using materials such as Cuisenaire rods. In this activity, two students are paired up and placed at a table. A divider is placed between the students so that they can't see what the other is doing. One student is designated the leader and the other the follower. Both are given a set of Cuisenaire rods. The leader builds a structure using the rods and provides the follower with oral directions for duplicating the structure. The follower must listen to the leader's oral directions and duplicate the structure. The directions must be followed exactly as given. After the activity is completed, the partition is removed and the two structures are compared. If the two structures aren't identical, the process is repeated until they are identical.

During repetition, flaws in the directions, direction following, or both will usually be discovered and corrected.

When you teach following written directions, you should also begin with simple directions and move progressively to more complex directions. You can also make use of emphasis cues in written directions. The simplest way to use emphasis cues in written directions is to underline key words in the directions. With younger students, Burns (1980) suggests that games be used to teach written direction following. Burns has students write out the directions for playing a game they like, e.g., how to play Tic-Tac-Toe. After the directions have been written, they are given to another student, who doesn't know how to play the game. The student who wrote the directions and the other student play the game according to the directions. If the game doesn't work out, the directions are revised and the game repeated. Another approach is to use various activities. One activity used for demonstration purposes is a direction-following test (see Box 3–1). You may have seen a test like this before or even taken one. You can construct several versions of this test for variability in the directions each time the activity is done. More closely related to academics are the activities suggested by Burmeister (1978). Activities for teaching written direction following in English, in mathematics, in science, and in social studies are illustrated. Box 3–2 is an example of an activity for English. Another activity, suggested by Thomas and Robinson (1977), is to provide students with direction-reading assignments using the three-times-over process described earlier. Students are given a checklist to complete while reading the directions. The checklist is designed to help them monitor their understanding of the directions.

**Box 3–1**  A quiz on proper direction following that can be given to students to demonstrate the importance of reading directions

---

**EVALUATION SHEET**

Name_____ Date_____

*Directions:* Read over the items below carefully and fully before answering.
1. In the upper right-hand corner of this page, draw a small square.
2. Put a circle around the square.
3. Place a dot in the center of the circle.
4. The _____ root of 4 is 2.
5. The square of 3 is _____.
6. As a slang term "square" can mean someone who isn't_____.
7. A tool called a square is used by _____.
8. As a figure, a square might be used in a branch of math called _____.
9. If two parallel sides of a square are lengthened, the resulting figure is called a _____.
10. If you are a square, complete the items above and throw this sheet away. Otherwise, turn it in blank.

---

**Box 3–2**    An example of a direction-following exercise in the area of English

---

**IN ENGLISH**

 1.  Look up the word "genre" in your dictionary and write the first two definitions given.
   _____
   _____

 2.  Look in your dictionary to find in what year Thomas Gray was born and in what year he
   died. Write the dates here: born _____, died _____.
 3.  Complete the following sentence by inserting two adjectives that make sense: The
   _____  _____ building collapsed when the tornado struck.
 4.  Insert two common nouns and any additional words necessary to complete the following
   sentence:_____ and _____ tied in the race.
 5.  If all the words in the following sentence are spelled correctly, circle every third word in
   this complete item; if not, circle every second word: "The dinosaur is a prehistoric animal."
   .
   .
   .
   .
10.

                                                        Time: _____

---

Source:   L. Burmeister, *Reading Strategies for Middle and Secondary School Teachers* (2nd ed.), 1978, Addison-Wesley Publishing Co.

### Library and Reference Skills

One thing that has to be done in order to teach library and reference skills is to stimulate students' interest in these skills. Petreshene (1982) suggested a procedure that can be used to stimulate interest. She conducts a weekly exercise with her students called Monday's Question. The idea is to ask an intriguing question that will engage students' interest. The students are given all week to find an answer to the question. Participation is voluntary and no written response is required. Students are also asked to keep their answers secret. At the end of the week, the students who have found an answer to the question are asked to stand. Each student is asked to state one fact about the topic of the question without repeating anything already said. When a student runs out of material, he or she is eliminated from the game and sits down. This process continues until there is only one student left standing. The game is repeated every week. The game can be age graded by varying the question topics. Once you have stimulated some interest in reference skills, it is much easier to teach them to your students.

There is an almost endless list of library and reference skills that could be taught. In Table 3–1, you will find a list of things that might be considered essential for making good use of a library and reference materials. The list is divided into three broad areas. The first division includes things a student needs

**Table 3-1**    A curriculum outline for library and
reference skills

---

    I.  Organization
        1. Dewey Decimal System
        2. Library of Congress System
        3. Card catalog
           a. Author index
           b. Subject index
        4. Locating shelved material

    II.  Reference
        1. Guides to periodical literature
           a. General
           b. Specialized
        2. Indexes to newspapers
        3. Dictionaries
        4. Encyclopedias
        5. Almanacs
        6. Atlases

    III.  Services
        1. Librarians
        2. Borrowing and reserving material
        3. Interlibrary loans
        4. Computer searches
        5. Copying

---

to know about library organization. The second division includes several common reference materials that a student should know how to use. The last division contains some of the services usually available in a good library of which a student should be aware. Usually the items contained in this curriculum outline can be taught in a school library, although a few of the items may require a larger library. Burmeister (1978) and Devine (1981) both devote a lot of attention to what and how to teach students about libraries.

One reference skill that can be taught right in the classroom is the use of a dictionary. This is a good first skill to teach because it is probably the most used reference skill. The skills required for good dictionary usage can also be readily transferred to many other reference resources, e.g., encyclopedias. Basic dictionary skills that need to be taught include alphabetizing using more than one letter, how to use guide words, what entry words are, common dictionary abbreviations, pronunciation guides, and how definitions are organized.

Both games and activities can be useful in teaching dictionary usage. Kaluger and Kolson (1978) provide examples of alphabetizing and guide word activities that can be used to teach dictionary skills. Cunningham, Cunningham, and Arthur (1981) describe several games that rely on the use of a dictionary. One of these games, the Dictionary Game, asks students to think of unusual words that may not be known by other students. Students look up and write down the definition of their unusual word. In addition, three fake definitions are constructed for the word. The game is for students to try to identify a word's correct definition. Correct identification earns a student or the student's team a point. The student or team with the most points wins the game. Cunningham et al. also describe a procedure used to help students keep up with new words and their definitions. They suggest that instead of having students keep a notebook of new words, you have them construct a "living dictionary." The dictionary is constructed on 3 × 5 cards kept on a shower curtain ring. The cards and ring allow students to add or delete words at any time and keep the "dictionary" correctly alphabetized.

### Test-Taking Skills

Like any skill, test-taking skills can be taught. Two skill areas stand out as particularly important. First, students need to know how to study for tests. Second, students need to know strategies that can be applied to taking a test.

We will briefly discuss two approaches developed to give students a systematic way of studying and preparing for a test. The first of these approaches was originally developed at the end of World War II by F. P. Robinson. In a recent publication, Robinson (1970) described the system he originally developed in 1946. His system has proven useful to many students over the years. The system Robinson developed is known as the *SQ3R method*. The method begins by teaching students to *Survey* all the topic headings, subheadings, and summaries. In the second step, students are taught to turn all the headings and subheadings into *Questions*. In the third step, students are taught to *Read* the material for answers to the questions. In the fourth step, students are taught to *Recite* the answers to the questions. This step should be done without any reference to the material. This step helps students fix the answers in memory. The fifth and final step is to *Review*. In this step, students are taught to review the material to double check the appropriateness of the questions and the accuracy of their answers. The second approach was developed by Hill and Eller (1964). Their approach is called the *POINT system*. The first step is to establish the *Purpose* for studying. This involves teaching students to set objectives for studying. Objectives are best stated in the form of questions. The second step is to *Overview* the material. Students are taught to survey the material to determine the scope of the material and to identify key facts and ideas. The third step is to *Interpret* the material. Students are taught to read carefully and relate detail to the major organizing ideas identified. In the fourth step, students are taught to develop a systematic set of *Notes* on the material. Notes should be in outline form. Emphasis is placed on students stating ideas in their own words. The fifth and final step is to *Test*. Students are taught to test themselves on the material by using the questions developed in the first step. In their book, Hill and Eller (1964) provide detailed discussion of the POINT system, a student checklist, and exercises useful for teaching students to use the system.

Next, students need to be taught strategies for taking tests. Campanile (1981) discussed some points that need to be covered when teaching students to be good test takers. First, she recommends that you go over tests in class and discuss the likely reasoning used in different responses to each item. The discussion will help identify faulty strategies that students may be using on tests. Second, she recommends demonstrating to students the importance of correctly following and interpreting directions on a test. Some of the suggestions given earlier on following directions can be used to work on this problem area. One of the most common problems in interpreting directions is failure to understand what is being asked for by various commonly used terms. Carlson (1979) identified some terms often critical to correct interpretation of directions. The following words were identified: compare, contrast, criticize, define, diagram, discuss, enumerate, evaluate, explain, illustrate, interpret, justify, list, outline, prove, relate, state, review, summarize, and trace. It is important for students to recognize that each term is asking for a different kind of response and how the responses differ from one another. Working under time limits is a third area that Campanile believes is important. She suggests giving students experience with timed activities of variable length. One activity she uses is sitting idle for a timed interval, e.g., 5 minutes. After the timed period ends, she and the students discuss what could have been accomplished in that amount of time.

In Table 3–2, you will find several strategies for improving performance on tests. The strategies are divided into three groups. The first group applies primarily to objective tests. The second group applies to tests requiring student comprehension of written material. The questions on this type of test may be either objective or require written responses. The third group applies to essay tests which require complex written responses.

Carman and Adams (1972) discuss a system that is easy to remember and includes some of the suggestions in Table 3–2. Their system is called *SCORER* and can be applied to any type of test. This system helps students remember to *Schedule* their time, look for *Clue* words, temporarily *Omit* difficult items, *Read* questions carefully, *Estimate* what the correct answer is (which is particularly helpful on items involving mathematics), and *Review* their completed test for errors.

Raphael (1982) discusses a system for approaching items on a comprehension test. The system is called *QAR*. QAR teaches students to classify questions based on the *Question-Answer Relationship*. The critical step in classifying a question is to identify the source of the information need to answer it. Raphael's first QAR is called "Right There," which means that the answer is explicit in the material and in one place. The second QAR is called "Think and Search," which means that the answer to the question is explicit in the material but will be found in more than one place, and the parts will have to be integrated. The third QAR is called "On My Own," and means that the answer is implicit in the material and will require the answer to be formulated by the student. Raphael (1982) provides a week-long sample lesson sequence for teaching this system.

Stewart and Green (1983) emphasize the importance of practice for learning to use new skills. They recommend practice take place under conditions similar to actual testing situations. Both the practice materials and the testing rules should be realistic. The arrangement of the room and the atmosphere should be similar to actual test conditions. Practice sessions should end with a discussion of problems students had with the test.

**Table 3–2**    A set of general guidelines to be followed by students when taking objective, comprehension, and essay-type tests

---

I. Objective tests
1. If an answer sheet is used, be sure that the organization of it is understood.
2. If demonstration items are provided, work through them.
3. Determine the number of items and the amount of time available and allocate each item a proportional amount of time, but reserve a few minutes to review for careless errors when the test is finished.
4. Begin by answering the readily known items first.
5. If items are skipped, mark them on the answer sheet, on the test, or on scratch paper, so they won't be forgotten.
6. Read each question completely and identify what it is asking for, e.g., who, what, when, where, why, or how.
7. Read all answer choices and give extra consideration to choices such as *all of the above* or *none of the above*.
8. Be alert for overly inclusive words such as *all*, *always*, and *never* in questions or answer choices.
9. Be very careful of items containing negatives, e.g, *no* and *not*.
10. Use the process of elimination to narrow down choices.
11. On difficult items, look for clues to the answer in other items on the test.
12. If guessing isn't penalized, select an answer choice which repeats a term of phrase used in the question, or select the longest answer choice.

II. Comprehension tests
1. Read the questions first.
2. Read the passage fully.
3. Answer the questions based only on what is provided.
4. Use scanning to locate key words or phrases in a reading passage that relate to a question.

III. Essay tests
1. Begin by reading over each of the questions. As you read, note key direction words, such as *compare* and *contrast.* Be sure that you know what each question is asking.
2. If choices are permitted, select the easier questions.
3. Make a brief outline for each question to be answered.
4. Budget your time and allow a few minutes for review at the end of the test.
5. Be sure that your answers are written legibly.
6. Give examples and cite references whenever possible.
7. When you finish, review your answers for errors in grammar, punctuation, spelling, etc.
8. If you should run out of time before you get to a question, answer it with the brief outline.

---

### Time Management

McCabe (1982) believes that the first step in developing time management skills is to help students become aware of how they spend their time. To this end, she has students keep a chart of how they spend their time. The chart is drawn up with days of the week across the top and time of day, in one-hour intervals, down the left-hand side. You might sometimes want to use intervals smaller than one hour. Students are asked to write in each day/time block on the chart what they did during the time. From the chart, summaries are developed by categories. For example, a summary for a day or week can be done showing how much time was spent on studying compared to watching TV. It is not enough to know how time is spent. Students must learn how to use time better. To use time better, students need to learn how to schedule time. Before a useful schedule can be developed a student must learn to set priorities and to do time estimates.

Learning to set priorities requires students to consider three things: immediacy, complexity, and importance. Students should first be taught to develop a list of things they are responsible for getting done. The list can initially be limited to a single day and then gradually expanded to cover longer periods. Next, they should be taught to evaluate various tasks on the list according to complexity. Each task should be designated at least as simple, complex, or very complex. Each task should also be rated according to its importance, e.g., unimportant, important, and very important. Some students may have to be taught how to judge both complexity and importance. This can best be done with examples, practice in making the judgments, and feedback on correctness. Learning to do accurate time estimates is a difficult skill to master.

The best way to acquire this skill is practice. Students should be asked to keep a chart of things they are going to be doing. These should be written in a column labeled "Activity." The chart should have two other columns, labeled "Estimated Time" and "Actual Time" (see Table 3–3). Beside each item on the chart, students should enter their estimate of how much time is going to be needed. Later, students should write in the adjacent column the actual time required. A fourth column (see Table 3–3), labeled "Difference," should show how much over or under the estimates were.

**Table 3–3**    An activities chart to aid students in learning to make accurate time estimates

| ACTIVITY | ESTIMATED TIME | ACTUAL TIME | DIFFERENCE |
|---|---|---|---|
| 1. Read Chapter 2 | 30 min | 72 min | +42 min |
| 2. Wash dishes | 40 min | 21 min | -19 min |
| 3. *and so on* | | | |
| 4. | | | |
| 5. | | | |
| 6. | | | |
| 7. | | | |
| 8. | | | |
| 9. | | | |
| 10. | | | |

The final step is to teach students how to develop schedules. First, students should be asked to develop a set of categories covering the various things they need to do. This set of categories may include such things as homework, school projects, chores or work, and recreation. Second, students should be asked to list all activities coming up in each category. At first, a short time period should be used, e.g., a day or week. After students have learned to develop and use schedules, longer time periods can be used, e.g., a month or a quarter. Third, students should be told to set priorities for all the activities that have been listed. Initially, this should be done with supervision. Fourth, the activities on the list should be assigned time estimates. Fifth, students should be helped to plan a schedule. The planning should begin with a time chart divided into convenient intervals with a separate page for each day the schedule will cover. Let's assume that the first schedule will cover only a single day (see Table 3–4). Sixth, students should be helped to go over the chart and assign enough time blocks to the highest-priority activity to cover the time estimate for the activity. The process is then repeated with the second-highest-priority activity, and so on, until all activities have been covered or the available time has been used up. If the available time is used up before all the activities are covered, students should be assisted in reexamining the time estimates to be certain they are reasonable. If the time estimates are reasonable, the priorities should be reexamined to be sure they are appropriate. If changes are indicated in either the time estimates or priorities, the planning should be redone after making the changes. If no changes can be made, students should be counseled about their tendency to overextend themselves and given help in finding ways to modify their commitments

**Table 3–4**   An initial attempt at developing a daily schedule[a]

| ACTIVITY | TIME |
|---|---|
| I. Schoolwork | |
|    1.   Math homework | 7:30–8:00 |
|    2.   English homework | 8:00–8:30 |
|    3.   History homework | 8:30–9:00 |
|    4.   Science project | ? |
| II. Chores | |
|    1.   Cut grass | 5:30–6:30 |
|    2.   Wash dishes | 7:00–7:20 |
|    3.   Take out trash | 7:20–7:30 |
|    4.   Get ready for bed | 10:00–10:15 |
| III. Recreation | |
|    1.   Play soccer | 3:30–5:00 |
|    2.   Watch TV | 9:00–10:00 |
|    3.   Call Bill | ? |

[a]Note that the schedule is in need of revision. The students gets out of school at 3:00 and must be in bed by 10:00. Assuming that the time estimates are reasonable, the student would need to use prioritizing to adjust the schedule.

to fit the available time. Finally, students should be asked to use the schedule they developed to see how appropriate it is in practice. If the schedule is appropriate, it is time to try working with longer periods. If it isn't appropriate, you should go back to the planning stage and make revisions. In the application stage, you may find some students need an incentive to help them use and stick to their schedule. Usually a contract that provides a reward for following the schedule should be used. Once the usefulness of the schedule is understood, its use will become rewarding and the external reward can be dropped.

### Memory Skills

There is little doubt that good memory skills are essential to success in school. The most common method of assessing how much students have learned is to determine how much they have remembered. Gladstein (1967) pointed out two basic divisions in memory skills. First, there is recognition. Students must recognize something when presented; e.g., "Which is the correct spelling for something you do with a pencil, *right* or *write?*" Second, there is recall. Recall requires students to generate the requested fact or idea; e.g., "Spell 'write,' as in, "I will write a letter." In this section, we will be concerned with recall, since this is the type of memory task that gives students the most difficulty. When trying to help students with remembering factual information such as names and dates, Devine (1981) suggested the use of two strategies. First, mnemonic devices, such as numeric pegwords, can be helpful. In this strategy, a numeric list, e.g., 1 through 10, is used to organize the material. The numbers and items in the list can be related by rhyme, e.g., 1 son, 2 blue, and 3 free. The numbers and items can be related by shape, e.g., 1 stick, 2 question, and 3 camel. The relationship between the items and numbers can be sequential or chronological, e.g., 1 private, 2 private first class, and 3 corporal. Second, the use of mental imagery can be useful. In this strategy, easily remembered symbols are associated with facts or details to be recalled. For example, if students need to remember the names of historical figures, they might use such associations as cherry tree/Washington, top hat/Lincoln, vacuum cleaner/Hoover, and so on. Devine (see Table 3–5) also suggested a list of questions that students should ask themselves, as they study, to help them develop memory aids for the material.

Students are often faced with memory tasks more complex than simply recalling words and names. A complex memory task requires a systematic way of organizing the material for memory. Burmeister (1978) suggested that the material be organized around main ideas and then details associated with the appropriate main idea. For example, if students are studying national political alliances, the organizing concepts might include Western bloc, Eastern bloc, and independent. Specific countries being studied could be associated with the appropriate organizer. For example, countries in the Western bloc are the United States, Britain, France, West Germany, and Japan. Countries in the Eastern bloc are the Soviet Union, China, East Germany, Cuba, and Vietnam.

**Table 3–5**   A set of questions that a student should always keep in mind
while studying, as an aid in developing memory strategies

---

1. How does *this* relate to what I already know?
2. What does it remind me of?
3. What can I associate it with?
4. Can I picture it in my mind?
5. What can I link this picture to?
6. How does it relate to the topic as a whole?
7. What crazy things pop into my mind when I think of it?
8. How can I use the crazy associations to help remember?
9. How does this relate to what I learned before?
10. How does it relate to my life outside this class?

---

SOURCE:   Thomas G. Devine, *Teaching Study Skills: A Guide for Teachers.* Copyright 1981 by Allyn and Bacon, Inc. Reprinted with permission.

Independent countries are India, Brazil, Mexico, Kenya, and Egypt. Burmeister (1978) offers suggestions on how to develop teaching activities to help students learn to use main ideas to organize and remember academic material.

While students will find an appropriate memory strategy helpful, the necessity of drill should not be forgotten. A memory strategy will only reduce, not eliminate, the need for drill. A student will still find some self-recitation or recitation to a monitor helpful. The role of motivation in memory should not be forgotten either. We all find it easier to remember things that we find interesting, e.g., statistics on our favorite athlete or team. The more interesting and relevant to students you make material, the easier it will be for them to remember it.

## LISTENING SKILLS

Otto and Smith (1980) say that listening is an essential skill for students. To convince yourself of the truth of this, you need only think about the extent to which spoken exchanges dominate instruction in classrooms at all levels. Otto and Smith say that students need to be made aware of how oral and written communications differ from one another. Understanding these differences is the first step in learning good listening skills. One way that oral communication differs from written material is in greater variability in both sentence length and structure. A second difference is that there will be more use of fragmentary sentences in oral communication. Finally, students should be aware that oral communications will make greater use of personal pronouns, contractions, and slang.

### Comprehension

Devine (1981) has stated that one of the most important factors in listening comprehension is listening with a purpose. He suggested three general purposes for listening: listening for directions, main ideas, and sequence or organization. We will not deal with listening for directions in this section. We have already discussed this topic in the section on following directions. Listening for main ideas means knowing to listen for various emphasis cues often used by speakers. Emphasis cues are such terms and phrases as *remember, the point is, specifically, in conclusion, note that.* Two writers, Lewis and Nichols (1965), emphasize the need to teach students to listen for organizational patterns in oral presentations.

Listening for organizational patterns requires the student to be aware of these patterns and the cue words that identify them. One pattern is related to chronology. In this pattern the students should listen for cue words suggesting that a chronological or time sequence is to be used. For example, the speaker may say something like "The three critical periods in the evolution of...." Use of this phrase tells the listener that the discussion will be organized around three time periods. A second pattern is spatial organization. The speaker may say, for example, "Ships can best be described in terms of their different decks or levels." Enumeration or listing is the third pattern. In this pattern students listen for such phrases as, "There are five reasons why we must...." The fourth pattern is the topical pattern. In this pattern, students listen for cues indicating that the discussion will be divided into topics. For example, the speaker may say, "The outbreak of World War II will be discussed relative to population, economics, political ideology, and cultural values." A fifth pattern is cause and effect. A speaker might say, "The current shortage of teachers can be attributed to three factors." A sixth pattern is organization through questions. In this pattern, a speaker might say, "In this discussion, I will limit myself to answering three critical questions." While there are a few other patterns, these six represent the ones students are most likely to encounter. Teaching ideas and activities for working on listening comprehension can be found in Devine (1981), Otto and Smith (1980), and Russell and Russell (1959). An interesting and potentially motivating approach to working on listening skills is to use tapes of old radio shows (Weiner, 1974).

### Questioning Skills

Gladstein (1967) suggests that questions can be an excellent aid to concentration when listening to oral presentations. Questions do not have to be directed to the speaker to produce this effect but can be self-directed. In other words, ask yourself questions to be sure you understand the speaker. Questions, according to Gladstein, can have several purposes. Questions can satisfy curiosity, obtain information or clarification, and challenge. Students should be taught how to use wording and tone of voice to ask a question in a nonoffensive way. They should be taught to use a polite tone of voice and to avoid provocative words such as *stupid, racist, treason,* and *sexist.* Students should also be taught how to time their questions, so that they don't interrupt a speaker's train of thought. Teach students to listen for natural breaks in a presentation or pauses in delivery. Students also need to be taught the importance of question signals, e.g., raising a hand when they want to ask a question. Finally, students should be cautioned against the use of questions simply as attention-getting devices or as a means of showing off their knowledge.

## READING

In this section, we will not be concerned with reading in its conventional sense. We will not look at reading skills like decoding or comprehension but at various supplementary skills. These reading-related skills include understanding what the parts of a textbook are, how to use them, and how to approach the reading of text material. The importance of these supplementary skills have been discussed by several writers on study skills (Burmeister, 1978; Devine, 1981; Kaluger & Kolson, 1978; Otto & Smith, 1980).

### Previewing

Previewing helps students grasp the framework in which reading will take place. Devine (1981) suggests that a teacher introduce a new text by discussing the book's structure. The discussion should focus on such topics as: what the title of the text means, the author's qualifications, why the author wrote the book, for whom the book was written, and how current the material in the book is. Burmeister (1978) suggests that examination of the text begin with a discussion of the table of contents as an outline of the book. Devine (1981) suggests including how the topics in the table of contents are related, what topics appear to be missing, and what topics could or will be added by class discussion or supplemental readings.

Next, Burmeister (1978) suggests teaching students to read the preface and introduction for the author's point of view. The next step, according to both Burmeister (1978) and Devine (1981), is to teach students the importance of the glossary, index, and appendices. Discuss the difference between an index and a table of contents, and how a glossary differs from a dictionary. Explain why these components are included, how they are used, and when they should be used. Burmeister also believes that it is important to teach students the purpose of appendices, and how and when to use them. Devine also suggests including a discussion of references and footnotes. Discuss their purpose, use, and possible locations in the text. With older students, include various styles used in references and footnotes, e.g., American Psychological Association style conventions. Also, introduce older students to common abbreviations used in citing references both in text and in footnotes, e.g., *et al.* (and others), *ibid.* (in the same place), *loc. cit.* (in the place cited), and *op. cit.* (in the work cited).

Finally, Burmeister (1978) suggests teaching students to preview the content of a book by reading the chapter titles, headings, subheadings, and illustration captions. Devine (1981) would add to this: coverage of various typographical aids that may be encountered in the text. These include such aids as notes placed in the margin by the author, oversized print, use of boldface lettering, italicized words, graphs, charts, and illustrations. Devine (1981), in his chapter "Reading for Study," has several teaching ideas and activities for previewing.

### Scanning and Skimming

Burmeister (1978) and Cunningham et al. (1981) define *scanning* as a very rapid survey of text material for locating specific details, e.g., names, dates, or key words. They define *skimming* as a thorough survey of material that is faster than reading for full comprehension. Teach students to skim to identify point of view, get an overview of content, identify organizational patterns, or develop an outline or summary. According to Maxwell (1979), skimming is what is often meant by "speed reading."

Pauk (1983) adds to the purposes noted above for skimming the identification of advance organizers. By *advance organizers*, he means key words and terms, around which an author organizes a discussion. Pauk describes the use of an athletic analogy to explain to students the importance of skimming. He discusses how athletes use a warming-up period before a contest to fine tune their concentration. He suggests that skimming is like a warm-up for studying. Next, Pauk teaches his students to use a four-step skim-and-think procedure. First, teach students to read the title of the book and think about what it means. The second step is to read the chapter titles and think about what they mean. Third, he asks students to review several chapter titles and think about how they might be related. Finally, he tells students to read all chapter headings and subheadings, the lead sentence under each, and the summaries at the end of sections or chapters. After this, students are asked to think about the overall theme, purpose, and structure of the text.

One technique for helping students with scanning and some types of skimming is the use of graphic organizers (Alvermann, 1983). Alvermann describes an eight-step process for developing graphic organizers, which is too detailed to cover fully here. The basic idea is for the teacher to review text material and identify the main ideas and supporting details. The teacher uses the ideas and details to construct graphs like the one in Figure 3–1. The students are given the graphs and asked to fill in the blanks with the information omitted. The exercise should be done under a time limit short enough to prevent a complete reading of the source material. This technique will give focus to students' practice and provide a structure for evaluating performance and giving feedback.

### Underlining

A common mistake made by students when underlining, pointed out by Devine (1981), is to use underlining to focus attention on print. This indiscriminate underlining is too extensive to be useful for review. Devine suggests

Graphic Organizer

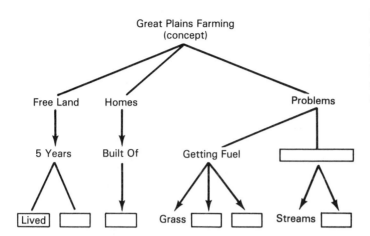

**Figure 3–1**
An example of a graphic organizer that could be used as an exercise to help students learn to use skimming. From Alvermann, 1983.

teaching students to use a coding system for underlining. A coding system will give the process a specific purpose and will reduce indiscriminate underlining. There are several possible approaches to coding. We will look at only one for illustration purposes. A simple coding system can be based on the use of different color pens. For example, teach students to use red to underline main ideas, blue for supporting detail such as examples, and green for new words. For practice, Devine gives students a copy of an article and has them use the coding system. The teacher applies the coding system to the article and uses it as an evaluation standard. Students' performance on the task is evaluated and the results used to identify problems and provide feedback.

### Study Guides

Devine (1981) equates study guides with maps. Study guides map out for students where they are going and how to get there. Study guides can be useful for reading, homework assignments, and test preparation. Study guides may be either teacher-made or available commercially from textbook publishers. Common elements in a study guide include new vocabulary and technical terms introduced and questions about main ideas and important details. The questions included in a study guide may range from simple to complex. For teacher-made study guides, Devine suggests several ways to control the complexity of the questions. One approach uses Bloom's *Taxonomy of Educational Objectives* (Bloom, 1959) for controlling the complexity of questions. The study guide may be focused at a particular level of complexity or there may be a range of complexity. Whether to use a single level or multiple levels within a study guide will depend on the teacher's purpose and instructional objective. Devine (1981), in his chapter on study guides, offers several teaching ideas.

## WRITING

When we talk about writing, we usually mean either handwriting or composition. In this section, we will focus on two specialized writing skills. These skills are taking notes and making outlines from either written or spoken material.

### Notetaking Skills

Notetaking is often taught as a format for recording information. Pauk (1978), however, correctly points out that notetaking involves more than learning a format. Notetaking, according to Pauk, requires learning a way of thinking as much as learning a recording format. He believes that the key to good notetaking is understanding the material. Understanding allows students to restate the material in their own words. Only after this cognitive task is accomplished can students appropriately use a recording format for the material.

Lewis and Nichols (1965) discuss several major approaches to outlining. First, there is *annotation*. This refers to taking notes within reading material such as textbooks. These writers suggest that most annotation can be done in the page margins while reading. They recommend using a coding system for annotating. A simple coding system should allow coding of two major types of content. One code would mark different kinds of material. The second code would mark interrelated material. For example, you might use stars to code different kinds of material. A single star could be used to code new words appearing in the text. Two stars could be used to code examples. Three stars could mark supporting details. Finally, four stars could identify main ideas or events. After coding these different types of material, you might use an alphabet code to show relationships within the material. For example, "A's" could be placed beside the stars indicating two or more related main ideas, and "B's" could be placed beside the stars indicating supporting detail common to two or more main ideas and so on.

Second, there is *précis writing*. In this type of notetaking, students are taught to write a short paragraph that summarizes a lengthy piece of material. Students should be taught that good précis writing depends on two things: identifying the organizing cues in the material, and understanding the main ideas in the material.

Third, there is the *columns approach* to notetaking. When using this technique, students divide a note page into three vertical columns. The first column is for main ideas, the middle for supporting detail, and the last column for questions.

The fourth technique uses outlining to take notes. We will discuss outlining shortly.

Maxwell (1979) discusses some general guidelines for notetaking. If notetaking is to be done on lecture material, she recommends teaching students to read related text material before the lecture. Students should also be advised to use only one side of a page for notes. Pauk (1978) would add that students should also be instructed to leave a wide left-hand margin of about 2 1/2 inches. The margin can be used later for summarizing the notes. Maxwell also stresses the importance of teaching students to use abbreviations to conserve time. Maxwell suggests that students include in their notes the major ideas presented, relationships between these ideas, questions about unclear points, and any useful examples, charts, or diagrams.

Several different systems for notetaking are available using mnemonic devices. Pauk (1974) suggests teaching a system called the *five R's*. *Record* the main ideas and details. *Reduce* the notes by summarizing. *Recite* the notes aloud for memory. *Reflect* on the meaning of the material in the notes. *Review* the notes on a regular schedule. Duffelmeyer (in Maxwell, 1979) offers a system called *WRECK*. *Wonder* or be curious about the topic. *Record* the main ideas and details. *Edit* the notes to refine them. *Correlate* notes from lectures and text material. *Keep* the notes for review. Devine (1981) recommends a system called *REAP*. In this system, students are taught to use the right-hand page in a notebook for notetaking. Shifts in topics or major ideas are shown by leaving blank lines between them. Next, students are taught to use the left-hand page in the notebook for refining the notes. The left-hand page is divided into two columns. In the first column, labeled "Triggers," students place key words or phrases for the parallel notes on the right-hand page. The second column is labeled REAP. Students are taught to *Relate* the material to their own lives. They are taught to *Extend* the material to the world at large. They are taught to *Actualize* the material by showing how it could be applied and to *Profit* by applying the material.

Devine (1981) offers two teaching ideas for notetaking. First, he suggests giving students notes on material with some of the details omitted. Next, students complete the notes while reading or listening to a lecture. After some practice, all the detail is omitted. Next, place only the main ideas in the prepared notes. Now, the students are responsible for adding all the details. Next, some of the main ideas are left out of the prepared notes. Now, the students add the missing main ideas and all the details. Finally, students are taught to develop a complete set of notes on their own. Devine also recommends linking notetaking practice and homework assignments. Homework should include instructions to the students to identify certain kinds of material in reading assignments. For example, the students might be told to write down, in their own words, the three main ideas covered on pages 32 through 49 or to write a five-sentence summary of the main points in an assigned chapter.

Berman (1979) discusses a more detailed teaching procedure for notetaking. In this procedure, the teacher must identify material in which each paragraph has a clear point to make. There must be several selections that meet this criterion. Next, the teacher records the material on tape. The first time a tape is played for students, they are told simply to listen and take no notes. The teacher next provides the students with a set of questions to help focus their attention on the important points. The tape is replayed and stopped at the end of each paragraph. At each pause, students write down the answer to the question related to the paragraph. At the end, the exercise is evaluated. The students are given feedback on their performance along with suggestions for improvement. After students can complete this exercise satisfactorily, the process is repeated without the questions. Next, the pauses are omitted. Finally, the initial preview of the tape is omitted.

### Outlining Skills

According to Devine (1981), before students can learn to outline, they must be able to identify sequences, chronological patterns, and cause-and-effect relationships. We discussed identification of organizational patterns in the listening skills section. Burmeister (1978) agrees that outlining depends on an understanding of organizational patterns. Essentially, outlining requires students to divide and classify material. It is important for students to recognize that something must consist of at least two parts before it can be divided. The most conventional approach to outlining uses Roman numerals for major divisions, capital letters for subdivisions, and Arabic numerals for details within a subdivision. Burmeister also discusses a recent adaptation of this outlining approach using only Arabic numerals (see Table 3–6). In addition, he discusses the use of flow charts, time lines, tree charts, graphs, diagrams, and maps as outlines. Burmeister (1978) discusses several activities for teaching outlining.

Devine (1981) recommends that students practice using outlines before learning to construct them. He recommends giving students teacher-prepared outlines to follow while reading or listening to lecture material. This will help students recognize that most writers and speakers follow an outline. Next, Devine suggests giving students incomplete outlines to complete while reading or listening to the outlined material. They are then asked to develop complete outlines on their own. Finally, when students can construct outlines from reading and lecture material, have them construct outlines for material they need to present, e.g., a class paper or oral report. Several teaching activities for this skill are discussed in Devine's (1981) book.

Friedland and Kessler (1980) discuss a detailed sequence of lessons for teaching outlining. As they point out, students are usually not very enthusiastic about learning to outline. The lack of enthusiasm is due to failure to under-

**Table 3–6**    An example of the outline using the numerical format based on the beginning of this chapter

---

1.0. Learning skills

1.1. Introduction
      1.1.1. Needed by all students
      1.1.2. Especially needed by handicapped students
      1.1.3. Transferrable

2.0. General skills

2.1. Following directions
      2.1.1. Why students don't follow directions
      2.1.2. Teacher considerations for directions
      2.1.3. Importance to students of following directions
      2.1.4. Instruction on following directions
            2.1.4.1. Instruction on written directions
            2.1.4.2. Instruction on oral directions

2.2. Library and reference skills, and so on

---

stand the usefulness of the skill. Friedland and Kessler begin teaching outlining without mentioning outlining. They also teach the skill using concrete tasks. First, they draw a four-drawer chest of drawers on the chalkboard. Next, they list the contents of each drawer. The content list for each drawer appears to have no order. Students are told that this is a child's chest of drawers, and the child can never find anything. Then they ask the students what the solution to the child's problem might be. Almost always, students say that the solution is organization. The students are asked to organize, on paper, the contents of the drawers. They teach the students to use Roman numerals to designate the drawers and capital letters to indicate the contents of each drawer. Students are told to omit items that don't belong in any of the drawers, e.g., toys. The second lesson uses a classroom inventory task. In this lesson, an inventory is taken of all the things in the classroom. Students are asked to organize the contents of the inventory into categories. Roman numerals are used for major categories, e.g., storage cabinet. Capital letters are used for divisions within a category, e.g., "A" for the first shelf, "B" for the second shelf, and so on. Arabic numbers are used for items within a division; e.g., on shelf A they might have 1. writing paper, 2. notepads, and 3. drawing paper. After practice with these concrete tasks, the third lesson is organization of information in a short news article. The fourth lesson uses the content of a textbook chapter. Although not covered, it would be a simple matter to extend the lessons to include reading and organizing a set of lecture notes taken in class. This last lesson would be particularly useful for older students.

## THINKING SKILLS

Thinking skills is a very complex topic with a considerable body of research and opinion. We cannot do justice to this topic in this chapter. However, we will take a brief look at two important areas: critical thinking and problem solving. Material useful for planning instruction will be presented. You should, however, study this topic in more detail if you plan to do extensive instruction on thinking skills.

### Critical Thinking

Gladstein (1967) states that critical thinking is making judgments about correctness and value. For those familiar with Bloom's (1959) taxonomy of cognitive processes, the definition above is at Bloom's highest level, i.e., evaluation. Since Bloom's taxonomy is hierarchical, students must have lower-level skills before they can do evaluation. For those not familiar with Bloom's sequence, it has six levels of cognitive processing. The first level is the *knowledge* level. This level requires only that material be recognized or recalled and is related primarily to memory. The second level is the *comprehension* level. This level requires that material not only be remembered but that it be understood. Understanding is usually evidenced by the ability to reconstruct material in one's own words.

At the third level, *application*, it is necessary to go beyond comprehension by demonstrating the ability to apply what has been understood. Beginning with the fourth level, *analysis*, we have what are sometimes called the higher cognitive processes. Analysis requires that a complex whole be analyzed into the distinctive parts of which it is composed. The fifth level is *synthesis*. Synthesis requires the ability to integrate into a new organization ideas, principles, and facts from diverse sources and disciplines. Finally, the sixth level, *evaluation*, requires judgments about correctness and value using appropriate standards. Obviously, students cannot be expected to function at the evaluation level without first developing lower-level skills.

There are alternatives to Bloom's sequence for looking at critical thinking. Devine (1981) suggested a six-stage model of thinking processes (see Table 3–7). In Devine's model, *critical thinking* is placed at stage 5. In his model, critical thinking is the ability to distinguish between fact and opinion, to evaluate sources, to identify bias, and to recognize emotional appeals. Adams, Hirsh, Hipple, and Hipple (1983) offer another set of thinking skills. Their set includes observing, comparing, classifying, imagining, hypothesizing, looking for assumptions, collecting and organizing data, summarizing, interpreting, problem solving, and decision making. Both Devine (1981) and Adams et al. (1983) suggest ideas and activities for teaching critical thinking skills.

Davidson (1982) suggests using story maps to aid comprehension and to develop critical thinking. Davidson's discussion focuses on using reading material. It could easily be adapted for use with lecture material as well. A *story map* is a diagram (see Figure 3–2) relating ideas and events in a reading assignment or lecture. There are no rules for constructing maps, since they are in-

**Table 3–7**  A six-stage model of thinking in which stage is associated with different types of thinking or cognitive processes

1. Stage 1 probably includes recognizing a problem or recognizing the source of a problem.

2. Stage 2 may include noting possible approaches to the problem or selecting an approach.

3. Stage 3 probably includes such mental processes as distinguishing between relevant and irrelevant, organizing material, sequencing material, noting main points, relating the new to the old, and relating the unknown to the known.

4. Stage 4 may include anticipating endings, predicting events, making inferences, judging inferences, organizing and reorganizing material, and distinguishing between relevant and irrelevant material.

5. Stage 5 includes such critical thinking processes as distinguishing fact from opinion, evaluating sources of information, noting bias in sources, and recognizing emotional appeals.

6. Stage 6 would include those processes associated with "testing out " and inductive-deductive thinking.

Source: Thomas G. Devine, *Teaching Study Skills: A Guide for Teachers.* Copyright 1981 by Allyn and Bacon, Inc. Reprinted with permission.

Map

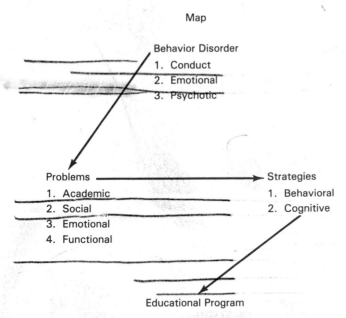

**Figure 3–2**

A broad map of the content of this book, showing the relationships between type of student, problem areas, educational strategies, and program development.

dividual creations, and there is no right or wrong way to do a map. What is correct is what best represents a student's understanding of the material. After a mapping assignment is completed, ask students to explain the reasoning and interpretations used in their map. Encourage questions about the maps and challenges of the reasoning and interpretations. The questioning and challenging phase of the procedure is a stimulus for developing critical thinking. The teacher is permitted to ask questions to stimulate discussion but otherwise stays in the background. Questions should be carefully phrased to stimulate complex processing of material. Bloom's (1959) taxonomy, discussed above, is one way to develop and target questions for this purpose. Another important guideline is always to use *open-ended questions*. An open-ended question is one that cannot be answered by *yes* or *no*. Open-ended questions are often called how and why questions and are the type of question that best stimulate critical thinking skills.

### Problem Solving

*Problem solving* is defined by Gladstein (1967) as a process to produce the best answer to a question with no prior answer. A study of poor problem solvers (Whimbey & Whimbey, 1975) identified some characteristics descriptive of students poor at problem solving. The researchers found that poor problem solvers were too hasty, frequently skipped steps in the process, showed a lack of motivation for doing the necessary analysis, were guilty of careless reasoning, and usually failed to check their solutions. All these characteristics are related to the cognitive style called impulsive. In short, poor problem solvers fail to be sufficiently reflective in their approach. McKinney and Haskins (1980) demonstrated that impulsive problem solvers can be taught to be more reflective. These researchers compared three remedial procedures: memory support, teaching a response rule, and teaching a focusing rule. The strategy most effective in remediating poor problem solving was teaching a focusing rule. A focusing rule is an efficient strategy to help eliminate possible but incorrect solutions. Academic areas where poor problem-solving skills are most apparent are math and science. Maxwell (1979) offers some suggestions for helping students with problem-solving tasks in math and science.

There are many descriptions of the problem-solving process, ranging from the simple to the complex. We will discuss only one of these. Sherry and Franzen (1977) discuss a simple, three-step process useful for both academic and nonacademic problems. In their process, you first teach students to define the problem. Students must recognize that a problem cannot be solved until the nature of the problem is clear. These writers suggest teaching students to apply who, what, when, where, why, and how questions to a problem to develop their definition. After the problem is clearly defined, the second step is to brainstorm as many potential solutions to the problem as possible. Students should be taught to be nonjudgmental in this phase of the process. Potential solutions are not evaluated but simply accepted as possibilities even if they appear unlikely. In the third step, evaluate the potential solutions and eliminate those that are not appropriate. Sherry and Franzen (1977) suggest three criteria for identifying those solutions that aren't appropriate: examination of the resources required and their availability, a projection of a solution's likely consequences and their acceptability, and a determination of the probable permanence of a solution. A good solution satisfies all three criteria.

## RESOURCES

Of the many resources cited above, Alley and Deshler (1979), Burmeister (1978), and Devine (1981) are especially useful. In addition, Adelman's (1982) and Carlson's (1979) curriculum guides have teaching activities covering many of the skills discussed in this chapter.

Several commercially prepared teaching materials addressing learning skills are also available. Learning Skills, a program available from Developmental Learning Materials, is based on the curriculum guide and teaching activities in Carlson's (1979) handbook. Some other useful materials include Library Reference Skills and Advanced Library Reference Skills from Encyclopaedia Britannica Educational Corporation, Basic Dictionary Skills from the SRA Organizing and Supporting Kit from Science Research Associates, and the listening activities in the SRA Reading Laboratory, also from Science Research Associates. In the area of thinking skills, there is the Thinking Skills Development Program from Coronado Publishers. The Institute for the Advancement of Philosophy for Children at Montclair State College in New Jersey has several thinking skills programs for specific areas, including logic, social studies, and language arts.

# REFERENCES

ADAMS, D., HIRSH, J., HIPPLE, T., & HIPPLE, M. (1983, February). Classroom fun that builds thinking skills. *Instructor*, pp. 117–118.

ADELMAN, M. (1982). *School survival skills*. Media, PA: Delaware County Public Schools.

ALLEY, G., & DESHLER, D. (1979). *Teaching the learning disabled adolescent: Strategies and methods*. Denver, CO: Love Publishing.

ALVERMANN, D. (1983). Putting the textbook in its place: Your students' hands. *Academic Therapy*, *18*(3), 345–351.

BERMAN, M. (1979). Note-taking practice. *English Language Teaching Journal*, 34(1), 39–40.

BLOOM, B. (Ed.). (1959). *Taxonomy of educational objectives: Handbook I. Cognitive domain*. New York: McKay.

BLOOM, B. (1979). *Human characteristics and school learning*. New York: McGraw-Hill.

BURMEISTER, L. (1978). *Reading strategies for middle and secondary school teachers* (2nd ed.). Reading, MA: Addison-Wesley.

BURNS, M. (1980, October). Why don't they follow directions? *Learning*, pp. 98–100.

CAMPANILE, P. (1981, March). Evening up the score. *Instructor*, pp. 58–59.

CARLSON, S. (Ed.). (1979). *Learning how to learn*. Lawrence, KS: Project STILE, Lawrence High School.

CARMAN, R., & ADAMS, W. (1972). *Study skills: A student's guide for survival*. New York: Wiley.

CUNNINGHAM, J., CUNNINGHAM, P., & ARTHUR, S. (1981). *Middle and secondary school reading*. New York: Longman.

DAVIDSON, J. (1982, October). The group mapping activity for instruction in reading and thinking. *Journal of reading*, pp. 52–56.

DEVINE, T. (1981). *Teaching study skills: A guide for teachers*. Boston: Allyn and Bacon.

FRIEDLAND, J., & KESSLER, R. (1980, September). A top (to bottom) drawer way to teach outlining. *Teacher*, pp. 110–111.

GLADSTEIN, G. (1967). *Individualized study*. Skoakie, IL: Rand McNally.

HILL, W., & ELLER, W. (1964). *Power in reading skills*. Belmont, CA: Wadsworth.

KALUGER, G., & KOLSON, C. (1978). *Reading and learning disabilities*. Columbus, OH: Merrill.

LEWIS, R., & NICHOLS, R. (1965). *Speaking and listening*. Dubuque, IA: Wm. C. Brown.

MAXWELL, M. (1979). *Improving student learning skills*. San Francisco: Jossey-Bass.

McCABE, D. (1982). Developing study skills: The LD high school student. *Academic Therapy*, *18*(2), 197–201.

McKINNEY, J., & Haskins, R. (1980). Cognitive training and the development of problem-solving strategies. *Exceptional Education Quarterly*, *1*(1), 41–51.

OTTO, W., & SMITH, R. (1980). *Corrective and remedial teaching* (3rd ed.). Boston: Houghton Mifflin.

PAUK, W. (1974). *How to study in college* (2nd ed.). Boston: Houghton Mifflin.

PAUK, W. (1978, October). A notetaking format: Magical but not automatic. *Reading World*, pp. 96–97.

PAUK, W. (1983, March). A new way to skim. *Reading World*, pp. 252–254.

PETRESHENE, S. (1982, January). The Monday question. *Instructor*, pp. 46–47.

RAPHAEL, T. (1982, November). Question answering strategies for children. *The Reading Teacher*, pp. 186–190.

ROBINSON, F. (1970). *Effective study* (4th ed.). New York: Harper & Row.

RUSSELL, D., & RUSSELL, E. (1959). *Listening aids*. New York: Columbia University Press.

SHERRY, M., & FRANZEN, M. (1977). Zapped by zinging: Students and teachers develop successful problem solving strategies. *Teaching Exceptional Children*, *9*(2), 46–47.

STEWART, O., & GREEN, D. (1983, March). Test-taking skills for standardized tests of reading. *The Reading Teacher*, pp. 634–638.

THOMAS, E., & ROBINSON, H. (1977). *Improving reading in every class*. Boston: Allyn and Bacon.

WEINER, K. (1974). From out of the past: Old time radio rides again. *Teaching Exceptional Children*, *6*(4), 210–213.

WHIMBEY, A., & WHIMBEY, L. (1975). *Intelligence can be taught*. New York: Dutton.

# 4

# REDUCING
# INAPPROPRIATE SOCIAL
# BEHAVIOR

## INTRODUCTION

Whenever possible, avoid the use of formal, structured behavioral interventions for modifying students' behavior. Formal behavior change programs are very powerful when properly conducted. They are also very time consuming. You should use a formal intervention only after informal techniques have failed. There are several informal behavior change techniques that you should try first. These include such things as teacher conferences with the student, with the student's parents, with the principal, or some combination of these. Formal techniques use operant learning theory or what we have called applied behavior analysis.

## THE OPERANT MODEL

The operant learning model is a research-based model of how behavior is learned and eliminated. There are many detailed discussions of this model and its application to human behavior (Karen, 1974; Skinner, 1953). We can describe this model using a symbol system to represent it (see Figure 4–1).

The "S" on the left side of Figure 4–1 is an antecedent stimulus. Antecedents signal possible reward ($S^D$); e.g., "When everyone is seated we'll begin the film." They signal possible punishment ($S^D$-); e.g., "If everyone doesn't sit down, there will be no recess." Finally, they may not signal either reward or punishment (S); e.g., "Everyone please sit down." The "R" in the middle of Figure 4–1 is an operant response or behavior. The "S" on the right side of Figure 4–1 is a

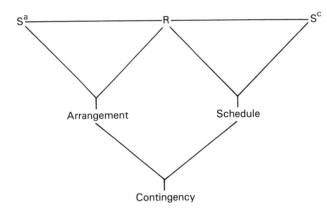

**Figure 4–1**
The three-term operant paradigm with labels for the various relationships between the terms.

consequent stimulus. Consequences are positive reinforcers ($S^R+$), e.g., being given a ball; negative reinforcers ($S^R-$), e.g., getting out of a boring lecture; punishment ($S^P$), e.g., getting slapped; or neutral (S), i.e., a stimulus with no value (positive or aversive). The relationship of "S" to "R" is called an *arrangement*. The relationship of "R" to "S" is called a *schedule*. The relationship of all three terms to one another is called a *contingency*.

Some attention has been given to control of behavior through the manipulation of antecedent stimuli alone (Center, Deitz, & Kaufman, 1982). Most behavior control emphasizes manipulation of consequent stimuli. There are two basic categories of consequences: reinforcers and punishers.

*Reinforcers* are, by definition, stimuli following a target behavior, which maintain the behavior or strengthen it. In other words, if you consequate a behavior and the behavior diminishes, the consequent stimulus is not a reinforcer. There are two reinforcement operations: the presentation of a valued stimulus (appetitive stimulus), or the withdrawal of a noxious stimulus (aversive stimulus) following a desired response. In the first case, the operation is called *positive reinforcement*. In the second case, it is called *negative reinforcement*.

*Punishers* are stimuli following a behavior, which weaken or eliminate it. In other words, if you consequate a behavior and the behavior is unchanged or increases, the consequent stimulus is not a punisher. There are three punishment operations: presenting an aversive stimulus, withdrawing an appetitive stimulus, or withholding an appetitive stimulus following an undesired behavior. The first two operations are called *punishment* and the third operation is called *extinction*. Extinction is a special case of punishment.

There is one final point that needs to be mentioned. Consequences are not limited to stimuli but may also be responses. That is, instead of giving or taking a stimulus, you permit, prohibit, or require some response following a target behavior, e.g., playing ball, losing a privilege (line leader), or doing 50 push-ups. Table 4–1 summarizes the operations noted above.

Consequences may be either prepotent, e.g., food or physical pain (primary consequences), or learned, e.g., money or admonishment (secondary consequences). In Table 4–2 are some examples of reinforcing consequences in both categories. When you select consequences, there are several rules to fol-

**Table 4–1**    A summary of various operations involving either stimuli or responses used as consequences and the effect produced[a]

|  | PRESENT | WITHDRAW | WITHHOLD |
|---|---|---|---|
| Appetitive stimulus | Positive reinforcement behavior → or ↑ | Punishment behavior ↓ | Punishment behavior ↓ |
| Aversive stimulus | Punishment behavior ↓ | Negative reinforcement behavior → or ↑ | ✕ |

|  | Permit | Prohibit | Require |
|---|---|---|---|
| Appetitive response | Positive reinforcement behavior → or ↑ | Punishment behavior ↓ | ✕ |
| Aversive response | ✕ | ✕ | Punishment behavior ↓ |

[a]Crossed-out positions are very unlikely.

low. First, a consequence is appropriate only if it produces the desired effect. Second, a secondary consequence is preferable to a primary consequence. Finally, an uncontrived secondary consequence, e.g., verbal praise, is preferable to a contrived secondary consequence, e.g., a toy.

     Whenever you select a consequence, you must have an objective rule to guide its use, e.g., sitting quietly for 5 continuous minutes. The schedule for delivery of a consequence is also important. The two basic types of schedules are continuous and intermittent. A *continuous schedule* provides for one consequence for each occurrence of the target behavior. Punishment should always be on a continuous schedule. Reinforcement should be on a continuous schedule when you establish a new behavior or strengthen a weak behavior. Set a criterion for a useful level of your target behavior before beginning an interven-

**Table 4–2**    Examples of primary and secondary reinforcers.[a]

| PRIMARY | SECONDARY | | |
|---|---|---|---|
| Edible | Material | Activity | Social |
| Peanuts | Toy car | Playing games | "Good" |
| Candy | Stars | Free time | "Terrific" |
| Raisins | Puppets | Line leader | Hand shake |
| Juices | Smelly stickers | Run errands | "Great" |
| Cereal | Marbles | Listen to records | Pat on back |
| Chips | Beads | Art activity | Hugs |

[a]Intrusiveness of the reinforcers ranges from high (left side) to low (right side).

tion, e.g., raises hand before speaking 90% of the time on five consecutive school-days. When you reach your criterion, begin shifting your reinforcement to an intermittent schedule.

There are four basic *intermittent schedules*. First, there are *fixed interval* (FI) *schedules*, based on a time criterion; e.g., the first occurrence of the target behavior after 3 minutes (FI3) is reinforced. Second, there are *variable interval* (VI) *schedules*, also based on time; e.g., the first occurrence of the target behavior after 3 minutes (VI3), on the average, is reinforced. The major difference between these two interval schedules is that the FI schedule is predictable and the VI schedule is not. This difference has implications for the consistency of behavior reinforced on these schedules. Third, there are *fixed ratio* (FR) *schedules* based on a frequency criterion; e.g., the third occurrence (FR3) of the target behavior since the last reinforced response is reinforced. Finally, there are *variable ratio* (VR) *schedules*, also based on frequency; e.g., each third occurrence (VR3), on the average, of the target behavior is reinforced. Again, the major difference between these two ratio schedules is predictability. The different effects of the schedules on behavior are summarized in Table 4–3.

When you first shift from a continuous to an intermittent schedule, *schedule stretching* has begun. This should be done so that there is a gradual and progressive reduction in the reinforcement density, e.g., stretching a continuous schedule to a FR3 schedule, then to a FR6, FR10, VR5, VR10, and VR15. Each schedule change is made only after you meet your criterion for a useful level of the target behavior. After you stretch a schedule, the variability of the target behavior will often increase temporarily. If this becomes too great, you have a condition called *schedule strain*. Schedule strain occurs when a schedule is stretched too soon or too far or both. It is usually a good idea to set a criterion to judge if you need to adjust the schedule. If, following a change in the schedule, the behavior deviates by more than 25%, in an undesirable direction, adjust the schedule to make it more like the previous schedule.

There are three reasons for stretching a reinforcement schedule. First, it is difficult for a teacher to keep a behavior under high-density reinforcement over a long time. Second, it provides a systematic method for using reinforcement operations to end interventions. Finally, it strengthens the target behavior's resistance to extinction; i.e., it makes it more likely that after the intervention ends the target behavior will be maintained.

Another planning consideration is generalization of treatment effects, e.g., from a special education classroom to a regular classroom. Stokes and Baer (1977) identified several strategies that promote a generalization of treatment effects. First, conduct the intervention sequentially in the settings where you want the behavior changed. Second, carefully select new or alternative behaviors to established or strengthen. Select behaviors with a high probability of being reinforced in the generalization setting. Third, conduct the intervention in a variety of settings using several different behavior change agents. Fourth, apply the intervention to several target behaviors concurrently. Fifth, shift the target behavior to an intermittent reinforcement schedule. A variable schedule is best because it is difficult for a student to identify the reinforcement schedule.

**Table 4–3**  A summary of the four basic intermittent reinforcement schedules and their effects on behavior

| NAME OF SCHEDULE | DEFINITION OF SCHEDULE | EFFECTS ON BEHAVIOR | |
|---|---|---|---|
| | | Schedule in Effect | Schedule Terminated (Extinction) |
| Fixed ratio (FR) | Reinforcer given after each X responses | High response rate | Irregular burst of responding; more responses than in continuous reinforcement, less than in variable ratio |
| Fixed interval (FI) | Reinforcer given for first response to occur after each X minutes | Stops working after reinforcement; works hard just prior to time for next reinforcement | Slow gradual decrease in responding |
| Variable ratio (VR) | Reinforcer given after X responses on the average | Very high response rates; the higher the ratio, the higher the rate | Very resistant to extinction; maximum number of responses before extinction |
| Variable interval (VI) | Reinforcer given for first response after each X minutes, on the average | Steady rate of responding | Very resistant to extinction; maximum time to extinction |

SOURCE:  From Hill M. Walker, *The Acting-Out Child: Coping with Classroom Disruption.* Copyright 1979 by Allyn and Bacon, Inc. Reprinted with permission.

Sixth, conduct the intervention under conditions as similar to the generalization setting as possible. Seventh, train students to mediate generalization of their own behavior by teaching and reinforcing the use of self-management techniques, e.g., self-monitoring and self-reinforcement. Finally, use generalization itself as a target behavior, i.e., monitor and reinforce instances of response generalization.

### Research Support

The amount of research supporting the operant model for modifying children's behavior is extensive. To do justice to this body of literature in the space available here is impossible. There are several extensive reviews of this literature available. Kazdin (1978) examined the experimental foundations of behavior modification. This book-length review covers all aspects of behavior modification research. Ross (1981) reviews and critiques many and varied studies of behavior therapy with children. Ross organizes the material in his book around specific problem areas, e.g., social isolation, hyperactivity, and aggression. S. O'Leary and K. O'Leary (1976) review behavior modification research conducted in school settings. Finally, Nelson and Polsgrove (1984) examine the impact of behavior modification research on special education. In general, all these reviews strongly support the effectiveness of behavioral procedures with children and youth. They also point out various limitations, issues, and unexamined questions that need study.

## ASSESSMENT

### Rating Scales and Checklists

Often, the first step in the assessment of behavior problems is collection of data on a student's behavior by indirect methods. Usually, a teacher or some other staff member supplies information about the student's behavior. This assessment may use techniques as informal as anecdotal records or as formal as standardized behavior rating scales. One example of an informal data collection instrument is the School Behavior Status Checklist (Cautela, Cautela, & Esonis, 1983). This checklist covers both appropriate and inappropriate behaviors. It also asks for estimates of frequency, duration, and need for change (see Figure 4–2). An example of a more formal instrument is the Walker Problem Identification Checklist (Walker, 1976). This is a standardized rating scale for behaviors typically observed in classrooms. The scale has five subscales: acting out, withdrawal, distractibility, disturbed peer relations, and immaturity. There are many other indirect data collection instruments available. Most of these instruments are useful for the initial identification of problem areas that may need attention. However, to conduct a formal behavior change program, it is necessary to collect data directly by observation.

### Behavioral Observation

The first step in direct assessment is to develop an operational definition of the target behavior. A good operational definition promotes reliable measurement. An operational definition should specify the response properties of a target behavior with overt, observable features of the behavior. When needed, the definition should include intensity, frequency, or duration criteria. An example of an operational definition of physical aggression might read as follows.

> Physical aggression is defined as physical contact between any part of the body of one student and any part of the body of another student or any contact mediated by an object, e.g., a stick, a rock, a pencil, etc. Such contact must produce a reaction in the contacted student which suggests pain, e.g., crying, hitting back, etc.

**SCHOOL BEHAVIOR STATUS CHECKLIST (S)**

Name of student _____ Date _____

Person describing student _____

Title/relationship to student _____

Amount of time spent with student during school week _____

Length of time have known student _____

School _____ Grade of student _____

Circle the number in the first column that best describes how often the student performs the listed behavior and circle the number in the second column that indicates the degree to which you would like the frequency of the behavior to change.

1 — Not at all
2 — A little
3 — A fair amount
4 — Much
5 — Very much

| | Behavior Occurs | Need to Change |
|---|---|---|
| 1. Completes tasks or activities | 1 2 3 4 5 | 1 2 3 4 5 |
| 2. Works within time limits | 1 2 3 4 5 | 1 2 3 4 5 |
| 3. Refrains from making noises in the classroom | 1 2 3 4 5 | 1 2 3 4 5 |
| 4. Raises his or her hand before speaking out | 1 2 3 4 5 | 1 2 3 4 5 |
| 5. Stays in his or her seat when required | 1 2 3 4 5 | 1 2 3 4 5 |
| 6. Participates in extracurricular school activities | 1 2 3 4 5 | 1 2 3 4 5 |
| 7. Does what he or she is told | 1 2 3 4 5 | 1 2 3 4 5 |
| 8. Gets attention in appropriate ways | 1 2 3 4 5 | 1 2 3 4 5 |
| 9. Leaves the room only with permission | 1 2 3 4 5 | 1 2 3 4 5 |
| 10. Pays attention when given instructions | 1 2 3 4 5 | 1 2 3 4 5 |
| 11. Follows instructions | 1 2 3 4 5 | 1 2 3 4 5 |
| 12. Does what he or she is told without crying or tantrum behavior | 1 2 3 4 5 | 1 2 3 4 5 |
| 13. Does what he or she is told without arguing or talking back | 1 2 3 4 5 | 1 2 3 4 5 |
| 14. Has adequate eating and table manners in the cafeteria | 1 2 3 4 5 | 1 2 3 4 5 |
| 15. Is clean and well-groomed | 1 2 3 4 5 | 1 2 3 4 5 |
| 16. Has control of bowel movements | 1 2 3 4 5 | 1 2 3 4 5 |
| 17. Has bladder control | 1 2 3 4 5 | 1 2 3 4 5 |
| 18. Does homework | 1 2 3 4 5 | 1 2 3 4 5 |
| 19. Accepts failure well | 1 2 3 4 5 | 1 2 3 4 5 |
| 20. Refrains from complaining about physical symptoms | 1 2 3 4 5 | 1 2 3 4 5 |
| 21. Makes age-appropriate decisions | 1 2 3 4 5 | 1 2 3 4 5 |
| 22. Protects himself or herself from physical injury | 1 2 3 4 5 | 1 2 3 4 5 |
| 23. Laughs at appropriate times | 1 2 3 4 5 | 1 2 3 4 5 |
| 24. Spends time alone | 1 2 3 4 5 | 1 2 3 4 5 |
| 25. Handles new situations well | 1 2 3 4 5 | 1 2 3 4 5 |

**Figure 4–2**    A sample portion of an informal behavior checklist. *Reprinted with permission from J. R. Cautela and J. S. Esonis, 1983,* Forms for Behavior Analysis with Children *(p. 105). Champaign, IL: Research Press.*

**Table 4–4**    The classification of recording techniques according to the most pertinent behavioral characteristic (frequency or time) and the precision of measurement (exact or estimate)

|          | FREQUENCY | TIME |
|----------|-----------|------|
| Exact    | Event recording | Duration recording |
|          |           | Latency recording |
| Estimate | Partial interval recording | Whole interval recording |
|          | Time-sampling |      |

The second step in direct observation is selection of an appropriate behavior recording technique. We will classify recording procedures by their use of (1) frequency or time, and (2) exact or estimated data (see Table 4–4). Event recording is simply a tally of the number of times a relatively distinct behavior occurs, e.g., throwing objects. Duration recording is a timed measure of how long a behavior lasts, e.g., a temper tantrum. Latency recording is a timed measure of the lag between a stimulus and a response to it. For example, "Put the puzzle away now" would be a stimulus, and compliance with the instruction would be a response. The time between the stimulus and response is the latency. All the above provide exact data.

Behavior sampling to obtain estimates is done using timed intervals (see Figure 4–3). Let each interval in Figure 4–3 represent 10 seconds of observation time. The intervals could be used for partial interval recording by marking an interval with a check (✓) if the target behavior occurs during the interval. The interval is scored only once, however, even if the target behavior occurred four times. Or, the intervals could be used for whole interval recording. Each 10-second interval is scored only if the target behavior occurred throughout the interval's 10-second duration. Thus, an occurrence of the target behavior lasting only 6 seconds is not scored. If the intervals were being used for time sampling, each interval might represent 10 minutes. Observation might then take place for only 1 minute out of each 10. The observation minute might occur on a predetermined schedule or be randomly selected from each interval. An interval is scored only if the target behavior occurs during the observation period within the interval. Cooper (1974) and Miller (1980) provide a more complete discussion of behavior measurement in classroom settings.

| ✓ | o | o | o | ✓ | ✓ |
|---|---|---|---|---|---|
| o | ✓ | o | o | o | ✓ |
| ✓ | o | o | ✓ | ✓ | o |
| ✓ | o | ✓ | o | ✓ | ✓ |
| o | ✓ | o | ✓ | o | ✓ |

**Figure 4–3**
Thirty timed recording intervals for a behavior sample.

Many writers on behavioral measurement stress the importance of obtaining interobserver reliability estimates (Cooper, 1974; Miller, 1980). In a dozen years, I have not observed a classroom teacher collecting reliability data except to meet a course requirement. No matter how desirable such data are, it is seldom feasible for a classroom teacher to collect them. Therefore, we will not discuss the topic any further. For additional information see the references cited above.

## FORMAL TECHNIQUES

### Group Interventions

One group intervention is the Good Behavior Game (Barrish, Saunders, & Wolf, 1969). Divide the classroom into two or more teams; e.g., the left side of the class is team A and the right side is team B. Establish a set of rules.

1. Stay in your seat.

2. Get permission before talking.

3. Be courteous to others.

Establish some rewards for following the rules.

1. Extra recess time

2. Free time

3. First to go to lunch

4. No homework

Mark off a section on the chalkboard to keep score on the teams.

| TEAM A | TEAM B |
|--------|--------|
|        |        |
|        |        |
|        |        |
|        |        |

Give a check (✓) to the appropriate team each time a member of the team breaks a rule. At the end of the game, e.g., a class period, the team with the fewest checks wins the game and gets a reward. Another variation is to set a maximum number of checks, e.g., 10, and if neither team goes over that number, both win and get a reward. Otherwise, the team with the fewest checks wins. You can also use this variation without dividing the class into teams by treating the class as a team. Sometimes a team will have one member that causes them to get most of their checks. When this happens, you can let the team vote to "kick" this student off their team for a day. You should allow this no more often than one day in any week. The intent of this procedure is to put peer pressure on the student through negative peer feedback.

Another group intervention is the Timer Game (McGookin cited in Sulzer-Azaroff & Mayer, 1977). In this game, you select a target behavior (either academic or conduct) and a menu of rewards. Put a kitchen timer on your desk. Set the time for variable periods, e.g., 3, 5, 9, 4, 6, and 2 minutes. When the bell goes off, award a point, check, or token to all who are busy with their work or behaving. The points are cashed in for reinforcers at a specified time, e.g., at the end of the day. Each time the bell goes off, you reset the timer at a new interval. A variation on this procedure is to give each student a fixed number of points, e.g., 25, at the beginning of the class or day. Then, start the game and when the bell goes off, remove a point from any student who is not working or behaving.

A third group intervention is Sweepstakes. In this procedure, you put a box, bowl, or can on your desk. Whenever you think that a student deserves a reward, e.g., working hard, behaving well, or turning in homework, you give the student a slip of paper. The student can write his or her name on the slip of paper and put it in the container. At the end of the game period, you hold a drawing and the winning student or students (if you have first, second, and third places) get a prize.

In any of the foregoing procedures, the longer the game runs, the bigger the reward should be. Also, be sure to use care in selecting rewards, so they are things truly valued by the students earning them. What you think is rewarding, students may not consider a reward.

### Token Economy

Finally, a classroom token economy can be a very effective method of managing the behavior of a group (Ayllon & Azrin, 1968; Kazdin, 1977). It is more difficult to plan and run a token economy than the group procedures discussed above. However, once established, a token economy is easy to manage, and it will handle most of the classroom problems faced by special education teachers. Thus, it will greatly reduce the need for individual behavior change programs. The following description is from a model developed by Center and Arnault (1984), which is a more detailed account than the following. Four major components will be discussed.

*1. Income Production.* Produce income by payment for productive work using classroom work periods as payment periods. Payment is made at the end of each work period according to a predetermined payment schedule. Payment based on productive work is determined in one of two ways. Payment can be based on an objective standard such as percent correct of an assigned task. For example, let's use 60% as a zero point (assuming that below 60% correct is not passing work). You would give one point or token for each percentage point from 61 to 100%. Thus, a total of 40 points or tokens could be earned on a task. Under this system, the percent correct converts into points, i.e., 88% correct is 28 points or 28 tokens. Second, payment can be based on a subjective standard such as teacher judgment. You should use this approach when students do tasks that are difficult to score objectively. Under this type of payment, you judge the work and assign a letter grade, e.g., B. The letter grade converts into points or tokens according to a fixed schedule; e.g., a grade of B converts to 25 points.

If you use the percent method for payment, you can avoid the problem of a disparity in income potential. Unequal quantities of work are often assigned to students when you individualize. If you base payment on simple quantity, students will have unequal earning potential. For example, let's assume that one student has a 10-response task and gets 8 correct, and another student has a 20-response task and gets 16 correct. Both students have 80% correct and get the same payment.

Another source of income you can include in the classroom microeconomic system is payment for independent functioning. To do this, you must establish a payment schedule for various desirable work practices (see Table 4–5). The amount paid for each item on the independent work schedule can vary. By varying the amount paid for different items, you can place a premium on the items you consider most desirable or those in need of improvement. When your priorities change, the payment schedule is revised to reflect those changes. It is also important to pay an amount that allows some flexibility in payment. For example, beginning work on time earns three points, a slight delay earns two, and a marked delay earns nothing. Following this procedure, it is possible to reward movement toward the desired behavior.

It is also a good idea to include in your classroom system a bonus points component. This allows you to award extra points to students who do particularly well. You can also use bonus points to reward targeted prosocial behaviors, e.g., helping others or sharing, you want to promote.

**Table 4–5**    An example of possible independent behaviors that could be targeted with associated point values.

| BEHAVIOR | VALUE |
| --- | --- |
| 1. Getting work out of the folder | 2 points |
| 2. Getting started immediately | 2 points |
| 3. No unnecessary questions | 2 points |
| 4. Work completed on time | 2 points |
| 5. Work done neatly | 2 points |

**2. Expenditures.**    A very important element in your system is consumer items that students can buy with their income. The goods, services, and activities selected must be motivating for your students. You can select these by surveying students, observation, experience, or by sampling trials. When a token system like this fails, it is almost always because of one of two problems. Either inappropriate consumer items were selected or there is an imbalance between income and purchasing power. You should arrange the consumer items in a hierarchy from desirable to very desirable, with appropriate increases in costs. The pricing system should be arranged so that even marginally acceptable behavior is worth something.

An additional source of consumer items is the home. Parents control many things that you can use to individualize consumer goods. This is particularly important for students who are difficult to motivate. With parental cooperation, you can tie your system to such things as TV time, bedtime, allowances, and special privileges. If parents are involved in the control of consumer goods, it is important to provide them with regular feedback about what their child has earned. One way of doing this is to send home a daily report on a parent information card (see Box 4–1). You must also devise methods to prevent alteration of the card and deliberate "loss" of the card.

The next component you must plan for the token economy is a set of class rules. There should be no more than five to seven simply stated rules. Each rule should cover several different but related behaviors. The rules should always be visible to students. You can do this by posting the rules or putting a copy in each student's work folder (See Table 4–6).

The next step is to establish a set of fines for violations of the classroom rules. Fines can be as simple as one point per infraction or variable fines levied according to the value placed on a rule. For example, you might consider speaking-out a minor problem and fine 5 points for each occurrence. You might consider out-of-seat more serious and fine 10 points for each occurrence. Don't make your fines too stiff or they will be considered unfair and unrealistic. You will also make your system so rigid that a few infractions will result in a student having nothing left to work for.

The token economy can also help you with bothersome routine problems and possibly help develop students' sense of responsibility. For example, a price

**Box 4–1**    An example of a possible means of informing parents of earned points to be rewarded through parent control

---

**PARENT INFORMATION CARD**

Name_____

Earned_____

Date_____


Signed_____

---

**Table 4–6**    An example of possible rules that could be targeted with associated fines

| RULE | FINE |
|---|---|
| 1. Get permission before speaking | -2  points |
| 2. Get permission before leaving your desk | -4  points |
| 3. Maintain a good sitting position | -2  points |
| 4. Be courteous to others | -5  points |
| 5. Do your work | -10 points |

can be put on certain activities and omissions, using a price sheet like the one shown in Table 4–7.

**3.  Balancing the Economy.**    The best way to balance your classroom token economy is to use a zero point. This can be set at any level you wish but is equivalent to the lowest level of acceptable work. If a student's performance falls below this point, he or she should have few or no points to spend on consumer goods. For example, assume that you set your zero point at 60%. A student with minimally acceptable academic performance (60 to 70%), some independent functioning, and few or no fines will have a small number of points to spend, e.g., 100. A student with moderately good performance will have more points to spend, e.g., 300. However, a student with moderately good work behavior combined with misbehavior will have fewer points to spend, e.g., 150. A student with an optimal level of performance will have a large number of points to spend, e.g., 500. Balancing the token economy will be easier if each student has the same earning potential. If you have students for variable periods of time, you should equalize their earning potential by interfacing your system with the students' other classes and teachers. You can do this by having other teachers rate a student's performance and behavior in their classes (see Chapter 11). The ratings are converted to points in your token economy on a fixed schedule.

Second, you need to compute the maximum number of points a student can earn in a day under your income system. Next, set an optimal level of income based on a portion of the maximum, e.g., 90%. You now have a range of earning from zero to the optimal amount. You should use an amount lower than

**Table 4–7**    An example of possible avoidable behaviors with associated fines.

| BEHAVIOR | FINE |
|---|---|
| 1. Going to the bathroom at unscheduled times | 20  points |
| 2. Going for water at unscheduled times | 20  points |
| 3. Sharpening pencils at unscheduled times | 10  points |
| 4. Borrowing a pencil | 6  points |
| 5. Buying paper to do work | 10  points |
| 6. Borrowing a book needed for lesson | 10  points |
| 7. Asking unnecessary or inappropriate questions | 6  points |

**Table 4–8**    An example of a possible listing of rewards and the associated purchasing values

| REWARD | VALUE |
| --- | --- |
| 1. Read comic book for 10 minutes | 40 points |
| 2. 10 minutes at activity table | 40 points |
| 3. Use of phonograph for 10 minutes | 80 points |
| 4. Use of tape player for 10 minutes | 80 points |
| 5. Candy bar (small) | 200 points |
| 6. Coke | 400 points |
| 7. Line leader (to lunch, etc.) for 1 week | 400 points |
| 8. Messenger for 1 week | 400 points |
| 9. Rent an office space for 1 week | 600 points |

the maximum to allow for minor losses for fines and task errors (no one is perfect). Third, you need to set up your reinforcement menu (see Table 4–8), arranged in order from the least to the most valuable items. Next, examine your consumer goods and determine "life-style" levels: poverty, middle, and affluent. Finally, set prices so a student with low, middle, and high levels of income can afford the corresponding "life-styles." You now have an approximately balanced token economy. As you put the program into operation, you may find that some adjustments will have to be made. The first two or three weeks of operation will be a trial period for fine tuning to get all the components working well together.

*4. Records.*    Record keeping will be made easier if you use a weekly or daily recording sheet. You can put the sheet in each student's work folder (see Box 4–2). The sheet is divided into days and subject areas and other categories, such as independent functioning and fines. Although it is usually not too much trouble to pay for productive work when you check tasks, it is often more bothersome to keep a record of fines. There are two methods of keeping track of fines. First, a running record can be kept on the chalkboard. Second, an individual record can be kept on the back of each student's daily record sheet (see Box 4–3). By using these two methods, you can apply a fine at a distance, i.e., on the board or directly on the back of the offending student's record sheet. If you use both methods, enter the combined total daily in the summary space on the student's record sheet.

### Individual Interventions

A brief discussion of the major operant-based behavior modification techniques follows. More complete descriptions of these techniques are available in any good textbook on behavior modification (Alberto & Troutman, 1982; Deitz & Hummel, 1978; Sulzer-Azaroff & Mayer, 1977).

**Box 4-2**  An example of a sheet for recording appropriate and inappropriate behaviors on a daily basis.

## DAILY PERFORMANCE RECORD

Name _____

Date _____

| Period: | 1 | 2 | 3 | 4 | 5 | Line totals | Income: Subtotal |
|---|---|---|---|---|---|---|---|
| **INCOME**<br>1. Classwork: grade received | | | | | | | |
| 2. Independent functioning | | | | | | | |
|   a. getting work out of folder | | | | | | | |
|   b. getting started immediately | | | | | | | |
|   c. no unnecessary questions | | | | | | | |
|   d. work completed on time | | | | | | | |
|   e. work done neatly | | | | | | | |
| 3. Bonus Points | | | | | | | Subtotal: |
| **FINES** | | | | | | Line totals | Fines: Subtotal |
| 1. Rules: response cost fines | | | | | | | -_____ |
|   a. get permission before speaking | | | | | | | |
|   b. get permission before leaving your desk | | | | | | | |
|   c. maintain a good sitting position | | | | | | | |
|   d. be courteous to others | | | | | | | |
|   e. do your work | | | | | | | |
| **EXPENDITURES** | | | | | | Line totals | Expenditures: Subtotal |
| 1. Maintenance costs | | | | | | | -_____ |
|   a. going to bathroom at unscheduled times | | | | | | | |

**Box 4-2**   Continued

| | | | | | | |
|---|---|---|---|---|---|---|
| b. going for water at unscheduled times | | | | | | |
| c. sharpening pencils at unscheduled times | | | | | | |
| d. borrowing a pencil | | | | | | |
| e. buying paper to do work on | | | | | | |
| f. borrowing a book needed for lesson | | | | | | Total points Earned _____ |
| g. asking unnecessary or inappropriate questions | | | | | | Debt _____ |

**Box 4-3** An example of a weekly record keeping sheet.

**RECORDING SHEET**

Name _____          Date _____

| COMPONENT | MONDAY | TUESDAY | WEDNESDAY | THURSDAY | FRIDAY |
|---|---|---|---|---|---|
| Period 1 | | | | | |
| Indep. Fun. | | | | | |
| Period 2 | | | | | |
| Indep. Fun. | | | | | |
| Period 3 | | | | | |
| Indep. Fun. | | | | | |
| Period 4 | | | | | |
| Indep. Fun. | | | | | |
| Period 5 | | | | | |
| Indep. Fun. | | | | | |

**Box 4-3** Continued

| | | | | | |
|---|---|---|---|---|---|
| Period 6 | | | | | |
| Indep. Fun. | | | | | |
| Bonus Pts. | | | | | |
| Subtotal 1 | | | | | |
| Fines | | | | | |
| Subtotal 2 | | | | | |
| FB Mean ST2 / 6 | | | | | |
| Main. Costs | | | | | |
| Purchases | | | | | |
| Sum Expend. | | | | | |
| Balance ST2 - S.E. | | | | | |

*Differential Reinforcement of Other Behavior (DRO).*    D R O reduces misbehavior by increasing appropriate behavior. The basic idea here is that if you can reinforce and increase the amount of appropriate behavior, there will be less time and fewer opportunities for misbehavior. DRO is done in three ways.

1. *DRO of incompatible behavior* (DRO-I). In DRO-I, you look for an appropriate behavior incompatible with the misbehavior; e.g, on-task is incompatible with off-task. In other words, the student can't do both behaviors at the same time. Once you select an incompatible behavior, reinforce it to increase its occurrence.

2. *DRO of alternative behavior* (DRO-A). In DRO-A, you look for an appropriate behavior that's an acceptable alternative to the misbehavior, e.g., asking for something instead of taking it. In this case, the behaviors are not mutually exclusive; i.e., they could both be done at the same time. Once you select an alternative behavior, reinforce it to increase its occurrence.

3. *DRO of the omission of behavior* (DRO-O). DRO-O reduces misbehavior by reinforcing its omission. The basic idea in DRO-O is to reinforce the student for periods when the misbehavior has not occurred. Usually, the reinforcement is given for short periods of omission at first and then the interval is gradually expanded. You might, for example, reinforce a student for working for a set period of time without asking for unnecessary assistance.

*Differential Reinforcement of Low Rates of Behavior (DRL)*. DRL reduces misbehavior by decreasing the frequency, duration, or intensity of the target behavior. The basic idea in DRL is to reinforce lower levels of the behavior. Often this is done using a series of small steps. Use DRL when you can't or don't want to eliminate a behavior but would like to reduce it to a more tolerable level. DRL is done in three ways.

1. *DRL using full sessions* (DRL-F). DRL-F is done by setting an interval, e.g., a class period, and placing a ceiling on the behavior. The ceiling is an upper limit on the behavior lower than its usual level. If the behavior stays below the ceiling for the full time interval, reinforce the behavior. For example, if voice level stays below a specified point during an activity period, you reinforce the student. At the end of the interval after the behavior level either has or has not been reinforced, the interval starts over.

2. *DRL using variable intervals* (DRL-I). DRL-I is done by setting an interval, e.g., 15 minutes, and setting a ceiling on the behavior. If the behavior stays below the ceiling, reinforce it at the end of the interval. For example, if the number of times a student is off-task during the interval doesn't exceed the ceiling, you reinforce the student. After reinforcement, the interval starts over. However, if at any time during the interval, the level of behavior exceeds the ceiling, start the interval over right then. Thus, only intervals resulting in reinforcement will run for the set time. Intervals not resulting in reinforcement will vary in length.

3. *DRL using spaced responding* (DRL-S). DRL-S is done by setting an interval, e.g., 5 minutes. This interval is the length of time you would like to see separate occurrences of the response. Responses separated by at least the interval of time set are reinforced. Don't reinforce any response with less than the set interval separating it from the last similar response. For example, if a student asks too many questions, you might respond only to those questions 5 or more minutes apart. If you want a fairly long latency between responses, use a series of small steps, e.g., first 5 minutes, then 10 minutes, then 14 minutes, and so on.

*Satiation.*    Satiation reduces misbehavior by diminishing the incentive value of the reinforcer maintaining it. The basic idea here is that if the reinforcer supporting a behavior is no longer reinforcing, the behavior will decrease or stop. The method used is to provide the reinforcer in such quantities that it loses its value. For example, if a student finds it "fun" to use profanity, you might have the student say the word or words repeatedly until it is no longer rewarding. When the reinforcer is a response rather than a stimulus, as was the case in the example, the procedure is called *response satiation* or *negative practice*. When the reinforcer is a stimulus, the procedure is called *stimulus satiation*.

*Extinction.*    Extinction reduces misbehavior by ending the reinforcement maintaining the misbehavior. The basic idea here is that if the reinforcer supporting a behavior is no longer available, the behavior will decrease or stop. The method used to accomplish this is to identify the reinforcer supporting a behavior and end the reinforcement. For example, a student always calls out instead of raising his or her hand to get your attention. If you respond, it is probably your attention to the behavior that is maintaining it. Thus, if you ig-nore calling out, the behavior will diminish because it no longer produces the intended result, i.e., your attention.

***Overcorrection (OC).***   OC reduces misbehavior by providing a con-sequence with a logical relationship to the misbehavior. OC has both positive and corrective aspects and a punitive aspect. The basic idea here is that if you have a student make amends for misbehavior, it will be both corrective and puni-tive. OC is done in three ways.

1. *OC through positive practice* (OC-P). In OC-P a student must repeatedly prac-tice the correct rather than the incorrect way of doing something. For example, if a student always slams a door shut, you would have the student practice opening and closing the door gently 25 times on each occurrence.

2. *OC through restitution* (OC-R). OC-R has a student overcorrect the effect produced by misbehavior. For example, if a student writes on the wall, you might require the student to scrub down the whole wall. Another example, if a student steals something from another student, you might have the student return what was stolen. The student would then give the victim something of greater value than what was stolen.

3. *OC through the full use of both methods* (OC-F). OC-F is done simply by combin-ing both OC-P and OC-R and applying both techniques to the same misbehavior. For example, a student drags the needle across another student's record while using the phonograph. You might have the student pay for the damaged record and give the victim another record. Next, you would have the errant student practice 25 times how to lift and move the phonograph arm properly.

***Response Cost (RC).***   RC reduces misbehavior by withdrawing a specified amount of a student's reinforcers for misbehavior. RC is equivalent to fining a student for misbehavior. RC is frequently used in a token economy, al-though it doesn't have to be. There are three ways to do RC.

1. *RC using bonus reinforcers* (RC-B). RC-B is done by giving a student a certain number of reinforcers free. The reinforcers are taken away in a specified quan-tity following each instance of misbehavior. For example, a student is annoy-ing a classmate by kicking his or her desk. You might place a bowl on the student's desk with 15 poker chips in it. You would take one each time the stu-dent kicks the classmate's desk. At the end of the day, the student would be able to spend any remaining poker chips for free time at one minute per chip.

2. *RC combined with earned reinforcement* (RC-C). You do RC-C the same way as RC-B with one difference. The student has earned the reinforcers you take away. Usually, the reinforcers were earned for either academic work or good conduct behavior.

3. *RC using a transfer of reinforcers* (RC-T). RC-T is a facilitative condition used with either RC-B or RC-C. It doesn't matter whether the student was given the reinforcers or had to earn them. RC-T imposes a fine of a specified quantity of reinforcers on a student for misbehavior. You then transfer these reinforcers

to another student in the class, whose behavior is appropriate. This procedure is often used in the context of a token economy where all students are under a uniform management system (Center & Wascom, 1984).

***Time-Out from Reinforcement (TO).***    TO reduces misbehavior by eliminating the opportunity to receive reinforcement. The basic idea here is to set a relatively brief time, immediately following misbehavior, when reinforcement is not available. There are three ways to do TO.

1.  *TO from earning reinforcement* (TO-E). TO-E is done by suspending for a brief period the opportunity to earn reinforcement. Immediately following a misbehavior, tell a student that he or she cannot earn any reinforcers for a specified time, e.g., 10 minutes. You can do this simply by informing the student or by taking away his or her point sheet for a specified interval. For example, students are earning reinforcers on an intermittent basis for appropriate behavior. You might, after a misbehavior, tell a student that he or she will not be eligible to receive reinforcement for the next 10 minutes.

2.  *TO by suspension of spending or consumption* (TO-S). TO-S is done by suspending the opportunity to use reinforcers. A student is told, immediately following a misbehavior, that he or she cannot use reinforcers for a specified time, e.g., 30 minutes. Reinforcers can still be earned but can't be used during the period of suspension. For example, if a student is receiving a consumable reinforcer, he or she could not eat or drink any of the earnings during the suspension period. If the student is on a token system, he or she cannot exchange any of the tokens for backup reinforcers during the suspension period. This procedure would only be workable if tokens could be exchanged at any time. If the student is in a token system where there are specified times for exchanging tokens for reinforcers, the suspension would have to be for the next exchange period. Finally, TO-S can be done if the student misbehaves while engaging in consuming) a reinforcing activity. For example, a student misbehaves while playing a game of kickball. He or she might be suspended from the game for a specified time and required to just sit and watch.

3.  *TO by isolation from reinforcement* (TO-I). TO-I is done by isolating the student from the source of reinforcement. Whenever a student engages in misbehavior, he or she is immediately isolated from reinforcement for a brief time. You do TO-I by socially isolating the student from sources of reinforcement. This is the procedure associated with the use of a time-out room. TO-I doesn't necessarily require a time-out room. You can socially isolate a student behind a partition in the classroom or a similar arrangement. For example, a student engages in a destructive temper tantrum. He or she might be removed from the classroom and secluded in a time-out room until calm. For many students, social isolation is an aversive experience. It will reduce misbehavior even if there are no reinforcers available in the classroom for the misbehavior.

***Presentation of an Aversive Stimulus (PAS).***    PAS reduces misbehavior by presenting an aversive stimulus immediately following a misbehavior. This type of punishment can result in undesirable side effects. There are several undesirable side effects of the use of punishment. First, punishment results in avoidance and escape behaviors which may aggravate a student's problems. Second, there are undesirable, negative emotional responses associated with these avoidance and escape behaviors. Third, punishment tends to suppress behavior in general rather than being highly specific. There is then a risk that not only undesirable behavior will be suppressed by punishment but also desirable behaviors. Fourth, punishment often suppresses behavior only temporarily. This is particularly true when no constructive alternative to the punished behavior has been established. Finally, the use of punishment by authority figures models, for students, aggressive behavior as an appropriate way to handle differences with others. An informative debate on the use of punishment in special education can be found in McGinnis, Scott-Miller, Neel, and Smith (1985). An extensive discussion of the use of punishment in special education can be found in Wood and Lakin (1978).

In my view the use of punishment should be restricted to one of two conditions. First, PAS is justifiable if a behavior has not yielded to other reductive techniques and is interfering with learning important behavior. For example, a student is engaging in a self-stimulation behavior, e.g., twirling. This behavior is preventing important behavior for learning, e.g., attending. If other procedures have failed to reduce it, you might present a mildly aversive stimulus, e.g., smelling salts, immediately following each occurrence. Second, PAS is justifiable if a behavior is dangerous to the student or to others. For example, if a student deliberately trips another student while going down a flight of stairs, you might give the student a paddling.

***Combinations.*** The effects produced by the techniques described above are enhanced by combining them. Generally, reductive techniques using reinforcement are combined with reductive techniques such as extinction or punishment, e.g., DRO with extinction, or DRL with RC. Antecedent and consequent control should always be combined.

### Selecting a Technique

When you select a technique to use in an individual behavior change procedure, you must consider three things: ethics, effectiveness, and efficiency (Deitz & Hummel, 1978). *Ethics* requires you to match the seriousness of a problem with the intrusiveness of the intervention. You should use the least intrusive technique appropriate for treating the problem. *Effectiveness* requires you to select a technique demonstrated to be successful with the problem behavior. *Efficiency* requires you to select a technique that you can plan and conduct in the least amount of time possible. Table 4–9 ranks orders techniques along the three dimensions just discussed.

The selection of a technique often depends on the nature of the target behavior. Deitz and Hummel (1978) recommend that you develop a continuum of behavior problems, ranging from minor, everyday problems to serious, less frequent problems (see Table 4–10). By doing this, you have a rationale for determining the seriousness of a problem behavior before selecting an intervention technique. Deitz and Hummel (1978) also rank order techniques based on the

**Table 4–9**  A rank ordering of intervention procedures along the three dimensions of concern in technique selection

| ETHICS | EFFECTIVENESS | EFFICIENCY |
|---|---|---|
| Most | | |
| 1. DRO-I | 1. Punishment | 1. Extinction |
| 2. DRL-F | 2. Response Cost | 2. Punishment |
| 3. DRL-I | 3. Extinction | 3. DRL-F |
| 4. DRL-S | 4. Time-out | 4. Response cost |
| 5. DRO-A | 5. DRL-F | 5. DRO-I |
| 6. OC-P | 6. DRO-I | 6. Satiation |
| 7. Extinction | 7. DRO-A | 7. OC-P |
| 8. Satiation | 8. DRL-I | 8. Time-out |
| 9. OC-R | 9. DRL-S | 9. OC-R |
| 10. Time-out | 10. OC-R | 10. DRO-A |
| 11. Response cost | 11. OC-P | 11. DRL-I |
| 12. Punishment | 12. Satiation | 12. DRL-S |
| Least | | |

SOURCE: Adapted from Deitz and Hummel, 1978.

**Table 4–10**  A continuum of inappropriate behavior ranging from everyday nuisance behaviors to serious problem behaviors with a rank ordering of interventions appropriate for use with behaviors at different levels of seriousness

| Usual | | | Serious |
|---|---|---|---|
| Talking | Teasing | Fighting | Murder |
| Out-of-seat | Poor sportsmanship | Lying | Rape |
| Littering | Crying | Stealing | Vandalism |
| Showing-off | Screaming | Chronic failure | Arson |
| Time to start | Not doing work | Rebelliousness | Drug use |
| Ignoring rules | Sleeping | Swearing | Assault |

| | USUAL | SERIOUS |
|---|---|---|
| Most Recommended | | |
| | 1. DRO-I | 1. DRO-A |
| | 2. DRL-F | 2. Punishment |
| | 3. Extinction | 3. Response cost |
| | 4. DRL-I | 4. Timeout |
| | 5. DRO-A | 5. OC-R |
| | 6. Satiation | 6. DRO-I |
| | 7. DRL-S | 7. DRL-I |
| | 8. OC-R | 8. DRL-F |
| | 9. OC-P | 9. OC-P |
| | 10. Time-out | 10. Extinction |
| | 11. Response cost | 11. Satiation |
| | 12. Punishment | 12. DRL-S |
| Least Recommended | | |

SOURCE:  Adapted from Deitz and Hummel, 1978.

seriousness of the problem behavior and the ethicalness, effectiveness, and efficiency of treatments (see Table 4–10).

### Evaluation

Evaluation of behavior modification interventions uses single-subject research designs and graphic analysis of data (Tawney & Gast, 1984). All but one of the single-subject designs available are experimental designs. Most texts on behavioral interventions advocate that classroom teachers use experimental designs for evaluation. The need for this is debatable since most classroom teachers are not trying to demonstrate experimental control of a target behavior. Presumably, teachers will usually limit themselves to techniques already demonstrated to be effective. From a practical perspective, teachers simply don't have the time or circumstances necessary for conducting experimental evaluations.

What is essential is that a teacher monitor the effects of an intervention so that any needed adjustments can be made. Teachers also need a way to assess the overall effect of their intervention. There is a single-subject design adequate to meet a classroom teacher's needs. This is the A-B design or clinical teaching design. This design can be thought of as an accountability design rather than an experimental design. The A-B design has only two phases. The first is the baseline phase in which you collect contrast data under nonintervention conditions. The second phase is the phase in which you collect intervention data. You evaluate the data by graphic analysis. In graphic analysis, treatment data are visually examined to see if they are discontinuous with baseline data.

As the discussion above implies, you must graph the data collected if they are to be useful for monitoring and evaluation. Since the data collection process is continuous, you must graph the data as they are collected to monitor the intervention. A graph for behavioral data should include the following.

1. A vertical and horizontal axis

2. A measurement scale along the vertical axis

3. A time scale along the horizontal axis

4. A phase-change line

5. Data lines

6. Descriptive labels for the axes and phases

The phase-change line divides a graph into baseline and intervention phases. It is a vertical line of dashes. You center the line between the points on the time scale on the horizontal axis which mark the end of the baseline phase and the beginning of the intervention phase. Data lines never cross phase-change lines. They are discontinuous within a phase if there is missing data (see Figure 4–4).

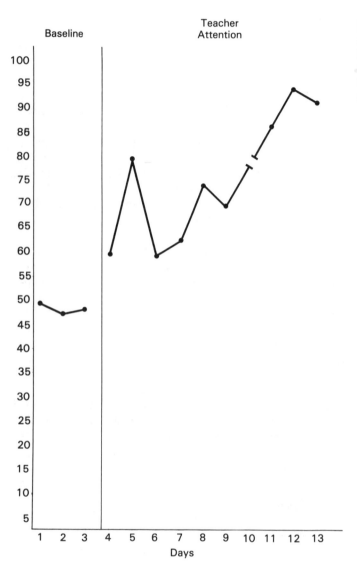

**Figure 4-4**
An example of a graph displaying data collected within an A-B design structure. Note the way that a day of missing data on day 9 is represented.

## PHYSICAL MANAGEMENT

Occasions will arise when all your behavior management strategies fail. Or, you haven't planned and begun an intervention yet and you have a student so disruptive or dangerous that an immediate and direct intervention is required. There are techniques that you can use in these situations. These techniques minimize the possibility of injury to either the student or the teacher (Harvey

& Schepers, 1977; Samuels & Moriarty, 1975; Upchurch, Ham, Daniels, Mc-Ghee, & Burnett, 1980). The following discussion is based on Samuels and Moriarty (1975).

### Evaluate Yourself

Before moving into a physical management situation, determine if you are wearing anything that could be used as a weapon against you, e.g., necklace or mechanical pencil. If so, remove these objects. Other possible problems include long hair that is loose and easy to grab hold of, clothing that restricts movement, or shoes that impede movement. Some of the latter items are impossible to alter on the spot. This means that you need to consider potential problems in advance so that you are always in a state of readiness.

### Evaluate the Situation

You should also consider several situational influences before becoming physically involved with an acting-out student. You should determine if there are any nearby objects that can be used as weapons or serve as obstacles. Also, consider if there are any students who you can depend on to take over the class, go for help, or assist you by doing things like opening doors.

### Taking Action

As you move into position to become directly involved with the student, maintain a nonthreatening stance (see Figure 4–5a). Act calmly, and try to use your voice and persuasion to bring the situation under control. If you must physically intervene, have a clear objective. Make contact with the student in a way that will make it easy to direct his or her movement (see Figure 4–5b). If the student strikes out, use his or her body to block the blow (see Figure 4–5c). If you must restrain the student, use the basket hold (see Figure 4–5d–f). If you must move the student after using restraint, use the side carry (see Figure 4–5g).

The techniques covered here are only a few of those available. The proper use of the techniques requires instruction and practice. You should obtain a copy of the training manual (Samuels & Moriarty, 1975) covering the techniques discussed for a more complete treatment of the topic of physical management.

## RESOURCES

There are several resources in addition to the references already cited that you will find useful. Two books on behavior change programs are suggested (Millman, Schaefer, & Cohen, 1980; K. O'Leary & S. O'Leary, 1977). There is also an excellent series of how-to booklets published by H & H Enterprises under a variety of titles, e.g., *How to Use Overcorrection*, and by a variety of authors (Reference Note 1). An excellent resource on the token economy is a book by

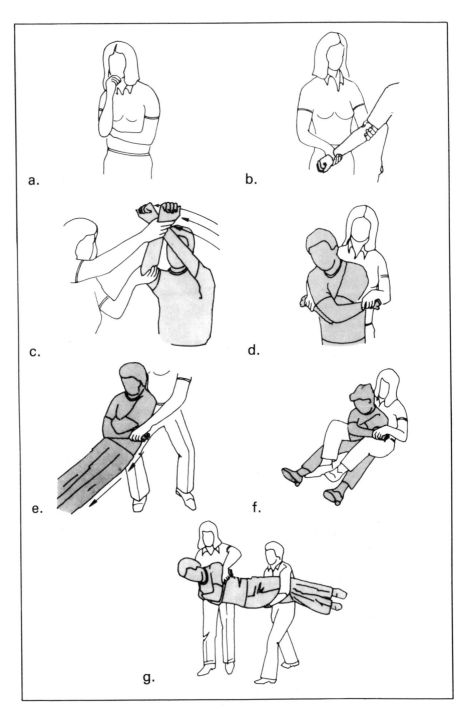

**Figure 4–5**  Illustrations of several physical management techniques from the film *Classroom Crisis Control*, Hinzman Productions, 354 Hookstown Grade Rd., Clinton, PA 15026. *The illustrations are adapted from the accompanying training manual developed by Martin Samuels and Peter Moriarty, 1975.*

Payne, Polloway, Kauffman, and Scranton (1975). Finally, Algozzine (1982) has developed a resource manual that includes material on individual behavioral techniques, token economies, and physical management as well as some other topics.

## REFERENCE NOTE

1.  How to Teach Series (16 titles) published by H & H Enterprises and distributed by PRO-ED, 5341 Industrial Oaks Blvd., Austin, TX 78735.

## REFERENCES

ALBERTO, P., & TROUTMAN, A. (1982). *Applied behavior analysis for teachers.* Columbus, OH: Merrill.

ALGOZZINE, B. (1982). *Problem behavior management.* Rockville, MD: Aspen.

AYLLON, T., & AZRIN, N. (1968). *The token economy.* New York: Appleton-Century-Crofts.

BARRISH, H., SAUNDERS, M., & WOLF, M. (1969). Good behavior game: Effects of individual contingencies for group consequences on disruptive behavior in a classroom. *Journal of Applied Behavior Analysis, 2,* 119–124.

CAUTELA, J. R., CAUTELA, J., & ESONIS, S. (1983). *Forms for behavior analysis with children.* Champaign, IL: Research Press.

CENTER, D., & ARNAULT, L. (1984). *Establishing and balancing a classroom token economy.* Mississippi State, MS: Mississippi State University. (ERIC Document Reproduction Service No. ED 245 487)

CENTER, D., DEITZ, S., & KAUFMAN, M. (1982). Student ability, task difficulty, and inappropriate classroom behavior. *Behavior Modification, 6,* 355–374.

CENTER, D., & WASCOM, A. (1984). Transfer of reinforcers: A procedure to enhance response cost. *Educational and Psychological Research, 4*(1), 19–27.

COOPER, J. (1974). *Measurement and analysis of behavioral techniques.* Columbus, OH: Merrill.

DEITZ, S., & HUMMEL, J. (1978). *Discipline in the schools.* Englewood Cliffs, NJ: Educational Technology Publications.

HARVEY, E., & SCHEPERS, J. (1977). Physical contact techniques and defensive holds for use with aggressive retarded adults. *Mental Retardation, 15*(5), 29–31.

KAREN, R. (1974). *An introduction to behavior therapy and its applications.* New York: Harper & Row.

KAZDIN, A. (1977). *The token economy: A review and evaluation.* New York: Plenum Press.

KAZDIN, A. (1978). *History of behavior modification: Experimental foundations of contemporary research.* Baltimore, MD: University Park Press.

MCGINNIS, E., SCOTT-MILLER, D., NEEL, R., & SMITH, C. (1985). Aversives in special education programs for behaviorally disordered students: A debate. *Behavioral Disorders, 10,* 295–304.

MILLER, L. (1980). *Principles of everyday behavior analysis* (2nd ed.). Monterey, CA: Brooks/Cole.

MILLMAN, H., SCHAEFER, C., & COHEN, J. (1980). *Therapies for school behavior problems.* San Francisco: Jossey-Bass.

NELSON, C., & POLSGROVE, L. (1984). Behavior analysis in special education: White rabbit or white elephant? *Remedial and special education, 5*(4), 6–17.

O'LEARY, K., & O'LEARY, S. (1977). *Classroom management.* Elmsford, NY: Pergamon Press.

O'LEARY, S., & O'LEARY, K. (1976). Behavior modification in the school. In H. Leitenberg (Ed.), *Handbook of behavior modification and behavior therapy.* Englewood Cliffs, NJ: Prentice-Hall.

PAYNE, J., POLLOWAY, E., KAUFFMAN, J., & SCRANTON, T. (1975). *Living in the classroom: The currency-based token economy.* New York: Human Sciences Press.

ROSS, A. (1981). *Child behavior therapy.* New York: Wiley.

SAMUELS, M., & MORIARTY, P. (1975). *CRYCON: The concept of classroom crisis control* (a training manual). (Available from Martin Samuels, 142 Pennlear Dr., Monroeville, PA 15146 or (412) 622-4619)

SKINNER, B., (1953). *Science and human behavior.* New York: Free Press.

STOKES, T., & BAER, D. (1977). An implicit technology of generalization. *Journal of Applied Behavior Analysis 10,* 349–367.

SULZER-AZAROFF, B., & MAYER, G. (1977). *Applying behavior-analysis procedures with children and youth.* New York: Holt, Rinehart and Winston.

TAWNEY, J., & GAST, D. (1984). *Single subject research in special education.* Columbus, OH: Merrill.

UPCHURCH, T., HAM, L., DANIELS, R., McGHEE, M., & BURNETT, M. (1980). *A better way: An illustrated guide to protective intervention techniques.* Butner, NC: Murdock Center.

WALKER, H. (1976). *Walker problem behavior identification checklist.* Los Angeles: Western Psychological Services.

WALKER, H. (1979). *The acting-out child: Coping with classroom disruption.* Boston: Allyn and Bacon.

WOOD, F., & LAKIN, C. (1978). *Punishment and aversive stimulation in special education: Legal, theoretical, and practical issues in their use with emotionally disturbed children and youth.* Minneapolis, MN: University of Minnesota Press. (Reprinted by Council for Exceptional Children, 1982)

# 5

# TEACHING APPROPRIATE SOCIAL BEHAVIOR

## Social Skills

### INTRODUCTION

There is some debate among professionals about what is meant by "social skill." We will use a general definition of social skill developed by Libet and Lewinsohn (1973). In their definition, *social skill* is the ability to exhibit behaviors that are either positively or negatively reinforced and to avoid exhibiting behaviors that are extinguished or punished by others. Argle (1980), more simply, defines social skill as behavioral competence in social situations. Phillips (1978) broadly defined *disturbance* as a deficit in social skill. *Deviance* is characterized by maladaptive behaviors in situations calling for the use of social skills. Argle (1980) estimates that at least 7 percent of the "normal" population has significant problems in coping with social situations. Based on the above, it would seem reasonable to conclude that most, if not all, disturbed children and youth have some degree of social skill deficit.

An extensive review of the research literature led Cartledge and Milburn (1978) to conclude that social behavior is clearly related to achievement and school success. They found evidence that teachers respond differently to students depending on the students' social behaviors. Cartledge and Milburn argue that the most effective place to teach social skills is in the classroom. In another review of the research literature, Gresham (1982) concludes that the success of mainstreaming efforts depends largely on peer acceptance of the handicapped. Peer acceptance, in turn, depends on the level of a student's social competence. Cartledge and Milburn (1978) would probably add that not only is peer acceptance critical but also teacher acceptance. Teacher acceptance is, in part, also related to a student's level of social skill.

### Social Learning Theory

The development of social learning theory was the result of the collective effort of several psychologists (Miller & Dollard, 1941; Rotter, 1954; Bandura & Walters, 1963; Statts, 1975). Our discussion of this theory will follow the presentations of Bandura (1971, 1977). Social learning theory largely accepts the operant learning theory model of how behavior is acquired. It does differ in one important respect. In social learning theory social behavior may be acquired not only through direct experience but also through vicarious experience or observation. The theory suggests that observation is an important additional consideration in human learning. Observational learning is considered important for understanding how people acquire behavior. It is important because people have cognitive abilities superior to those of other members of the animal kingdom.

In social learning theory, a person demonstrating behavior is called a *model*. Models influence learning in observers through their ability to convey information. The observer acquires information from a model through perceptual processes. However, the critical factor is what the observer does with information once it is received. Because of the cognitive abilities in human observers, the observer can develop a symbolic representation of what is observed. From this symbolic representation, a person can retrieve information at any time and use it to guide behavior.

Social learning theory describes several processes that regulate observational learning. First, it is necessary for an observer to attend to the model. *Attention* to the model is influenced by several things. The observer's judgment about the functional value of the model's behavior will be important. You do not attend carefully to behavior you see no need for in yourself. Various characteristics of the model will also influence attention. You will attend more to a model you see as similar to yourself than to one you cannot identify with. An observer will also attend more carefully to a model whose behavior results in an outcome seen as desirable by the observer. That is, you will attend carefully to behavior in a model that produces a consequence you would like for yourself. While motivation will influence attention, its greatest effect is on retention and reproduction.

The second process regulating social learning is retention. *Retention* means long-term memory. It is at this point the higher cognitive abilities mentioned earlier become very important. Memory in people is greatly aided by the ability to code information using symbol systems. Primarily, we use two methods of coding information. One way we represent information symbolically is through visual images. You can, no doubt, recall information you have stored in memory using images, for example, the appearance of various traffic control signs you must respond to when you see them. Another way we represent information symbolically is through linguistic symbols or words. You can, no doubt, also recall information you have stored in memory using words, for example, verbal directions on how to make something. Another aid to memory our higher cognitive abilities make possible is rehearsal. Rehearsal means cognitively reviewing information. You have also, no doubt, done this, for example, silently reciting a number of times a poem you must say to your teacher and other students.

The third process regulating social learning is *reproduction* or *imitation*. Before you can exhibit behavior that has been acquired observationally, you must be able to produce responses corresponding to the behavior you have observed. Reproduction will, of course, be limited by the accuracy of the symbolic representation you have stored in memory. Accurate reproduction may also be limited by physical factors. For example, you may have an accurate memory of the behavior observed but simply not have the physical ability to perform it due to size, strength, disabilities, and so on. There are two types of imitation in social learning. The simplest type of imitation is a matching response to a sample. For example, you are shown how to operate a combination lock. If your imitation is not a perfect match to the demonstration, it will be unsuccessful. A more complex type of imitation is a rule-governed response to a sample. Rule-governed imitation doesn't require a perfect matching response to the sample. It requires a match with the form or rule implicit in the sample. For example, you learned the form for a simple sentence from samples provided by models, probably your parents. At first you made simple imitative responses to the model sentences. Once you recognized the rule controlling the construction of simple sentences, you were able to generate sentences you had never heard before. Even though these sentences were not exact matching responses to samples, they did correspond to the rule you had learned.

### Research

Earlier, both operant and social models of learning were mentioned. There is little doubt that social behavior can be taught using operant principles. This is done by direct reinforcement of a target behavior or approximations of it. The latter operation is called *shaping*. Under naturalistic conditions the application of the operant principles tends to be unsystematic, inconsistent, and inefficient (Mischel, 1973). When the principles are applied systematically and consistently, they are more effective but tend to be very time consuming. With most children, the systematic use of social learning principles is more efficient and less time intensive. The one exception is severely disturbed children who aren't responsive to social stimuli.

The basic research supporting social learning theory is available in two book-length presentations (Bandura & Walters, 1963; Bandura, 1977). One important and well-researched antecedent is model characteristics. Bandura identified several important model characteristics. Briefly, they are as follows.

1. *The age of the model.* Similarity in age is particularly important when teaching children and youth.

2. *Sex of the model.* Same sex models are more effective than opposite sex models.

3. *Likability of the model.* Models that are personable are more effective.

4. *Similarity of the model.* Models the observer can identify with are more effective.

5. *Status of the model.* Competent models with social status are more effective.

Research also shows that the observed consequences to a model affect learning in observers. The vicariously experienced consequences have an effect similar to but less potent than those of directly experienced consequences. Reinforcing consequences delivered to a model will aid learning in observers. Punitive consequences delivered to a model will inhibit learning in observers. The absence of consequences for a model, which are anticipated or expected by the observer, will also affect behavior. When a model exhibits a prohibited behavior and is not punished, the observer's behavior is disinhibited. That is, the observer becomes more likely to engage in the same behavior. Likewise, when the model performs a permitted behavior and isn't reinforced, the observer's behavior is inhibited. That is, the observer becomes less likely to engage in the same behavior. Thus, the lack of consequences for behavior performed by a model appear to be just as important as the type of consequence delivered.

Other researchers have demonstrated the effectiveness of social learning for teaching social skills to children. O'Connor (1969, 1972) demonstrated modeling was more effective than shaping in treatments designed to affect social behavior. Evers and Schwarz (1973) demonstrated modeling was effective regardless of whether or not it was paired with reinforcement of the observer for imitation. It should be noted that Gottman (1977) has cast some doubt on the subject selection procedures used in these studies. Gottman, Gonso, and Schuller (1976) demonstrated the effectiveness of modeling over naturalistic interaction for teaching social behavior. Several reviews of the research literature on teaching social skills are available to the interested reader (Foster & Ritchey, 1979; Gresham, 1981; Michelson & Wood, 1980; Van Hasselt, Hersen, Whitehill, & Bellack, 1979).

## ASSESSMENT

Before you can begin planning social skills instruction, you need to assess students' skills. Otherwise, the instruction process will be haphazard and may waste time on skills that don't need to be taught. A variety of methods can be used to assess social behavior. Unfortunately, no single method is clearly superior to the others. Each method has its uses and some are better for one purpose and others better for another purpose. Unless what is being measured is actual behavior using a direct measurement technique, there will always be some question about how well the assessment reflects actual behavior. Even when using a direct measurement technique, there is the question of what behaviors should be measured, when, and where they should be assessed. The assessment will only be as good as the appropriateness of the behaviors selected for measurement and the setting and time selected for the assessment. We will now review some of the approaches available for assessing social behavior.

## Testing

Tests, in the conventional sense, for assessing social behavior are cognitive in nature. In other words, the test supplies a set of stimuli to which the testee makes either a verbal or a written response. The responses made to the stimuli are then scored and interpreted. Johnson (1975) demonstrated a significant relationship between an ability for role-taking and prosocial behavior. That is, the more adept you are at taking the perspective of others, the better your social skills tend to be. One test based on this approach is the Role-Taking Test (RTT) developed by Feffer and Gourevitch (1960). The RTT was originally developed for use with adults but has been modified for use with children (Reardon, Hersen, Bellack, & Foley, 1979). Another instrument is the Roberts Apperception Test for Children (McArthur & Roberts, 1982), which is a projective test. This test uses a set of picture stimulus cards illustrating various interpersonal situations involving a child with either a peer or an adult. The situations illustrated are deliberately vague. The child is asked to describe what is going on in the picture, what took place immediately prior to what is being shown, what the outcome will be, and how they feel about it.

Tests of the type just described can be useful in getting a measure of overall social development or for comparing social development in two or more children. The major problem with tests of this type is that they do not assess individual skills. In short, they are not specific enough for planning instruction.

## Self-Report

Self-report or interviewing is another approach to assessing social behavior. In this approach, the subject is interviewed about his or her behavior and the problems being experienced. Although this is one of the most widely used techniques by psychologists, it is usually not standardized. That is, there is a great deal of variation from one interviewer to the next in what is asked and how the responses are interpreted (O'Leary & Turkewitz, 1978). Probably a better approach to interviewing is the structured interview. This approach provides a framework in which the interview takes places. The structure reduces some of the variability in interviewing mentioned above. One type of structured interview particularly appropriate for use with children is the fictitious story. The interview focuses on the situation and characters in a story to provide some consistency to the interview process. A discussion of this approach to interviewing can be found in Meichenbaum (1976).

There is some evidence (Rutter & Graham, 1968) that interviewing can be a very useful approach to assessment with children. How useful interview data will be depends on a number of things. First, the skill of the interviewer will be critical. Second, the appropriateness of the questions asked will be important. Finally, the usefulness of the data will depend on the accuracy of the responses given. This last consideration can, of course, vary greatly from one interviewee to the next.

### Self-Rating

Another way to structure information collection from students is to have students rate themselves on a set of social behaviors. Students are asked to use a numeric rating to estimate how often they exhibit the behavior. The rating scale may also use labels to help students select the most accurate numeric rating. Sometimes only the labels are supplied and numeric ratings are assigned by the assessor later (see Box 5–1). An alternative to this approach is to supply descriptions of various social situations. Students are asked to select from a set of choices provided under each item. A student's choice, hopefully, represents the most likely action by the student in a similar situation. This type of scale resembles a multiple-choice test. A few sample items from a scale developed by Cautela, Cautela, and Esonis (1983) are shown in Box 5–2.

There are several concerns about self-rating scales. First, they can only be used with students who have sufficient reading skill to complete the scale independently. Of course, you could use a self-rating scale like a structured interview with students who can't read or don't read well. However, if you do, the efficiency of a self-rating scale is lost. Second, Ledingham, Younger, Schwartzman, and Bergeron (1982) found that self-report scales completed by children did not correlate well with either peer or teacher ratings. Teacher and peer ratings, however, correlated well with one another. Ledingham et al. also found self-ratings to be biased by social desirability and to yield the lowest estimate of deviance.

### Informant Reports

Several approaches use informants to obtain data on students rather than using the students themselves. One technique is the *informant interview*.

**Box 5–1**   Examples of the use of numerals and labels on social skills rating scales

---

**Numeric Rating Scale**

1. The students laughs at other people's jokes and funny stories. (Circle one)

   Almost never   1   2   3   4   5   Almost always

**Labeled Rating Scale**

1. The student laughs at other people's jokes and funny stories. (Circle one)

   | Almost never | Sometimes | Often | Very frequently | Almost always |
   |---|---|---|---|---|

**Labeled and Numeric Rating Scale**

1. The student laughs at other people's jokes and funny stories. (Circle one)

   | Almost never | Sometimes | Often | Very frequently | Almost always |
   |---|---|---|---|---|
   | 1 | 2 | 3 | 4 | 5 |

**Box 5–2**   An example from a situation-specific social skills assessment scale using a multiple-choice format

Name_____Date_____

Age_____        Sex: Boy_____        Girl_____

School_____        Grade_____

I. What would you do if these things happened to you? Circle the number that tells best what you think you would do.

A.  You are constantly being picked on or hit by another kid in your class.
   1.   I say, "If you do that again, I'm warning you, I'll have to hit you back hard."
   2.   I say, "Cut it out" or tell a grownup.
   3.   I cry or say nothing.
B.  Your friends always decide what to do after school and don't ask you what you would like to do.
   1.   I say, "Once in a while I'd like to be the one to say what we'll do."
   2.   I complain, "I never get to pick what we're going to do."
   3.   I say nothing and always go along with the other kids.
C.  Your lunch at the school cafeteria is badly burned or not cooked well enough.
   1.   I take it back, explain what's wrong with it, and ask for another lunch.
   2.   I complain to my friends about the school's food.
   3.   I say nothing and eat it anyway.

SOURCE:   Reprinted with permission from J. R. Cautela, J. Cautela, and S. Esonis 1983, *Forms for Behavior Analysis With Children*. Champaign, IL: Research Press.

The earlier discussion of interviewing applies to this approach as well. You need only keep in mind that an informant is being interviewed rather than the student. The informant should be someone who is knowledgeable about the student. This often means one or both parents, although other types of informants can be used. As we stated earlier, a structured interview is probably the best approach. A well-known informant-based structured interview with which teachers are familiar is the Vineland Social Maturity Scale (Doll, 1965; Sparrow, Balla, & Ciccagetti, 1984).

The *sociogram* is a widely used technique for assessing social behavior in children. This approach uses peers as informants. It usually is done in one of two ways. The first method is called the *nomination method*. In it, students are asked to write down on a piece of paper their nominations for the students they like the most and those they like the least. The number of nominations a student gets in either category is used as an indicator of the student's social standing. The second method is called the *roster method*. In it students are supplied a list of all the students in the class or group. By using a roster,  you can eliminate the possibility, under the nomination method, that some students will be left out. Students are asked to rate each peer on the roster, for likability, using a numeric, labeled, or combination scale. Hymel and Asher (1977) discuss these two methods and their associated merits and problems. One problem is that they often do not correlate well with direct measures of behavior. Another problem is that they are broad measures and do not identify specific behaviors. The Behavior Rating Profile (Brown & Hammill, 1983) is one source of an easily obtainable sociogram procedure.

A third informant-based procedure is a rating scale completed by a knowledgeable person such as a teacher. The informant is usually given a list of social behaviors and asked to rate a student on each one. The ratings are usually done using a bipolar scale for each item. An example from some recent research (Center & Wascom, 1987) is in Box 5–3. A major advantage of this approach is that a large number of specific behaviors of interest can be assessed in a short time. Teacher rating scales are widely used and many examples can be found. Virtually all the commercially available social skills training programs are accompanied by this type of instrument.

The informant rating scale is criticized for being subject to several biasing influences (Sulzbacher, 1973; Sroufe, 1975). However, Siegel, Dragovitch, and Marholin (1976) demonstrated that this type of scale is quite resistant to bias if specific items of behavior, e.g., hitting, are used instead of global trait labels, e.g., hostility. Even with a well-constructed instrument, the quality of the data obtained depends on how well the informant knows the student being rated.

### Direct Observation

Direct observation, in a natural setting, is a widely used approach to behavioral assessment of children and youth (Johnson & Bolstad, 1973).

**Box 5–3**    Some sample items from a social skills rating instrument using a bipolar scale

Circle one number per item.

1. The student has eye contact when speaking.

    Almost never    1    2    3    4    5    Almost always

2. The student asks questions when talking with others.

    Almost never    1    2    3    4    5    Almost always

3. The student apologizes when s/he wrongs someone.

    Almost never    1    2    3    4    5    Almost always

4. The student asks if s/he can be of help.

    Almost never    1    2    3    4    5    Almost always

5. The student keeps commitments s/he makes.

    Almost never    1    2    3    4    5    Almost always

SOURCE:   Center and Wascom, 1987.

Usually in this approach a specific behavior is assessed as it actually occurs in a given setting. The behavior assessed must be operationally defined, continuously monitored, and each occurrence individually recorded. It is a time-consuming approach, but if done correctly it provides accurate data. The training requirements for users of this approach are quite rigorous (Jones, Reid, & Patterson, 1974). Use of direct observation was discussed in some detail in Chapter 4.

Direct observation can be more efficient if you use a set of behaviors in combination with a coded observation system. An example of such a system (Wahler, House, & Stambaugh, 1976) uses a set of 18 response categories, e.g., sustained noninteraction and six stimulus categories, e.g., social attention child, aversive. A list of the category codes for this instrument is given in Table 5–1. The coding sheet used with the codes is shown in Figure 5–1. Durlak and Mannarino (1977) discuss the use of this system to assess socially deficient children. While the direct observation of behavior in a naturalistic setting is believed to yield good data, it isn't without its problems (Kent & Foster, 1977).

In addition to use in naturalistic settings, direct observation can also be done in analogue settings. *Analogue settings* are contrived situations such as role plays. An analogue setting is often used to help ensure that the behavior of interest will occur at a suitable time. That is, instead of waiting for the behavior to occur under natural circumstances, a situation is contrived to stimulate its occurrence. An example of this approach is the Behavioral Assertiveness Test for Children (Bornstein, Bellack, & Hersen, 1977). In the BAT-C, nine standard interpersonal situations commonly encountered by children are used to aid observation. Although this is a more convenient approach than naturalistic observation, there is some question about its use. The major question raised is whether or not the observed behavior in the analogue settings correlates well with actual behavior in natural settings (Bellack, Hersen, & Lamparski, 1979).

Regardless of other considerations, there are three limitations in particular to bear in mind about direct observation. First, it usually addresses only a small number of specific behaviors. This is not a problem if you know what you want to assess. It may be a problem, however, if your assessment is exploratory. Second, the approach requires a lot of training to execute properly. Finally, it is a time-intensive approach to assessment.

In summary, probably the best approach for classroom teachers is the teacher rating scale. These scales do not require a high level of training to use properly and don't take a lot of time to complete. They also cover a broader range of behaviors than any of the other approaches discussed. In addition, most of the social skill training programs developed for teachers come with a rating scale based on the curriculum in the program. Several cautions are in order for teachers planning to use a rating scale. First, be certain you understand the proper use of the scale. Second, don't use a rating scale on a student unless you know the student well. Third, be sure that the scale you plan to use covers specific behaviors rather than global traits. Finally, try to confirm your ratings through informal observations.

**Table 5–1** A list of the observation category codes used in *Ecological Assessment of Child Problem Behavior*

| | | |
|---|---|---|
| *Response Categories* | C | Compliance |
| | O | Opposition |
| | O- | Aversive opposition |
| | CP | Complaint |
| | S | Self-stimulation |
| | OP | Object play |
| | T | Self-talk |
| | NI | Sustained noninteraction |
| | SS | Sustained schoolwork |
| | ST | Sustained toy play |
| | SW | Sustained work |
| | SA | Sustained attending |
| | MA | Mand adult |
| | MC | Mand child |
| | AA | Social approach adult |
| | AC | Social approach child |
| | SIA | Social interaction adult |
| | SIC | Social interaction child |
| | SL | Slash |
| | | |
| *Stimulus Categories* | IA+ | Instruction adult, nonaversive |
| | IA- | Instruction adult, aversive |
| | SA+ | Social attention adult, nonaversive |
| | SA- | Social attention adult, aversive |
| | SC+ | Social attention child, nonaversive |
| | SC- | Social attention child, aversive |
| | | |
| *Procedural Category* | Obs. | Obstruct |

SOURCE: R. Wahler, A. House, and E. Stambaugh II, 1976.

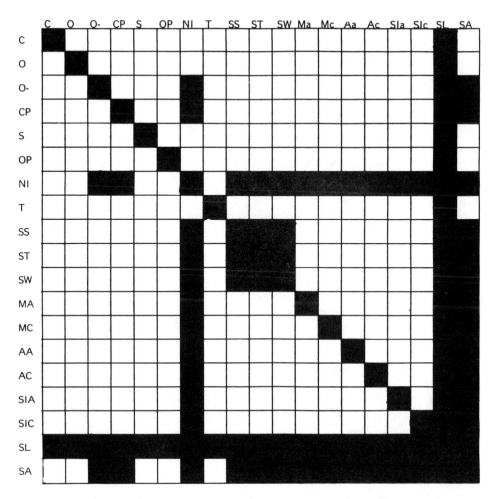

**Figure 5–1**    An observational recording matrix used in conjunction with category codes. From R. Waller, A. House, and E. Stambaugh II, 1976, *Ecological Assessment of Child Problem Behavior.*

## Curriculum

Curriculum is what is taught in a social skills training program. You can either develop your own curriculum or use a commercial program. In either case, you need some knowledge about what should go into a social skills curriculum. At the beginning of this chapter, I gave a general definition of social skill by Libet and Lewinsohn (1973). A more comprehensive definition was given by Argle (1980) in a discussion of social competence. The definition includes skills in nine areas:

1. Accurate perception of others

2. Ability to take the role of others

3. Nonverbal communication of attitudes and emotions

4. Nonverbal support of speech

5. Emitting behavior rewarding to others

6. Planning behavior and responding to feedback

7. Appropriate self-presentation

8. Understanding of situations and their rules

9. Appropriate sequencing of behavior during interaction

### Social Skills Research

A number of studies have attempted to identify the social skills needed by children and youth. Drabman and Patterson (1982) reviewed the research literature on the characteristics of socially accepted children. They identified six characteristics of socially accepted children:

1. The children conformed to acceptable standards for social behavior

2. The children exhibited extroverted behavior

3. The children were cooperative

4. The children adapted well to the demands of routine

5. The children accepted situations as they found them

6. The children conformed to the requirements of situations

These characteristics are based on research with "normal" children. The authors of this paper, however, believe the limited research they found on handicapped children suggests that similar characteristics would apply to them as well.

Gresham (1982) reviewed the research literature on social skills and successful mainstreaming of handicapped children. Gresham identified six social skills critical for the social integration of handicapped children:

1. Cooperative skills

2. Positive interaction skills

3. Sharing skills

4. Skill in greeting others

5. Skill in asking for and giving information

6. Conversation skills

Gresham's (1982) review suggested that handicapped children deficit in these skill areas could not be successfully mainstreamed into regular classrooms. This appeared to be true even if the children had the academic skills needed to function successfully in the regular classroom.

Finally, in a survey of teacher perceptions of social behavior in behavior-disordered children and youth, Center and Wascom (1987) identified 47 prosocial behaviors seen as deficit in behavior-disordered students. This study was conducted using a modified version of the Social Performance Survey Schedule (Lowe & Cautela, 1978). The study accumulated data on a total of 410 students. Half of these students were behavior disordered and half were socially normal. The students ranged in age from 8 to 15. Half of the students were between 8 and 11 and half between 12 and 15 years of age. Approximately 75% of the students were male and 25% were female. Approximately 70% of the students were white and 30% were black. Most of the 47 prosocial behaviors identified were perceived as deficient in both sexes. Seven of the identified behaviors, however, applied only to males and one only to females. These eight behaviors were as follows:

*Males only:*

1. Has eye contact when speaking

2. Laughs at other people's jokes and funny stories

3. Listens when spoken to

4. Remembers and discusses topics previously discussed with others

5. Does things others like to do

6. Reevaluates his position after receiving new information

7. Mentions people's names when talking to them

*Females only:*

1. Stands up for her rights

The 47 prosocial behaviors identified by Center and Wascom (1987) are more extensive than those identified in the other studies discussed above. However, the small number of characteristics in the previous studies are more general and broader in scope. The Center and Wascom study deals with more

**Table 5–2**   A table of the 47 prosocial behaviors that teachers identified as deficit in behavior-disordered students[a]

| | |
|---|---|
| *Positive Interaction* | 1. The student makes other people laugh (with jokes, funny stories, etc.). |
| | 2. The student shows appreciation when someone does something for him/her. |
| | 3. The student demonstrates concern for others' rights. |
| | 4. The student is able to accept other people despite their faults. |
| | 5. The student, when facing conflict with others, knows what to do or say to avoid offending. |
| | 6. The student laughs at other people's jokes and funny stories. |
| | 7. The student keeps the significance of his/her accomplishments in perspective. |
| | 8. The student knows when to leave people alone. |
| | 9. The student shows appreciation when people seek him/her out. |
| | 10. The student admits to mistakes or errors s/he makes. |
| | 11. The student gives positive feedback to others. |
| | 12. The student is able to recognize when people are troubled. |
| | 13. The student keeps in touch with friends. |
| | 14. The student apologizes when s/he wrongs someone. |
| | 15. The student finds something to be optimistic about in hard times. |
| | 16. The student compliments others on their clothes, hairstyle, etc. |
| | 17. The student stands up for his/her rights. |
| | 18. The student stands up for his/her friends. |
| | 19. The student expresses concern to others about their misfortunes. |
| | 20. The student takes care of others' property as if it were his/her own. |
| | 21. The student gets to know people in depth. |
| | 22. The student reevaluates his/her position when s/he receives new information. |
| | 23. The student keeps commitments s/he makes. |
| | |
| *Conversation* | 24. The student has eye contact when speaking. |
| | 25. The student is able to accept other people despite their faults. |
| | 26. The student smiles when s/he first sees someone s/he knows. |
| | 27. The student asks others how they've been, what they've been up to, etc. |
| | 28. The student listens when spoken to. |
| | 29. The student remembers and discusses topics previously discussed with others. |
| | 30. The student shows interest in what another is saying (e.g., with appropriate facial movements, comments, and questions). |
| | 31. The student directs conversation with other people toward topics the other person is interested in. |
| | 32. The student asks questions when talking with others. |
| | 33. The student considers the opinions given by others. |
| | 34. The student has eye contact when listening. |
| | 35. The student asks if s/he can be of help. |
| | 36. The student discusses a variety of topics with others. |
| | 37. The student considers the effects of his/her statements and actions on others' feelings. |
| | 38. The student mentions people's names when talking to them. |
| | 39. The student talks about interesting topics. |

**Table 5–2**    Continued

| *Cooperation and Sharing* | 40. The student shows enthusiasm for others' good fortunes. |
| | 41. The student keeps secrets or confidential information to him/herself. |
| | 42. The student shares what s/he has with others. |
| | 43. The student tries to work out problems with others by talking to them. |
| | 44. The student does things others like to do. |
| | 45. The student shows a willingness to compromise to resolve conflicts. |
| | 46. The student tries to help others find solutions to problems they face. |
| | 47. The student shares responsibility equally with the members of groups s/he belongs to. |

[a]The behaviors have been organized into three broad categories, which are a modification of Gresham's (1982) six categories.
SOURCE:   Center and Wascom, in press.

specific behaviors and therefore identified a larger number of behaviors. The more specific behaviors identified in the Center and Wascom study could be grouped using the broader characteristics identified in the other studies as categories. Table 5–2 is a classification of these behaviors using Gresham's (1982) characteristics. Gresham's six characteristics are collapsed into three categories by combining cooperation and sharing into one category and by combining greeting, asking for and giving information, and conversation into another category.

### Social Skills Training Programs

There are several social skills training programs available for use by teachers. The skills included in these programs are usually research based. The skills included in the programs, however, do vary. In addition, the number of skills included vary from one program to another. Jackson, Jackson, and Monroe (1983) include 17 skills in their Core Social Skills program. This program includes such skills as like giving and receiving positive feedback, joining a conversation, and saying "no" to stay out of trouble.

The ACCEPTS program (Walker et al., 1983) includes 28 social skills divided into five categories. The five categories are as follows:

1. Classroom skills

2. Basic interaction skills

3. Getting along skills

4. Making friends skills

5. Coping skills

Stephens (1978) developed a program for classroom social skills, with 136 social skills. These skills are divided into four broad categories with 30 sub-categories. The four broad categories are as follows:

1. Environmental behaviors

2. Interpersonal behaviors

3. Self-related behaviors

4. Task-related behaviors

McGinnis and Goldstein (1984) and Goldstein, Sprafkin, Gershaw, and Klein (1980) developed programs for teaching prosocial behaviors to children and adolescents. These are called *skillstreaming programs*. The child program includes 60 skills divided into five categories:

1. Classroom survival skills

2. Making friends skills

3. Dealing with feelings skills

4. Alternatives to aggression skills

5. Dealing with stress skills

The adolescent skillstreaming program includes 50 prosocial skills divided into six categories:

1. Beginning social skills

2. Advanced social skills

3. Dealing with feelings skills

4. Alternatives to aggression skills

5. Dealing with stress skills

6. Planning skills

Although there is a good deal of overlap between these two programs, they aren't identical. The 50 social skills in the adolescent skillstreaming program are listed in Table 5–3. Each skill is followed by a clarifying question.

The programs described are representative of those available. The actual skills covered by each program vary in both number and focus. There is, however, a good bit of agreement between the programs concerning the kinds of skills that need to be taught. To get a better understanding of the curriculum

**Table 5–3**   A list of the 50 prosocial skills contained in the adolescent skillstreaming program[a]

1. *Listening:*   Does the student pay attention to someone who is talking and make an effort to understand what is being said?
2. *Starting a Conversation:*   Does the student talk to others about light topics and then lead into more serious topics?
3. *Having a Conversation:*   Does the student talk to others about things of interest to both of them?
4. *Asking a Question:*   Does the student decide what information is needed and ask the right person for that information?
5. *Saying Thank You:*   Does the student let others know that he or she is grateful for favors, and so on?
6. *Introducing Yourself:*   Does the student become acquainted with new people on his or her own initiative?
7. *Introducing Other People:*   Does the student help others become acquainted with one another?
8. *Giving a Compliment:*   Does the student tell others that he or she likes something about them or their activities?
9. *Asking for Help:*   Does the student request assistance when he or she is having difficulty?
10. *Joining In:*   Does the student decide on the best way to become part of an ongoing activity or group?
11. *Giving Instructions:*   Does the student clearly explain to others how they are to do a specific task?
12. *Following Instructions:*   Does the student pay attention to instructions, give his or her reactions, and carry the instructions out adequately?
13. *Apologizing:*   Does the student tell others that he or she is sorry after doing something wrong?
14. *Convincing Others:*   Does the student attempt to persuade others that his or her ideas are better and will be more useful than those of the other person?
15. *Knowing Your Feelings:*   Does the student try to recognize which emotions he or she is feeling?
16. *Expressing Your Feelings:*   Does the student let others know which emotions he or she is feeling?
17. *Understanding the Feelings of Others:*   Does the student try to figure out what other people are feeling?
18. *Dealing with Someone Else's Anger:*   Does the student try to understand other people's angry feelings?
19. *Expressing Affection:*   Does the student let others know that he or she cares about them?
20. *Dealing with Fear:*   Does the student figure out why he or she is afraid and do something to reduce the fear?
21. *Rewarding Yourself:*   Does the student say and do nice things for himself or herself when the reward is deserved?
22. *Asking Permission:*   Does the student figure out when permission is needed to do something, and then ask the right person for permission?
23. *Sharing Something:*   Does the student offer to share what he or she has with others who might appreciate it?
24. *Helping Others:*   Does the student give assistance to others who might need or want help?
25. *Negotiating:*   Does the student arrive at a plan that satisfies both the student and others who have taken different positions?

**Table 5–3** Continued

26. *Using Self-Control* Does the student control his or her temper so that things do not get out of hand?
27. *Standing up for Your Rights:* Does the student assert his or her rights by letting people know where he or she stands on an issue?
28. *Responding to Teasing:* Does the student deal with being teased by others in ways that allow the student to remain in control of himself or herself?
29. *Avoiding Trouble When with Others:* Does the student stay out of situations that might get him or her into trouble?
30. *Keeping Out of Fights:* Does the student figure out ways other than fighting to handle difficult situations?
31. *Making a Complaint:* Does the student tell others when they are responsible for creating a particular problem for the student, and then attempt to find a solution for the problem?
32. *Answering a Complaint:* Does the student try to arrive at a fair solution to someone's justified complaint?
33. *Sportsmanship after the Game:* Does the student express an honest compliment to others about how they played a game?
34. *Dealing with Embarrassment:* Does the student do things that help him or her feel less embarrassed or self-conscious?
35. *Dealing with Being Left Out:* Does the student decide whether he or she has been left out of some activity, and then do things to feel better about the situation?
36. *Standing Up for a Friend:* Does the student let other people know when a friend has not been treated fairly?
37. *Responding to Persuasion:* Does the student carefully consider the position of another person, comparing it to his or her own, before deciding what to do?
38. *Responding to Failure:* Does the student figure out the reason for failing in a particular situation, and what he or she can do about it, in order to be more successful in the future?
39. *Dealing with Confusing Messages:* Does the student recognize and deal with the confusion which results when others tell him or her one thing, but say or do things which indicate that they mean something else?
40. *Dealing with an Accusation:* Does the student figure out what he or she has been accused of and why, and then decide on the best way to deal with the person who made the accusation?
41. *Getting Ready for a Difficult Conversation:* Does the student plan on the best way to present his or her point of view prior to a stressful conversation?
42. *Dealing With Group Pressure:* Does the student decide what he or she wants to do when others want the student to do something else?
43. *Deciding on Something to Do:* Does the student deal with feeling bored by starting an interesting activity?
44. *Deciding What Caused a Problem:* Does the student find out whether an event was caused by something that was within his or her control?
45. *Setting a Goal:* Does the student realistically decide on what he or she can accomplish prior to starting on a task?
46. *Deciding on Your Abilities:* Does the student realistically figure out how well he or she might do at a particular task?

**Table 5–3**    Continued

---

47. *Gathering Information:*  Does the student decide what he or she needs to know and how to get the information?
48. *Arranging Problems by Importance:*  Does the student decide realistically which of a number of problems is most important and should be dealt with first?
49. *Making a Decision:*  Does the student consider possibilities and make choices which he or she feels will be best?
50. *Concentrating on a Task:*  Does the student make those preparations which will help him or her get a job done?

---

[a]Each skill is followed by a clarifying question for that skill
SOURCE:   A. P. Goldstein, S. J. Apter, and B. Harootunian, *School Violence*, 1984, pp. 168–170. Reprinted by permission of Prentice Hall, Englewood Cliffs, NJ.

content of these programs, you should inspect the manual that accompanies each program.

## INSTRUCTION

The most efficient instructional strategy for social skills training is social modeling. This is the strategy used in most of the commercially prepared social skills training programs (Kelly, 1982; Goldstein et al., 1980; McGinnis & Goldstein, 1984; Stephens, 1978; Walker et al., 1983). It was pointed out earlier that shaping may need to be used with some severely disturbed students. Shaping is usually required when students are unresponsive to interpersonal stimuli. Shaping will be discussed in Chapter 9.

### Modeling

When we use modeling as our instructional strategy, we have two choices about the type of models to use. The first type is called a *mastery model.* The mastery model is what most of us first think of when we hear the term "modeling." The mastery model is a model who has mastered the skill to be taught and provides a flawless demonstration of it. For example, if the skill is how to initiate a telephone conversation, the mastery model will demonstrate exactly how this skill is performed without any errors or mistakes. The second type is called a *coping model.* The coping model is a model who, like the mastery model, has mastered the skill to be taught and could deliver a flawless demonstration of the skill. However, when we use the coping model, we do not want the model to provide an error-free demonstration.

We would only use a coping model for a skill we have experience in teaching. This would also be a skill that students find difficult to acquire from a mastery model. From our teaching experience with this skill, we would have identified particular components of the skill students have problems with. In other words, we would have observed that certain common mistakes occur when students tried to imitate the mastery model. These would be points we often have to go back over and provide additional instruction on. The purpose of the coping model is to incorporate this additional instruction into the initial modeling performance.

When setting up a demonstration using a coping model, we would teach the model where the difficult components are located in the skill sequence. The coping model is taught to make deliberate mistakes at those points where students frequently err. The coping model is also taught to stop after those mistakes and correct the error. The model would first point out what the error was, why it was made, provide instruction on how to avoid the error, and demonstrate the coping strategy used to avoid the mistake. The coping model has several advantages. First, it alerts the student to difficult components and focuses their attention on these difficult points. Second, it reduces errors by providing instruction on how to deal with the difficult components. Finally, it saves time, in the long run, because it reduces the amount of time spent reteaching a skill.

Using the skill mentioned above, initiating a telephone conversation, let's take a look at how this approach might be used. Suppose that you have noticed students frequently failing to identify themselves initially when imitating the demonstration of the skill. Following is a partial illustration of what was modeled, using a mastery model, the flawed imitation, and how the coping model's demonstration might go.

*Mastery Model*

1. Dials phone number and waits for an answer.

2. Call is answered with "Hello."

3. Model says, "Hello, this is Andy Anxious. May I speak to Denise?"

*Student Imitation*

1. Dials phone number and waits for an answer.

2. Call is answered with "Hello."

3. Student says, "May I speak to Denise?"

*Coping Model*

1. Dials phone number and waits for an answer.

2. Call is answered with "Hello."

3. Model says, "May I speak to Denise?

4. Model says, "No! That isn't correct. I goofed. I have to remember the person on

the line can't see me, so they don't know who is speaking. Many people find it irritating to talk with an unidentified person on the phone. They may also have doubts about what information they should give out to an unidentified caller. I should have identified myself first, before asking to speak to Denise!"

    5. Model says, "Hello, this is Andy Anxious. May I speak to Denise?"

    Remember, you would only want to use the coping model for teaching skills you have good reason to believe will give students problems. To use this approach when it isn't necessary will waste valuable instruction time.

    Another decision you may have to make about the use of modeling is whether to use live or symbolic modeling. A *live model* is a real model performing the demonstration for the students in the classroom. A *symbolic model* is some type of representational media. This will usually be either a filmed model or a videotaped model. Both types of presentation can be effective demonstrations. The live model has the major advantage of giving you control over the demonstration, which gives you instructional flexibility. This instructional flexibility is particularly important when you need to use a coping model or are working with a very diverse group of students. The major disadvantage is the problem of locating appropriate models who can demonstrate the skills you need to teach. The symbolic model's major advantage is convenience. The major disadvantage is that you are limited to the model characteristics, modeling style, and skills available in the film or videotape.

    A final consideration when using modeling is the characteristics of the model. You may recall, one factor contributing to the effectiveness of modeling is how closely the observer identifies with the model. Identification with the model will affect attention to and recall of what is modeled. Identification with the model will be affected by the similarity of the model's characteristics with those of the observer. Such characteristics as the age, sex, social status, and perhaps race of the model will influence the observer's identification with the model. Evidence also suggests that modeling effects will be enhanced if the observer and the model have had cooperative experiences with one another in the past. Modeling effects may also be enhanced if the model has previously imitated the observer. When selecting a model, whether for live or symbolic presentations, these factors should be taken into consideration. For example, you would not want to select a filmed model that is very different from your students or from very many of them.

### Teaching Strategy

    Although you may find some variation among different explanations of the modeling strategy, the following is representative. Virtually all explanations will include most of the steps below. A few will add or delete a step for various reasons. You should find the sequence below satisfactory. In practice you may want to experiment some with the strategy and possibly modify it according to your needs or situation.

***1. Setting the Stage.***    Prior to instruction, it is a good practice to introduce the skill to be taught. This introduction can be done through discussion, stories, or films. The purpose, regardless of the method used, is to communicate to the students what the nature of the skill is, why it is the preferred way of acting, and how it can be useful to the students in their everyday lives. This last point is particularly important because it will help motivate the students to learn the skill. All of us are more motivated to learn when we can see the personal relevance of what is to be taught.

For example, let's look at an assertiveness skill, saying "No!" to an invitation to engage in inappropriate behavior. You might introduce this skill by using a story or film illustrating the difficulties a student got into when invited by friends to do something inappropriate, e.g., skip school with them. You would point out how these difficulties could have been avoided if the student had said "No!" You would also make it clear that this is the preferred way of acting because it puts the student in control of the situation, rather than others. Finally, you would discuss with the students how the skill might be personally relevant to their everyday lives. One way of doing this is to ask students to provide examples of similar situations they have recently experienced. These should be things they have been asked to do which they knew were wrong or they did not care to do but went along with anyway. How these situations might have worked out better if the student involved had been more assertive and said "No!" should be discussed.

***2. Specifying the Skill Components.***    Before exposing the students to the modeling demonstration of the skill, you should specify the specific components in the skill. This will work like an advance organizer for observing the demonstration and attending to the components included. Being able to specify the components in the skill to be taught is critical. Not only can knowing these in advance be helpful to the observer, but the model must be aware of them also. If you are developing your own curriculum, you will have to work out the specific components for each skill. This can be accomplished using the task analysis procedures discussed in Chapter 2. Even if you are using a commercially prepared curriculum, you may find it necessary, at times, to work out the specific components for yourself. This may occur if the program you are using has not included this information or if you have a student that needs the skill broken down into smaller pieces than those provided. As an example, let's continue with the assertiveness skill used above. What are the specific components you might want to include in the skill of saying "No!" to something a student shouldn't or might not want to do? The following is one possible sequence.

a. Look directly at the person and make eye contact.

b. In a calm, normal voice say, "No! I don't want to do that."

c. Suggest an appropriate alternative.

d. If the alternative is declined and the original suggestion is repeated,

e. In a calm, normal voice say, "No! I don't want to do that."

f. If the No statement is still not accepted,

g. In a calm, normal voice say, "I'm sorry. I've got to go now. I'll see you later."

h. Walk away.

**3. Modeling the Skill.** You are now ready to demonstrate the skill for the students. You should already have selected your model and modeling type. The model should have previously been through the modeling strategy with you so that everything is clear. You will also need to have a role-playing situation to provide the context for the demonstration. You should have more than one role-playing situation ready so that the demonstration can be repeated if necessary. You will also need some role-playing situations to use with students to rehearse the modeled skill. The situations selected should be realistic for the students who will be observing the demonstration. Be sure you provide social reinforcement to the model at the end of the demonstration sequence.

Let's continue with our example and illustrate the modeling phase of the teaching strategy.

The role-playing situation will be a conversation between Chuck and his friend Lisa in the hallway between first and second periods at school. Lisa is standing at her locker and Chuck walks up to her.

CHUCK: "Hi, Lisa. How goes it?"

LISA: "Great! How about you?"

CHUCK: "Not so good. I'm really sweating that sixth-period math test."

LISA: "Oh, I don't think it will be very hard."

CHUCK: "Well maybe not for you. You're good at that stuff. Listen. How about helping a friend out. I could sit beside you during the test and you could kind of help me out with a few hints. O.K.?"

Lisa looks directly at Chuck and makes eye contact and then calmly and in a normal tone of voice speaks.

LISA: "No! I won't do that, Chuck. I'll tell you what, why don't you meet me at lunch and we'll go over the problems you're having trouble with."

CHUCK: "I don't have time for that, Lisa. I've got to meet Mel at lunch time to talk about this movie I saw last night. Come on. It won't hurt you to give me a few hints during the test."

Lisa looks directly at Chuck and makes eye contact and then calmly and in a normal tone of voice speaks.

> LISA:   "No! I won't do that, Chuck."
>
> CHUCK:   "Come on, Lisa. Give me a break. All I want is a few hints. That's not much to ask."

Lisa looks directly at Chuck and makes eye contact and then calmly and in a normal tone of voice speaks.

> LISA:   "I'm sorry, Chuck. I've got to go now. It's almost time for the bell. I'll see you later."

Lisa turns and walks away from Chuck.

> TEACHER:   "Good! That was very well done, Lisa. You handled that just right. Thank you."

**4. _Cognitive Rehearsal._**   In this phase, you will select a student to practice the modeled skill. Before the student imitates the modeled skill, you should have the student verbally describe for you the specific components in the skill. This description should closely follow the components provided just before the modeling demonstration. If the student makes errors in the verbal description, go back over the components with the student, referring to the demonstration for illustrative purposes. Have the student continue describing the skill components until they can be given in their entirety without any errors or prompting from you. Once this phase is completed successfully, the student is ready to imitate what has been observed.

**5. _Behavioral Rehearsal._**   In this phase, the student is given a role-playing situation in which to practice the skill. You may, if you wish, use the same role-playing situation used for the modeling phase for the first behavioral rehearsal. The student should, however, get practice with different situations before the behavioral rehearsal phase is over. During this phase, you should give the student feedback on his or her performance. If you have criticisms of the performance, present them using the _sandwich technique_. First, present one instance of positive feedback; i.e., comment on something that was done properly. Second, present one of your critical observations. This should be accompanied by an explanation of how to correct the problem. Third, present another instance of positive feedback. The presentation of the positive feedback should clearly specify what was done correctly and why what was done was correct. This positive feedback should be worded so that it includes social reinforcement. For some students social reinforcement may not be sufficiently motivating. In those cases, you should plan for an alternative form of reinforcement. See the discussion on reinforcement in Chapters 2 and 4 for additional information on reinforcement strategies.

The following example will illustrate the use of the sandwich technique described above.

POSITIVE FEEDBACK:    "You did an excellent job in the first step, Marie. You looked right at Shawn, had good eye contact, and spoke very calmly. Good work!"

CRITICAL FEEDBACK:    "Marie, you had a bit of a problem with the No statement. You should not have followed the No statement with an excuse for why you wouldn't do what Shawn asked. You don't need to make excuses or explain yourself. When you do that you are opening up the possibility for an argument or debate about your reasons. That you don't want to do it is sufficient. Remember how Lisa phrased her statement to Chuck? She kept her statement simple and directly to the point and did not try to explain herself to Chuck.

POSITIVE FEEDBACK:    "I liked your alternative suggestion. It was very appropriate and a good alternative to what Shawn asked you to do. Marie, that was well done!"

If the student has made errors, you should give additional practice opportunities, so your feedback can be used to correct mistakes. If the mistakes were serious enough, repeat the modeling phase before giving additional practice. Even if the student performs correctly the first time, additional practice is needed to firmly establish the skill. Don't forget to use different role-playing situations in the practice. This will keep the practice interesting and aid generalization of the skill. You don't want the skill to be too situation specific, or it will be too limited in its applications for the student.

Another possibility for providing feedback is videotaping equipment. If this equipment is available, it can be a useful aid. You can tape student practice of the skill and then replay the sequence for the student. During this replay, you can enhance your feedback by stopping at various places, making your point, and then backing up and replaying the part related to your feedback. If the modeling sequence has been taped, you can also use it to go back over points with the student during feedback.

**6. *Evaluation of Performance.*** After the student has been instructed and has had practice and feedback on performance, you are ready to evaluate the student. You should use the components making up the skill as a basis for the evaluation. One approach is to use the specific components of the skill to develop a checklist or rating scale (See Box 5-4). To evaluate the student use a new role-playing situation and observe the student's performance. As you observe the performance, complete the checklist or rating scale. If the student meets the criterion that you have set for mastery of the skill, you are ready to move on to a new skill. If the student does not meet the criterion, you should provide additional instruction and practice until the evaluation criterion has been met.

**7. *Generalization.*** This is the last phase in the instructional strategy. Often, it is also the most difficult to arrange. It should not be omitted,

**Box 5-4**   A checklist and a rating scale based on the specific components in the assertiveness skill of saying "No!"

---

**Checklist**

No     Yes

_____  _____   1. Looks directly at the person and makes eye contact.

_____  _____   2. In a calm, normal voice says, "No! I don't want to do that."

_____  _____   3. Suggests an appropriate alternative.

_____  _____   4. Repeats "No!," if necessary.

_____  _____   5. If necessary, says, "I'm sorry, I've got to go now."

_____  _____   6. Walks away.

**Rating Scale**

1. Looks directly at the person and makes eye contact.

| Not done or poorly done | Acceptable | Well done |
|---|---|---|
| 1 | 2 | 3 |

2. In a calm, normal voice says, "No! I don't want to do that."

| Not done or poorly done | Acceptable | Well done |
|---|---|---|
| 1 | 2 | 3 |

3. Suggests an appropriate alternative.

| Not done or poorly done | Acceptable | Well done |
|---|---|---|
| 1 | 2 | 3 |

4. Repeats "No!," if necessary.

| Not done or poorly done | Acceptable | Well done |
|---|---|---|
| 1 | 2 | 3 |

5. If necessary, says, "I'm sorry, I've got to go now."

| Not done or poorly done | Acceptable | Well done |
|---|---|---|
| 1 | 2 | 3 |

6. Walks away.

| Not done or poorly done | Acceptable | Well done |
|---|---|---|
| 1 | 2 | 3 |

---

however, since it is a critical phase. In this phase, you want the student to gain experience in using the skill in real situations that arise in the student's life. You should negotiate a contract with the student in which it is agreed that the skill will be tried out in a real situation. The contract should provide for a reward to the student if the skill is used successfully used (see Box 5-5).

**Box 5-5**    An example of a teacher-made contract on applying a newly learned social skill

---

**CONTRACT**

When _____ Lisa Lightfoot _____ completes

three uses of social assertiveness skill of saying,

"No! I don't want to do that," when actually asked

to do something inappropriate and

_____

by  May 30                                                                                            ,

he/she will be able to        take home for the

weekend, 3 records of her choice                                                              .

_____    _____        _____        _____
Date        Student                                        Witness                    Teacher

---

        The most difficult aspect of the contract is monitoring it. Sometimes the skill will be one you, another teacher, a parent, or some other adult will have an opportunity to observe. If this is the case, monitoring should not be a great problem. If another person is going to be involved, you will need to explain what should be looked for and how to judge the adequacy of the performance. Your checklist or rating scale can be useful for this task. If you have been able to videotape the modeling phase or if you have used a commercial film or tape, this can be useful also. If the skill is one that a responsible adult will not have an opportunity to observe, you will have to rely on self-report from the student. Often you can get a fairly good idea about whether or not the skill was used by requiring a detailed verbal report of the situation the skill was used in and how it was used. This is the least desirable way to monitor, but often it is your only choice.

## RESOURCES

There are many excellent resources available to guide the teacher who wants to do social skills training with students. In recent years there has been a virtual explosion in the publication of materials on this topic. Several resources you should find useful include books by Cartledge and Milburn (1980), Dowrick and

Gilligan (1985), and Michelson, Sugai, Wood, and Kazdin, (1983). Many of the books and papers cited previously should also be useful.

We have already discussed several commercially available programs that include social skills curricula, assessment procedures, and teaching strategies. Among these you should find one or more that will be useful in starting a program. The Getting Along with Others: Teaching Social Effectiveness to Children program (Jackson, Jackson, & Monroe, 1983) covers 17 social skills. This program makes less use of modeling than most of the other programs. The program includes planning guides, activities, and teaching strategies. In addition, there is a complete training package on the use of the program available on videotape. Skillstreaming the Elementary School Child (McGinnis & Goldstein, 1984) and Skillstreaming the Adolescent (Goldstein et al., 1980) are social skills training manuals for children and adolescents, respectively. These manuals cover 60 social skills for children and 50 social skills for adolescents. The manuals also provide rating scales, record-keeping forms, and lesson plans. The instructional approach used in these programs is social modeling. The authors call their instructional procedure *structured learning*. There is a set of audiotapes available for the adolescent program. These tapes provide instruction on the implementation of the program with several examples of lessons being conducted using the structured learning approach.

Another excellent program is the Walker Social Skills Curriculum: The ACCEPTS Program (Walker et al., 1983), which covers 28 social skills. The program includes screening and assessment instruments, instructional procedures, and teaching scripts. The program is based on a social modeling approach. In addition to the manual, video training tapes for teachers are available, as well as taped models for use in teaching the social skills covered in the curriculum. Finally, there is Social Skills in the Classroom (Stephens, 1978). This program covers a total of 136 social skills for children and youth. The manual includes record-keeping forms, assessment procedures, and lesson plans. The instructional approach is called *directive teaching* and relies to a large extent on social modeling.

The list of resources and materials above is by no means exhaustive. There are many good programs available besides the ones discussed above. You can create your own curriculum, designed to meet your specific needs, or you can select a program from one of those commercially available. If you do the latter, be sure that you examine the program carefully to ensure that it meets your needs and your situation.

## REFERENCES

ARGLE, M. (1980). Interaction skills and social competence. In P. Feldman & J. Orford (Eds.), *Psychological problems: The social context.* New York: Wiley.

BANDURA, A. (1971). *Social learning theory.* Morristown, NJ: General Learning Press.

BANDURA, A. (1977). *Social learning theory.* Englewood Cliffs, NJ: Prentice-Hall.

BANDURA, A., & WALTERS, R. (1963). *Social learning and personality development.* New York: Holt, Rinehart and Winston.

BELLACK, A., HERSEN, M., & LAMPARSKI, D. (1979).

Role play tests for assessing social skills: Are they valid? Are they useful? *Journal of Consulting and Clinical Psychology, 47,* 335–342.

BORNSTEIN, M., BELLACK, A., & HERSEN, M. (1977). Social skills training for unassertive children: A multiple baseline analysis. *Journal of Applied Behavior Analysis, 10,* 183–195.

BROWN, L., & HAMMILL, D. (1983). *Behavior rating profile: An ecological approach to behavioral assessment.* Austin, TX: PRO-ED.

CARTLEDGE, G., & MILBURN, J. (1978). The case for teaching social skills in the classroom: A review. *Review of Educational Research, 1,* 133–156.

CARTLEDGE, G., & MILBURN, J. (Eds.). (1980). *Teaching social skills to children: Innovative approaches.* Elmsford, NY: Pergamon Press.

CAUTELA, J. R., CAUTELA, J., & ESONIS, S. (1983). *Forms for behavior analysis with children.* Champaign, IL: Research Press.

CENTER, D., & WASCOM, A. (1987). Teacher perceptions of social behavior in behavior disordered and socially normal children and youth. *Behavioral Disorders, 12*(3), 200–206.

DOLL, E. (1965). *Vineland Social Maturity Scale.* Circle Pines, MN: American Guidance Services.

DOWRICK, P., & GILLIGAN C. (1985). *Social survival for children: A trainers resource.* New York: Brunner/Mazel.

DRABMAN, R., & PATTERSON, J. (1982). Disruptive behavior and the social standing of exceptional children. In P. Strain (Ed.), *Social development of exceptional children.* Rockville, MD: Aspen.

DURLAK, J., & MANNARINO, A. (1977). The social skills development program: Description of a school based preventive mental health program for high risk children. *Journal of Clinical Child Psychology, 6,* 48–52.

EVERS, W., & SCHWARZ, J. (1973). Modifying social withdrawal in preschoolers: The effects of filmed and teacher praise. *Journal of Abnormal Child Psychology, 1,* 248–256.

FEFFER, M. (1959). The cognitive implications of role-taking behavior. *Journal of Personality, 27,* 152–168.

FEFFER, M., & GOUREVITCH, V. (1960). Cognitive aspects of role-taking in children. *Journal of Personality, 28,* 384–396.

FOSTER, S., & RITCHEY, W. (1979). Issues in the assessment of social competence in children. *Journal of Applied Behavior Analysis, 12,* 625–638.

GOLDSTEIN, A., APTER, S., & HAROOTUNIAN, B. (1984). *School Violence.* Englewood Cliffs, NJ: Prentice-Hall.

GOLDSTEIN, A., SPRAFKIN, R., GERSHAW, N., & KLEIN, P. (1980). *Skillstreaming the adolescent.* Champaign, IL: Research Press.

GOTTMAN, J. (1977). The effects of a modeling film on social isolation in preschool children: A methodological investigation. *Journal of Abnormal Child Psychology, 5,* 69–78.

GOTTMAN, J., GONSO, J., & SCHULLER, P. (1976). Teaching social skills to isolated children. *Child Development, 4,* 179–197.

GRESHAM, F. (1981). Social skills training with handicapped children: A review. *Review of Educational Research, 51,* 139–176.

GRESHAM, F. (1982). Misguided mainstreaming: The case for social skills training with handicapped children. *Exceptional Children, 48,* 422–433.

HYMEL, S., & ASHER, S. (1977). Assessment and training of isolated children's social skills. Paper presented at the meeting of the Society for Research in Child Development, New Orleans.

JACKSON, N., JACKSON, D., & MONROE, C. (1983). *Getting along with others: Teaching social effectiveness to children.* Champaign, IL: Research Press.

JOHNSON, D. (1975). Affective perspective taking and cognitive predisposition. *Developmental Psychology, 11,* 869–870.

JOHNSON, S., & BOLSTAD, O. (1973). Methodological issues in naturalistic observation: Some problems and solutions for field research. In L. Hamerlynck, L. Handy, & E. Mash (Eds.), *Behavior change: Methodology, concepts. and practice.* Champaign, IL: Research Press.

JONES, R., REID, J., & PATTERSON, G. (1974). Naturalistic observation in clinical assessment. In P. McReynolds (Ed.), *Advances in psychological assessment* (Vol. 3). San Francisco: Jossey-Bass.

KELLY, J. (1982). *Social skills training: A practical guide for interventions.* New York: Springer.

KENT, R., & FOSTER, S. (1977). Direct observation procedures: Methodological issues in naturalistic settings. In A. Ciminero, K. Calhoun, & H. Adams (Eds.), *Handbook of behavioral assessment.* New York: Wiley.

LEDINGHAM, J., YOUNGER, A., SCHWARTZMAN, A., & BERGERON, G. (1982). Agreement among teacher, peer, and self-ratings of children's aggression, withdrawal, and likeability. *Journal of Abnormal Child Psychology, 10,* 363–372.

LIBET, J., & LEWINSOHN, P. (1973). Concept of social skill with special reference to the behavior of depressed persons. *Journal of Consulting Psychology, 40,* 304–312.

LOWE, M., & CAUTELA, J. (1978). A self-report measure of social skill. *Behavior Therapy, 9,* 535–544.

McARTHUR, D., & ROBERTS, G. (1982). *Roberts apperception test for children.* Los Angeles: Western Psychological Services.

McGINNIS, E., & GOLDSTEIN, A. (1984). *Skillstreaming the elementary school child.* Champaign, IL:

Research Press.

MEICHENBAUM, D. (1976). A cognitive-behavior modification approach to assessment. In M. Hersen & A. Bellack (Eds.), *Behavioral assessment: A practical handbook*. Elmsford, NY: Pergamon Press.

MICHELSON, L., SUGAI, D., WOOD, R., & KAZDIN, A. (1983). *Social skills assessment and training with children: An empirically based handbook*. New York: Plenum Press.

MICHELSON, L., & WOOD, R. (1980). Behavioral assessment and training of children's social skills. *Progress in Behavior Modification, 9*, 241–291.

MILLER, N., & DOLLARD, J. (1941). *Social learning and imitation*. New Haven, CT: Yale University Press.

MISCHEL, W. (1973). Cognition in self-imposed delay of gratification. In L. Berkowitz (Ed.), *Advances in social psychology* (Vol. 1). New York: Academic Press.

O'CONNOR, R. (1969). Modification of social withdrawal through symbolic modeling. *Journal of Applies Behavior Analysis, 2*, 15–22.

O'CONNOR, R. (1972). Relative efficacy of modeling, shaping, and the combined procedures for modification of social withdrawal. *Journal of Abnormal Psychology, 79*, 327–334.

O'LEARY, K., & TURKEWITZ, H. (1978). Methodological errors in marital and child treatment. *Journal of Consulting and Clinical Psychology, 46*, 747–758.

PHILLIPS, E. (1978). *The social skills basis of psychopathology*. New York: Grune & Stratton.

REARDON, R., HERSEN, M., BELLACK, A., & FOLEY, J. (1979). Measuring social skill in grade school boys. *Journal of Behavioral Assessment, 1*, 87–105.

ROTTER, J. (1954). *Social learning and clinical psychology*. Englewood Cliffs, N.J.: Prentice-Hall.

RUTTER, M., & GRAHAM, P. (1969). The reliability and validity of the psychiatric assessment of the child: I. Interview with the child. *British Journal of Psychiatry, 114*, 563–579.

SIEGEL, L., DRAGOVITCH, S., & MARHOLIN D., II. (1976). The effects of biasing information on behavioral observations and rating scales. *Journal of Abnormal Child Psychology, 4*, 221–233.

SPARROW, S., BALLA, D., & CICCHETTI, D. (1984). *Vineland Adaptive Behavior Scales*. Circle Pines, MN: American Guidance Services.

SROUFE, L. (1975). Drug treatment of children with behavior problems. In F. Horowitz (Ed.), *Review of child development research* (Vol. 4). Chicago: University of Chicago Press.

STATTS, A. (1975). *Social behaviorism*. Homewood, IL: Dorsey.

STEPHENS, T. (1978). *Social skills in the classroom*. Columbus, OH: Cedars Press.

SULZBACHER, S. (1973). Psychotropic medication with children: An evaluation of procedural biases in results of reported studies. *Pediatrics, 51*, 513–517.

VAN HASSELT, V., HERSEN, M., WHITEHILL, M., & BELLACK, A. (1979). Social skills assessment and training for children: An evaluative review. *Behavior Research and Therapy, 17*, 413–437.

WAHLER, R., HOUSE, A., & STAMBAUGH, E., II. (1976). *Ecological assessment of child problem behavior*. Elmsford, NY: Pergamon Press.

WALKER, H., McCONNELL, S., HOLMES, D., TODIS, B., WALKER, J., & GOLDEN, N. (1983). *The Walker social skills curriculum: The ACCEPTS program*. Austin, TX: PRO-ED.

# 6

# TEACHING APPROPRIATE SOCIAL BEHAVIOR

Social Reasoning

## INTRODUCTION

### The Cognitive-Developmental Model

Values development is an important component in affective curriculum (Krathwohl, Bloom, & Masia, 1964), and public education should be concerned with the affective development of students. The National Support Systems Project at the University of Minnesota (1980) produced a document concerned with a common body of practice for teacher preparation programs. The paper suggests 10 clusters of abilities that teachers should have. One of these clusters, "teaching basic skills," has three components: literacy skills, life maintenance skills, and personal development skills. The latter component is concerned with affective curriculum. A basic assumption of this component is that everyone must deal with values, moral behavior, and the basic issues of life. All teachers should be prepared to help students develop in these areas. A need for values education in programs for children who have behavior or learning disorders is also recognized (Hammill & Bartel, 1978; Haring & Phillips, 1962; Hobbs, 1967; Kauffman, 1985; Lerner, 1981; Mann, Goodmman, & Wiederholt, 1978; Newcomer, 1980; Redl & Wineman, 1952). The importance of values education for behavior-disordered children is supported by recent research (Selman, 1976a; Selman & Jaquette, 1978; Selman, Jaquette, & Lavin, 1977). This research examined reasoning skills involving social values and interpersonal problems. The research suggests that children deficient in social reasoning are likely to be impulsive, aggressive, or hyperactive.

Traditionally, moral education has taught adult values to children by moralizing and by example. One recent alternative to the traditional approach is values clarification (Raths, Merrill, & Simon, 1966; Simon, Howe, & Kirschenbaum, 1976; Simon & O'Rourke, 1977). The emphasis in this approach is not on transmission of values but on development of valuing, i.e., process rather than content. Valuing as a process, according to Raths et al. (1966), involves prizing, choosing, and acting on beliefs (values). The values clarification approach to moral education attempts to help students explore and apply their existing and emerging values. Perhaps the greatest shortcoming of this approach is its lack of a clear developmental frame of reference. A developmental frame of reference would aid curriculum development, assessing students, selecting instructional strategies, and planning lessons.

The work of Lawrence Kohlberg (1964, 1966, 1969, 1973, 1984) offers educators a developmental framework. Kohlberg's approach is also process oriented, but brings to the process-oriented approach a developmental dimension. The approach used by Kohlberg in studying moral reasoning has been called the *cognitive-developmental approach* (Kohlberg, 1969). The cognitive-developmental approach to the study of reasoning rests upon several assumptions.

1. Development involves changing cognitive structures.

2. Development is not the direct result of maturation or of learning but depends on their interaction.

3. Cognitive structures depend on the organization of experience.

4. Development moves toward balance.

5. Affective development and cognitive development are parallel.

6. There is a basic unity of cognitive organization and social development called *self*.

7. The basic processes underlying changes in cognition are also important for social development.

8. Social development moves toward a balance in the actions between self and others.

The interaction between a child and the environment results in stages or levels of cognitive organization. The movement from one level of organization to another is called a *transformation*. One of the most important influences on transformations is the discrepancy between a child's current cognitive stage and level of reasoning and an experienced event. A low-to-moderate level of discrepancy is probably best for bringing about change. A large discrepancy is too difficult to accommodate.

At the heart of the cognitive-developmental position is the theory of cognitive stages. According to Piaget (Gruber & Voneche, 1977), cognitive stages have the following characteristics:

1. Stages imply different types of thinking at different points in the growth cycle.

2. The different types of thought form an invariable sequence of development. The rate of development can vary, but not the sequence.

3. Each stage represents a cognitive structure with a characteristic organization.

4. Cognitive stages are hierarchical in nature. Each move upward through the hierarchy represents a reintegration of the lower stages.

Kohlberg (1964) defines morality "as a set of cultural rules of social action which have been internalized by the individual." Moral development, then, is the progressive internalization of basic cultural rules. This process has three different aspects: behavioral, emotional, and judgmental. It is the latter aspect that is the focus of Kohlberg's moral reasoning studies. Kohlberg's work is an extension of the work of Jean Piaget on moral reasoning in children and uses Piaget's intensive case study approach.

The initial study by Kohlberg (1964) was of 72 boys between 10 and 16 years of age. Twenty-five aspects of morality were investigated, including "concepts of rights," "basis of respect for social authority," and "motivation for moral action," among others. This study resulted in a developmental sequence of moral reasoning with three levels and two stages per level.

I. The preconventional level

1. Good behavior is what satisfies superior powers.

2. Good behavior is what satisfies one's own needs and occasionally the needs of others.

II. The conventional level

3. Good behavior is what satisfies others and is approved by them.

4. Good behavior is what satisfies the expectations of social authorities.

III. The postconventional level

5. Good behavior is what satisfies standards examined and agreed upon by society.

6. Good behavior is what satisfies one's conscience and self-chosen universal, comprehensive, and logically consistent ethical principles.

Recently, Kohlberg (1984) has dropped the sixth stage in the developmental sequence, leaving a five-stage model. Each stage can involve up to 25 different aspects of morality. For example, the five stages could be described for the aspect called "motivation for rule obedience" as follows:

1. Conform to avoid punishment

2. Conform to obtain rewards and have favors returned

3. Conform to avoid disapproval or dislike by others

4. Conform to avoid censure by authorities and feelings of guilt

5. Conform to maintain the respect of the "impartial spectator," judging one in terms of community welfare

The five-stage developmental hierarchy has been examined in relation to culture, social class, age, and sex. The sequence, without variation, was found in all groups studied. Differences were found for rate of development but not for the sequence of development. Social influences appear to affect the developmental rate but not the nature of moral reasoning.

Kohlberg (1966) asserts that education should be involved in the moral education of children. Furthermore, the development of moral maturity appears to have a critical period in the life cycle. Kohlberg's studies suggest if a child does not reach stage 3 or 4 by age 13, there is little chance that the child will achieve morally mature thinking. The critical point appears to be 10 to 13 years of age, when most children make the shift from preconventional to conventional thinking. If this shift is not made by age 13, the child often becomes fixated at a preconventional level of moral thinking.

Moral development is related to the development of social perception and the ability to organize and integrate social experience in a consistent manner. To accomplish this each child needs to have a variety of social experiences and to become familiar with many social roles and perspectives. Education can make contributions toward meeting all of these needs.

Turiel (1966, 1969, 1973) experimentally validated two important principles for moral education. First, students can only assimilate moral reasoning that is developmentally appropriate. Exposure to reasoning below the current stage of reasoning serves no purpose. Reasoning more than one stage above the current stage will not be understood. Second, developmental progress is not ensured by mere exposure to higher levels of reasoning. Development is promoted by cognitive conflict. Cognitive conflict is produced by attempts to resolve meaningful moral dilemmas.

A former student of Kohlberg's (Selman, 1976a, 1980; Selman & Jaquette, 1978; Selman et al., 1977) has extended Kohlberg's work to the study of the reasoning process applied to interpersonal relations. Selman calls this reasoning process *social reasoning*. Selman (1980) identified four areas of social reasoning. These four areas include conceptions of individuals, conceptions of friendships, conceptions of peer groups, and conceptions of parent-child relations. Each of these four interpersonal areas has five developmental stages.

In the conceptions of individuals, the first stage is "individuals as physical entities." In this stage, the child bases conceptions of self and others on observable behavior and physical characteristics. The second stage is "individuals as intentional subjects." In this stage, the child recognizes the importance of psychological states in understanding behavior but has a rather simple view of their role. The child tends to take at face value such things as a statement by someone that s/he is angry. The child also has trouble recognizing that conflicting thoughts or feelings about the same person or event can occur together, for example, that you can feel both happy and sad about a given event. The third stage is "individuals as introspective selves." In this stage, the child has learned that you can have a dual sense of self. The child also recognizes that you can convey to others an impression that does not have to coincide with your own self concept. The child recognizes that multiple and conflicting psychological states may occur together. For example, you might be happy to see your father, but sad because seeing him reminds you that your father and mother are divorced. The fourth stage is "individuals as stable personalities." In this stage, the child develops a sense of self-as-observer which organizes thoughts and feelings into a unified whole (personality). Still missing is the recognition that all thoughts and feelings do not have to be in conscious awareness. The fifth and final stage is "individuals as complex self-systems." In this stage, the child recognizes that some thoughts and feelings may not be accessible through self-reflection but that they can still influence behavior.

In the conceptions of friendship, the first stage is called "friendship as momentary physical interaction." In this stage, the child defines friendship by brief and frequent interactions with others who are judged similar to self. For example, she is a girl and likes to play with dolls, and I am a girl and like to play with dolls. The second stage is "friendship as one-way assistance." In this stage, the child recognizes the existence of psychological states and their influence on behavior. Friends are those who recognize what one likes or wants and behaves accordingly. To make a friend you reverse this process. The third stage is "friendship as fair-weather cooperation." In this stage, the child recognizes that perspective taking is a mutual process. Perspective taking is limited to specific situations and is mostly governed by self-interest rather than mutual interests. The fourth stage is "friendship as intimate and mutual sharing." In this stage, the child begins to see friendship as a relationship that has duration over time. Friendship is also seen to depend on mutual interests and attributes. The fifth and final stage is "friendships as autonomous interdependence." In this stage, the child recognizes that people have complex and possibly conflicting needs which may be met through a variety of relationships. Friendships are seen as flexible and subject to growth and change.

In the conceptions of peer groups, the first stage is "the peer group as physical connections." In this stage, the child is unaware of psychological relationships that exist within the peer group. The view of the peer group is limited to the observable activities and aspects of the group. The second stage is "the peer group as unilateral relations." In this stage, the child views the peer group as a cooperative process limited to overt activities. Cooperation is seen as one-sided and justified by some concrete outcome. Prosocial behavior is motivated by self-interest. Group leadership is based on obedience to authority. The third stage is "the peer group as bilateral partnerships." In this stage, the child views the peer group as a group of interlocked pairs. Each member of the group has a mutual relationship with every other member of the group. The group is believed to depend on equality among the members. The group depends on a commonality of interest related to some overt activity, e.g., playing football. The fourth stage is "the peer group as a homogeneous community." In this stage, the child achieves the ability to view the peer group as a unit based on a set of shared interests and values. This results in a common set of expectations for members of the group and a requirement for conformity. The fifth and final stage is "the peer group as a pluralistic organization." In this stage, the child views the peer group as a community of related but independent individuals. The group process becomes more democratic, and different points of view are both tolerated and encouraged. The group's diversity is organized by the members' common interests and goals. The group is managed by formal and informal agreements among the members.

In the conceptions of parent-child relations, the first stage is "the parent-child relation as boss-servant." In this stage, the child believes that his or her role is to satisfy the desires of parents. The child believes that the parents' role is to meet his or her immediate needs. Conflicts between these roles, in the child's view, are not resolved but forgotten. The second stage is "the parent-child relation as caretaker-helper." In this stage, the child begins to identify with parental attitudes, opinions, and values. The child views the parents' reasons for having children as practical in nature. For example, parents have children to have someone to do chores, to play with, and for companionship. Parents show love for the child by caretaking. Children show love for parents by obedience. Obedience is motivated by the child's view of the parents as "wise" and to avoid punishment. The third stage is "the parent-child relation as guidance counselor-need satisfier." In this stage, the child recognizes the parents' role in providing psychological and emotional support and in giving advice and guidance. The child acquires some ability to appreciate the demands and sacrifices of parenthood. The relationship between child and parents is no longer defined by mutual actions, but by mutual feelings. The fourth stage is "the parent-child relation as tolerance-respect." In this stage, the child develops the ability to take a third-person perspective and has a more mature understanding of the relationship. The child recognizes that the relationship has important implications for his or her development as an individual. It is understood that the relationship does not require complete agreement between child and parents but rather, sensitivity to and respect for one another's positions. The fifth and final stage in this area has not been sufficiently examined to provide a complete description. Tentatively, this stage appears to involve a view of the parent-child relationship as involving a system in which both independence and dependence are present and vary over time.

The various stage sequences from both Kohlberg and Selman are summarized in Table 6–1. There is no intention to equate the stages across areas.

**Table 6-1**  A summary of the cognitive-developmental domains of reasoning from Kohlberg and Selman[a]

| STAGE | KOHLBERG MORAL JUDGMENT | SELMAN INDIVIDUALS | SELMAN FRIENDSHIP | SELMAN PEERS | SELMAN PARENTS | DEVELOPMENTAL PERIOD |
|---|---|---|---|---|---|---|
| First | Punishment-obedience orientation | Individuals as physical entities | Friendship as momentary physical interaction | Peer group as physical connections | Parent-child relation as boss-servant | Early childhood |
| Second | Instrumental-exchange orientation | Individuals as intentional subjects | Friendship as one-way assistance | Peer group as unilateral relation | Parent-child relation as care-taker-helper | Early middle childhood |
| Third | Good-boy, nice-girl orientation | Individuals as introspective selves | Friendship as fair-weather cooperation | Peer group as bilateral partnership | Parent-child relation as counselor-need satisfier | Late middle Childhood |
| Fourth | Authority-rules orientation | Individuals as stable personalities | Friendship as intimate and mutual sharing | Peer group as homogeneous community | Parent-child relation as tolerance-respect | Early adolescence |
| Fifth | Social-contract orientation | Individuals as complex self-systems | Friendship as autonomous interdependence | Peer group as a pluralistic organization | Parent-child relation as ongoing changing system | Late adolescence |
| | | | | | | Adult |

[a]The parallel stages for each sequence should be viewed as only an approximate equivalence, and the associated developmental period as only a rough guideline.

There probably is, however, some rough equivalence between them. The table also provides some developmental guidelines, but again, these are only suggestive. It should be remembered, too, that development does not progress evenly across all of the developmental sequences.

Table 6–2 is an adaptation of a table from Selman (1980) suggesting a possible relationship between the development of social reasoning and ego development. The sequence for ego development is based on Loevinger (1976). This table provides some possible parallels between social reasoning, impulse control and character development, interpersonal style, and conscious preoccupations. The table is not intended to establish equivalence and is only suggestive.

### Research Support

Looking at the cognitive-developmental model of reasoning developed by Kohlberg and extended by Selman, three questions arise. First, is there any research support for the model? Second, is there any relationship between moral/social reasoning and behavior? Third, is it possible to aid the development of moral/social reasoning by educational techniques?

In reply to the first question, there is Kohlberg's report on his longitudinal study. The results of this study (Kohlberg, 1969) support the stages and developmental sequence identified by Kohlberg in his original cross-sectional study (Kohlberg, 1964). In addition to studies done in the United States, the model has been investigated cross-culturally in Taiwan, Mexico, Turkey, and Israel (Kohlberg, 1969; Reimer, 1977). Other studies (Kuhn, Langer, Kohlberg, & Haan, 1977; Blatt & Kohlberg, 1975) investigating age trends and social class also support the model. Although Kohlberg has his critics (Kurtines & Greif, 1974), the available data generally support his theoretical model (Brown & Hernstein, 1975). It should also be noted that Gilligan (1982) questions the validity of the model when applied to women. Gilligan points out that Kohlberg's initial study, on which the model is based, included only male subjects and in her opinion has a male bias.

In response to the second question, there are a number of studies that support a relationship between reasoning and behavior. Kohlberg and Candee (1974) reviewed three studies that examined the relationship between reasoning and behavior and concluded that a relationship exists. Scharf (1978), Candee (1975), and Krebs and Kohlberg (1973) all report evidence supporting a relationship between reasoning and behavior.

Other studies also suggest a link between reasoning and behavior. These include a study by Jurkovic and Prentice (1977) which found psychopaths deficit in moral reasoning in comparison to neurotics, subcultural delinquents, and normal subjects. A study by Freundlich and Kohlberg (in Scharf, 1978) found significant deficits in moral reasoning in delinquents compared to normal adolescents. Similar results were found by Fodor (1972) and Hudgins and Prentice (1973) in their studies of delinquents. All of these studies found a pattern of preconventional reasoning associated with antisocial behavior. Rothman

**Table 6–2** The possible relationship between stages of social reasoning and ego development relative to three different ego characteristics

| STAGE OF SOCIAL REASONING | IMPULSE CONTROL AND CHARACTER DEVELOPMENT | INTERPERSONAL STYLE | CONSCIOUS PREOCCUPATIONS |
|---|---|---|---|
| 0 | Impulsive, fear of retaliation | Receiving, dependent exploitative | Bodily feelings, especially sexual and aggressive |
| 1/2 | Fear of being caught, externalizing blame, opportunistic | Wary, manipulative, exploitative | Self-protection, trouble, wishes, things, advantage, control |
| 2/3 | Conformity to external rules, shame, guilt for breaking rules | Belonging, superficial niceness | Appearance, social acceptability, banal feelings behavior |
| 3/2 | Differentiation of norms, goals | Aware of self in relation to group, helping | Adjustment, problems, reasons, opportunities (vague) |
| 3 | Self-evaluated standards, self-criticism, guilt for consequences, long-term goals and ideals | Intensive, responsible, mutual, concern for communication | Differentiated feelings, motives for behavior, self-respect, achievements, traits, expression |
| 3/4 | Add: respect for individuality | Add to previous level: dependence as an emotional problem | Add to previous level: development, social problems, differentiation of inner life from outer |
| 4 | Add: coping with conflicting inner needs, toleration | Add to previous level: respect for autonomy, interdependence | Vividly conveyed feelings, integration of physiological and psychological, psychological causation of behavior, role conception, self-fulfillment, self in social context |

Source: Adapted from Selman, 1980 and Loevinger, 1976.

(1980), in a review of the research literature, concluded that there is a relationship, although it is a complex one, between stage of moral reasoning and moral conduct. It appeared that moral reasoning was one of several influences on moral conduct. Since moral reasoning appears to influence behavior, it should be a variable of interest to behavior change agents such as special educators.

In response to the third question, there is an experimental study (Blatt & Kohlberg, 1975) of classroom discussions with junior high and high school students. This study assessed the impact of structured, developmental discussions of moral issues on moral reasoning. There was a significant gain for the experimental groups over the control group. Further, the gains were still evident in a follow-up study a year later. These findings were replicated with other public school students, prisoners, and college students. Hickey (in Scharf, 1978) obtained similar results in a moral education program with delinquents.

Another issue is whether or not teachers can produce similar results in their classrooms. Colby, Kohlberg, Fenton, Speicher-Dubin, and Lieberman (1977) investigated this question. There was a significant improvement in moral reasoning in students given a moral education program by trained teachers in contrast to the students of untrained teachers. Another study (Gardner, 1983), conducted by a classroom teacher trained by Kohlberg, was successful in significantly increasing moral reasoning in emotionally disturbed adolescents. These students were in a special education program in a public school setting. Follow-up studies of the students two years later found that all had either maintained their gains or continued to progress.

One final point needs to be made concerning differences in reasoning evident with different types of material. Jaquette (in Selman, 1980) found that the reasoning level in a naturalistic context with real-life content was below the level of reasoning exhibited with purely hypothetical material. Further, Jaquette found slower development and greater variability in reasoning in disturbed compared to normal children.

## CURRICULUM

The major task in developing curriculum materials is constructing value-based dilemmas. There are two basic types of dilemmas: hypothetical and real dilemmas. Scharf (1978) discusses some qualities common to good dilemmas. A good dilemma should contain conflicting positions that appear reasonable. It should involve life experiences relevant to students. An issue is required in which dispute about facts is not likely. It needs to be accompanied by questions to help bring into focus the values issue. Finally, probe questions targeted at particular stages of reasoning are needed.

Hypothetical dilemmas are believable dilemmas with no basis in fact: in other words, a fictitious but believable story with a values issue. Hypothetical dilemmas are particularly useful for generating discussion because they are not usually threatening to students. Students are often more willing to make public statements, express their attitudes, and generalize principles when dealing with a hypothetical situation. Unlike hypothetical dilemmas, real dilemmas are based on fact. Material for dilemmas can be found in either subject-matter content or daily-life events.

### Sources for Dilemmas

Educational subject matter is a major source of material for values dilemmas in school programs. Taking material from subject matter promotes integration of values education with the regular school curriculum. It will also help stimulate student interest and involvement in course content. Several writers (Hersh, Paolitto, & Reimer, 1979; Scharf, 1978) discuss the use of course content as a source of material for values education. There are at least five curriculum areas from which to draw material. Literature is an excellent source of material. An example from literature would be the dilemma faced by Huckleberry Finn, created by his conflicting loyalties to his friend and runaway slave, Jim, and to Miss Watson. Social studies is also an excellent source of material. Recent history, for instance, provides an example in the issues surrounding Truman's decision to drop the atomic bomb on Hiroshima. Science, too, is an area where conflicts in values often arise. Walter Reed's deliberate decision to infect a group of subjects with yellow fever to conduct an experiment involves important ethical issues. Vocational education also provides opportunities to raise questions related to values. Temptations to steal from an employer or knowledge of illegal or unethical behavior in fellow workers are examples of values issues in vocational education. Finally, school athletic programs can be a source of values education material. An example in this area would be the issues raised by illegal recruiting activities to build a school's or a coach's reputation.

To use subject matter for values education material, you must carefully examine texts and other material for situations involving values conflicts. After potential material is identified, you must select material appropriate for your students considering their interests and level of reasoning. Consideration should also be given to the availability of audiovisual materials related to an issue. The potential of the material for dramatic involvement through class skits or role-playing exercises is also important. Finally, when you use subject matter material you should focus on the development of units or mini-units rather than on one-shot lessons. For example, you might develop a mini-unit on values issues in the decisions made by Eisenhower as a military leader or a unit on values issues raised within some families with divided loyalties during the Civil War.

A third source of values education materials is daily life. Dilemmas in this area can be from current events in the school, community, nation, or world. Perhaps the most useful source of material is school-based events. Many issues in school have potential for use in a values education program, for example, issues related to theft, cheating, sharing, sex, truth, rule violation, drugs, and friendship. School-based issues have considerable potential for working with problem students since many of the difficulties they get into are related to some of the issues suggested above. When you use school-based issues, you should be careful to present the issue in an impersonal way. That is, don't identify it with any individual in your class or school. When you use dilemmas of this type, you should try to relate it to the lives of the students, have a character or characters on whom the issue is focused, and require judgments by the character(s) with clear implications for behavior.

### Focus of Dilemmas

A dilemma of any type can have either of two focuses, i.e., moral or interpersonal. Dilemmas with either focus can vary in the breadth of their implications. Kohlberg (reported in Hersh et al., 1979) has identified 10 universal moral issues. These issues can be useful to the dilemma writer. The issues can serve as a source of ideas or as an organizing scheme. The 10 issues identified by Kohlberg follow.

1. Laws and rules

2. Conscience

3. Personal roles of affection

4. Authority

5. Civil rights

6. Contract, trust, and justice in exchange

7. Punishment

8. The value of life

9. Property

10. Truth

Box 6–1 is an example of a dilemma based on the eighth issue (the value of life). The sample dilemma is real, derived from daily-life events, and has a moral focus, i.e., is the value of life absolute? Before you could use this dilemma, various questions need to be constructed to help channel the issue at the appropriate stage or stages for your students.

Selman and Jaquette (1977) and Selman (1980) provide a set of issues to guide the dilemma writer when constructing dilemmas in his four areas. The four issues for the first area, concepts of individuals, follow.

1. Conflicts between thoughts, feelings, or motives within the individual

2. Awareness of one's ability to observe one's own thoughts, feelings, and actions

3. The nature of personality traits, e.g., extroversion

**Box 6–1**    A moral dilemma focused on issue 8 from Kohlberg's 10 universal moral issues

---

**LEUKEMIA**
**A LIFE SITUATION DILEMMA**

The following story was reported in the *Boston Globe*, March 3, 1978:

MGH Will Fight to Treat Boy, 2

by Richard A. Knox
Globe Staff

Massachusetts General Hospital officials decided last night to fight a Brockton probate judge's ruling that 2-year-old Chad Green be returned to the legal custody of his parents, who plan to discontinue conventional medical treatment for his leukemia and seek unorthodox "dietary" therapy.

Plymouth County Probate Judge James Lawton ruled yesterday morning that Gerald and Diane Green of Scituate are "not unfit" to retain custody of Chad merely because they wish to abandon the conventional chemotherapy that medical experts say is the child's only hope of survival.

MGH spokesman Martin Bander said yesterday evening that hospital officials feel "morally obligated" to pursue other legal avenues to ensure Chad's continued treatment. "To stop treatment now," Bander said in a prepared statement, "would be not only to abandon Chad but also in a sense to abandon thousands of future Chads whose parents unwittingly wish to condemn their children to a painful death—children too young to decide for themselves."

The boy's father said after the Brockton hearing that he and his wife would fight further attempts by the hospital to continue chemotherapy.

The MGH's decision to pursue its legal battle makes it likely that Chad's case will become a landmark confrontation between established medical opinion and adherents of unorthodox cancer therapies as well as a test of who should decide about the treatment of a minor.

Dr. John T. Truman of the MGH, who has managed the boy's care, said yesterday: "If treatment is discontinued at this point, it can be said with 100 percent confidence that the disease will recur and he will die within a period of one to six months."

With treatment, Truman said, his chances of survival are less than 50 percent but still substantial.

Diane Green said after the hearing: "For my husband and me, quality of life is more important than quantity. We would rather see Chad have a short, wonderful life as himself than to have a life extended by poisonous drugs and needles."

Truman said that the two-year-old, who is at home with his parents, has so far suffered "minimal side effects" from the anticancer drugs he took last fall and again this month. The Greens, who moved to Boston from Nebraska to find the best available treatment for their son, contradicted Truman, saying that the therapy has terrified the child and has been "physically and emotionally exhausting."

"Have you ever seen a child turn into a mad dog?" the father said. "That's what our child does because of the poisons they have been giving him…There has to be a better way than to poison the human system in order to cure it."

Last November, the Greens discontinued Chad's chemotherapy without informing the doctors, substituting a regiment of organic foods, vitamins and distilled water. Though the boy had been in remission, he suffered a recurrence of his blood cancer in February, when the

**Box 6–1**    (Continued)

Greens admitted they had stopped the prescribed treatment.

In ruling in favor of the parents' motion to regain legal control over their son, Judge Lawton agreed with the recommendation of Chad's temporary guardian, Atty. John H. Wyman of Plymouth, who was appointed by the court to represent the boy's best interests.

Wyman told the judge that the parents' decision to forego further chemotherapy is "a rational parental decision, perhaps one that I might not personally make, but one that I can respect."

Without taking further testimony from doctors or from parents of children who have been successfully treated for leukemia, Lawton announced that "there is no way we are going to be able to establish that the parents of Chad Green are unfit. I am satisfied that they are not."

**Questions**

Did Judge Lawton make the right decision, or should he have ordered Chad's parents to continue chemotherapy treatments?
Why or why not?

Source:   Landenburg, Landenburg, & Scharf, 1978.

4. Factors that influence change in individuals, e.g., peer influences

There are six issues for the second area, concepts of friendship.

1. The motives and mechanisms involved in friendship formation

2. The degrees and types of friendships

3. The mutual nature of friendships and the role of trust

4. Feelings of jealousy that arise when a new person becomes involved in a relationship

5. The resolution of conflict between friends

6. Why friendships fail

There are seven issues for the third area, concepts of peer groups.

1. The motives and mechanisms involved in the formation of peer groups

2. How unity is achieved within a peer group

3. The reasons for and degrees of conformity in peer groups

4. The rationale for and types of rules that govern peer groups

5. Decision making, goal setting, cooperation, and conflict resolution in peer groups

6. The nature and role of leadership in peer groups

7. Individual exclusion from and the breakup of peer groups

There are five issues for the fourth area, concepts of parent-child relations.

1. The motives, needs, and personal characteristics involved in parent-child relations

2. Affective relations between parents and children

3. Obedience of children to parents and the nature of parental authority

4. The role of punishment in the parent-child relationship

5. The process of conflict resolution in the parent-child relationship

Box 6–2 is an example of a dilemma based on the fourth issue in the second area, concepts of friendship. The sample dilemma is hypothetical,

**Box 6–2**    An interpersonal dilemma focused on issue 4 from Selman's second domain

---

**THE FRIEND'S DILEMMA (Children's Version)**

Kathy and Becky have been best friends since they were five years old. They went to the same kindergarten and have been in the same class ever since. Every Saturday they would try to do something special together, go to the park or the store, or play something special at home. They always had a good time with each other.

One day a new girl, Jeanette, moved into their neighborhood and soon introduced herself to Kathy and Becky. Right away Jeanette and Kathy seemed to hit it off very well. They talked about where Jeanette was from and the things she could do in her new town. Becky, on the other hand, didn't seem to like Jeanette very much. She thought Jeanette was a showoff, but was also jealous of all the attention Kathy was giving Jeanette.

When Jeanette left the other two alone, Becky told Kathy how she felt about Jeanette. "What did you think of her, Kathy? I thought she was kind of pushy, butting in on us like that."

"Come on, Becky. She's new in town and just trying to make friends. The least we can do is be nice to her."

"Yeah, but that doesn't mean we have to be friends with her," replied Becky. "Anyway, what would you like to do this Saturday? You know those old puppets of mine, I thought we could fix them up and make our own puppet show."

"Sure, Becky, that sounds great," said Kathy. "I'll be over after lunch. I better go home now. See you tomorrow."

Late that evening Jeanette called Kathy and surprised her with an invitation to the circus, the last show before it left town. The only problem was that the circus happened to be at the same time that Kathy had promised to go to Becky's. Kathy didn't know what to do, go to the circus and leave her best friend alone, or stick with her best friend and miss a good time.

---

SOURCE: Selman, 1980.

derived from daily-life events, and has an interpersonal focus, i.e., a friendship conflict. Again, before using this dilemma, you would need to construct questions to channel the issue at the stage or stages of your students.

Finally, Beck (1971) offers some guidelines for selecting issues for different age groups. Beck suggests that primary-age children are concerned with issues such as cooperation and sharing, while intermediate-age children are concerned with issues related to the family and friendships, and high school students are most concerned with abstract issues such as truth and justice. A more complete list of Beck's guidelines appears in Table 6–3. Beck offers suggestions about the interests of children between 5 and 18 years of age. These suggestions are useful for selecting age-appropriate material focused on the concerns typical of children. You should take into consideration the developmental level of your students when using these suggestions.

Hersh et al. (1979) provide a set of planning procedures to follow when you develop a cognitive-developmental curriculum for teaching reasoning. Their 10 procedures follow.

1. Develop a rationale, i.e., a clear purpose for your use of the theory.

2. Identify issues appropriate for your students.

3. Relate the issues to your students' lives.

4. Develop material that promotes role taking.

5. Expose students to reasoning slightly above their current level.

6. Encourage students to identify issues themselves.

7. Work with other teachers to generate ideas and material.

8. Try out material and procedures on a limited basis first.

9. Look beyond subject content for material.

10. Provide for experiences that will allow students to act on their reasoning.

## ASSESSMENT

### Interviewing

To assess moral reasoning in his research subjects, Kohlberg developed a questionnaire based on nine brief stories. Each story contains a moral dilemma. Subjects are asked to respond to the story with their opinions and ideas. The responses are scored using scoring criteria developed by Kohlberg. Porter and Taylor (1972) developed an assessment guide for use by teachers based on Kohlberg's original questionnaire.

The teachers' questionnaire uses only five stories instead of nine. Porter

**Table 6–3** Five sets of age-graded topics, of interest and relevance to children and youth, useful in developing dilemmas

*Personal and Social Values (5–9)*
1. Helping other people
2. The self and others
3. The value of rules to ourselves and others
4. Exceptions to rules
5. The need to look ahead
6. Parent-child relationships
7. Attitudes toward teachers
8. Other authorities in society
9. The need to learn
10. The need for advice
11. Making up one's mind
12. Valuable goals in life
13. The legitimacy of happiness as a goal
14. The place of work

*Human Relations (10–11)*
1. Rules people give us
2. The place of rules in society
3. Exceptions to society's rules
4. The individual's need for other people
5. Helping other people
6. The self and others
7. The place of laws, judges, and police
8. The place of governments and other authorities
9. Law-breaking and the place of punishment
10. Different values and rules in our society
11. Different values and rules around the world
12. Loyalty and patriotism
13. The place of the inner group of relatives and friends
14. Parent-child relationships
15. Prejudice against races, social classes, and other groups
16. Differences in taste in our society and around the world
17. Settling conflicts of interest in society
18. The role of the school in solving society's problems
19. Students, teachers, and schools
20. The individual and society
21. Studying society and working out solutions to its problems

*Decision Making (12–13)*
1. Worthwhile personal goals to pursue in life

2. The place of education in one's life
3. Work and leisure, so called
4. The place of leisure, recreation, and exercise
5. Alcohol and drugs
6. Vocational decision making
7. Personal moral virtues
8. The need to look ahead
9. The need to stop and think (at times)
10. The need for self-control
11. Personality differences and problems
12. Dependence/independence
13. Introversion/extroversion
14. Emotional elements in one's makeup
15. Emotional needs
16. Sexual needs
17. Personal decision making in general
18. Multiple and mixed motives
19. Intuition
20. Conscience
21. Feelings
22. Authorities
23. Rules
24. What is right, "all things considered"
25. A working understanding of the world
26. Using one's mind effectively
27. Managing one's time and abilities
28. Adapting to change

*Human Issues in the World Today (14–15)*
1. Democracy, fascism, socialism, and communism in the world today
2. Freedom and equality in the world today
3. Means to ends: political process
4. Means to ends: national and international law
5. International trade: protection policies
6. National and international monetary policy
7. Science, engineering, commerce: various moral issues
8. War
9. Disarmament
10. Underdeveloped nations, so

called
11. Pollution
12. Population control
13. Abortion
14. Euthanasia
15. Eugenics
16. Nationalism
17. Racism
18. Women's liberation
19. Civil liberties, e.g., in commerce, speech, alcohol, drugs, marriage, and divorce
20. Civil disobedience
21. Welfare and the minimum wage
22. Social work
23. Old age
24. Medical insurance

*Value Theory (17–18)*
1. The purpose of morality
2. Moral and nonmoral law
3. The self and others
4. Favoring an inner group
5. Justice
6. Compromise
7. What is morality?
8. Stages of moral development
9. Moral character and personality traits
10. Human needs and moral ideals
11. Elements in human decision making
12. Elements in human action
13. Politics, law and morality
14. Business, economics, and morality
15. National, racial, and cultural distinctions
16. The movement toward internationalism
17. Future planning
18. Value theories emphasizing function and purpose
19. Authority-oriented value theories
20. Hedonistic value theories
21. Utilitarian theories
22. Subjectivism, relativism, and objectivism
23. Developing a value theory
24. The place of beliefs and rules in moral decision making
25. The place of conscience and feelings in moral decision making
26. Decision making in general

SOURCE: C. Beck, 1971, *Moral Education in the Schools*. Toronto, Canada: Ontario Institute for Studies in Education.

and Taylor (1972) state that an adequate assessment can be done using only four stories. Each story is a brief description of a moral dilemma faced by an individual under a specified set of circumstances. A set of questions accompany each story to aid getting a full response from a student. The questionnaire can be used with both elementary and secondary students. However, it is not recommended for students below the fourth grade unless the teacher is a skilled interviewer.

At the elementary level or with poor readers, the stories are read aloud by the teacher. The teacher asks the questions and records responses either on tape or by taking notes. Secondary-level students with good reading skills can be given the questionnaire to complete independently. However, if a student at any level has difficulty with written expression, the interview approach should be used. In an interview the teacher can probe and seek clarification where needed and record a student's responses.

Box 6–3 is a sample from the Kohlberg questionnaire as adapted by Porter and Taylor (1972). In Box 6–3, there is a brief story that contains an ethical dilemma. Following the story, there are five probe questions. Answers to these questions are scored according to criteria and examples given in the manual. There are sample responses to the first question in Box 6–3. As these sample responses illustrate, an answer may not be easily classified at a given stage. In these cases, the answer is given a mixed classification. Often, these mixed classifications indicate that a student is in a transition phase.

There are also interview materials to assess social reasoning based on the extension of Kohlberg's work done by Selman. This assessment material uses a testing procedure similar to the one just described. The manual provides the interview material and scoring guidelines (Selman, Jaquette, & Bruss-Saunders, 1979).

**Box 6-3** An illustrative moral dilemma story with a set of probe question and sample responses to the first question at various stages of reasoning

---

**STORY IV**

Joe is a 14-year-old boy who wanted to go to camp very much. His father promised him he could go if he saved up the money for it himself. So Joe worked hard at his paper route and saved up the $40 it cost to go to camp and a little more besides. But just before camp was going to start, his father changed his mind. Some of his friends decided to go on a special fishing trip, and Joe's father was short of the money it would cost. So he told Joe to give him the money he had saved from the paper route. Joe didn't want to give up going to camp, so he thought of refusing to give his father the money.

20. Should Joe refuse to give his father the money? Why?

21. Does his father have the right to tell Joe to give him the money?

22. Does giving the money have anything to do with being a good son?

23. Which is worse, a father breaking a promise to his son or a son breaking a promise to his father?

24. Why should a promise be kept?

**Box 6-3    Continued**

The following responses are answers given to question 20 at various stages of reasoning.

**STAGE**

| | |
|---|---|
| 1 | No. His father is in command. He can boss his son around. |
| 1(2) | I think so. His father should save up the money himself because he promised Joe he could go. |
| 2 | Yes. Because he saved it up himself and why should he give it to his father? His father wouldn't give him any. |
| 2(3) | Yes. Because he got that money on his own. His father should get the money on his own. |
| 3 | It would depend on what kind of father. If it was a father like I have, he would want to give it to him. |
| 3(4) | No. Joe should refuse his father. His father has done a lot more for Joe than Joe can ever repay him for. |
| 4 | No, he owes his father his life and his father has supported him all this time. |
| (6) | Yes. Because Joe trusted his father would let him go to camp if he earned his own money and, therefore, his trust should be upheld. |
| 5 | Yes. Because it was rightfully his and most likely he felt his cause was more worthy. If he didn't, his passiveness would show he accepted authority blindly. |
| 6 | The father may have legal right but no moral right to the son's money. |

SOURCE: N. Porter and N. Taylor, 1972, *How to Assess the Moral Reasoning of Students*. Toronto, Canada: The Ontario Institute for Studies in Education.

## Testing

There is another approach to assessing moral reasoning developed by Rest and his associates (Rest, Cooper, Coder, Masanz, & Anderson, 1974). Rest et al. call their instrument the Defining Issues Test (DIT). The DIT also makes use of stories which contain moral dilemmas. Each story is followed by a series of 12 issues bearing on the story. These issues are related to different stages of reasoning. Each issue is rated on its importance using a five-category scale. After the issues for each story are rated, the issues are ranked.

Box 6–4 is an example from the Defining Issues Test (Rest, 1979). The DIT uses six moral dilemmas like the one illustrated. First, a student is asked to make a judgment about the story using a multiple-choice item. Next, the student is asked to rate a set of issues related to making a judgment about the story. The four most important issues are then ranked. After a student responds to all the dilemmas, the responses are profiled (see Box 6-5) and scored. The DIT manual also provides reliability data, validity data, and norms. A procedure for doing an abbreviated assessment using only three stories is also described in the manual. The earlier comments concerning reading ability would apply to this approach as well.

The DIT is a better approach to assessing students who have difficulty expressing themselves either orally, in writing, or both. It also has the advantage of being relatively well researched and normed. The norms, however,

**Box 6-4**  An illustrative moral dilemma story with a multiple-choice question related to the reader's judgment about the story and 12 questions concerning issues that might be important in making a judgment[a]

---

**ESCAPED PRISONER**

A man had been sentenced to prison for 10 years. After one year, however, he escaped from prison, moved to a new area of the country, and took on the name of Thompson. For 8 years he worked hard, and gradually he saved enough money to buy his own business. He was fair to his customers, gave his employees top wages, and gave most of his own profits to charity. Then one day, Mrs. Jones, an old neighbor, recognized him as the man who had escaped from prison 8 years before, and whom the police had been looking for.

Should Mrs. Jones report Mr. Thompson to the police and have him sent back to prison? (Check one)

_____ Should report him     _____ Can't decide     _____ Should not report him

Rate the <u>importance</u> of the following questions in judging the situation above. Rate by checking the appropriate box to the left of each item.

| GREAT | MUCH | SOME | LITTLE | NO | | |
|---|---|---|---|---|---|---|
| | | | | | 1. | Hasn't Mr. Thompson been good long enough to prove he isn't a bad person? |
| | | | | | 2. | If someone escapes punishment for a crime, does that encourage more crime? |
| | | | | | 3. | Wouldn't we be better off without prisons and the oppression of our legal system? |
| | | | | | 4. | Has Mr. Thompson really paid his debt to society? |
| | | | | | 5. | Would society be failing what Mr. Thompson should fairly expect? |
| | | | | | 6. | What benefits would prisons be apart from society, especially for a charitable man? |
| | | | | | 7. | Would it be cruel and heartless to send Mr. Thompson to prison? |
| | | | | | 8. | Would it be fair to all the prisoners who had to serve out their full sentences if Mr. Thompson was let off? |
| | | | | | 9. | Was Mrs. Jones a good friend of Mr. Thompson? |
| | | | | | 10. | Wouldn't it be a citizen's duty to report an escaped criminal, regardless of the circumstances? |
| | | | | | 11. | How would the will of the people and the public good best be served? |
| | | | | | 12. | Would going to prison do any good for Mr. Thompson or protect anybody? |

**Box 6-4**    (Continued)

From the list of questions above, select the four most important:

Most important _____

Second most important _____

Third most important _____

Fourth most important _____

ᵃ Each of the 12 issues are rated on a five-point scale and them ranked in importance from first to fourth in importance.

SOURCE: Rest, 1979.

are limited because they do not include elementary-age students. Unfortunately, there is no similar test available based on Selman's work.

There is another approach to assessing moral reasoning which makes use of a combination of techniques and is not entirely an interview or an objective test. This third approach is the Sociomoral Reflection Measure (SRM)

**Box 6-5**    An illustration of the profile and scoring matrix used with the Defining Issues Test.

| STORY | | | | | | | | | | RATE-RANK |
| STAGES | 2 | 3 | 4 | 5A | 5B | 6 | A | M | P | INCONSISTENCIES |
|---|---|---|---|---|---|---|---|---|---|---|
| *Heinz* | | | | | | | | | | |
| *Students* | | | | | | | | | | |
| *Prisoner* | | | | | | | | | | |
| *Doctor* | | | | | | | | | | |
| *Webster* | | | | | | | | | | |
| *Newspaper* | | | | | | | | | | |
| *Raw Stage Score* | | | | | | | | | | |
| *Storage Percentages* | | | | | | | | | | |

SOURCE: Rest, 1979.

developed by Gibbs and Widaman (1982). The SRM provides dilemma situations and then asks for a decision from three choices about what should be done. This is followed by several additional questions to which answers are selected and explanations given.

Finally, if you are well acquainted with the developmental model and the hierarchy of stages, you can determine a student's developmental stage by informally evaluating a student's reasoning in comments and written work. However, it is important, for planning purposes, to know at what stage a student is functioning. Thus, the latter approach should be followed only after you have a good deal of experience assessing moral reasoning in students.

## INSTRUCTION

There are a variety of approaches to instruction in values education programs. One approach to values education was suggested by a study of the effect of teaching counseling to high school students (Mosher & Sullivan, 1978; Mosher & Sprinthall, 1971). In the study, adolescents were taught counseling skills. After the training, students prepared a problem or ethical issue suitable for taking to a counselor. Students divided into pairs and alternated roles as client and counselor. Part of the evaluation used in this study was Kohlberg's moral development scale. The post-test showed significant gains in moral reasoning. The gains were explained by students' learning to understand other people's beliefs, feelings, and attitudes. In short, the students had learned to be empathetic.

Another approach (Ulschak & Nicholas, 1977) uses Transactional Analysis (TA). In this approach, the reasoning associated with various ego states in TA (child, adult, and parent) is used to do ethical analysis and make decisions. The teacher serves as both a model and a trainer in this approach. Using guidelines based on TA, the teacher helps students analyze value conflicts. In addition to analysis, the teacher uses the structure of a contracting process to promote conflict resolution. The contracting process involves the following components.

1. Present the situation and help students develop an awareness of the dilemma.

2. Aid students in understanding what their objective or desired outcome is and what values they have related to the situation.

3. Help students determine what actions are necessary to get to the desired outcome and which ego state appears to be involved.

4. Promote the identification and establishment of criteria to evaluate the results of the solution.

5. If the results of the process do not produce the desired outcome, recycle.

A third approach (Goldiamond, 1968) to values education uses applied behavior analysis. Goldiamond offers a functional analysis of moral behavior in which morality or conscience is simply a set of behavior/consequence relations.

In other words, moral behavior is understood through operant learning theory. Goldiamond suggests that if moral behavior can be understood in these terms, then it can be modified using techniques based on learning theory. Specifically, he argues that morality might be teachable through errorless discrimination learning and reinforcement procedures.

An indirect approach to moral education is parent training (Bunzl, Coder, & Wirt, 1977). Using this strategy, Bunzl et al. successfully increased the level of moral maturity in children. These investigators designed a parent-intervention program to teach parents skills to improve role-taking opportunities for children in the home. A major focus of this program was to improve self-expression skills in parents with the intent of promoting children's participation in decision making in the home. The parent education program had five weekly sessions of two hours each and covered alternative ways of communicating, identification and modification of family relationships, and problem solving.

Finally, there is the most widely used approach, the developmentally based group discussion (Beyer, 1978; Galbraith & Jones, 1976; Gardner, 1983; Hersh et al., 1979; Scharf, 1978). The first task in this approach is to create an appropriate classroom atmosphere. Hersh et al. (1979) discuss several influences on classroom atmosphere.

*1. Physical Arrangement.* Whatever physical arrangement is used, it must encourage communication, e.g., a circle arrangement that allows each member of the group to see all other members of the group.

*2. Grouping.* Students should work in small groups of from three to five. These groups can be formed in several ways. First, group students based on agreement. Second, if students are reluctant to take a public position, assign them to a group and ask the group to be responsible for arguing and defending a particular position. Third, assign students to groups randomly. Whatever grouping procedure is followed, you must bear in mind the reasoning levels of the students involved. It is important to ensure that there is a mix of stages with no more than two stages between the lower and upper end of the range in the group. When there is such a spread, it is important there be at least one student at each stage being used, since development is best promoted by exposure to reasoning from adjacent stages.

*3. Model Acceptance.* You must model and encourage a nonjudgmental attitude. Critical to this effort is your acceptance and respect for students' thoughts, ideas, and feelings.

*4. Listening And Communication Skills.* Meaningful communication can only take place if all parties can listen to and communicate with others. You can model good communication skills by asking questions to verify comprehension, to clarify, or to seek elaboration on what students say. Selman and Jaquette (1978) found that communication skill deficits were particularly important in handicapped students with interpersonal problems. Planned instruction in communication skills should be included in a social reasoning program for problem students. Three sources of material on teaching communication skills are Alley and Deshler (1979), Koopman, Hunt, and Cowan (1978), and Robin (1979).

   **5. *Encourage Student-to-Student Interaction.*** A major purpose of the discussion group is to create interaction among students. Your purpose for creating a good classroom atmosphere is to promote interaction. The work of Kohlberg and his colleagues suggest that development is stimulated more by exposure to the reasoning of peers than to a teacher or other adult.

   The second task is to create conflict. Turiel's (1966, 1969, 1973) research suggests that one critical element in stimulating development is cognitive conflict. This is accomplished by challenging the students' reasoning about a dilemma. Challenge comes from student-teacher interaction, student-student interaction (which is critical), and reflection, i.e., internal dialogue within a student. Challenge and cognitive conflict depend upon your careful selection or development of dilemmas and creation of an appropriate classroom atmosphere.

   The third task is the effective use of questioning strategies. Hersh et al. (1979) divide questioning strategies into initial strategies and in-depth strategies. Your initial questioning should be directed at ensuring the following:

1. Understanding the issue

2. Confronting the values component in the problem

3. Drawing out students' opinions and reasoning

4. Creating interaction among students with different points of view

5. Bringing the values issue into focus

6. Stimulating students to examine why they hold a particular position

7. Extending or complicating the issue, e.g., by "what if " questions

8. Encouraging presentation of personal experiences related to the issue under discussion

The in-depth strategies should be directed at the following:

1. Explanation of terms used in the discussion

2. Exploration of the issue beyond the immediate problem

3. Generating discussion of the conflicting values identified

4. Encouraging students to take the perspective of different persons in the conflict

5. Asking students to consider the implications for everyone taking a particular position

6. Getting students within the group who are at adjacent stages to interact with one another

7. Clarification of the reasoning at different stages present in the discussion

8. Maintaining focus by requesting summary statements of positions and the reasoning behind them

Figure 6–1 is a diagram that summarizes the teaching process. This diagram illustrates the four basic steps in the process. These four steps include confrontation of the dilemma, statement of a position, testing the reasoning, and adopting a position. Each of these four steps involves additional substeps, which are also illustrated.

Most of the discussion above draws on sources concerned with the use of Kohlberg's model in moral education programs. It can also be applied directly or adapted to interpersonal education programs based on Selman's extension of Kohlberg's work. Jaquette (in Selman, 1980) suggests a set of principles to follow when conducting class discussions. These principles are based on Jaquette's experiences in conducting social reasoning programs with disturbed preadolescents. These principles are as follows:

1. Emphasize positive peer interactions in discussion groups with supportive feedback.

2. Emphasize the adequacy of the interpersonal problem solving when judging ideas.

3. Stress the real-life concerns of students.

4. Ensure that real consequences follow from the group's discussion and decisions.

5. Require that decision making be based on democratic principles, e.g., consensus.

6. Develop a formal organization for discussion groups to avoid looseness and negative behavior, e.g., rotating group leadership among students.

7. Create a sense of interdependence so that resolution of problems is a cooperative effort.

Jaquette also suggests some rules to govern group discussion. These rules are presented in Box 6–6.

One cautionary note is due at this point. Values conflict can be a very unsettling and painful experience for some students and teachers (Joseph, 1977). Whenever a student is observed going through a period of doubt or confusion, you should take time to talk individually with the student. In this way, you can provide personal support and reassurance as well as gain a better idea of how to help the student through a transitional period. You should also have a publicly announced open-door policy for any student who feels the need for a private discussion.

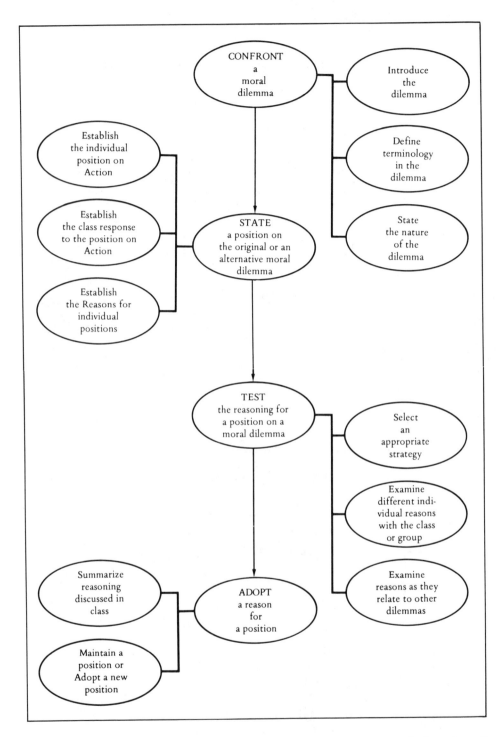

**Figure 6–1**    A diagram of the basic steps and the associated components in the values discussion process. *From Scharf, 1978.*

152

**Box 6–6**    A set of rules adopted for group discussions involving disturbed preadolescents

---

**RULES FOR CLASS DISCUSSION**

Initial class meetings are used to propose, debate, and vote class rules into operation. The following rules were adopted by the class during class meetings.

1. One person should talk at a time.

2. Respect others—no hollering or swearing at people.

3. Be cool.

4. Talk to the whole group, not just one other person.

5. Pay attention; know what is going on.

6. No threats or intimidation in class.

---

Source:    Jaquette in Selman, 1980.

## EVALUATION

Evaluation of instruction can be done either informally or through formal assessment. Any of the assessment procedures previously described can be used to do the evaluation. Since what is being worked on is related to cognitive development, you should not expect to find measurable change over brief periods of time. Based on some previous studies, e.g., Blatt and Kohlberg (1975), it appears that interventions should not be expected to yield measurable change in less than 9 to 12 weeks.

## RESOURCES

A great deal of material has been published during the past 15 years for use in education programs directed at moral and social reasoning. In this section, only a few materials and resources will be described. Much of the additional material referred to is referenced in the materials and resources described. Four resources you will find particularly useful are Galbraith and Jones (1976), Hersh et al. (1979), Scharf (1978), and Selman (1976b). Two books of dilemmas are available for use in discussion groups (Blatt, Colby, & Speicher, 1974; Ladenburg, Ladenburg, & Scharf, 1978). Two sets of filmstrips with teacher's guides, one set for elementary-age students and the other for secondary-age students, have been developed by Selman, Byrne, and Kohlberg (1974) and Selman and Kohlberg (1972). These materials are of particular interest because they illustrate a merger of Kohlberg's and Selman's work. A better understanding of this merger can be gained through another filmstrip program, designed to train teachers (Selman & Kohlberg, 1976). Of course, the best materials are those created to fit your particular situation and students. However, until you develop the skills needed to function independently, the resources and materials noted above should prove both helpful and instructive.

## REFERENCES

ALLEY, G., & DESHLER, D. (1979). *Teaching the learning disabled adolescent: Strategies and methods.* Denver, CO: Love Publishing.

BECK, C. (1971). *Moral education in the schools.* Toronto, Canada: The Ontario Institute for Studies in Education.

BEYER, B. (1978). Conducting moral discussion in the classroom. In P. Scharf (Ed.), *Readings in moral education.* Minneapolis, MN: Winston Press.

BLATT, M., COLBY, A., & SPEICHER, B. (1974). *Hypothetical dilemmas for use in moral discussion.* Cambridge, MA: Moral Education and Research Foundation.

BLATT, M., & KOHLBERG, L. (1975). The effects of a classroom moral discussion on children's level of moral judgement. *Journal of Moral Education, 4,* 129–161.

BROWN, R., & HERNSTEIN, R. (1975). *Psychology.* Boston: Little, Brown.

BUNZL, M., CODER, R., & WIRT, R. (1977). Enhancement of maturity of moral judgement by parent education. *Journal of Abnormal Child Psychology, 5*(2), 177–186.

CANDEE, D. (1975). The moral psychology of Watergate. *Journal of Social Issues, 31,* 183–192.

COLBY, A., KOHLBERG, L., FENTON, E., SPEICHER-DUBIN, B., & LIEBERMAN, M. (1977). Secondary school moral discussion programs led by social studies teachers. *Journal of Moral Education, 6,* 90–111.

FODOR, E. (1972). Delinquency and susceptibility to social influence among adolescents as a function of level of moral development. *Journal of Social Psychology, 86,* 257–260.

GALBRAITH, R., & JONES, T. (1976). *Moral reasoning: A teaching handbook for adapting Kohlberg to the classroom.* St. Paul, MN: Greenhaven Press.

GARDNER, E. (1983). *Moral education for the emotionally disturbed early adolescent.* Lexington, MA: Lexington Books.

GIBBS, J. C., & WIDAMAN, K. F. (1982). *Social intelligence: Measuring the development of sociomoral reflection.* Englewood Cliffs, NJ: Prentice-Hall.

GILLIGAN, C. (1982). *In a different voice: Psychological theory and women's development.* Cambridge, MA: Harvard University Press.

GOLDIAMOND, I. (1968). Moral behavior: A functional analysis. *Psychology Today, 2*(4), 31–34.

GRUBER, H., & VONECHE, J. (1977). *The essential Piaget.* New York: Basic Books.

HAMMILL, D. D., & BARTEL, N. R. (1978). *Teaching children with learning and behavior problems.* Boston: Allyn and Bacon.

HARING, N. G., & PHILLIPS, E. L. (1962). *Educating emotionally disturbed children.* New York: McGraw-Hill.

HERSH, R. H., PAOLITTO, D. P., & REIMER, J. (1979). *Promoting moral growth: From Piaget to Kohlberg.* New York: Longman.

HOBBS, M. (1967). The reeducation of emotionally disturbed children. *Behavior Science Frontiers,* pp. 339–354.

HUDGINS, W., & PRENTICE, N. (1973). Moral judgements in delinquent and nondelinquent adolescents and their mothers. *Journal of Abnormal Psychology, 82,* 145–152.

JOSEPH, P. (1977). Value conflict: The teacher's dilemma. In L. Stiles & B. Johnson (Eds.), *Morality examined: Guidelines for teachers.* Princeton, NJ: Princeton Book Co.

JURKOVIC, G., & PRENTICE, N. (1977). Relation of moral and cognitive development to dimensions of juvenile delinquency. *Journal of Abnormal Psychology, 86,* 414–420.

KAUFFMAN J. (1985). *Characteristics of children's behavior disorders* (3rd ed.). Columbus, OH: Merrill.

KOHLBERG, L. (1964). Development of moral character and moral ideology. In M. Hoffman (Ed.), *Child development research.* New York: Russell Sage Foundation.

KOHLBERG, L. (1966). Moral education in the schools: A developmental view. *The School Review, 74,* 1–30.

KOHLBERG, L. (1969). The child as moral philosopher. In D. A. Goslin (Ed.), *Handbook of socialization theory and research.* Skokie, IL: Rand McNally.

KOHLBERG, L. (1973). *Collected papers on moral development and moral education.* Cambridge, MA: Graduate School of Education, Harvard University.

KOHLBERG, L. (1984). *The psychology of moral development: Essays on moral development* (Vol. 2). New York: Harper & Row.

KOHLBERG, L., & CANDEE, D. (1984). The relation of moral judgement to moral action. In W. Kurtines & J. Gewirtz (Eds.), *Morality, moral behavior, and moral development.* New York: Wiley.

KOOPMAN, E. J., HUNT, E. J., & COWAN, S. D. (1978). *Talking together.* Kalamazoo, MI: Behaviordelia.

KRATHWOHL, D. R., BLOOM, B. S., & MASIA, B. B. (1964). *Taxonomy of educational objectives: The classification of educational goals: Handbook II. Affective domain.* New York: David McKay.

KREBS, R., & KOHLBERG, L. (1973). *Moral judgement and ego controls as determinants of resistance to cheating.* Cambridge, MA: Harvard University Press.

KUHN, D., LANGER, J., KOHLBERG, L., & HAAN, N. (1977). The development of formal operations in logical and moral judgement. *Genetic Psychology Monographs, 95,* 97–188.

KURTINES, W., & GREIF, E. (1974). The development of moral thought: Review and evaluation of Kohlberg's approach. *Psychological Bulletin, 81,* 453–470.

LANDENBURG, T., LANDENBURG, M., & SCHARF, P. (1978). *Moral education: a classroom workbook.* Davis, CA: Dialogue Books.

LERNER, J. (1981). *Learning disabilities, theories, diagnosis, and teaching strategies.* Boston: Houghton, Mifflin.

LOEVINGER, J. (1976). *Ego development.* San Francisco: Jossey-Bass.

MANN, L., GOODMAN, L., & WIEDERHOLT, J. L. (1978). *Teaching the learning disabled adolescent.* Boston: Houghton Mifflin.

MOSHER, R., & SPRINTHALL, N. (1971). Psychological education: A means to promote personal development during adolescence. *The Counseling Psychologist, 2,* 3–81.

MOSHER, R., & SULLIVAN, P. (1978). A curriculum in moral education for adolescents. In P. Scharf (Ed.), *Readings in moral education.* Minneapolis, MN: Winston Press.

NATIONAL SUPPORT SYSTEMS PROJECT (1980). *A common body of practice for teachers: The challenge of Public Law 94-142 to teacher education.* Washington, DC: American Association of Colleges of Teacher Education.

NEWCOMER, P. L. (1980). *Understanding and teaching emotionally disturbed children.* Boston: Allyn and Bacon.

PORTER, N., & TAYLOR, N. (1972). *How to assess the moral reasoning of students.* Toronto, Canada: The Ontario Institute for Studies in Education.

RATHS, L., MERRILL, H., & SIMON, S. (1966). *Values and teaching.* Columbus, OH: Charles E. Merrill.

REDL, F., & WINEMAN, D. (1952). *Controls from within.* New York: Free Press.

REIMER, J. (1977). *A study in the moral development of kibbutz adolescents.* Unpublished doctoral dissertation, Harvard University.

REST, J. (1979). *Revised manual for the Defining Issues test.* Minneapolis, MN: Minnesota Moral Research Projects, University of Minnesota.

REST, J., COOPER, D., CODER, R., MASANZ, J., & ANDERSON, D. (1974). Judging the important issues in moral dilemmas—An objective measure of development. *Developmental Psychology, 10,* 491–501.

ROBIN, A. (1979). Problem-solving communication training: A behavioral approach to the treatment of parent-adolescent conflict. *American Journal of Family Therapy, 7,* 69–82.

ROTHMAN, G. R. (1980). The relationship between moral judgement and moral behavior. In M. Windmiller, N. Lamber, & E. Turiel (Eds.), *Moral development and socialization.* Boston: Allyn and Bacon.

SCHARF, P. (1978). Creating moral dilemmas for the classroom. In P. Scharf (Ed.), *Readings in moral education.* Minneapolis, MN: Winston Press.

SCHARF, P. (1978). *Moral education.* Davis, CA: Dialogue Books.

SELMAN, R. L. (1976a). Toward a structural analysis of developing interpersonal relations concepts: Research with normal and disturbed preadolescent boys. In A. D. Pick (Ed.), *Minnesota symposia on child psychology* (Vol. 10). Minneapolis, MN: The University of Minnesota Press.

SELMAN, R. (1976b). Social-cognitive understanding: A guide to educational and clinical practice. In T. Lickona (Ed.), *Moral development and behavior.* New York: Holt, Rinehart and Winston.

SELMAN, R. (1980). *The growth of interpersonal understanding.* New York: Academic Press.

SELMAN, R., BYRNE, D., & KOHLBERG, L. (1974). *First things: Social reasoning.* Mount Kisco, NY: Guidance Associates.

SELMAN, R., & JAQUETTE, D. (1977). Stability and oscillation in interpersonal awareness: A clinical-developmental analysis. In C. Keasey (Ed.), *Nebraska symposium on motivation: Social cognitive development.* Lincoln, NE: University of Nebraska Press.

SELMAN, R., & JAQUETTE, D. (1978). To understand and to help: Implications of developmental research for the education of children with interpersonal problems. In P. Scharf (Ed.), *Readings in moral education.* Minneapolis, MN: Winston Press.

SELMAN, R., JAQUETTE, D., & BRUSS-SAUNDERS, E. (1979). *Assessing intrapersonal understanding: An interview and scoring manual.* (Available from Harvard-Judge Barker Social Reasoning Project, Judge Barker Guidance Center, 295 Longwood Ave., Boston, MA 02115)

SELMAN, R., JAQUETTE, D., & LAVIN, D. (1977). Interpersonal awareness in children: Toward an integration of developmental and clinical child psychology. *American Journal of Orthopsychiatry, 47,* 264–274.

SELMAN, R., & KOHLBERG, L. (1972). *First things: Values.* Mount Kisco, NY: Guidance Associates.

SELMAN, R., & KOHLBERG, L. (1976). *Relationships and values.* Mount Kisco, NY: Guidance Associates.

SIMON, S., HOWE, L., & KIRSCHENBAUM, H. (1976). *Values clarification*. New York: Hart Publishing Co.

SIMON, S., & O'ROURKE, R. (1977). *Developing values with exceptional children*. Englewood Cliffs, NJ: Prentice-Hall.

TURIEL, E. (1966). An experimental analysis of developmental stages in children's moral judgment. *Journal of Personality and Social Psychology*, *3*, 611–618.

TURIEL, E. (1969). Developmental processes in the child's moral thinking. In P. Mussen, J. Langer, & M. Covington (Eds.), *New directions in developmental psychology*. New York: Holt, Rinehart and Winston.

TURIEL, E. (1973). Stage transition in moral development. In R. Travers (Ed.), *Second handbook of research in teaching* (pp. 732–758). Skokie, IL: Rand McNally.

ULSCHAK, F., & NICHOLAS, J. (1977). Transactional analysis: A framework for ethical decision making. In L. Stiles & B. Johnson (Eds.), *Morality examined: Guidelines for teachers*. Princeton, NJ: Princeton Book Co.

# 7

# REDUCING INAPPROPRIATE EMOTIONAL BEHAVIOR

## A Behavioral Approach

## INTRODUCTION

Besides operant learning, applied behavior analysis uses respondent learning. Applied behavior analysts believe that respondent learning is the best model for explaining and changing emotional behavior. They consider affective responses to be reflexive, physiological responses. Thus, in respondent learning, you learn not a new response but to respond with an existing response to a new stimulus. To explain emotional behavior, these psychologists use both the respondent and operant models. Respondent learning explains how a new stimulus elicits an existing response. Operant learning helps explain maintenance of the response without the presence of the original eliciting stimulus. Since we have covered operant principles in an earlier chapter, we will focus only on respondent principles in this chapter.

### The Respondent Model

Respondent learning is based on the work of Pavlov (1927). Respondent behavior is an involuntary response elicited by some class of stimuli. They are called either unconditioned or conditioned stimuli. An *unconditioned stimulus* (US) is called *prepotent*. This means that you do not have to learn to respond to it, e.g., heat. A *conditioned stimulus* (CS) is a stimulus to which you have learned to respond, e.g., a gun. Your response to a US is an *unconditioned response* (UR). Your response to a CS is a *conditioned response* (CR). A stimulus or response may be either positive or negative. This is shown notationally by a plus (+) or minus (-) sign, e.g., UR-.

A CS is learned by stimulus pairing. A formerly neutral stimulus (C)S paired with a potent US or CS acquires some of the eliciting properties of the US or CS by association. If the eliciting stimulus is a US, the process is called *conditioning*. If the eliciting stimulus is a CS, the process is called *secondary*, or *higher-order*, *conditioning*. A diagram of this process is shown in Figure 7–1. The CR produced will not have exactly the same properties as the UR, but it will be similar. If the eliciting stimulus is mild, the conditioning takes repeated trials. If the eliciting stimulus is intense, the conditioning may occur in a few or even one trial. Intense eliciting stimuli produce a pattern of anatomic and physiological responses. The pattern includes increased heart rate, increased blood pressure, sweating, and muscle tension. The resulting CR is called a *conditioned emotional response* (CEr).

Figure 7–2 is a diagram, with labels, illustrating the conditioning process in a school setting. In the figure, the eliciting stimulus is a US- labeled "paddling." The associated UR- is labeled "pain, fear, and escape behavior." The (C)S, which will become a CS- by pairing or association with the US-, is labeled "teacher." The CR- developed by this process is labeled "anxiety and avoidance behavior." The CS- will have the power to elicit the CR- even when the US- is not present. Now, the operant overlap referred to earlier becomes important. If the CS- is eliciting a CR-, the conditions for negative reinforcement are present. Avoidance behavior in the child, e.g., cutting class, reduces or eliminates the CR- (anxiety). The result is negative reinforcement of avoidance behavior. You will recall that negative reinforcement maintains or strengthens the behavior it follows. Thus, the operant overlap will maintain the avoidance behavior even though the US- does not reoccur and the CS- is seldom if ever encountered.

Respondent Conditioning

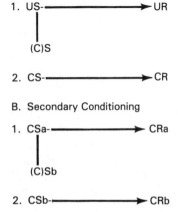

A. Primary Conditioning

1. US-——————————▶ UR

  |

  (C)S

2. CS-——————————▶ CR

B. Secondary Conditioning

1. CSa-——————————▶ CRa

  |

  (C)Sb

2. CSb-——————————▶ CRb

**Figure 7–1**
A representation of the respondent learning model. Part (A) illustrates conditioning involving a prepotent stimulus as the initial stimulus. Part (B) illustrates conditioning involving a conditioned stimulus as the initial stimulus.

Respondent Conditioning

A. Primary Conditioning

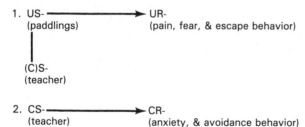

B. Secondary Conditioning

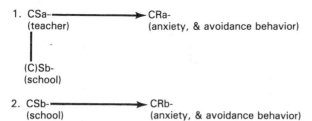

**Figure 7–2**
A labeled representation of respondent conditioning as it might occur in an educational setting.

We also need to discuss respondent generalization. In Figure 7–2, we labeled the CS- "teacher." However, other stimuli were present. We can consider the entire classroom and even the school as a complex of associated stimuli. The teacher is simply the most immediate association. There may actually be several pairings, and they may be diverse. For example, punishment may occur in different locations, at different times, and involve different teachers. Under these conditions, the CS- will become generalized. That is, it will come to represent a complex of associated stimuli. When this happens, the CR- is elicited by a variety of stimuli and the avoidance response becomes pervasive. The result will be what we sometimes call school phobia (a CEr-).

### Research Support

You can find good reviews of the research literature on respondent learning in any basic text on learning theory (Bower & Hilgard, 1981). The earliest research on respondent learning and emotional behavior used children (Jones, 1924; Watson & Rayner, 1920). Subsequent work focused mostly on adults (Wolpe, 1958). Wilson (1984) discusses an unpublished meta-analysis by Andrews, Moran, and Hall of 26 studies using respondent procedures with adults. Andrews et al. concluded that respondent interventions are more effective than a placebo or no intervention. Barlow and Wolf (1981), Mathews,

Gelder, and Johnston (1981), and Paul (1969) also concluded that respondent interventions are the most effective treatment for emotional disorders in adults.

Recently there has been an increased interest in respondent interventions with children. There are several reviews of the research literature on these applications. Graziano, DeGiovanni, and Garcia (1979) did a review covering almost 60 years of research with children. They found that until very recently there has been little research on respondent procedures with children. These reviewers concluded that of the procedures researched, modeling was the most successful. They also caution that it has not been demonstrated that the findings in experimental studies are actually useful in clinical practice. In another review by Hatzenbuelhler and Schroeder (1978), the reviewers state that the research on respondent procedures with children is hardly better than anecdotal reports. Drawing on their review, they suggest that you should treat children with severe anxiety disorders with procedures not requiring direct participation with the anxiety-eliciting stimulus. They define a severe disorder as one in which the child is too inhibited to have any voluntary involvement with the anxiety stimulus. They further suggest that you should treat children with mild to moderate anxiety disorders with procedures requiring direct participation with the anxiety-eliciting stimulus. In spite of the lack of extensive research with children, many psychologists believe that respondent procedures hold much promise for treating anxiety disorders in children (Gelfand, 1978; Morris & Kratochwill, 1983).

## ASSESSMENT

The assessment of emotions focuses on one of three dimensions of behavior or some combination of these dimensions. Assessment is done at the physiological level by using such measures as galvanic skin response. It is done at the cognitive level using various psychological tests. Finally, it is done at the behavioral level using observation. A basic problem with these three approaches is they don't correlate well with one another. In short, the results of one approach usually don't confirm the results of either of the other approaches.

Leaving aside this measurement problem, the physiological approach is not suitable for use in educational settings. The necessary equipment and conditions usually aren't present. In addition, teachers don't have the background to do this type of assessment. The use of psychological tests is common in educational settings and many teachers have the necessary background to use them. However, the validity of these tests has been seriously questioned (Mischel, 1968). The behavioral approach appears to be the best choice for educational settings. It is an approach that teachers can learn to use. The approach also focuses on responses most likely to be of concern to teachers. Finally, the measurement techniques have good reliability and validity when properly used.

Whenever you are going to assess a student, you should consider several things before proceeding. First, is the student's fear normal? MacFarlane, Allen, and Honzik (1954) in a longitudinal study of normal children found that many children experience fears during normal development. Second, you should consider the student's age. There are age differences in the kinds of stimuli that children fear. There is evidence that the frequency of normal fears declines with increasing age (Rachman, 1968). Third, you must consider the seriousness of the fear. Usually, our concern is only for clinical fear or serious anxiety. Normal fear is usually a response to a rational stimulus, that is, a fear response to a stimulus we can understand. Clinical fear or anxiety is usually elicited by an irrational stimulus or no identifiable stimulus and is a persistent and long-lasting response; for example, we can understand why one is anxious around a dog even if we aren't. It is more difficult to understand why one is anxious around a mailbox. One is rational and the other is irrational. Finally, the most critical test is the degree of impairment caused by the anxiety response. We can't say that an anxiety response is an emotional disorder until it has become serious enough to interfere with normal functioning. When the response is dysfunctional and pervasive or when it is highly dysfunctional in an important area of life, it is serious enough to call an emotional disorder.

Borkovec, Weerts, and Bernstein (1977) suggest several questions to ask when planning an assessment. First, what are the specific stimuli or classes of stimuli that elicit the anxiety response? Second, what are the specific responses made that comprise the problem behavior? Third, does the anxiety response occur in anticipation of the eliciting stimulus? If so, what are the conditions needed for an anticipatory anxiety response? Fourth, is the child's anxiety response appropriate or inappropriate? Finally, what are the current and probable long-term effects of the anxiety response and the associated behaviors for the child?

### Checklists and Observation Scales

Most self-report measures are checklists or rating scales. Students either put a check beside the items that apply to themselves or rate the intensity of their response to the items. In rating scales, a bipolar scale with three to five intensity levels is typical. The scale may use numeric indicators of intensity, e.g., 1 is very low and 5 is very high. It may label levels of intensity with descriptive words or phrases such as *not at all, somewhat,* and *extremely.* Sometimes a combination of numerals and labels are used. Rating scales may focus on specific fears, e.g., answering in class or teasing. Figure 7–3 illustrates a self-report measure for adolescents that uses specific fears. Or, the rating scale may focus on specific symptoms associated with anxiety problems, e.g., dizziness or shaking. Figure 7–4 is an example of a self-report measure for children that uses symptoms. Both of these scales use labeled levels of intensity rather than numeric ratings of intensity.

One problem with using self-report measures is that young children may not have sufficient reading or language skills to read the items or understand the intensity scale used. You can handle a lack of adequate reading skill by reading the items and asking for oral responses. For children who may not understand the intensity scale, Kelly (1976) suggests using colors or pictures of faces

---

## ASSESSMENT OF FEARS

### FEAR INVENTORY (A)

Name _____ Date _____

Age _____ Sex _____

School (if in school) _____ Grade _____

Occupation (if employed) _____

The items in this questionnaire refer to things and experiences that may cause fear. Read each item. Then decide which of the following sentences is most true:

I'm not afraid of   (for example, being alone)   at all.

I'm slightly afraid of _____ .

I'm terribly afraid of _____ .

Put a check mark in the column that best describes how you feel about that item. At the end there is a question for you to answer on your own. Write as much as you want.

| | Not afraid at all | Slightly afraid | Terribly afraid |
|---|---|---|---|
| 1. Being alone | | | |
| 2. Being in a strange (new) place | | | |
| 3. Being in an accident | | | |
| 4. Being teased by others | | | |
| 5. Going to the dentist | | | |
| 6. Answering in class | | | |
| 7. Failing in school | | | |
| 8. Entering a room where other people are already seated | | | |
| 9. Being in high places | | | |
| 10. Seeing people who are handicapped | | | |
| 11. Seeing harmless snakes | | | |
| 12. Having nightmares | | | |
| 13. Getting an injection from a doctor or nurse | | | |
| 14. Being around strangers | | | |

---

**Figure 7–3** An illustration of part of a self-report measure for use with adolescents, which addresses specific fears. *Reprinted with permission from J. R. Cautela, J. Cautela, & S. Esonis, 1983, Forms for Behavior Analysis with Children. Champaign, Il: Research Press.*

to indicate intensity. Another problem with self-report measures is that they don't have good reliability and validity. If possible, you should only use them for initial screening. You may, however, have to use them in treatment when the procedure is imaginal. In imaginal treatments, it isn't possible to get an overt behavioral response to the actual anxiety stimulus. Here, you must use caution in interpreting the assessment data because of reliability and validity problems associated with self-report measures.

---

### ASSESSMENT OF SYMPTOMS

**BODILY CUES FOR TENSION AND ANXIETY (C)**

Name _____ Date _____

Age _____ Sex: Boy _____ Girl _____

School _____ Grade _____

When you are scared of something or worried about something, you feel bad. But everyone is not the same—when some kids are worried, their stomachs feel sick; when other kids are worried, their hands shake. How does each part of *your* body feel when you are scared or worried? Put an X in the box that tells best how each part feels.

|  | Not at all | A little | Very much |
|---|---|---|---|
| 1. My head feels light. | | | |
| 2. My head aches. | | | |
| 3. My head feels tight. | | | |
| 4. My head feels heavy. | | | |
| 5. My eyes squeeze shut. | | | |
| 6. My forehead gets wrinkled. | | | |
| 7. My mouth feels dry. | | | |
| 8. I hold my shoulders stiffly. | | | |
| 9. My mouth shuts very tightly. | | | |
| 10. I can't breathe. | | | |
| 11. I feel dizzy. | | | |
| 12. I breathe fast. | | | |
| 13. My arms get stiff. | | | |
| 14. My hands shake. | | | |

**Figure 7–4**  An illustration of part of a self-report for use with children, which addresses symptoms often associated with anxiety. *Reprinted with permission from J. R. Cautela, J. Cautela, & S. Esonis, 1978, Forms for Behavior Analysis with Children. Champaign, IL: Research Press.*

### Observation Scales

These scales are similar to self-report measures. The major difference is that they obtain data from an informant rather than from a student. The informant completes the scale on a student based on his or her past experience with the student. An improvement on this approach is to use an observer who completes the scale on the student using observations of current behavior. Although this approach also has limitations (Kent & Foster, 1977), it will yield better data than self-report measures.

### Observational Recording

You obtain the best data by observing and recording overt behavior. This approach has the additional advantage of individualizing assessment for the problem behavior. We will not go into great detail about observational recording. You should review the material in Chapter 4 on observational recording if you need additional information. The first thing you do is select for observation a behavior directly related to the anxiety problem. One of the most commonly used behaviors for assessing anxiety problems is approach behavior. You measure approach behavior by the distance between the student and the anxiety stimulus. You also need to consider how long a student can maintain an approach distance. Various symptomatic behaviors associated with an anxiety problem are also used for observational recording. For example, a student suffers from dysfunctional public-speaking anxiety with speech dysfluencies. Here, you can use the student's speech as the assessment behavior. After you select an appropriate behavior for assessment, you must define the behavior operationally. Next, you must decide what recording procedure to use for the behavior. With approach behavior, you need to record two dimensions of a student's behavior. First, you need to record the distance, in feet, of the approach response. This assumes that you are using free approach rather than controlled approach for responding. In the former case the student is free to end the approach response at will. In the latter case you ask the student to move to a specified approach distance. Second, you need to use latency recording, in minutes and seconds, to measure how long the student can maintain the approach distance without anxiety.

If you use controlled approach, you need a record of latency on each trial at each specified approach distance. To avoid extending the length of trials beyond a useful duration, you need to set a time criterion for ending a trial. Let's assume that you have determined there is no reason to extend a trial beyond 10 minutes. That is, if the student can maintain the approach distance for 10 minutes, it can be maintained indefinitely. For example, you ask a student to move to a predetermined approach distance and it's maintained for 10 minutes. You have reached your time criterion and would end the trial. When your consistency criterion for this distance is attained, you are ready to move to the next approach distance. With a behavior such as dysfluent speech, you would need to use event recording. You could give the student a script of fixed length and record the number of dysfluencies during recitation. If part of the student's speech problem is hesitations, you might also record the number of words spoken per minute and the number of dysfluencies.

You also need to decide whether to assess under natural conditions or to use controlled presentations. Controlled presentations are commonly used in this type of assessment. They are frequently used because the natural environment may not provide sufficient assessment opportunities. There may also be too many confounding variables in the natural environment. With controlled presentations you set up and control the conditions under which you do the assessment. This allows you to chose the times for assessment. It also helps you control confounding variables that might interfere with the assessment. If feasible, you can establish reliability for your assessment procedure by having two observers record the behavior. You then compare the records of the two observers to determine how closely they agree. You will find a more detailed discussion of how this is done in any good textbook on behavior modification (Alberto & Troutman, 1986). You can evaluate the validity of your assessment procedure by having your assessment behavior and operational definition appraised by others who are familiar with the student's problem.

You should collect assessment data before treatment is begun to establish a baseline. You should also collect data during treatment. You use the treatment data to monitor the effect of the treatment. You can also compare the baseline and treatment data to evaluate the treatment. The data collected should be visually displayed and continuously updated during assessment on a graph. Figure 7–5 is an example of graphed data.

**Figure 7–5**   A graph representing the number of speech dysfluencies in a student's verbalization of a series of 200 word presentations.

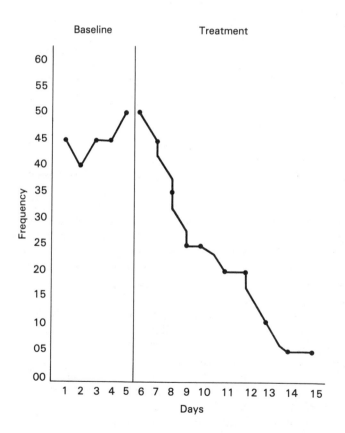

## INTERVENTION

Earlier we discussed suggestions by Hatzenbuelhler and Schroeder (1978) for selecting an appropriate intervention technique. You will recall that their suggestions depended on the severity of a child's problem. They suggested that if a child has a severe disorder, you should not use a technique that requires direct participation with the anxiety-eliciting stimulus. They defined a severe problem as one in which the child will not have any voluntary involvement with the anxiety stimulus. The suggestion for mild to moderate disorders was to use a technique that requires direct involvement with the anxiety stimulus. You can modify most of the techniques discussed below so that they are appropriate for either severity level. When direct involvement is required, we will say that the technique is done in vivo. When there is no direct involvement, we will say that the technique is done imaginally.

Another consideration in selecting a technique is the ethicalness of the procedure. Some techniques are ethically questionable when used with children. You should avoid any technique potentially dangerous to a child. Two techniques particularly inappropriate for children are *flooding and implosion therapy*. Both techniques are classified as forced extinction procedures. They require maximizing anxiety under conditions where avoidance or escape are not possible. These techniques are too threatening to use with children. You should also consider the effectiveness and efficiency of a technique before selecting it.

### Respondent Extinction

Recall from our earlier discussion of respondent principles that a CS- acquires its potency by association with some US- or another CS-. Repeatedly present the CS- without the original US- or potent CS-, and it gradually loses its ability to elicit a CEr-. Respondent extinction uses this phenomenon. You present the CS- repeatedly without the original eliciting stimulus until it loses it potency, assuming, of course, that there is no operant overlap to complicate the situation. Respondent extinction probably occurs to everyone at some time under natural conditions. When used as a planned intervention, it is done systematically and progressively and is called *graduated extinction*.

Graduated extinction is usually done in vivo with the CS- attenuated, i.e., reduced in potency. You can attenuate the CS- by adjusting the proximity of the CS- to the child or by removing various stimuli associated with the CS-. For example, let's suppose that you were going to work with a child who had serious anxiety associated with public speaking, e.g., speaking before a class. You would set up a graduated set of stimulus conditions similar to those in Box 7–1. As you can see, the graduated set of stimulus conditions reduces the potency of the CS- by removing stimulus features. The sequence begins with an empty classroom and gradually progresses to a normal classroom condition.

The first step in the graduated sequence is a set of conditions that the child can tolerate with only minor discomfort. You ask the child to speak under that condition until comfortable with it. You need to set a criterion for telling

**Box 7–1**   An illustration of a graduation of stimulus conditions that might be used for *in vivo* extinction of public-speaking anxiety[a]

---

**GRADUATED EXTINCTION CONDITIONS**

1. Speaking in an empty classroom with the teacher present but shielded from view

2. Speaking in an empty classroom with the teacher present

3. Speaking in a classroom with the teacher and a close friend present

4. Speaking in a classroom with the teacher and several (3–5) friends present

5. Speaking in a classroom with the teacher and a small (8–11) group of students, including both friends and other peers, present

6. Speaking under normal classroom conditions

---

[a]The CS- has been attenuated by modifying the characteristics associated with the CS-.

when to end each condition and move on to the next. For example, you might set the criterion as at least three consecutive sessions of 10 minutes each with no anxiety evident or reported by the child. When you reach the criterion under the first condition, you move to the second condition until you reach the criterion again. The process continues in this fashion until you reach the criterion under the last stimulus condition.

Earlier in our discussion of assessment, we mentioned using both observational and self-report measures of anxiety. In a case like the one just described, you might want to use both types of assessment. You would operationally define anxiety with observable behaviors such as speech dysfluencies for an observational measure. You would also combine this with a self-report measure, using a rating scale, to measure the level of experienced anxiety. The latter measure would be useful for avoiding too quick a shift to the next most potent level of the CS-. In other words, the child may still experience some residual anxiety even after the observable signs are no longer present.

When you use graduated extinction with a child, be sure you do three things. First, you must be patient. Be certain you allow enough exposure under each condition before going on to the next condition. It is better to err by giving more exposure than needed than to err by not giving enough exposure to extinguish the anxiety. Second, you need to be supportive. At each step, provide the child with positive feedback about progress toward the treatment goal. Finally, be alert for possible problems. If the child exhibits too much anxiety or has difficulty in making the transition from one step to the next, reconsider the sequence. You may need a finer gradation of conditions than you have or you may need to revise your criterion for changing conditions.

A variation on graduated extinction combines it with participant modeling. In this procedure, you proceed in much the same manner as described above. However, each session begins with a modeling presentation of a child comfortably engaging the anxiety stimulus under the conditions in the current step in the graduated sequence. After the child observes the model, you ask the child to imitate the model's behavior. Modeling can be either live or symbolic, e.g., on videotape. If you use this approach, follow the guidelines in Chapter 5 for selecting models and for conducting modeling procedures. You should use the modeling approach with children who have more serious problems. Keep the child in the modeling condition at each step in the graduated sequence until there is no anxiety observed or reported while watching the model. When you achieve this objective, the participant component is begun. The child again observes the first step modeled and you ask the child to imitate the model. When there is no anxiety observed or reported during imitation in the first step, you begin the next step in the graduated sequence. For children with severe problems, you should use symbolic modeling first. This will not be as threatening as live modeling. Next, you would go to live modeling and then to the participation component.

### Counterconditioning

Earlier we said that respondent learning involved learning to make an existing response to a new stimulus. This is the basis for counterconditioning. In counterconditioning, you help the child exhibit an anxiety antagonistic response, e.g., relaxation. You then introduce the CS- to the child while the anxiety antagonistic response is present. Over several trials, you establish the anxiety antagonistic response as the response associated with the CS-. Of course, when that takes place the CS- has changed into a CS+. Thus, you have counterconditioned the stimulus by changing it from a negative stimulus associated with an anxiety response to a positive stimulus associated with an anxiety antagonistic response.

There are two ways of producing anxiety antagonistic responses. First, you can chose an existing response that is immediately available, e.g, eating. Here, all you have to do to produce the response is to present stimuli that elicit it. The eliciting stimuli for eating would be well-liked foods that you can present in quantities easy to administer, e.g., small candies. Second, you can chose a response that you must teach before it is used, e.g., relaxation. Here, you will want to teach the child a relaxation technique easy to use under a variety of conditions. Certain cues for relaxation are taught that can quickly elicit the relaxation response, e.g., rhythmic breathing to a numerical count.

There are several types of anxiety antagonistic responses. First, one of the earliest reported anxiety antagonistic responses was of a child eating an appetizing food while exposed to a CS- (Jones, 1924). Second, the most commonly used response is relaxation. Bergland and Chal (1972) used relaxation to treat a behavior problem in a junior high school student. In their procedure, they taught deep muscle relaxation to a student as an anxiety antagonistic response. The child learned to elicit the relaxation response whenever the presence of the anxiety stimulus was anticipated. Third, Lazarus and Abramovitz (1962) used "emotive imagery" as an anxiety antagonistic response. In their procedure, the child imagined scenes with positive images of heroes or imaginal acts involving him or herself with strong positive affect associated with them. The child used emotive imagery as an alternative to relaxation during counterconditioning. Fourth, Gershman and Stedman (1971) used directed muscular activity as an anxiety antagonistic response. In their procedure, they used Oriental self-defense exercises as an alternative to relaxation during counterconditioning. However, any directed muscular activity would probably work. Finally, Smith (1973) reports using humor as an antagonistic response to anger in a counter-conditioning treatment.

Systematic desensitization (Wolpe, 1973) is the most common counter-conditioning procedure for both adults and children. This procedure is done either *in vivo* or imaginally. Your first step in this procedure, in either case, is to develop a desensitization hierarchy. This hierarchy is a series of graduated steps where each step is a closer approximation to the stimulus conditions elicit-ing the CEr-.

You can develop the steps for a sequence in two ways. First, you can use avoidance to construct the approximations. As you may recall, one of the respon-ses associated with a CS- is avoidance. Thus, you can construct the approxima-tions by having each step in the sequence reflect progressively less avoidance. This is easiest to do when proximity to the CS- is determined by either distance or time, e.g., school phobia or test anxiety (see Box 7–2). Second, when the CS- is a complex stimulus, you can use complexity to construct the hierarchy. Most CS-'s are complex stimuli with several components. Thus, you can construct the approximations by having each step in the sequence reflect progressively more complete approximations to the full CS-. You do this by beginning with only one or a few of the stimuli making up the complex stimulus functioning as a CS-. You then add additional stimuli from the CS- complex at each new step until you have a complete representation of the CS-. This is easiest to do when proximity to the stimulus is determined not by time or distance but by situa-tional stimuli, e.g., public-speaking anxiety (see Box 7–1).

**Box 7–2**  An illustration of a desensitization hierarchy that might be used in either imaginal or *in vivo* desensitization of test anxiety[a]

---

**DESENSITIZATION HIERARCHY**

  1. Reviewing for a test scheduled to be given in a week

  2. Reviewing for a test scheduled to be given in three days

  3. Reviewing for a test scheduled to be given in one day

  4. Sitting in one's homeroom prior to the period in which the test is scheduled

  5. Sitting in the class in which the test is scheduled prior to it beginning

  6. Receiving the test paper

  7. Beginning work on the test items

  8. Encountering a difficult item

---

[a]The CS- has been attenuated by modifying the time separating the student from the most potent anxiety condition.

Systematic desensitization is done either imaginally or *in vivo*. Sometimes both are used sequentially beginning with imaginal and moving to *in vivo*. When the procedure is done imaginally, your first step is to construct an anxiety hierarchy. Second, you select an anxiety antagonistic response, e.g., relaxation. Third, when necessary, you teach the response selected and rehearse it. Relaxation is one of the possible choices that would require training where eating would not. Fourth, you must develop a set of verbal cues that correspond to the steps in the hierarchy. You deliver the cues for any given step to the child either orally or on audiotape. Fifth, you set a criterion for moving from one step to the next. For example, the criterion might be three consecutive sessions with no observed or reported anxiety. Sixth, you must select techniques for assessing anxiety during the sessions. As we discussed earlier, these can be observational, self-report, or both. You should probably use a combination in most cases.

The easiest way to use self-report is to teach a child to use the following scale.

a. 0 is no anxiety.

b. 1 is low anxiety (a tolerable level).

c. 2 is moderate anxiety (a stressful level).

d. 3 is high anxiety (an intolerable level).

During desensitization tell the child to lay his or her hand flat with fingers extended. The flat-hand position is zero on the scale. Tell the child that if his or her anxiety increases, to raise the appropriate number of fingers for the level of anxiety experienced. You also observe the child during the sessions for overt signs of anxiety according to the operational definition. Having accomplished all these planning and preparation steps, you are ready to begin the intervention.

You do the *in vivo* desensitization procedure in almost the identical fashion as described above. The major exception is that the verbal cues for the steps in the hierarchy will not be necessary. These aren't necessary because the actual stimuli for each step will be present. The *in vivo* procedure is your first choice if a child's problem is mild to moderate in severity. If the problem is severe, your first choice is the imaginal procedure. The imaginal procedure is followed by the *in vivo* procedure if necessary. Sometimes it may not be practical to use the *in vivo* procedure even though it is otherwise appropriate. If this is the situation, use the imaginal procedure.

A few further comments on measurement are in order. When using an observational measure, you should establish a specific criterion for what is a stressful level of anxiety. You would measure the elapsed time between presentation of the anxiety stimulus and the first indication of a stressful level of anxiety. When you reach your criterion, the session ends and your measure for the session is the elapsed time recorded. You should also have a preset session length for the sessions. This should be the shortest time you believe necessary for eliciting anxiety. You should also follow a similar procedure for measurement of elapsed time with the self-report measure.

The simplest approach to evaluation of respondent interventions is to use an evaluation design called the clinical teaching or A-B design (see Chapter 4). This design begins with a baseline taken under the conditions eliciting the anxiety response and before treatment has begun. The treatment phases in the design correspond to the steps in the anxiety hierarchy. You enter a new phase in the design each time you meet your criterion for shifting from one step in the hierarchy to the next step. The data collected are recorded on a graph so that you can monitor the intervention as you conduct it (see Figure 7–6). The last step in the hierarchy should be the same set of conditions under which you took the baseline. For evaluation you contrast the level of the target behavior in baseline against its level in each phase of treatment. The most critical contrast is between baseline and the last phase of treatment.

One final point that needs discussion is the possibility of operant overlap. As we discussed earlier, the avoidance behavior associated with a problem is often negatively reinforced and strengthened by anxiety reduction. The ex-

**Figure 7–6**    An illustration of the clinical teaching design used with a respondent-learning-based treatment. Duration of exposure to an anxiety condition, while remaining relaxed, is measured in minutes. Each phase (P) in the treatment represents successive steps in the anxiety hierarchy. The baseline and P3 would represent data collected under the same stimulus conditions.

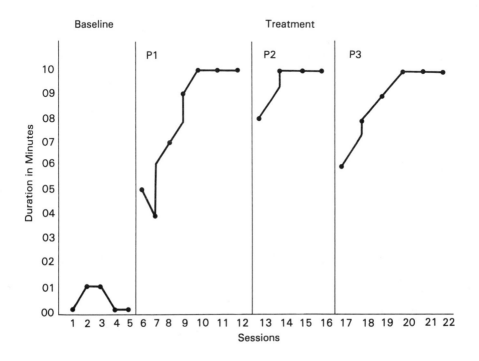

tinction or desensitization procedure will usually take care of this problem unless the avoidance is so powerful that you cannot conduct the procedure. If this is the case, specialized techniques using tranquilizers are employed. These techniques must be done by or with medical personnel because drugs are utilized. Another possibility with operant overlap is positive reinforcement. This may occur through sympathetic responses to the child by significant adults. It may also occur as a result of appetitive stimuli associated with the avoidance behavior. For example, in school phobia the child may not only avoid the CS- (school) but have access to various reinforcers such as TV, toys, etc. at home. If the child is older and is out in the community when avoiding school, the list of possible reinforcers is almost endless. In situations where positive reinforcers are maintaining the avoidance behavior, you must identify these reinforcers and ensure that they are not available during the intervention. Removing positive reinforcers will put the operant component of the avoidance response on operant extinction. We discussed this procedure in Chapter 4.

## RESOURCES

There are several good resources available for carrying out respondent procedures. An extensive discussion of behavioral assessment techniques is given in Mash and Terdal (1981). A short discussion of respondent procedures and their use, intended for educators, is given in Algozzine (1982). A more comprehensive discussion of respondent and operant techniques for use in treating children's fears and phobias is given in Morris and Kratochwill (1983). This book covers theoretical issues, assessment, and treatment and is an excellent resource. Finally, Cautela and Groden (1978) discuss in detail teaching the relaxation response to special needs children. Their book covers proper positioning, imitative skills, following instructions, relaxation procedures for arms, hands, and legs, and breathing techniques.

## REFERENCES

ALBERTO, P., & TROUTMAN, A. (1986). *Applied behavior analysis for teachers* (2nd ed.). Columbus, OH: Merrill.

ALGOZZINE, B. (1982). *Problem behavior management.* Rockville, MD: Aspen.

BARLOW, D., & WOLF, B. (1981). Behavioral approaches to anxiety disorders: A report on the NIMH-SUNY, Albany, Research Conference. *Journal of Consulting and Clinical Psychology, 49,* 448–454.

BERGLAND, B., & CHAL, A. (1972). Relaxation training and a junior high behavior problem. *The School Counselor, 19,* 288–293.

BORKOVEC, T., WEERTS, T., & BERNSTEIN, D. (1977). Assessment of anxiety. In A. Ciminero, K. Calhoun, & H. Adams (Eds.), *Handbook of behavioral assessment.* New York: Wiley.

BOWER, G., & HILGARD, E. (1981). *Theories of learning.* Englewood Cliffs, NJ: Prentice-Hall.

CAUTELA, J. R., CAUTELA, J., & ESONIS, S. (1983). *Forms for behavior analysis with children.* Champaign, IL: Research Press.

CAUTELA, J., & GRODEN, J. (1978). *Relaxation: A comprehensive manual for adults, children and children with special needs.* Champaign, IL: Research Press.

GELFAND, D. (1978). Social withdrawal and negative emotional states: Behavior therapy. In B. Wolman, J. Egan, & A. Ross (Eds.), *Handbook of treatment of mental disorders in childhood and adolescence.* Englewood Cliffs, NJ: Prentice-Hall.

GERSHMAN, L., & STEDMAN, J. (1971). Oriental defense exercises as reciprocal inhibitors of anxiety. *Journal of Behavior Therapy and Experimental Psychiatry, 2,* 117.

GRAZIANO, A., DEGIOVANNI, I., & GARCIA, K. (1979). Behavioral treatment of children's fears: A review. *Psychological Bulletin, 86,* 804–830.

HATZENBUEHLER, L., & SCHROEDER, H. (1978). Desensitization procedures in the treatment of childhood disorders. *Psychological Bulletin, 85,* 831–844.

JONES, M. (1924). A laboratory study of fear: The case of Peter. *Journal of Genetic Psychology, 31,* 308–315.

KELLY, C. (1976). Play desensitization of fear of darkness in preschool children. *Behavioral Research and Therapy, 14,* 79–81.

KENT, R., & FOSTER, S. (1977). Direct observational procedures: Methodological issues in naturalistic settings. In A. Ciminero, K. Calhoun, & H. Adams (Eds.), *Handbook of behavioral assessment.* New York: Wiley.

LAZARUS, A., & ABRAMOVITZ, A. (1962). The use of "emotional imagery" in the treatment of children's phobias. *Journal of Mental Science, 108,* 191–195.

MACFARLANE, J., ALLEN, L., & HONZIK, P. (1954). *A developmental study of the behavior problems of normal children between twenty-one months and fourteen years.* Berkeley, CA: University of California Press.

MASH, E., & TERDAL, L. (Eds.). (1981). *Behavioral assessment of childhood disorders.* New York: Guilford Press.

MATHEWS, A., GELDER, M., & JOHNSTON, D. (1981). *Agoraphobia: Nature and treatment.* New York: Guilford Press.

MISCHEL, W. (1968). *Personality assessment.* New York: Wiley.

MORRIS, R., & KRATOCHWILL, T. (1983). *Treating children's fears and phobias: A behavioral approach.* Elmsford, NY: Pergamon Press.

PAUL, G. (1969). Outcome of systematic desensitization: II. Controlled investigations of individual treatment, technique variations, and current status. In C. Franks (Ed.), *Behavior therapy: Appraisal and status.* New York: McGraw-Hill.

PAVLOV, I. (1927). *Conditioned reflexes.* (G. Anrep, Trans.). London: Oxford University Press.

RACHMAN, S. (1968). *Phobias: Their nature and control.* Springfield, IL: Charles C Thomas.

SMITH, R. (1973). The use of humor in the counterconditioning of anger responses: A case study. *Behavior Therapy, 4,* 576–580.

WATSON, J., & RAYNER, R. (1920). Conditioned emotional reactions. *Journal of Experimental Psychology, 3,* 1–14.

WILSON, G. (1984). Fear reduction methods and the treatment of anxiety disorders. In C. Franks, G. Wilson, P. Kendall, & K. Brownell (Eds.), *Annual review of behavior therapy* (Vol. 10). New York: Guilford Press.

WOLPE, J. (1958). *Psychotherapy by reciprocal inhibition.* Stanford, CA: Stanford University Press.

WOLPE, J. (1973). *The practice of behavior therapy* (2nd ed.). Elmsford, NY: Pergamon Press.

# 8

# REDUCING
# INAPPROPRIATE
# EMOTIONAL BEHAVIOR

## A Cognitive Approach

## INTRODUCTION

There are a number of cognitive approaches available for intervention into emotional problems (Berne, 1964; Freed, 1971; Freud, 1975; Chadbourn & L'Abate, 1975; Redl & Wineman, 1952). These as well as other approaches have their supporters. All could be adapted for use in a special education program serving students with emotional problems. However, we will focus our attention in this chapter on the work of Ellis (1962, 1971, 1974, 1977). Ellis's approach is known as Rational-Emotive Therapy (RET). One component of RET is Rational-Emotive Education (REE). The REE component in RET makes it attractive for special education programming. RET and REE have also been extensively applied to the problems of children and youth. Finally, there is an extensive body of literature and materials available to support programs using this approach.

### Rational-Emotive Theory

Ellis's (1962, 1971, 1974, 1977) theory rests largely on two assumptions. First, we humans have a biological predisposition toward irrational thinking, e.g., overgeneralization and illogical association. The human nervous system, by design, appears prone to errors in thinking (Wessler, 1977). Some of us are more affected by these biological tendencies than others. That is, there is individual variability in this as in other biological traits. Second, one of the major tasks of socialization is to establish a system of beliefs. Our belief system helps us interpret our experiences and observations. It also helps us organize our thoughts and our actions. Our tendency to think irrationally results in distortions, flaws, and inaccuracies in our belief system. Not only are belief systems distorted by *our* faulty thinking but by that of others as well. Parents, peers, community institutions (e.g., schools, churches, Scouts, political parties, etc.), and the media all try to teach children. Distortions are possible from any of these sources.

Ellis suggests that any theory of human behavior and behavior change must take values into consideration. Our behavior must be judged in terms of its appropriateness for achieving our goals. Our goals are a reflection of our values. The question of what is a good value is not a question of fact but of belief. Ellis assumes that we all value and therefore have as basic goals survival, happiness (satisfaction with life), acceptance, and relationship. Thus, RET judges the rationality or irrationality of our behavior by its appropriateness for achieving these basic goals.

Given a behavior with its associated affect, we must ask whether it is functional or dysfunctional for meeting one or more of the basic human goals. If the behavior is dysfunctional, it is a product of irrational thinking. RET uses a three-term model for the analysis of behavior. The analysis begins with (C), which is the behavior under examination. That is, behavior is a consequence of some prior activating event. For example, Bill becomes depressed and gives up in his math class. This is the (C) or the behavior. The analysis next looks for the activating event (A) that precipitated this response. Assume that the activating event was failing a unit test in math. Is the test failure the cause of Bill's depression and decision to give up trying? RET would say no! Getting depressed and giving up is an irrational behavior because it doesn't contribute to meeting one of the four basic goals. If the behavior is irrational, it must be due to faulty thinking. The analysis now asks, how did Bill construe the test failure? What does he believe (B) about it? Suppose that Bill believes that failing the test proves he is stupid and doomed to be a failure. He believes that to be a success he must not fail at anything. Thus, Bill's behavior (C) is not the consequence of failing the test (A) but of his beliefs (B) about the meaning of the event (A).

Bill's problem is a negative self-evaluation (stupid) based on an absolute belief (must not fail) that allows no compromise. This belief causes a dysfunctional emotion (depression) and a dysfunctional response (giving up) which interfere with goal attainment (happiness). RET takes the position that the best approach to dealing with problems like Bill's is to teach the logico-empirical method of science. Scientific method is the major tool available to us to combat our inherent, irrational tendencies. RET advocates persuasion and teaching as the most effective therapeutic techniques. Instruction is done while confronting a specific problem or by a broader educational process. A teacher (therapist) challenges, questions, and disputes (D) the irrational beliefs of a student (client) and teaches the student to recognize irrational thinking and to self-dispute. RET is a direct, active, present oriented, and educational approach to behavior change.

### Research Support

Ellis (1979) did an extensive review of the research literature on RET. This review examined 32 different clinical and personality hypotheses from RET. From this review, Ellis concluded "...that a vast amount of research data exists most of which tends to confirm the major clinical and theoretical hypotheses of RET" (p. 134). DiGiuseppe and Kassinove (1976) investigated the effects of an REE program on the emotional adjustment of elementary-age students. They concluded that elementary-age students can learn REE principles. They also found significant improvement in measures of emotional adjustment for the REE students, in contrast to alternative and no-treatment groups. The students came from fourth- and eighth-grade classes. Contrary to their expectations, the younger students showed more effect than the older students.

Other studies have, however, obtained good results with older students. Maultsby (1974) and Maultsby, Knipping, and Carpenter (1974) reported on a program for emotionally disturbed high school students. The program taught students how to use RET principles in analyzing their problems and solving conflicts. In contrast to a control group, the experimental group showed significant improvement on several measures of emotional adjustment. Block (1978) studied the effect of REE on underachieving, disruptive high school students. The students were blacks and Hispanics from lower socioeconomic backgrounds. The REE group was contrasted with alternative and no-treatment control groups. The REE group showed a significant increase in grade point average. The REE group also had a significant decrease in disruptive behavior and class cutting. The investigators attributed the success of REE, in part, to its active, directive, and structured procedures.

Bernard and Joyce (1984) reported on an extensive review of the research literature on RET and REE with children and adolescents. They drew several conclusions from their review. First, children of all ages can learn the principles of RET. Second, RET can help children with emotional problems. Third, RET can reduce emotional problems, prevent emotional problems, and aid emotional adjustment. Fourth, results are better in programs using multiple methods for teaching the principles of RET and their application. Fifth, little is known about the interactive effects of such variables as sex, age, race, and IQ on the efficacy of RET. Sixth, large changes on measures of personality are not usually found. Finally, Bernard and Joyce conclude that the full utility of RET with children and youth remains to be demonstrated.

## ASSESSMENT

In a discussion of RET assessment, Bernard and Joyce (1984) state that the primary focus of RET assessment is on psychological problems. Psychological problems are dysfunctional emotional reactions, e.g., anxiety, depression, or anger. To qualify as a problem, these emotional reactions must be accompanied by maladaptive behavior, e.g., avoidance, withdrawal, or aggression. The frequency, intensity, or duration of a behavior is important for judging if the response is maladaptive. Four general approaches to assessment are discussed.

### Interview

The interview can be formal and focused on a particular problem or an informal continuing process. In either case the teacher should attempt to determine the thoughts, feelings, and behavior present in problem situations. In particular, the teacher should listen for statements suggesting cognitive distortions of reality. Mahoney (1974) suggested four attentional problems that distort reality.

1. *Selective inattention*: ignoring relevant stimuli

2. *Misperception*: inaccurate labeling of stimuli

3. *Maladaptive focusing*: attending to irrelevant or inappropriate stimuli

4. *Maladaptive self-arousal*: generating irrelevant or negative, cognitive stimuli

Beck, Rush, Shaw, and Emery (1979) discussed six systematic errors in thinking that distort reality.

1. *Arbitrary inference*: drawing conclusions without evidence or in spite of contrary evidence

2. *Selective abstraction*: focusing on a detail taken out of context and construing the situation through this fragment

3. *Overgeneralization*: forming a general rule from an isolated observation or experience and applying it widely

4. *Magnification and minimization*: errors in evaluating the significance of an event

5. *Personalization*: relating external events to oneself when they are unconnected

6. *Dichotomous thinking*: black-and-white thinking, i.e., categorizing all experience into one of two opposite categories (male or female)

Here are three more errors in thinking that distort reality.

1. *Rigid thinking:* the inability to formulate alternatives

2. *Aconsequential thinking*: a failure to think through the consequences of behavior before acting

3. *False attribution*: assigning false causes to events

When interviewing or monitoring student talk, listen for statements that suggest irrational beliefs. There are four types: *should, awful, need,* and *worth* statements. Should statements suggest a belief certain things must be. Awful statements suggest a belief certain things are terrible and unbearable. Need statements suggest that certain things are an absolute necessity rather than merely wanted or desired. Finally, worth statements suggest a belief that the intrinsic value of persons can be judged.

The interview process is a good way to collect data on students in the classroom. You should recognize that the data collected will be subjective. How good the data are depends on your interviewing skills and deductive powers. The ability of students to discriminate feelings from one another and to self-analyze cognition also affect the quality of data collected by interview.

### Self-Monitoring

In self-monitoring you make use of self-report measures to obtain information from students. Self-report measures try to get information about beliefs and feelings in problem situations. Several self-report measures are available for use with children. Knaus (1974) developed two forms of a scale called the Children's Survey of Rational Beliefs. One scale is for children ages 7 to 10 and the other for children ages 10 to 13 (see Box 8-1). Shorkey and Whiteman (1977) developed a scale called the Rational Behavior Inventory, which has been used with children as young as 9. Plutchik (1976) developed the Self-Inventory using college students. It might be useful with adolescents. All of these scales have limited reliability and validity. You can use these scales in your classroom to aid your understanding of students' thinking. Data from these scales should be interpreted cautiously.

**Box 8-1**   Five sample items from the 10- to 13-year-old version of the Children's Survey of Rational Beliefs

---

*Directions*:   Next to each question there are four possible answers. You are to pick out the answer that you believe is best for you. Write the letter on the answer sheet beside the number of the question.

1.   A person who feels angry toward another person thinks:

   a.   he can't stand the other person's behavior
   b.   the other person has no right to act the way he does
   c.   nobody is perfect and this person is no different
   d.   all the above answers are correct

2.   If a person says it is human to make a mistake and then feels awful when he makes a mistake, he:

   a.   can't help feeling that way
   b.   generally is a liar
   c.   doesn't really believe it is right for him to make a mistake
   d.   will always correct his mistakes

---

**Box 8-1**    (Continued)

---

3. A person who is angry because the world is not perfect can help get rid of this feeling by:

   a. trying to force the world to be the way he wants it
   b. telling himself that it doesn't matter how the world is
   c. questioning why the world must be the way he wants it to be
   d. giving up and pretending not to care

4. If you see a person who is not acting his age, the first thing

   a. try to change him by teasing him out of his behavior
   b. ignore him completely
   c. tell him to grow up and act his age
   d. try to understand that not everybody can act their age

5. When a person hates herself when someone laughs at her:

   a. she thinks she needs the other person to like her so that she can like herself
   b. she has to believe the other person is unfair
   c. her grades will start to drop at school
   d. she will never get over feeling that way

---

SOURCE:    Knaus, 1974.


### Psychometric Tests

The tests available for assessing irrational beliefs are limited in both number and psychometric properties. The Idea Inventory (Kassinove, Crisci, & Tiegerman, 1977) is one RET test that appears promising. You can use this test with students in the fourth through twelfth grades. The test has limited reliability and validity. A set of norms, based on a somewhat limited population, is available. Wasserman (1983) developed the Children's Dysfunctional Cognition Scale, which appears to hold promise. This test has good reliability. It has been shown to discriminate between normal and emotionally disturbed children. The test also correlates well with teacher reported classroom behavior of emotionally disturbed children. Limited norms are available for the test (see Box 8-2). Another test with potential for RET assessment is the Intellectual Responsibility Achievement Questionnaire (Crandall, Kratovsky, & Crandall, 1965). This test has good reliability but limited validity. There are some norms available for it. The IRAQ is a measure of causal attribution or locus of control for children in educational settings. Some emotionally disturbed children are abnormally high in external locus of control (DuCette, Wolk, & Soucar, 1972; Finch & Nelson, 1974). Gorman and Simon (1977) found a possible relation between irrational beliefs and the adjustment vs. anxiety factor on Cattell's Sixteen Factor Personality Inventory. The neuroticism scale on the Junior Eysenck Personality Inventory appears to correlate well with measures of irrational thinking (Kassinove et al., 1977; MacDonald & Games, 1972).

**Box 8-2**    Ten sample items from the Children's Dysfuntional Cognition Scale

1. I will cry or be very sad if I think that my parents or my teachers are unhappy with me.

2. I will cry or be very sad if a boy or girl that I like won't be my friend.

3. My teacher must always like my school work.

4. It is O.K. if my friends say bad things about me. I may not like it but I can handle it.

5. When children do bad things, they must always be punished a lot.

6. If a child does a bad thing, the mother does not have to punish him or her; she can help him or her learn to behave better.

7. Children who cause trouble in the classroom should be thrown out.

8. Children who do not listen to their parents should be punished a lot.

9. Getting very angry at other children helps you get what you want from them.

10. I become very sad and cry when my parents do not give me what I want.

SOURCE:  Wasserman, 1983, "Development of the Children's Dysfunctional Cognition Scale," *Child and Family Behavior Therapy*, *5*, Haworth Press, Binghamton, NY.

### Behavioral

Observational measures using the methods discussed in Chapter 4 can be useful in RET assessment. We mentioned earlier that maladaptive behavior is an important indicator of dysfunctional emotional reactions. You can measure either overt motor behavior or verbal responses. The assessment can be in either a natural setting or an analogue setting. The latter is often used. When this approach is used the student is in a role-play situation about some type of problem or conflict. This approach gives you control over the assessment situation. The use of a naturalistic setting should, however, provide more valid data.

## CURRICULUM

This discussion of curriculum is based, in part, on Bernard (1979), Gerald and Eyman (1981), and Knaus (1974). The curriculum discussed below is not from any one of these sources, nor is it solely a synthesis of them. The organization and some of the content reflects my views on curriculum for a REE program. Rational-emotive education is a preventive and self-help program. It is not therapy in the traditional sense. Students who go through the REE curriculum should, however, be better able to benefit from RET counseling. Thus, the REE curriculum lays a foundation for more direct intervention and treatment of students' problems. We can divide curriculum into three major areas: feeling, thinking, and self-analysis.

## Feeling

You need to educate students about their emotions. It isn't possible to carry on meaningful educational or therapeutic interventions with a student who doesn't understand what is being talked about. The following topics need to be addressed.

*Labels.*    You need to familiarize students with the most frequently talked about emotions. There are several sources that you can use to obtain a list of affective labels. For illustrative purposes, let's use a model developed by Plutchik (1980). You can use whatever list suits your program or develop your own list. Plutchik's model begins with a list of primary emotions. You could use these for a basic program. The primary emotions are combined, like colors, to form a set of primary dyads (see Figure 8-1). You could use this second set to expand your program. The model allows further expansion. If you wish, you can obtain from the model a third and fourth set of emotions. You might use the different sets of emotions from this model for different age groups. For example, the primary emotions might be all that you try to cover with elementary students. You might want to use one or more of the expansion sets in a program with secondary-level students.

*Characteristics*    It is just as important to understand emotions as to label them. Thus, you need to teach the meaning of each emotional term you introduce to your students. You need to establish an agreed-upon meaning for the emotional terms. It is important for you and the students to use terms in the same way and mean the same things by them. Otherwise, there will be miscommunication, which is a major obstacle to effective education or counseling. You can use the "Emotional Dictionary" in Davitz (1969) to develop materials and activities for teaching the meaning of emotional terms. There is not, however, perfect agreement between Davitz and Plutchik in their use of labels. You can find similar or equivalent terms when identical terms have not been used.

*Dimensions.*    After students understand the terminology and meanings needed for emotional communication, you need to teach them that each emotion can vary along several dimensions. First, emotions can vary in frequency. Some emotions are much more common than others. Second, they can vary in intensity. The same emotion can be felt to varying degrees, depending on circumstances. Finally, emotions can vary in duration. The same emotion can persist for different periods of time on different occasions. You should teach students how to measure these dimensions informally when they experience emotions.

*Antecedents.*    After you have taught all the above, teach students what some of the more common antecedents are for different emotions. The antecedents for most emotions are either an interpersonal response or an intrapersonal response. Interpersonal responses are things that others do that elicit

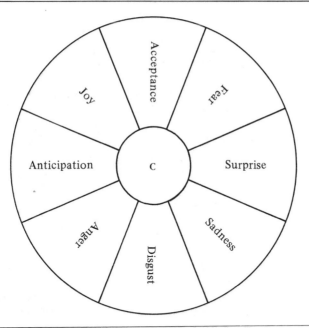

PRIMARY DYADS (*mixture of two adjacent emotions*)
  joy + acceptance = love, friendliness
  acceptance + fear = submission
  fear + surprise = alarm, awe
  surprise + sadness = embarrassment, disappointment
  sadness + disgust = misery, remorse
  disgust + anger = scorn, indignation, contempt, hate, resentment, hostility
  anger + anticipation = aggression, stubbornness
  anticipation + joy = optimism, courage

SECONDARY DYADS (*mixtures of two emotions, once removed*)
  joy + fear = guilt
  acceptance + surprise = curiosity
  fear + sadness = despair
  surprise + disgust = ?
  sadness + anger = envy, sullenness
  disgust + anticipation = cynicism
  anger + joy = pride
  anticipation + acceptance = fatalism

TERTIARY DYADS (*mixtures of two emotions, twice removed*)
  joy + surprise = delight
  acceptance + sadness = resignation, sentimentality
  fear + disgust = shame, prudishness
  surprise + anger = outrage
  sadness + anticipation = pessimism
  disgust + joy = morbidness (?)
  anger + acceptance = dominance (?)
  anticipation + fear = anxiety, caution, dread, cowardliness

**Figure 8-1**    A theoretical representation of the basic emotions and their relative similarity to one another and a list of emotions produced by blending pairs of basic emotions with different degrees of similarity. *From Plutchik, 1980.*

emotional reactions in us. For example, if someone insults you, you usually get angry. Intrapersonal responses are things that we do to ourselves. For example, if you fail to meet some personal goal and label yourself a failure, you will probably get depressed. There are also other events that elicit emotions. For example, an approaching tornado will probably elicit fear. Our emotional responses are usually appropriate and adaptive. That is, they motivate us to make a proper response. We also exhibit emotional responses to events or objects that aren't appropriate or adaptive. These events are often intrapersonal in nature. These inappropriate response are caused by irrational construing of the event or object. For instance, we construe telephones as threatening and experience anxiety whenever we have to use one.

### Thinking

In this curriculum component, students need to learn how to use causal thinking. Learning basic distinctions in the use of words is an important part of causal thinking. Students should also learn about the kinds of errors in thinking that result in irrational thinking. Finally, they need to learn the most common irrational beliefs found in children and youth.

*Causal vs. Magical Thinking.*    One of the most critical thinking skills you need to teach students with emotional problems is causal thinking. By causal thinking we mean the practice of working backward from an effect, in a logical manner, to the event that produced it. The event may be either overt, e.g., an external event such as being cheated by someone, or covert, e.g., a belief or attitude. Causal thinking also requires that logically deduced causes be tested or at least supported by objective evidence. Like many of us, students with emotional problems appear to use magical thinking. By *magical thinking* we mean a belief that things just "happen." We misattribute events to illogical causes or attribute events to causes that appear possible without seeking evidence to support the attribution. Our discussion of errors in thinking and irrational thought is related to this curriculum area. A good introductory text on logic (e.g., Copi, 1986) that covers informal fallacies in thinking can also be useful.

*Fact vs. Opinion.*    You need to teach students to discriminate between fact and opinion. A common problem in irrational thinkers is confusion of opinion with fact. Just because one believes a thing to be true does not make it so. Irrational thinkers often act as if belief were fact. Students with emotional problems should be taught the difference between a fact and an opinion and their relative credibility. You should teach your students that opinions vary in their credibility. An informed opinion, one held by someone with relevant expertise, is more credible than an uninformed opinion. They also need practice discriminating between facts and opinions. Students should learn to use the practice in science of holding all beliefs tentatively even when well supported by factual evidence.

*Want vs. Need.*    You need to teach your students to discriminate between wants and needs. Students with emotional problems often confuse wants with needs. Usually, these students treat all desires as if they were needs. We actually need few things, e.g., air, food, water, clothing, and shelter. Most of the things we seek are wants. We can manage quite well without most of them, e.g, to be liked by someone, to belong to a club, to watch TV, or to have a new bicycle. Irrational thinkers often give their wants the status of needs and then proceed to act as if it were imperative that these "needs" be satisfied. You must teach your students the difference between wants and needs. You should also give them practice in discriminating wants from needs.

Common irrational beliefs in children and youth have been identified by Waters (1982) and are listed below. Many irrational beliefs can be recognized by their use of oversimplification, overgeneralization, perfectionism, absolutism, and uninformed assumptions.

*Common irrational beliefs found in children*

1. It's awful if others don't like me.
2. I'm bad if I make a mistake.
3. Everything should go my way.
4. I should always get what I want.
5. Things should come easy to me.
6. The world should be fair.
7. Bad people must be punished.
8. I shouldn't show my feelings.
9. Adults should be perfect.
10. There's only one right answer.
11. I must win.
12. I shouldn't have to wait for anything.

*Common irrational beliefs found in adolescents*

1. It would be awful if peers didn't like me.
2. It would be awful to be a social loser.
3. I shouldn't make mistakes, especially social mistakes.
4. It's my parents' fault that I'm so miserable.

5. I can't help it, that's just the way I am.

6. I guess I'll always be this way.

7. The world should be fair and just.

8. It's awful when things do not go my way.

9. It's better to avoid challenges than to risk failure.

10. I must conform to my peers.

11. I can't stand to be criticized.

12. Others should always be responsible.

### Self-Analysis

If your students are going to be able to use their new vocabulary and knowledge for self-help, you must teach them how to do self-analysis. When you teach self-analysis, you need to consider the developmental level of your students. A discussion of developmental level follows in the next section of this chapter. There are three aspects of self-analysis that you should teach. First, teach a model for looking at the relationship between thoughts, feelings, and behavior. Second, teach how to challenge irrational beliefs. Third, teach how to restructure irrational self-talk.

*Relationship.*    You should teach your students the ABC model, discussed previously, as an aid to understanding the relationship between thoughts, feelings, and behavior. If self-help is to be effective, it is essential for students to understand that the antecedent event is not the source of their emotional problem and problem behaviors. They must learn that it is their beliefs about the antecedent event causing their emotional upset and problem behaviors.

*Challenge.*    After students understand the RET conceptual model, you should teach them *self-disputation*. The process of self-disputation has two basic steps. First, you must teach students to identify the belief that is causally linked to their problem. Identification of the responsible belief requires an analysis of *self-talk*. Self-talk is the words, phrases, and statements we make to ourselves under various circumstances. Teach students to identify the self-talk that always follows a particular antecedent event. Teach them to examine their self-talk and ask what belief about external events or about self it suggests. Second, you must teach them how to examine the belief to determine if it is rational or irrational. You can teach them that there are two ways to check out the belief. First, examine the belief against the list of commonly held irrational beliefs and see if it is similar to one of those. If so, it is an irrational belief. Second, if it doesn't appear on the list of commonly held irrational beliefs, it should be tested. The basic test of a belief's rationality is whether or not there is objective evidence to support it. If there is evidence to support it, teach them to ask themselves this question: Is this belief functional? In other words, is this belief consistent with basic human values and my goals? If the answer is yes, the belief is probably not the one causing the problem. In this case, students should be taught to reexamine self-talk. If the belief is irrational, it must be countered or changed.

*Restructuring.* The basic approach to countering an irrational belief is restatement of the belief in a rational form. You should teach your students that they can change many irrational beliefs by making them less absolute, that is, modify the belief by adding one or more conditional statements to it. Sometimes it is necessary to find an alternative belief. Alternative beliefs can often be identified by using imagery. Teach students to imagine themselves in a situation where the antecedent event occurs and more positive feelings and behaviors also occur. Or, teach them to imagine themselves in a problem situation where the negative feelings and behavior occur and to make them more positive. Next, teach students to examine the self-talk they used in the imaginal exercise. The beliefs suggested by their self-talk can help them to feel and behave more positively. You must also teach your students to practice using the new belief. Initially, they can practice imaginally, then in role-play simulations, and finally in real situations.

## INTERVENTION

When you plan interventions, it is important that you make use of developmental levels. Since RET is essentially a cognitive technique, you need to consider cognitive development. Bernard and Joyce (1984) and Rossi (1977) discuss the application of Piaget's model of cognitive development to RET. Preoperational children, usually those younger than 7 years old, are egocentric and concrete in their thinking. This means that these children need concrete materials such as pictures and stories. Students in this stage cannot learn to do self-analysis. The best approach to use at this level is instruction on the use of rational self-statements.

Children in the concrete operations stage, those between 7 and 11 years old, can learn concrete concepts and how to use them. Teach concepts in this stage with concrete illustrations in specific situations. The child should be able to relate personally to the situations used. In other words, the situations should be within the child's experience. Children in this stage can learn to do self-analysis. The results of their self-analysis will tend to be limited to specific situations and will not generalize very much. When students are at the formal operations stage (about 12 years old and up) more abstract concepts can be learned and used. Abstract concepts are more general concepts and are similar to broad inclusive beliefs or philosophical assumptions about the world. Youth who have reached this stage of thought can learn to do self-analysis at its deepest or most general level. They can learn effectively to examine their own beliefs, dispute them, develop alternative beliefs, and broadly apply them to various situations in their lives. Rossi (1977) discusses the implications of Piaget for guiding our use of vocabulary with children and our way of responding to them. Finally, Kassinove et al. (1977) studied developmental trends in rational thinking and found that thought becomes progressively more rational with age.

There are four types of intervention based on RET. They are educational, crisis intervention, problem solving, and counseling. When used as an instructional program, REE is the educational intervention. It can also be a component in each of the other three approaches to intervention.

All of the approaches, excluding crisis intervention, are done either individually or in groups. Group instruction is the most likely approach in most educational settings. There are several things to consider in group work. First, you must decide on the type of group you are going to form. This may be an instructional group, a problem-solving group, or a counseling group. You also need to decide, for the latter two groups, if the group will be homogeneous or heterogeneous. Homogeneous groups include only students with the same problem, and heterogeneous groups include students with varied problems. Second, you must decide on a schedule for the group. The following are rules of thumb that you can use when you schedule a group. You may have to make some adjustments after the group is under way, and you have had some experience with the students in it.

1. *Grades 1–3:*      about 15 minutes on a daily basis

2. *Grades 4–6:*      about 30 minutes on a daily basis

3. *Grades 7–9:*      about 45 minutes two or three times per week

4. *Grades 10–12:*    about 60 minutes two or three times per week

A third consideration is motivation. Rossi (1977) discusses what he considers to be the three most important ingredients for maximizing interest and involvement in children. They are enthusiasm, reinforcement, and contact. Enthusiasm is best communicated nonverbally by facial expression, animated gestures, and movement. Reinforcement of student participation with a liberal use of praise is recommended. For resistant students, you can make reinforcement more potent by using token reinforcement along the lines discussed in Chapter 4. Physical contact is very rewarding for most children and will help you get a positive response.

A fourth consideration is how to handle new members that arrive after a group is formed and under way. New members can present a problem. Since this approach is educational in nature, it can be difficult to bring someone into a group in progress. It may be necessary to plan some tutorial sessions to catch a new student up to where he or she can function in your group. You may be able to use peer tutors or a classroom aide to do the tutorial sessions.

Finally, you need a few general guidelines for conducting the group. You should use a seating arrangement that will aid interaction, e.g., circular. You assign seats to minimize disturbance, e.g., separate contentious students. Require students to get permission before speaking. Don't interrupt students to correct their grammar or for using slang or mild profanity. Keep the group process flowing; e.g., don't allow a student to dominate the group. Keep the group focused and on track. That is, have a purpose for the group and stick to it. Don't deviate in any significant way from your schedule once you have worked it out.

### Rational-Emotive Education

As an instructional program, REE has already received a good bit of discussion in the section on curriculum. Thus, our discussion of REE here will be brief. You can do REE using a variety of instructional techniques. Lecture, particularly when accompanied by examples and illustrations, is quite useful. Modeled demonstrations of principles or techniques done by role-play simulations are very concrete and effective. Guided discussions focused on applying principles or techniques presented by lecture or modeling are very useful. You can also do guided discussion following the procedures for discovery learning. In this type of discussion, you would try to help the students deduce a principle or point for themselves using stimulus materials you have presented and guided by questions you propose. Reading assignments can also be used profitably in the instructional program. Reading assignments can be textual presentations of vocabulary, principles, or techniques. Illustrative stories can also be assigned to students as reading assignments. For students who don't have adequate reading skills or for variety, this type of material can also be put on audiotape.

The most critical component of any instructional program is an adequate amount of practice or application of the things taught. Classroom applications may include paper-and-pencil tasks, activities, or games (see Boxes 8-3, 8-4, and 8-5).

**Box 8-3**    An example of paper-and-pencil activity that might be used in a REE classroom program

---

*Directions*:    There are two lists below. List I is a list of emotions and list II is a list of behaviors. Match the list of behaviors to the list of emotions by placing the letter beside a behavior in the blank next to the emotion with which you think it is associated.

| LIST I | LIST II |
|---|---|
| _____ Acceptance (affection) | a. to wait |
| _____ Anger | b. to hit |
| _____ Disgust | c. to cry |
| _____ Joy | d. to spit |
| _____ Fear | e. to tremble |
| _____ Anticipation (hope) | f. to laugh |
| _____ Sadness | g. to startle |
| _____ Surprise | h. to share |

---

**Box 8-4**  An activity that could be used in a REE program to help students practice making discriminations between labeling statements and descriptive statements

---

Read the following statements and sort them out according to *behaviors* (B) and *not behaviors* (N).

1. Greg played the drums for two hours last night. _____

2. Greg's a good drummer. _____

3. Alberta cooked Spanish rice for dinner. _____

4. Alberta is the greatest cook anywhere. _____

5. I ate two helpings of her Spanish rice. _____

6. Paul and Gail went roller skating last night. _____

7. Gail doesn't skate very well. _____

8. She fell three times. _____

9. Abby works till five every day. _____

10. Abby is a very good employee. _____

11. The boss said Abby's a good worker. _____

12. Lenny ran the mile in 5:20. _____

13. Lenny's our star. _____

14. Lenny told me being a star is no big thing. _____

15. Fifteen questions are a lot of questions. _____

---

SOURCE:  Gerald and Eyman, 1981.

**Box 8-5**  An example of a game that might be used in the classroom to reinforce a point made during REE instruction

---

**REINFORCEMENT**

1. *The Huddle Game, a game of assumptive rejection.* A group of eight children are organized to play a bean bag game and only these children are given game instructions:

   a. You will be given an envelope filled with cards which say either *yes* or *no*.
   b. While you play the game, I will send some classmates who will ask to join you. When someone asks to join, go into a huddle but make sure no one other than the team can see what you are doing. Draw a card from the envelope and if it says *yes*, the child can join. If it says *no*, he can't join.
   c. In the next huddle, if there is a new player, tell him the game plan.
      After five or six children have been rejected, ask these children to state what they *assume* are the reasons for their denial. List these responses on the board. Have each student check out his or her assumptions. Then announce that the basis of rejection was pure chance, and have the class help those students who had gotten upset by their irrational assumptions to challenge those beliefs.

---

SOURCE:  Knaus, 1974.

Another important type of application is homework assignments. Learning to make use of the RET model for the analysis of problem situations is one very important focus for homework assignments. Elkin (1983) suggests that younger children do as homework an events diary. Each page of the diary is structured by using four columns. The columns are labeled from left to right: What Happened, What I Thought, What I Felt, and What I Did. Goodman and Maultsby (1978) provide a homework format more appropriate for older students (see Box 8-6).

**Box 8-6**   A sample format for doing rational self-analysis that could be used to structure REE homework assignments for older students

| | |
|---|---|
| **A.**<br><br>State only the basic facts and events involved in the problem to be analyzed.<br><br>Example: "Waited five minutes before salesclerk appeared." | |
| **B.**<br><br>Express the thoughts implied by the feelings identified under (C) below.<br><br>Example: "Customers should not be kept waiting so long." | |
| **C.**<br><br>Identify the kinds of feelings you had during the situation.<br><br>Example: "Irritated." "Angry." "Outraged." "Upset." "Depressed." | |
| **D.**<br><br>Challenge each thought expressed in the (B) section. Develop each challenge fully, based on the five criteria for rational behavior, without regard to length of response or time required.<br><br>Example: "This is a vague demand, stated in a general form, and might not fit a particular situation. Maybe the clerk was on her break; maybe she's so underpaid she moves slowly. It is grandiose of me to expect always to be waited on promptly. Five minutes may seem like a long time, but it's not to the end of the world…" | |

SOURCE:   D. Goodman and M. Maultsby, 1978, *Emotional Well-Being Through Rational Behavior Training.* Courtesy of Charles C Thomas, Publisher, Springfield, IL.

### Crisis Intervention

Crisis intervention is appropriate for children and youth of almost any age. It is the method of choice with very young children, i.e, below 7 years of age. It is the most appropriate approach you can use with very young children because it is situation specific and thus very concrete. It is also highly directive and has rather limited objectives. A model for using RET principles for crisis intervention with emotionally disturbed children is available (Wasserman & Adamany, 1976; Wasserman & Kimmel, 1978). There are three goals for intervention in a crisis situation. Your first goal is immediate removal of the child from the crisis situation. Your second goal is reduction of the child's negative thoughts, affect, and behaviors. Your third goal is to teach the child more appropriate thoughts, feelings, and behaviors. The crisis intervention model uses a four-step process (see Figure 8-2).

1. The first step is to remove the child from the situation and obtain a description of the activating event.

2. The second step is to explore the child's self-talk to determine the beliefs involved and help the child understand their role in his or her problem.

3. The third step is to help the child verbalize more rational thoughts in the form of self-statements. You teach the child to repeat the new self-statements several times and exam how he or she feels. If feeling don't change, ask the child to con-

**Figure 8-2**   A diagram with step-by-step description of the Rational-Emotive Crisis Intervention Treatment Model. *From Wasserman and Kimmel, 1978.*

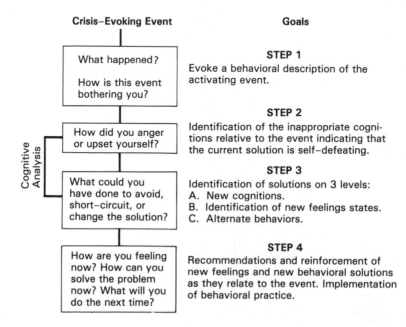

tinue saying the new self-statements until feelings do change. You should give social reinforcement during recitation of the self-statement(s).

4. After the child's feelings change, your emphasis is on discussion and rehearsal of the new behaviors that go with the new feelings. You should socially reinforce practice of the new behavior and if necessary, reinforce it in more concrete ways, e.g., with tokens.

### Problem Solving

Problem solving is used with both children and youth. It is the best approach to use with children under 12 years of age. As you recall from the discussion of developmental levels, children in the concrete operations stage are best able to deal with RET concepts when they are specific and concrete. You should limit RET work with children in this stage of cognitive development to finding a solution for a specific problem. Problem solving is also appropriate for youth who are in the formal operations stage of cognitive development. It is appropriate when time is limited, a problem needs immediate attention, or when the youth is reluctant to engage more fully in RET work.

Hafner (1981) discusses a problem-solving model based on RET. In his discussion, Hafner makes a distinction between two levels of belief. First, he discusses *underlying beliefs*, which are the most general and basic form of belief. Second, he discusses *immediate beliefs*, which are reflected in our conscious self-talk in specific situations. Immediate beliefs come from underlying beliefs that are less readily available for examination and communication. For example, in a particular situation such as a math class, you might express the thought "I have to make an A on the six-week-test this Friday" in your self-talk. An immediate belief like this is called an *upsetting belief*. This immediate belief may have come from a more basic underlying belief "I must win." An underlying belief like this is called an *irrational belief*. You can see that the immediate belief is more concrete and specific to a given situation than is the underlying belief. The focus of problem solving is on the immediate beliefs in a specific situation causing difficulties.

Problem solving using the Hafner (1981) model follows an eight-stage sequence.

1. Identify the negative feelings and designate them as cues that signal negative thinking.

2. Develop a positive self-statement to counter the negative thoughts temporarily.

3. Examine the problem situation associated with the negative feelings.

4. Identify the upsetting belief(s) about the problem situation.

5. Challenge the upsetting belief by requiring that its truth be supported by evidence.

6. Change the upsetting belief so that it is more realistic and set a specific, concrete goal for the problem situation.

7. Find constructive methods of achieving the goal and list the options available.

8. Select an option that appears to be feasible and has a good chance of producing the outcome desired and develop a plan to put the option into action. In many cases, problem solving will also require teaching specific skills needed to put a plan into action, e.g., social skills.

### Counseling

The meaning of the term *counseling* is rather varied, depending on who is using it. For our purposes we will reserve use of the term for describing more in-depth and long-range interventions. Counseling is appropriate for youth who have reached the stage of formal operations. To do in-depth RET work, students must be able to work with abstract concepts with broad implications. They must be ready to learn how to deal with the underlying beliefs (Hafner, 1981) discussed above.

Newman (1980) has discussed a model of belief structure with implications for exploring underlying or root beliefs. She suggests that beliefs may have either vertical or horizontal structure. Either structure may be involved in underlying beliefs. An underlying belief with *vertical* structure is the foundation for a sequence of linked beliefs. An underlying belief with *horizontal* structure appears in several different belief sequences. It does not, however, have to be the foundation belief for those sequences. Because of its structural position and generalized effect, an underlying belief is more resistant to change than are higher-order beliefs such as upsetting beliefs. Kelly (1955) discusses a detailed theory of belief structure and its relation to personality and psychopathology.

Before beginning counseling, you must satisfy two prerequisites. First, you (the counselor) need to establish rapport with the student(s) to be counseled. If you have done a REE program with your students, rapport will probably be present. A REE program also helps establish a good working context for RET counseling. The vocabulary, communication skills, and knowledge of principles learned will aid and speed up the counseling process. Second, your student(s) must recognize that a problem exists and want to work on it. Earlier work in REE, crisis intervention, or problem solving helps develop this awareness and motivation. To do serious counseling, you need many skills. There is insufficient space to present all those skills in this chapter. A basic text on helping relationships (e.g., Egan, 1986) will go into these skills in detail.

In the first phase of counseling, you should explore private thoughts associated with antecedent events related to a problem. This exploration will help bring to the surface thoughts not usually found in self-talk and personal communication. It also helps identify other belief sequences in which the belief under examination occurs. You can prompt belief exploration using open-ended, probe questions. Probe questions usually ask for *clarification*, *description*, or *discussion.* Be sure that you allow ample opportunity for exploring material evoked by a probe question. Counselors are sometimes too quick to follow up a probe question with another question. If too much resistance to belief exploration develops, you can use the resistance itself as the focus of a problem-solving session. Grieger and Boyd (1980) describe four counselor problems that can slow progress during the exploration phase. They are insufficient knowledge of RET, overexploration of past events, attempting too broad an understanding of a student, and putting too much emphasis on developing a relationship.

During belief system exploration, you must examine the thoughts presented and identify irrational beliefs. This often requires some deduction and inference by you because underlying beliefs are not always easy to verbalize clearly. You must be familiar with fallacies in reasoning, such as those discussed previously, and be adept at recognizing examples of them. You should not hesitate to seek additional information when you need it, nor to ask questions to check your understanding. When you believe that the relevant parts of the belief structure are known and the irrational beliefs identified, shift to the treatment phase.

In the treatment phase of counseling, you focus on disputation of the irrational beliefs identified. Work on each irrational belief by stating the belief and asking for confirmation that this is an accurate statement of the belief. Follow confirmation with an examination of the belief's consequences. The examination should include the affective and behavioral consequences of the belief. You should also help a student examine the probable response from the environment to the affective and behavioral effects of the belief. Following this examination, you should challenge or dispute the belief. Bernard and Joyce (1984) discuss three types of disputation: cognitive, emotional, and behavioral.

*Cognitive disputation* is done by questions that challenge a student to provide evidence to support the validity of the belief or at least provide logical justification for it. If a student gives another irrational belief in response to the challenge, challenge this irrational belief in the same way. You continue the process until the student recognizes irrational beliefs are indefensible. *Emotional disputation* is a technique for identifying new cognitions. In this technique you use *rational-emotive imagery* (REI). REI is done using either positive or negative imagery. In positive REI, the task is to imagine yourself in a problem situation feeling and acting positively. In negative REI, you imagine yourself in a problem situation feeling and acting negatively. The task in negative REI is to modify the negative feelings and behavior in a positive direction. When the task is accomplished successfully, you examine the self-talk used to produce the positive effect. This examination will aid the development of new cognitive formulations for use in the future. Sometimes, you use negative REI simply to demonstrate that negative affect can be tolerated. In *behavioral disputation*, you use role-play simulations and homework assignments to provide refutation of irrational beliefs. For example, a student feels ridiculous under certain circumstances; you ask the student to enter those circumstances deliberately and practice a new interpretation of the situation until positive feelings and behavior are produced. The result of successful counseling is called an effect (E). A successful result or (E) is a rational belief system that aids goal appropriate feelings and behaviors. Thus, the complete RET model is A-B-C-D-E.

## RESOURCES

There are a variety of resources available for teachers who want to learn more about RET and REE programs. *Rational-Emotive Therapy with Children and Adolescents* (Bernard & Joyce, 1984) is an excellent presentation of theory and intervention techniques. *Rational-Emotive Approaches to the Problems of Childhood* (Ellis & Bernard, 1983) provides background material, a number of chapters devoted to treatment of specific types of childhood problems, and chapters on working with parents and teachers. Another book that has many useful suggestions, although not directed specifically at children, is *A Practitioner's Guide to Rational-Emotive Therapy* (Walen, DiGiuseppe, & Wessler, 1980). There are several REE curriculum guides available to teachers. Knaus (1974) has a manual for use by elementary school teachers. Gerald and Eyman (1981) present an emotional education program aimed at secondary-level students. Bernard (1979) has a manual for REE using a group counseling approach. Additional curriculum materials are presented in Appendix One of Bernard and Joyce's (1984) book. All of these provide objectives, teaching strategies, procedures, and activities for doing a REE program. Both Kranzler (1974) and Vernon (1980) are books of REE activities and exercises.

A wide assortment of other materials are available from the Institute for Rational-Emotive Therapy; 45 East 65th Street; New York, NY 10021. Their catalog has many print, audio, and video materials for a person working in RET programs. Many of these materials are specifically for programs working with children and youth. For example, there are a series of paired booklets by Virginia Waters. One volume in each pair is a REE children's story related to a childhood problem. The other volume in each pair is a pamphlet for parents. Another book by Bedford (1974) presents a technique, called *instant replay*, which is useful when working with young children. There are many other story books and activity books in the catalog for working with children.

## REFERENCES

BECK, A., RUSH, A., SHAW, B., & EMERY, G. (1979). *Cognitive theory of depression*. New York: Guilford Press.

BEDFORD, S. (1974). *Instant replay*. New York: Institute for Rational Living.

BERNARD, M. (1979). *Manual for rational-emotive group counseling*. Unpublished manuscript, University of Melbourne, Department of Education, Melbourne, Australia.

BERNARD, M., & JOYCE, M. (1984). *Rational-emotive therapy with children and adolescents*. New York: Wiley.

BERNE, E. (1964). *Games people play*. New York: Grove Press.

BLOCK, J. (1978). Effects of a rational-emotive mental health program on poorly achieving, disruptive high school students. *Journal of Counseling Psychology, 25*, 61–65.

CHADBOURN, R., & L'ABATE, L. (1975). An evaluation of emotional maturity instruction: A review of assumptions, methods, and results. *Catalog of Selected Documents in Psychology, 5,* 237.

COPI, I. (1986). *An introduction to logic* (7th ed.). New York: Macmillan.

CRANDALL, V. C., KRATOVSKY, N., & CRANDALL, V. G. (1965). Children's belief in their own control of reinforcement in intellectual/academic achievement situations. *Child Development, 36,* 91–109.

DAVITZ, J. (1969). *The language of emotion.* New York: Academic Press.

DiGIUSEPPE, R., & KASSINOVE, H. (1976). Effects of a rational-emotive school mental health program on children's emotional adjustment. *Journal of Community Psychology, 4,* 382–387.

DuCETTE, J., WOLK, S., & SOUCAR, T. (1972). Atypical patterns in locus of control and nonadaptive behavior. *Journal of Personality, 40,* 287–297.

EGAN, G. (1986). *The skilled helper* (3rd ed.). Monterey, CA: Brooks/Cole.

ELKIN, A. (1983). Working with children in groups. In A. Ellis & M. Bernard (Eds.), *Rational-emotive approaches to the problems of childhood.* New York: Plenum Press.

ELLIS, A. (1962). *Reason and emotion in psychotherapy.* New York: Stuart.

ELLIS, A. (1971). *Rational-emotive therapy and its application to emotional education.* New York: Institute for Rational Living.

ELLIS, A. (1974). Rational-emotive therapy. In A. Burton (Ed.), *Operational theories of personality.* New York: Brunner/Mazel.

ELLIS, A. (1977). The basic clinical theory of rational-emotive therapy. In A. Ellis & R. Grieger (Eds.), *Handbook of rational-emotive therapy.* New York: Springer.

ELLIS, A. (1979). Rational-emotive therapy: Research data that support the clinical and personality hypotheses of RET and other modes of cognitive-behavior therapy. In A. Ellis & J. Whiteley (Eds.), *Theoretical and empirical foundations of rational-emotive therapy.* Monterey, CA: Brooks/Cole.

ELLIS, A., & BERNARD, M. (1983). *Rational-emotive approaches to the problems of childhood.* New York: Plenum Press.

FINCH, A., & NELSON, W. (1974). Locus of control and anxiety in emotionally disturbed children. *Psychological Reports, 35,* 469–470.

FREED, A. (1971). *T.A. for kids.* Sacramento, CA: Jalmar Press.

FREUD, A. (1975). *Introduction to the technic of child analysis.* New York: Arno Press.

GERALD, M., & EYMAN, W. (1981). *Thinking straight and talking sense.* New York: Institute for Rational Living.

GOODMAN, D., & MAULTSBY, M. (1978). *Emotional well-being through rational behavior training.* Springfield, IL: Thomas.

GORMAN, B., & SIMON, W. (1977). Personality correlates of rational and irrational beliefs. *Rational Living, 12,* 25–27.

GRIEGER, M., & BOYD, J. (1980). *Rational-emotive therapy: a skills-based approach.* New York: Plenum Press.

HAFNER, J. (1981). A problem-solving extension of the A-B-C format. *Rational Living, 16,* 29–34.

KASSINOVE, H., CRISCI, R., & TIEGERMAN, S. (1977). Developmental trends in rational thinking: Implications for rational-emotive school mental health programs. *Journal of Community Psychology, 5,* 266–274.

KELLY, G. (1955). *The psychology of personal constructs* (Vols. 1 & 2). New York: Norton.

KNAUS, W. (1974). *Rational-emotive education: A manual for elementary school teachers.* New York: Institute for Rational-Emotive Therapy.

KRANZLER, C. (1974). *Emotional education exercises for children.* Eugene, OR: Cascade Press.

MacDONALD, A., & GAMES, R. (1972). Ellis's irrational values. *Rational Living, 7,* 25–28.

MAHONEY, M. (1974). *Cognition and behavior modification.* Cambridge, MA: Ballinger.

MAULTSBY, M. (1974). The classroom as an emotional health center. *The Educational Magazine, 31,* 8–11.

MAULTSBY, M., KNIPPING, P., & CARPENTER, L. (1974). Teaching self-help in the classroom with rational self-counseling. *Journal of School Health, 44,* 445–448.

NEWMAN, H. (1980). A theory of belief systems. *Rational Living, 15,* 31–34.

PLUTCHIK, R. (1976). The self-inventory: A measure of irrational attitudes and behavior. *Rational Living, 11,* 31–33.

PLUTCHIK, R. (1980). *Emotion: A psychoevolutionary synthesis.* New York: Harper & Row.

REDL, F., & WINEMAN, D. (1952). *Controls from within: Treatment of the aggressive child.* New York: Free Press.

ROSSI, A. (1977). RET with children: More than child's play. *Rational Living, 12,* 21–24.

SHORKEY, C., & WHITEMAN, V. (1977). Development of the rational behavior inventory: Initial validity and reliability. *Educational and psychological measurement, 37,* 527–534.

VERNON, A. (1980). *Help yourself to a healthier you: Emotional education exercises for children.* Lanham, MD: University Press of America.

WALEN, S, DiGIUSEPPE, R., & WESSLER, R. (1980). *A practitioner's guide to rational-emotive therapy.* New York: Oxford University Press.

WASSERMAN, T. (1983). Development of the Children's Dysfunctional Cognition Scale. *Child and Family Behavior Therapy, 5,* 17–24.

WASSERMAN, T., & ADAMANY, N. (1976). Day treatment and public schools: An approach to mainstreaming. *Child Welfare, 50,* 117–124.

WASSERMAN, T., & KIMMEL, J. (1978). A rational-emotive crisis-intervention treatment model. *Rational Living, 13,* 25–29.

WATERS, V. (1982). Replies to frequently asked questions. *Retwork, 1,* 3.

WESSLER, R. (1977). Evolution of irrational thinking. *Rational Living, 12,* 25–30.

# 9

# PROGRAMMING FOR PSYCHOTIC STUDENTS

## INTRODUCTION

Historically, the study of childhood psychosis began with the publication of a book by Maudsley in 1867. In his book *Physiology and Pathology of Mind*, Maudsley included a chapter titled "Insanity of Early Life." Studies of childhood psychosis steadily increased in number from that time to the present. Today the study of childhood psychosis is a major research area in medicine, psychology, and education.

Goldenson (1970) gives the following general definition of psychosis:

A severe and disabling mental illness of organic and/or emotional origin characterized by loss of contact with reality, personality disorganization, and extreme deviation from normal patterns of thinking, feeling, and acting....They are so incapacitated that they are unable to work, study, or maintain relationships with other people. They often do not attend fully to their own physical needs, and their behavior may be uncontrolled and injurious to themselves, or, in a small minority of cases, to other people ...(p. 1078).

### Incidence

Studies of the incidence of childhood psychosis report figures ranging from a low of .7 case per 10,000 births (Treffert, 1970) to a high of 21 per 10,000 births (Wing & Gould, 1979). The variable results of these studies are a product of different diagnostic criteria. Treffert (1970) looked only at cases meeting the classic definition of autism. Wing and Gould (1979) used more liberal criteria and looked at all cases with psychotic features. Their cases included children diagnosed as autistic, autistic-like, and schizophrenic. Psychosis in children occurs more often in males than in females. The ratio of male to female psychotic children is about 4:1 (Ando & Tsuda, 1975; Rutt & Oxford, 1971).

### Classification

Psychotic children are often classified into two broad groups (Kolvin, 1971). This classification is based primarily on age of onset. Children who are diagnosed before 30 months of age usually get the label *infantile autism*. Those diagnosed between five and 15 years of age usually get the label *childhood schizophrenia*. The earlier the age of onset, the more severe the symptoms and the worse the prognosis. The diagnostic criteria for infantile autism were first proposed by Kanner (1943). The diagnostic criteria for childhood schizophrenia were first proposed by Potter (1933). Hingtgen and Bryson (1972) argue that the division of psychotic children into two distinct groups is an artificial distinction.

You may recall that in Chapter 1 when we discussed the P.L. 94-142 definition of severely emotionally disturbed, infantile autism was not included. Initially, autism was part of the definition. A subsequent revision of the definition removed autism from the emotional disturbance category and categorized it as a health impairment. Schizophrenia, however, remains a part of the definition. Autism was removed because an association of parents of autistic children objected to their children being classified as emotionally disturbed. Their objection was based on the generally accepted belief that autism has a biological basis rather than a psychological cause. Although this is probably true, it is also true, as Kauffman (1985) has pointed out, that autistic children clearly meet the criteria for and characteristics of severe emotional disturbance contained in the P.L. 94-142 definition. While the cause of autism may be biological, the characteristics of the disorder are very similar to emotional disturbance. Teachers trained to provide educational services to the emotionally disturbed are probably better prepared to meet the needs of autistic children than are teachers trained to serve health-impaired children. In our discussion we will not distinguish between infantile autism and childhood schizophrenia. Rather, we will use the more general term *childhood psychosis*, which includes both of these psychotic disorders.

Creak (1961) proposed a single classification for childhood psychosis with the features given below. Depending on the severity of the disorder, these features will vary in number and intensity.

1.  Severe and persistent impairment of emotional relationships with people

2.  A tendency toward preoccupation with inanimate objects

3.  Loss of speech or a failure to develop speech and language

4. Disturbances in sensory perception

5. Bizarre or stereotyped behavior and motility patterns

6. Marked resistance to environmental change

7. Outbursts of intense and unpredictable panic

8. Absence of a sense of personal identity

9. Blunted, uneven, or fragmented intellectual development.

### Cause

The cause of childhood psychosis is not known. There is evidence (Hanson & Gottesman, 1976) for a genetic influence on the disorder. Most authorities believe that there is an organic basis for the disorder. Environmental influences also play a contributing role, by interaction with the underlying organic condition.

### Learning Characteristics

Psychotic disorder in children and youth has serious implications for their education. The learning characteristics of this population make them very difficult to teach. Impaired attention is a major feature of this disorder. This problem is often described as stimulus overselectivity (Lovaas, Schreibman, Koegel, & Rehm, 1971). This means that the psychotic student tends to focus attention too narrowly. Attention to a complex stimulus is often limited to a single stimulus feature. For example, Lovaas et al. trained normal and psychotic students to make a response (bar press) to a complex stimulus consisting of visual, auditory, and tactile features. After training, the students were tested to see if they would respond to each of the components of the complex stimulus alone. The normal students responded to each of the three components. The psychotic students responded to only one of the three components. The psychotic students learned to respond to the complex stimulus during training but apparently attended to only one aspect of the complex stimulus. This overexclusive attention, even if to a relevant stimulus feature, impairs discrimination learning. Since discrimination is basic to all instruction, this is a very serious problem.

A second feature of this disorder with major implications for education is memory impairment. Hermelin and Frith (1971) showed that psychotic students have normal echo memory. These investigators, however, found impaired memory in psychotic students for material requiring organization. They found that psychotic students failed to recognize patterns in structured material when presented to them for recall. The psychotic students responded to the structured material as if it were random. For example, they gave normal and psychotic students a list of words, in random order, that were classifiable into several categories. When asked to recall the words, normal children reconstructed the word list in clusters. That is, their reconstruction grouped together all the words for a given category. Psychotic students reconstructed the word list randomly. The strategy used by the normal students is called *feature extraction*. Feature extraction is critical for meaningful reorganization of material. Meaning, in normal students, is a great aid to memory.

Hermelin and Frith found that psychotic students also have a problem with processing and using sequential structure in material presented to them. For example, they presented several words repeated in a rule-based, patterned sequence. Normal students extracted the rule and used it to reconstruct the sequence. Psychotic students reconstructed the sequence in a patterned way, but the pattern was self-generated and simplistic. The psychotic students failed to extract the rule governing the sequence and imposed their own rule on the reconstruction.

These attention and memory problems interfere with learning many important behaviors (Rincover & Koegel, 1978). Most important, they interfere with learning language and social behavior. Both of these are complex responses based on rules and patterns. In addition, these attention and memory problems help explain the failure of psychotic students to acquire secondary reinforcers. Secondary reinforcers are learned by pairing with primary reinforcers. If a student limits attention to the primary reinforcer in a pairing, the secondary reinforcer can't acquire reinforcing properties by association. The failure to acquire secondary reinforcers contributes to the motivation problems faced by educators working with psychotic students. Attention and memory problems also help explain the failure of psychotic students to learn to imitate. The failure to learn this important response eliminates a very efficient learning strategy used by normal children. These deficits in attention and memory also affect the psychotic student's ability to learn appropriate emotional responses. We learn emotional expression, in part, by imitation. Like secondary reinforcers, emotional responses to new stimuli are learned by association. Finally, these two cognitive processing deficits interfere with transfer of training or generalization.

### Problem Areas

The problems faced by educators working with psychotic students are of two types. First, there are problems of behavioral excesses. These include such problems as self-injurious behavior, repetitive behaviors, disturbed motility, and preservation of sameness. Second, there are problems of educational deficits. These include deficits in such areas as self-help, communication, social, and academic skills.

Cantor (1982) discusses some of the major problem areas in childhood schizophrenia for different developmental periods. During the preschool period significant problem areas include the following:

1.  Inability to function in a group

2.  Avoidance of eye contact

3. Hyperactivity

4. Extreme anxiety

5. Illogical associations in thinking

6. Negativism

7. Neologisms (meaningless, made-up words)

8. Word salad

9. Echolalia

10. Unintelligible speech

11. Talking to self

12. Voice disorders

13. Inappropriate gait, e.g., toe walking

14. Problems with balance

15. Poor gross and fine motor coordination.

During the childhood years the significant problem areas include problems carried over from the earlier period and the following:

1. Failure to understand social norms

2. Hallucinations

3. Delusions

4. Sleep disturbance

5. Unpredictable shifts in mood

6. Significant difficulties with abstract concepts

7. Academic problems, including particularly mathematics and reading comprehension

8. Difficulty in understanding idiom in speech.

During the adolescent years the significant problem areas include problems carried over from the earlier periods and the following:

1. Regressive response to nocturnal emissions

2. Regressive response to menstruation

3. Body-related delusions

4. Hypotonia (underdeveloped musculature and concern about it)

5. Negative response to awakening sexuality

6. Echopraxia (mimicry of others' body movements)

7. Anhedonia (inability to experience pleasure)

8. Identity formation and self-concept

9. Ambivalence and disorganized behavior

10. Suicidal tendencies

11. Independence striving

12. Vocational adaptation.

## ASSESSMENT

### Testing

The use of formal diagnostic tests are of limited value for assessing psychotic students, particularly those with the most severe symptoms. Most tests, such as intelligence tests and personality tests, require the testee to use language or at least understand language. Many psychotic students have no language or very limited language. Their communication deficit, along with some of their inappropriate behaviors, often makes them virtually untestable.

### Rating Scales and Checklists

Diagnostic scales and checklists used to assess psychotic students include Rimland's Diagnostic Checklist for Behavior Disturbed Children (Rimland, 1964), the British Working Party Diagnostic System (Creak, 1961), and the Autism Behavior Checklist (Krug, Arick, & Almond, 1979). The symptom areas covered by the ABC include sensory, relating, body and object use, language, and social behavior. Some sample items from the latter instrument are shown in Figure 9–1. The Behavior Problem Checklist Revised (Quay, 1983) includes a psychosis scale. The BPC-R is probably more useful for screening than for the diagnosis of psychosis. All these scales are useful aids for identifying psychotic disorder. However, you must use them with caution because none of them are well enough validated to be used alone.

There are also descriptive scales or checklists for assessing psychotic students. One often-used checklist is the Behavior Evaluation Scale (Kozloff, 1974), not to be confused with the scale of the same title by McCarney, Leigh, and Cornbleet. There is a summary of the tasks covered on the BES in Table 9–1. Schopler and Reichler (1979) developed two scales useful for obtaining a

Figure 9–1    Part of the Autism Behavior Checklist. *From Krug, Arick, and Almond, 1979.*

INSTRUCTIONS: Circle the number to indicate the items that most  accurately describe the child.

| Item | 1 | 2 | 3 | 4 | 5 |
|---|---|---|---|---|---|
| Whirls self for long periods of time | | | 4 | | |
| Learns a simple task but "forgets" quickly | | | | | 2 |
| Child frequently does not attend to social/environmental stimuli | | 4 | | | |
| Does not follow simple commands which are given once (sit down, come here, stand up) | | | | 1 | |
| Does not use toys appropriately (spins tires, etc.) | 2 | | | | |
| Poor use of visual discrimination when learning (fixates on one characteristic such as size, color or position) | | | 2 | | |
| Has no social smile | | 2 | | | |
| Has pronoun reversal (you for I, etc.) | | | | 3 | |
| Insists on keeping certain objects with him/her | | | 3 | | |
| Seems not to hear, so that a hearing loss is suspected | 3 | | | | |
| Speech is atonal and arhythmic | | | | 4 | |
| Rocks self for long periods of time | | | 4 | | |
| Does not (or did not as a baby) reach out when reached for | | 2 | | | |
| Strong reactions to changes in routine/environment | | | | | 3 |
| Does not respond to own name when called out among two others (Joe, Bill, Mary) | | | | 2 | |
| Does a lot of lunging and darting about, interrupting with spinning, toe walking, flapping, etc. | | | 4 | | |
| Not responsive to other people's facial expressions/feelings | | 3 | | | |
| Seldom uses "yes" or "I" | | | | | |
| Has "special abilities" in one area of development, which seems to rule out mental retardation | | | | | 4 |
| Does not follow simple commands involving prepositions ("put the ball on the box" or "put the ball in the box") | | | | 1 | |
| Sometimes shows no "startle response" to a loud noise (may have thought child was deaf) | 3 | | | | |
| Flaps hands | | | 4 | | |
| Severe temper tantrums and/or frequent minor tantrums | | | | | 3 |
| Actively avoids eye contact | | 4 | | | |
| Resists being touched or held | | 4 | | | |
| Sometimes painful stimuli such as bruises, cuts and injections evoke no reaction | 3 | | | | |
| Is (or was as a baby) stiff and hard to hold | | 3 | | | |
| Is flaccid (doesn't cling) when held in arms | | 2 | | | |
| Gets desired objects by gesturing | | | | 2 | |
| Walks on toes | | | 2 | | |
| Hurts others by biting, hitting, kicking, etc. | | | 2 | | |
| Repeats phrases over and over | | | | 3 | |
| Does not imitate other children at play | | | | | 2 |
| Often will not blink when a bright light is directed toward eyes | | 3 | | | |
| Hurts self by banging head, biting hand, etc. | 1 | | | | |

**Table 9–1**  A summary of the items covered on the Behavior Evaluation Scale

A.  *Learning readiness skills*
- ••(A1)  SPONTANEOUS EYE CONTACT
- ••(A2)  EYE CONTACT ON REQUEST
- (A3)  Responds to his name
- ••(A4)  COOPERATES WITH SIMPLE SPOKEN REQUESTS
- ••(A5)  SITS TO WORK AT SOME TASK
- (A6)  Approaches others
- (A7)  Smiles at others
- A8)  Responds to praise

B.  *Looking, Listening, and Moving Skills*
Large Motor Skills
- (B1)  Bend and stand
- (B2)  Balance when walking
- (B3)  Walks backwards
- (B4)  Kicks ball
- (B5)  Throws ball
- (B6)  Jumps in place
- (B7)  Balances on one foot
- (B8)  Broad-jumps
- (B9)  Hops on one foot
- (B10)  Heel-toe walks
- (B11)  Catches ball
- (B12)  Pedals tricycle
- ••(B13)  SKILL AT MANY LARGE MOTOR ACTIVITIES: SPENDS MUCH TIME AT THEM
Small Motor Skills
- ••(B14)  LOOKS AT OBJECTS. PARTS OF THE BODY, FACE, MOUTH
- (B15)  Moves objects from one hand to the other
- (B16)  Picks up objects with thumb and index finger
- (B17)  Stacks blocks
- (B18)  Works simple puzzles
- (B19)  Imitates drawing line
- (B20)  Imitates drawing circle
- ••(B21)  SKILL AT MANY SMALL MOTOR ACTIVITIES: SPENDS MUCH TIME AT THEM
- ••(B22)  GOOD WORK HABITS, SUCH AS SITTING, LISTENING AND WORKING AT A TASK

- ••(B23)  POINTS OR MATCHES BY NAME
Social Skills
- ••(B24)  USES EYE CONTACT TO GET NATURAL REWARDS
- (B25)  Plays with others
- (B26)  Cooperates on a task
- (B27)  Takes or waits his turn

C.  *Motor Imitation Skills*
Imitation of Movements
- ••(C1)  IMITATES LARGE MOTOR MODELS
- ••(C2)  IMITATES SMALL MOTOR MODELS
- ••(C3)  IMITATES OBJECT PLACEMENTS
- ••(C4)  IMITATES MOUTH MOVEMENTS AND POSITIONS
- (C5)  Plays imitation games
- (C6)  Imitates complex movements
Generalized Imitation
- ••(C7)  IMITATES SOME MODELS EVEN IF NOT REWARDED
- (C8)  Moves body as others do on his own
- (C9)  Imitates chores or tasks on his own
- ••(C10)  IMITATES MOTOR MODELS OF MANY PEOPLE

D.  *Verbal Imitation Skills*
Easing into Verbal Imitation
- (D1)  Pays attention to the speech of others
- (D2)  List of sounds child makes
- ••(D3)  MAKES MANY DIFFERENT SOUNDS ON HIS OWN, OFTEN
- (D4)  How does the child make sounds?
- (D5)  Makes more sounds if you imitate him
- ••(D6)  MAKES EYE CONTACT AND A SOUND AT THE SAME TIME TO GET THINGS
*Verbal Imitation*
- ••(D7)  IMITATES BASIC

SOUNDS
- ••(D8)  IMITATES SYLLABLES
- ••(D9)  IMITATES SIMPLE WORDS
- ••(D10(  IMITATES PHRASES AND SIMPLE SENTENCES
- ••(D11)  IMITATES VERBAL MODELS OF MANY PEOPLE

E.  *Functional Speech*
Kinds of Functional Speech
- ••(E1)  NAMES OBJECTS OR PICTURES
- ••(E2)  ASKS FOR THINGS HE WANTS
- ••(E3)  IDENTIFIES AND DESCRIBES WHAT HE SEES AND HEARS
- ••(E4)  ANSWERS SIMPLE QUESTIONS
- ••(E5)  SAYS "HELLO" AND "GOODBYE" CORRECTLY
- ••(E6)  USES PHRASES AND SIMPLE SENTENCES TO NAME, ASK, DESCRIBE, ANSWER QUESTIONS
- ••(E7)  IDENTIFIES AND DESCRIBES ONE AND MORE THAN ONE (PLURALS)
- ••(E8)  UNDERSTANDS AND USES PREPOSITIONS
- ••(E9)  UNDERSTANDS AND USES PRONOUNS
- ••(E10)  UNDERSTANDS AND USES OPPOSITES
- ••(E11)  USES WORDS ABOUT TIME (BEFORE/AFTER)
*Handling Special Problems*
- ••(E12)  USES THE FUNCTIONAL SPEECH HE KNOWS HOW TO USE
- ••(E13)  USES FUNCTIONAL SPEECH INSTEAD OF ECHOING OR PARROTING
- ••(E14)  USES FUNCTIONAL SPEECH IN MANY PLACES AND WITH MANY PEOPLE

F.  *Chores and Self-Help*

**Table 9–1    (Continued)**

| Skills | OWN, OFTEN | (G10) Stares at fingers or objects |
|---|---|---|
| Chores | G.  Problem Behaviors | (G11) Flaps hands or arms |
| ••(F1) DOES SIMPLE TASKS | Destructive Behaviors | (G12) Makes strange faces |
| ••(F2) DOES MORE COMPLEX TASKS AND CHORES ON HIS OWN, OFTEN | (G1) Bangs head | (G13) Strange postures |
| | (G2) Bites or scratches himself | (G14) Demands or does rituals |
| | | (G15) List of strange behaviors |
| | (G3) Throws tantrums | *Reaction to Certain Consequences* |
| Self-Help Tasks | (G4) Hits, bites, kicks others | |
| (F3) Feeds himself with the right utensils | (G5) List of destructive behaviors | (G16) Physical punishment |
| | | (G17) Verbal punishment |
| (F4) Undresses himself | Getting into Things | (G18) Time out |
| (F5) Dresses himself | (G6) Gets into or messes up things | (G19) Ignoring |
| (F6) Washes and dries face and hands | | ••(G20) PROBLEM BEHAVIORS ARE BEING REPLACED WITH GOOD BEHAVIORS FROM OTHER SKILL AREAS |
| | Strange Behaviors | |
| (F7) Brushes his teeth | (G7) Rocks himself | |
| (F8) Toilet trained | (G8) Spins himself | |
| ••(F9) DOES MANY SELF-HELP TASKS ON HIS | (G9) Spins things | |

SOURCE:   Kozloff, 1974.

psychoeducational profile of psychotic students. Their two scales are the Developmental Function Scale and the Pathology Scale. The broad areas covered in these scales follow.

*Developmental*

1. Imitation

2. Perception

3. Fine motor

4. Gross motor

5. Eye-hand integration

6. Cognitive performance

7. Cognitive verbal

*Pathology*

1. Affect

2. Relating, cooperating, and human interest

3. Play and interest in materials

4. Sensory modes

5. Language

In addition, various adaptive behavior scales such as the American Association on Mental Deficiency's (1975) Adaptive Behavior Scale are used to assess psychotic students. The descriptive scales are the most useful for educational planning.

### Observation

Lovaas et al. (1965) developed a useful observation measure called Multiple-Response Recording. This procedure focuses on observation of five types of behavior. The observation categories are self-stimulation, echolalic and bizarre speech, appropriate speech, social nonverbal behavior, and appropriate play. You observe the behaviors in these categories under three conditions. First, you observe them while the child is alone. Second, you observe them while the child is in the presence of a strange adult who does not interact with the child. Finally, you observe them while the child is with the adult and the adult encourages the child to interact. Another useful observational system, developed by Twardosz, Schwartz, Fox, and Cunningham (1979), focuses on affectionate behavior. This system looks at interaction between a caregiver and a child. The behavioral categories used include smiling, affectionate words, affectionate physical contact, speech, and other social interaction. This is an important area for assessment since a major deficit in psychotic disorder is positive affective interaction.

Perhaps the most useful and versatile approach to observational assessment is to use the recording techniques discussed in Chapter 4. These tech-niques have the advantage of allowing you to focus on the specific behaviors of interest. You can define the behaviors and select recording procedures that best meet your needs and situation. Observational measurement of specific behaviors is also the best assessment for monitoring and evaluating treatment. If necessary, you should review the recording procedures discussed in Chapter 4.

## CURRICULUM

Children and youth with psychotic disorders have many skill-deficit areas that need instruction. It is not possible to go into all these areas in great detail in the space we have available. We will discuss briefly below several of the major deficit areas. In the next section, we will discuss instruction in these areas.

### Attention

One of the most basic deficits found in these students is inappropriate attention. This is most often evident in either a failure to attend to relevant stimuli in the environment or overexclusive attention to some aspect of relevant stimuli in the environment. You may have to teach a student directly to attend to relevant stimuli. This usually means teaching the student to respond to oral and visual prompts for attention to stimuli. When the problem is overexclusive attention, you must teach the student to attend to all the relevant features of a complex stimulus. This often involves training on each individual feature and their combination.

Ross (1976) discusses a developmental model of attention (see Figure 9–2). This model suggests that all children begin attending predominantly in what he describes as overexclusive attention. Attention next shifts to predominance of the overinclusive mode of attending. Finally, attention shifts to predominance of the selective mode of attention. At any developmental level all three modes of attention may be functioning. What is important, developmentally, is which mode predominates. It has been shown that severely impaired children function in the overexclusive mode of attention (Wilhelm & Lovaas, 1976; Schover & Newsom, 1976). This research suggests that psychotic children have a significant developmental lag in attention. Experimental work on training changes in attention in children shows that attention can be fostered (Adams & Shepp, 1975; Koegel & Schreibman, 1977; Shepp & Swartz, 1976; Schreibman, Koegel, & Craig, 1977).

### Imitation Training

Imitation is a response class that is often absent or deficit in students with psychotic disorder. This is a serious hindrance to learning that you must remove if possible. Failure to teach imitation deprives you of the most efficient

**Figure 9–2**    A three-stage developmental model of attention, illustrating individual differences in the development of attention at different ages and rates of development. *From Ross, 1976.*

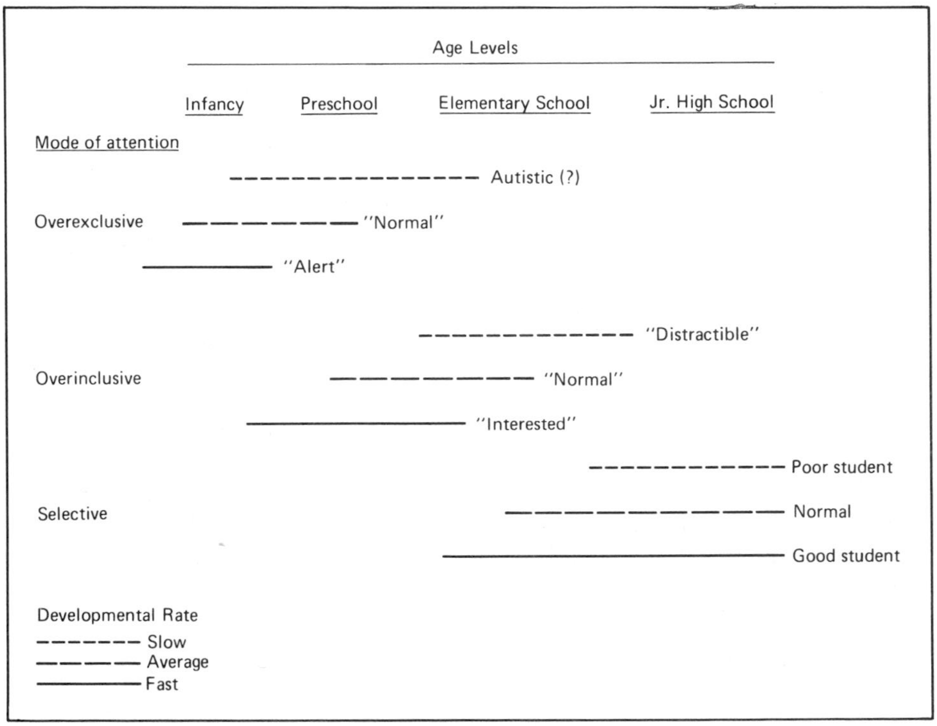

method (modeling) for teaching. As early as 1964, Baer and Sherman showed that imitation as a response class could be taught using reinforcement procedures. You should begin imitation training with motor tasks and then try to generalize the response to other types of behavior, e.g., speech (Bricker & Bricker, 1970; Hewett, 1965). Box 9–1 presents a sequence of motor responses used in a motor imitation training program. Severely impaired children can also be trained to imitate peers (Apolloni, Cooke, & Cooke, 1976; Peck, Apolloni, Cooke, & Raver, 1978; Talkington, Hall, & Altman, 1973). Learning to imitate peers is very important for acquiring both social and language behavior.

**Box 9–1**   A motor imitation training sequence beginning with an easy response and proceeding to progressively more difficult items

| | |
|---|---|
| 1. Step on board | 11. Swing feet |
| 2. Token in box | 12. Walk in place |
| 3. Sit on box | 13. Hand on Mouth |
| 4. Cups in cups | 14. Bow up and down |
| 5. Pat box with hand | 15. Raise foot |
| 6. Blow cotton | 16. Finger on feet |
| 7. Pat knees | 17. Turn around |
| 8. Open mouth | 18. Move head up and down |
| 9. Hands on head | 19. Arms waving |
| 10. Touch ear | 20. Wave arms extended |

SOURCE:  Bricker and Bricker, 1970.

### Motor Development

Training in motor skills will help develop attention and imitation skills by giving you some concrete tasks to work on that require both. It will also help to remediate problems in motor development that affect motility, self-help skills, preacademic, academic, and vocational skills. Usually, a psychotic student's motor skill deficits are due to diminished interaction with the environment and peers. That is, lack of development in this area is more likely to result from lack of learning opportunities than from physical disability. Reinforcement can increase motor behaviors such as walking (Harris, Johnston, Kelley, & Wolf, 1964). Interaction with play equipment and cooperative play can also be increased by reinforcement procedures (Buell, Stoddard, Harris, & Baer, 1968; Hall & Broden, 1967; Johnston, Kelley, Harris, & Wolf, 1966). You can find lists of motor development skills for both gross and fine motor behaviors in texts on early childhood development and physical education. An example of some of the kinds of tasks found in gross and fine motor curricula is presented in Box 9–2.

**Box 9–2**    A sequence of progressively more difficult gross and fine motor skills

| BASIC GROSS MOTOR SKILLS | BASIC FINE MOTOR SKILLS |
|---|---|
| Walking | Picking up small blocks |
| Running | Color with templates |
| Jumping | Scissors cutting |
| Hopping | Block building |
| Skipping | Pegboard activities |
| Climbing | String beads |
| Throwing | Tracing |
| Catching | Cutting-out shapes |
| Bouncing | Copying |
| Kicking | Drawing |

### Speech Training

Many psychotic students have no speech, or severely impaired speech. This is often, in part, caused by their failure to imitate (Lovaas, Berberich, Perloff, & Schaeffer, 1966). You should begin speech training by teaching a set of basic nouns and verbs (Lahey & Bloom, 1977; Stremel & Waryas, 1974). The nouns should be labels for the most common objects the child encounters and needs, e.g., clothing, food, and household objects. The verbs should be the most frequently used action words that relate to the student's needs and wants. Box 9–3 is a sample list of words you might include in your initial vocabulary training.

**Box 9–3**    Sample of common nouns and verbs for vocabulary instruction

| NOUNS | | VERBS |
|---|---|---|
| Head | Juice | Go |
| Hair | Milk | Sit |
| Ears | Cola | Stand |
| Nose | Cheese | Run |
| Mouth | Bread | Jump |
| Eye | Cereal | Ride |
| Hand | Cracker | Eat |
| Fingers | Chips | Drink |

**Box 9–3**    (Continued)

| | | |
|---|---|---|
| Arm | Meat | Push |
| Foot | Chicken | Cut |
| Toes | Fish | Wash |
| Leg | Bacon | Chew |
| Stomach | Egg | Take |
| Chest | Jelly | Give |
| Shirt/Blouse | Butter | Get |
| Pants/Skirt | Sugar | Button |
| Suit/Dress | Potato | Zip |
| Sweater | Tomato | Snap |
| Jacket | Beans | Pull |
| Coat | Peas | Tie |
| Hat | Carrot | Wipe |
| Belt | Hamburger | Throw |
| Shoes | Hot dog | Catch |
| Socks | French fry | Show |
| Gloves | Apple | Draw |
| Scarf | Orange | |
| Bed | Banana | |
| Pillow | Cookie | |
| Blanket | Cake | |
| Chair | Pie | |
| Couch | Ice cream | |
| Desk | Jello | |
| Rug | Dog | |
| Plate | Cat | |
| Bowl | Car | |
| Cup | Truck | |
| Glass | Bus | |
| Spoon | Airplane | |
| Fork | Boat | |
| Knife | Bike | |
| Water | Swing | |

Modeling is the most efficient way to teach these words if a student has become adept at imitation. Even if you have taught motor imitation, the response may not generalize to vocal responses. If generalization isn't present, you will have to teach it again with this new class of responses. It may also be necessary to use shaping and chaining during speech training (Koegel, Rincover, & Egel, 1982). Two special problems that you may encounter when doing speech training are echolalia and nonmeaningful vocalizations. Carr, Schreibman, and Lovaas (1975) describe how to deal with echolalia. Center (1984) describes a procedure for reducing nonmeaningful vocalizations.

When we talk about speech, we usually mean oral speech. Speech can also be manual signs such as those used by the deaf or other nonverbal symbol systems (Silverman, 1980). Some psychotic students learn speech terms more easily as manual signs than as oral sounds (Bonvillian & Nelson, 1976; Carr, Binkoff, Kologinsky, & Eddy, 1978). One advantage of using manual signing is that it relies on visual rather than auditory stimuli. Most psychotic students appear to respond better to visual stimuli (Hermelin & O'Connor, 1970). Another advantage to signing is a greater probably of generalization of motor imitation training to this form of speech.

### Language Development

It is difficult to teach some psychotic students to say words or make signs. It is even more difficult to teach them to use these terms in a meaningful way, that is, to teach them to use language. After a student can say or sign a word, the first and most basic thing that you must teach is meaning. Next, you must teach the student to use the word correctly in a realistic context, that is, make the word functional. After you have taught single words, you need to begin teaching word combinations. You are then teaching syntax or language structure. You may have to go through several steps with this instruction, that is, teach combinations, then meaning, and finally functional use. Besides the multiple steps often involved in teaching a structure, there are many structures to teach. There are several curricula available for language training with severely impaired students. A language training sequence for nonverbal children is given in Cole and Cole (1981). Stremel and Waryas (1974) discuss a teaching sequence based on psycholinguistic research. Lovaas (1977) presents a detailed curriculum and teaching procedures for language training in autistic children. The following is a very abbreviated outline of the Lovaas program.

1. Production of speech sounds and words

2. Association of verbal labels with objects and events

3. Development of words for abstract concepts

4. Verbal exchange using question-and-answer format

5. Obtaining information from another person

6. Development of grammar and sentence structure

7. Recall of past events

8. Responding to open-ended questions

9. Communication of ideas without concrete referents

### Self-Help Skills

Another area aided by motor imitation training is self-help. If a psychotic student is to become very self-sufficient, self-help skills must be mastered. Self-help skills include very basic skills such as toileting, dressing, and feeding. They also include more complex skills such as personal hygiene, grooming, cooking, cleaning, and first aid. Much of the work on teaching self-help skills has been with retarded students. As early as 1965, Bensberg, Colwell, and Cassel used shaping to teach self-help skills to the retarded. Good illustrations of the use of behavioral procedures for teaching self-help skills are available. Azrin and his colleagues developed excellent procedures for teaching skills such as toileting (Azrin & Foxx, 1971) and eating (Azrin & Armstrong, 1973). Good self-help skills will relieve caretakers of some of their burden. More important, self-help skills aid independence and self-concept in a student. They also lay a foundation for developing vocational skills. Box 9–4 is a partial list of some self-help skills you may have to teach.

**Box 9–4**    Examples of some of the basic self-help skills needed for minimal independence

|    |                    |     |                  |
|----|--------------------|-----|------------------|
| 1. | Toileting          | 12. | Buttoning        |
| 2. | Wash hands         | 13. | Snapping         |
| 3. | Wash face          | 14. | Zipping          |
| 4. | Brush teeth        | 15. | Buckling         |
| 5. | Comb/brush hair    | 16. | Tying            |
| 6. | Put on/remove coat | 17. | Use spoon        |
| 7. | Put on/remove shirt| 18. | Use fork         |
| 8. | Put on/remove pants| 19. | Use knife        |
| 9. | Put on/remove socks| 20. | Use cup or glass |
| 10.| Put on/remove shoes| 21. | Use light switch |
| 11.| Put on/remove belt | 22. | Open/close door  |

### Social Development

Social isolation is one of the most prominent features of psychotic disorder. The ability to relate to other people is nearly always impaired. At the most basic level the problem stems from a failure of the psychotic student to learn to be reinforced by social stimuli (Rincover & Koegel, 1977). Reinforcing social stimuli include such things as physical contact, e.g., hug, nonverbal expressions, e.g., smile, and verbal responses, e.g., praise. Your first task for social development is to attempt to teach the psychotic student to respond to social reinforcers (Lovaas, Freitag, et al., 1966). You also need to teach the psychotic student basic rules about social interaction, e.g., taking turns. Finally, you must teach the student more complex social skills, e.g., conversational skills. The development of social skills depends on learning to engage in behaviors that promote social interaction. Romanczyk, Diament, Goren, Trunell, and Harris (1975) developed a procedure for teaching toy play. Gaylord-Ross and Pitts-Conway (1982) developed a procedure for teaching psychotic adolescents "hanging out" behaviors. In another study, autistic adolescents learned to play video games to promote socialization in a free-play situation (Gaylord-Ross, Haring, Breen, & Pitts-Conway, 1982). Imitation and language training are important aids to socialization. Thus, your imitation and language programs are also components of social development. The material in Chapter 5 can be used once you have taught the basic foundations for social development.

### Preacademic Skills

The next area that you should address is the readiness skills needed for mastery of basic skills. These are the kinds of skills usually taught in preschool programs. Most texts on early childhood development explain these skills in detail. They include such things as color discrimination and shape discrimination. They can be taught using the procedures described in Chapter 2. Box 9–5 is a partial list of some of the preacademic skills that may need to be taught.

**Box 9–5**    Some of the basic preacademic skills and concepts

Auditory discrimination
Visual discrimination
Auditory memory
Visual memory
Concepts of size
Concepts of color
Concepts of shape
Concepts of position
Concepts of weight
Concepts of height
Concepts of temperature
Concepts of motion
Concepts of time
Concepts of number
Matching likes
Identifying opposites
Similarities and differences
Recognizing absurdities
Ordering and sequencing
Categorization

### Other Skills

Two other areas that need to be covered in programs with psychotic students are basic academic skills and vocational skills. You should refer to the material in Chapters 2, 3, and 10 for additional information on these areas.

## INTERVENTION

### Behavior Excesses

One of the major problems you must deal with in most psychotic students is excesses of inappropriate behavior. The individual behavior change techniques discussed in Chapter 4 are the best procedures to use for these problems. The range of inappropriate behavior that you might encounter is wide. Two major problem areas worth special mention are self-stimulation and self-injurious behaviors (Lovaas, Ackerman, & Taubman, 1983).

Self-stimulation behaviors are a major obstacle to learning (Koegel & Covert, 1972). They make the already present withdrawal and isolation from the environment even worse. Research suggests that these behaviors are maintained by either intrinsic or extrinsic reinforcement or both. When the reinforcement is of the former type, it is the feedback to the student produced by the behavior itself that is reinforcing. This creates a particularly difficult problem because reinforcement is under the student's control. Reinforcement of the latter type is usually social reinforcement. This reinforcement is the attention that the student receives from others because of the behavior.

Several approaches are possible when you want to control this type of behavior. One is *sensory extinction* (Rincover, 1978). In sensory extinction the aim is to eliminate the reinforcer by controlling the feedback to the student produced by the behavior. The feedback may be visual, auditory, or kinesthetic. It may also be some combination of these. For example, assume that the behavior is spinning an object on a table and the sensory reinforcer the sound of the object against the table. Sensory extinction might be obtained by covering the top of the table with felt. This would muffle the sound of the object against the table and reduce or eliminate the auditory feedback. If the reinforcer maintaining a behavior is social in nature, you can control the behavior by more conventional extinction procedures. For example, assume that the reinforcer is teacher attention to the behavior. Here, you can put the behavior on extinction simply by withholding your attention. That is, you can ignore it. Social isolation or time-out is also a possibility. However, you must be careful about the use of this technique with psychotic students. If the inappropriate behavior is maintained by both sensory and social reinforcers, social isolation may actually increase the self-stimulation behavior. This will happen because one of the sources of reinforcement is under the student's control and will not be affected by social isolation. In fact, social isolation will provide more opportunities to engage in the behavior and obtain sensory reinforcement.

Another possible intervention for self-stimulation behavior is *overcorrection* (Foxx & Azrin, 1973). This approach assumes that the problem behavior is due to an imbalance between the behaviors available to the student for obtaining reinforcement from self and the environment. Under these circumstances a student will tend to engage in the most available behaviors that produce reinforcement. For a psychotic student these are usually self-directed behaviors. When you apply overcorrection to self-stimulation, you should interrupt every instance of the self-stimulation behavior and physically guide the student repeatedly through some alternative behavior. The alternative behavior should be an externally directed behavior and one that is functional. Functional means a behavior that has a high probability of obtaining reinforcement from the environment. For example, assume that the inappropriate behavior is hand flapping. An overcorrection response that you could use would be toy play.

DRO could also be used to increase a behavior that is either incompatible with or an alternative to the self-stimulation behavior. With DRO you would still be trying to develop a functional and externally directed behavior as a means of obtaining reinforcement. The difference, in the example above, would be that the toy play would be an independent target behavior under DRO rather than a consequence for hand flapping as in the overcorrection procedure. Regardless of what approach you take to reducing self-stimulation, you should always attempt also to establish appropriate substitute behaviors.

Self-injurious behaviors are very serious problem behaviors because they are potentially dangerous to a student. They also interfere significantly with learning. Self-injurious behavior appears to be established and maintained by either positive or negative reinforcement or both (Carr, Newsom, & Binkoff, 1976). Positive reinforcement usually is in the form of social reinforcement provided by the attention given to the behavior. Negative reinforcement occurs as the result of escape from an onerous demand. That is, you make a demand on a student perceived as undesirable and the student engages in self-injurious behavior and avoids the task or situation.

One approach used with mild-to-moderate self-injurious behaviors is DRO (Repp & Deitz, 1974). This approach involves use of one of the three types of DRO discussed in Chapter 4. For example, assume that the student engages in a high rate of self-directed, face-slapping behavior. You might use an incompatible but related response as your target behavior, e.g., use of bongo drums. You would conduct a program to reinforce slapping the bongo drums with an open hand. As the amount of drum "playing" went up, the amount of face slapping would decrease. If the drum "playing" is reinforcing, you would, in time, be able to stretch and eliminate the extrinsic reinforcement for the behavior. If the drum "playing" had become intrinsically reinforcing, the behavior would maintain itself once established.

A mild punishment procedure used for mild-to-moderate self-injurious behavior is overcorrection (Azrin, Gottlieb, Hughart, Wesolowski, & Rahn, 1975). In this procedure, Azrin et al. used overcorrection on several self-injurious behaviors involving the hands. When a student engaged in a self-injurious behavior, the student was required to perform a relaxation response lasting 10 minutes. This response consisted of lying on a bed with arms and hands along the side of the body. If this response was not appropriate or didn't work, the student was given hand training. Hand training required the student to perform a series of hand movements that were incompatible with self-injury. With some self-injurious behaviors, particularly when they are serious, only the use of more aversive punishment procedures will work (Corte, Wolf, & Locke, 1971). Aversive stimuli in such punishment procedures may be physical, e.g., a slap (Koegel & Covert, 1972), chemical, e.g., aromatic ammonia (Altman, Haavik, & Cook, 1978), or electrical, e.g., electric shock (Lovaas & Simmons, 1969). Use of punishment to suppress self-injurious behavior must be accompanied by programming for alternative appropriate responses (Lovaas & Newsom, 1976).

### Behavior Deficits

l objectives and the greater need to use shaping and chaining procedures. That is, you will have to carry your task analysis of objectives further and teach a larger number of subcomponents to reach an objective. Since learning problems will be more severe in psychotic students, you will be more likely to use shaping when teaching a skill. You will also be more likely to use chaining since you will be teaching a larger number of subcomponents to more severely handicapped students. We will therefore limit our discussion in this section to the use of shaping and chaining. We will look at an example of each procedure. The examples will be from my experiences working with psychotic students.

Our example of *shaping* will be teaching a student to make the long *i* sound to a vocal imitative prompt. This sound was taught to a nonverbal student as one step in training the student to imitate a word vocally. The student had previously gone through a motor imitation training procedure but had no experience imitating vocal sounds. The first word selected for instruction was "pie." I selected this word because it was one that had a high probability of being established as a functional word. That is, it was a word that related to something liked by the student and often sought out. Another reason I selected this word was that the student already had an approximation to the long *i* sound in the vocal repertoire. The student, when irritated, would loudly vocalize repeated sounds approximating the long *i*. The following is a description of the teaching procedure with comments. The student's name was Joe.

1. Teaching begins with Joe sitting in a chair facing the teacher. The teacher is also seated. Joe is restricted to his chair by a wall behind him and a small table pushed up to him and over his legs. The teacher sits on the other side of the table.

2. The instruction begins by attempting to get the student to imitate the teacher vocally.

TEACHER: "Joe, do this 'eye.'"

COMMENT "Joe, do this" was an imitative prompt used during a motor imitation program done just before this program. "Joe" was also used as a preparatory prompt for attention in an earlier attention training program. Joe made no response to repeated presentations of the foregoing vocal prompt. It became apparent that the motor imitation training was not generalizing to vocal imitation and that a shaping procedure would need to be used.

3. TEACHER: "Joe do this 'eye.'" and reaches over and takes one of Joe's ears between his thumb and finger.

   JOE: Loudly and agitated, "eye, eye, eye, eye."

   TEACHER: Releases his grasp on the ear, says "good Joe!" and gives Joe a small sip of cola.

COMMENT The ear-touching procedure was used as a physical prompt for vocalizing the long *i* sound. It was known from past experience that Joe was irritated by anyone touching his ears. He usually expressed this with a loud and repeated vocalization of an approximation of the long *i* sound. The release of the ear functioned as a negative reinforcer for Joe's vocalization because the vocalization ended an aversive stimulus (ear touching). The statement "good Joe!" was a social stimulus presented in association with the sip of cola to help establish this social reinforcer by association with the primary reinforcement (cola). This procedure continued until Joe made the vocal response on 10 consecutive trials for three consecutive and independent sessions.

4. TEACHER: "Joe, do this 'eye.'" and reaches toward one of Joe's ears but does not make contact.

   JOE: Loudly, but less agitated, "eye, eye, eye."

   TEACHER: Pulls back his hand and says, "good Joe!" and gives Joe a sip of cola.

COMMENT The teacher has begun fading the physical prompt for vocalizing by reaching toward but not touching one of Joe's ears. The social and primary reinforcers remain unchanged. This continued until the same criteria given above were reached.

5. TEACHER: "Joe, do this 'eye.'" The teacher does not reach for Joe's ears.

   JOE: Loudly, with little evidence of agitation, "eye, eye, eye, eye, eye."

   TEACHER: Gives social and primary reinforcement.

COMMENT    The physical prompt has now been completely faded and Joe is responding to the vocal prompt. This step continued until the stated criteria were reached.

6.  TEACHER:    "Joe, do this." The teacher does absolutely nothing else.

    JOE:    Less loudly, "eye, eye, eye, eye."

    TEACHER:    No response.

COMMENT    This was a probe to see if Joe's responding was under appropriate stimulus control. Appropriate stimulus control was not present. Joe responded without the critical feature of the stimulus being present. That is, the "eye" vocalized by the teacher within the vocal prompt was missing.

7.  TEACHER:    "Joe, do this."

    JOE:    Loudly, "eye, eye, eye."

    TEACHER:    No response.

    TEACHER:    "Joe, do this 'eye.'"

    JOE:    Loudly, "eye, eye, eye, eye."

    TEACHER:    Gives social and primary reinforcement.

COMMENT    The teacher in this step is doing discrimination training to establish the "eye" component within the prompt as the critical feature. When the teacher makes no response, Joe's response is on extinction. When Joe responds to the appropriate form of the stimulus, he is reinforced. The "eye" component of the vocal prompt is being established as the critical feature of the prompt by differential reinforcement. Appropriate and inappropriate forms of the vocal prompt were presented in random order to avoid response set. This continued until Joe responded only to the appropriate stimulus and to the stated criteria. Once this was accomplished, Joe's behavior was under stimulus control, that is, under the control of the prompt for vocal imitation.

8.  TEACHER:    "Joe, do this 'eye.'"

    JOE:    Less loudly, "eye, eye, eye, eye."

    TEACHER:    No response.

    TEACHER:    "Joe, do this 'eye.'"

    JOE:    Loudly, "eye, eye, eye."

    TEACHER:    Gives social and primary reinforcement.

COMMENT    The teacher is now moving to a closer approximation of the target response. Before, Joe could say "eye" any number of times and be reinforced. Now the teacher has set a criterion for reinforcement that allows no more than three repetitions of the vocalization by Joe. That is, if Joe says "eye" more than three times, he is not reinforced. You will note in the examples above that there has been some variation in the number of time Joe emits the "eye" response. This natural variability in response production is used to aid the shaping procedure. When the stated criteria are reached using three repetitions, the criterion for reinforcement was changed to two. As the number of repetitions required for reinforcement went down, so did the range of variability for the response. This process was continued until Joe made only one response to each presentation of the vocal prompt.

You may have noted that the way Joe makes his response varied from loudly to less loudly. After the number of repetitions was brought down to one, the next step in the shaping procedure was to reduce progressively the loudness of Joe's response. This was done in the same way as reduction in repetitions was obtained. The criterion for reinforcement was changed so that only less loud vocalizations were reinforced. Loud vocalizations were put on extinction. After less loud vocalizations were consistently emitted, the criterion for reinforcement became quiet vocalizations. At the end of the shaping procedure, Joe emitted only quiet, single repetitions of "eye" and only to vocal prompts containing the appropriate stimulus features. We have looked at only a very small slice of the language training done with Joe to illustrate shaping. We have not, in this illustration, dealt with other issues, such as stretching the reinforcement schedule and shifting Joe from primary to secondary reinforcement.

Our second example will be of *chaining*. We could illustrate chaining using a continuation of the language training example. For the sake of variety, we will use the area of self-help to illustrate chaining. Our example of chaining will be putting on a pair of pants. The student in this example is Ben. Ben was evaluated on the dressing skill using a large dressing doll. Ben was tested on the following subskills: orientation of pants to body, inserting feet into legs, pulling pants up to waist, zipping, snapping, and buckling. Each skill was tested individually. Ben could not do any of the subskills. Ben was taught to do each skill individually using a large dressing doll. After Ben had learned the individual skills needed to put on a pair of pants, the individual skills were chained together. The complex skill putting on a pair of pants was first taught using a dressing doll and then taught on Ben himself. We will limit our description to chaining the individual subskills together on the dressing doll. A procedure called *backward chaining* was used.

1. TEACHER:    Stands behind Ben, who is sitting at a table, and places a dressing doll on the table in front of Ben. A pair of pants are on the doll and need only to have the belt buckle buckled to be complete. The teacher says, "Ben, buckle the belt."

   BEN:    Reaches over and runs the belt through the buckle and fastens it.

TEACHER:    "Good work Ben!" and gives Ben a small piece of dry cereal.

COMMENT    The dressing doll and the teacher's instructions are antecedents for buckling the belt. Later the vocal prompt, i.e., the teacher's instructions, will need to be faded. Ben did the correct response and was given both social and primary reinforcement. The social reinforcement was paired with the primary reinforcement to aid establishment of it as a secondary reinforcer. This task was repeated until Ben completed five trials without error during each of three different sessions. The task was started with the last step in the process rather than the first. This served several purposes. First, it kept the task brief. Second, it ended the training task with the end step so there was closure on the task. Third, it put the reinforcer on the last step in the task. The reason for this will become apparent below.

2. TEACHER:    Places the dressing doll on the table in front of Ben. The pants are complete except for the snap and the buckle. The teacher says, "Ben, snap the pants."

BEN:    Reaches over and snaps the snap and buckles the belt.

TEACHER:    Gives Ben both social and primary reinforcement.

COMMENT    The backward chaining continued. Note that the teacher gave only one vocal prompt and did not provide reinforcement until the end of the task. Snapping functioned as an antecedent for buckling, and buckling served as a secondary reinforcer for snapping because it led to extrinsic reinforcement. This phase continued until the stated criteria were reached.

3. TEACHER:    Places the dressing doll on the table in front of Ben. The pants are complete except for the zipper, snap, and buckle. The teacher says, "Ben, zip the pants."

BEN:    Reaches over and zips the zipper, snaps the waist snap, and buckles the buckle.

TEACHER:    Gives Ben both social and primary reinforcement.

COMMENT    Zipping functioned as an antecedent for snapping, and snapping served as a secondary reinforcer for zipping. Snapping still functioned as an antecedent for buckling, and buckling still served as a secondary reinforcer for snapping. This phase continued until the stated criteria were reached. The process continued in this fashion until all steps trained for putting on pants were linked together.

When this process was complete the teacher was able to give Ben the doll, a pair of pants, and the vocal instruction to put the pants on the doll. Ben was able to go through the sequence of steps with only this initial set of antecedents and with extrinsic reinforcement delayed until the end of the sequence. Once this process was complete, training shifted to working with Ben actually putting a pair of pants on himself. When this generalization training was complete, the vocal prompt was faded. After this was done, Ben's behavior was under the control of natural antecedents. That is, Ben's behavior was prompted only by not having pants on and by being given a pair of pants. The primary reinforcer still needed to be stretched and eliminated and the secondary reinforcer stretched before the training was complete. Further, generalization training also had to be done. For example, generalization training had to be done in several locations, e.g., home and school, and with several agents, e.g., teacher, aide, and parent.

### Parent Programming

Educators have long recognized the need for parent involvement in a child's education if optimal results are to be obtained. This is even more true for psychotic students. In fact, it is virtually essential for psychotic students. Lovaas, Koegel, Simmons, and Long (1973) conducted an extensive follow-up study of treated psychotic children. They found that the most important influence on maintenance and continuation of progress was the post-treatment environment. If the child went into an environment where the treatment procedures were continued, the child maintained gains and continued to progress. If the child went into an environment where treatment procedures were not continued, the child regressed. The best post-treatment environment was a home setting where the parents were trained to continue the treatment procedures. In addition, if the parents are trained to work with the child and the educational program can be extended into the home, more rapid progress can be expected.

Research by Koegel, Russo, and Rincover (1977) identified the essential components that need to be taught to someone who works with a psychotic child. Five skills were identified:

1. The ability to present instructions clearly and consistently

2. The ability to effectively use prompts and to fade them

3. The ability to teach using shaping

4. The ability to deliver appropriate consequences immediately following responses

5. The ability to use learning trials with clear beginning and end points and to separate each trial by a brief and discrete interval

Training parents in these skills needs to be done by someone skilled in their use. Training should be structured and carried out in a formal manner. The training will be most effective if it is done first in the treatment setting, where the procedures can be modeled using a parent's child in the training. It is helpful, though not necessary, to use videotapes of parent practice. In this way, the trainer can easily review a parent's procedures with the parent and point out problem areas and corrective procedures. The same feedback and instruction can be provided without videotapes through oral descriptions of what was observed. After formal training in the treatment setting, the training can be extended into the home setting to aid generalization. Educator's who work with the child should give parents specific tasks to work on. These should complement the school-based program. They should also be for limited objectives that can be accomplished in a short time.

## RESOURCES

Many excellent resources are cited in this chapter. You should refer to those dealing with topics of particular interest or concern. There are several resources of particular value. These are broad inclusive resources useful for a variety of needs. First, there are three volumes related to Project TEACCH (Treatment and Education of Autistic and Related Communication Handicapped Children). The first volume in the set provides extensive assessment materials for developing a psychoeducational profile on a student (Schopler & Reichler, 1979). The second volume is devoted to teaching strategies for use by both teachers and parents (Schopler, Reichler, & Lansing, 1980). The last volume covers teaching activities for autistic children (Schopler, Lansing, & Waters, 1983). A somewhat briefer description of programming for psychotic children is also available (Koegel, Rincover, & Egel, 1982). An excellent resource for language training for psychotic children is a book by Lovaas (1977). There is also a resource manual for providing services to psychotic children in rural areas (Lowry, Quinn, & Stewart, n.d.). Kozloff (1974, 1979) has prepared two volumes that provide detailed step-by-step guidance to teachers and parents for the use of behavioral procedures with handicapped children. Finally, a volume by Ross (1981) described in Chapter 4 is particularly useful for reviewing the behavioral research on intervention into many of the problems of psychotic children.

## REFERENCES

ADAMS, M., & SHEPP, B. (1975). Selective attention and the breadth of learning: A developmental study. *Journal of Experimental Child Psychology, 20,* 168–180.

ALTMAN, K., HAAVIK, S., & COOK, J. (1978). Punishment of self-injurious behavior in natural settings using contingent aromatic ammonia. *Behaviour Research and Therapy, 16,* 86–96.

AMERICAN ASSOCIATION ON MENTAL DEFICIENCY (1975). *Adaptive behavior scale* (Revised). Washington, DC: Author.

ANDO, H., & TSUDA, K. (1975). Intrafamilial incidence of autism, cerebral palsy, and mongolism. *Journal of Autism and Childhood Schizophrenia, 5,* 267–274.

APOLLONI, T., COOKE, S., & COOKE, T. (1976). Establishing a normal peer as a behavioral model for developmentally delayed toddlers. *Perceptual and Motor Skills, 43,* 1155–1165.

AZRIN, N., & ARMSTRONG, P. (1973). The "minimeal"— A method of teaching eating skills to the profoundly retarded. *Mental Retardation, 11,* 9–13.

AZRIN, N., & FOXX, R. (1971). A rapid method of toilet training the institutionalized retarded. *Journal of Applied Behavior Analysis, 4,* 89–99.

AZRIN, N., GOTTLIEB, L., HUGHART, L., WESOLOWSKI, M., & RAHN, T. (1975). Eliminating self-injurious behavior by educative procedures. *Behaviour Research and Therapy, 10,* 14–19.

BAER, D., & SHERMAN, J. (1964). Reinforcement control

of generalized imitation in young children. *Journal of Experimental Child Psychology, 1*, 37–49.

BENSBERG, G., COLWELL, C., & CASSEL, R. (1965). Teaching the profoundly retarded self-help activities by behavior shaping techniques. *American Journal of Mental Deficiency, 69*, 674–679.

BONVILLIAN, J., & NELSON, K. (1976). Sign language acquisition in a mute autistic boy. *Journal of Speech and Hearing Disorders. 41*, 339–347.

BRICKER, W., & BRICKER, D. (1970). A program of language training for the severely language handicapped child. *Exceptional Children, 37*, 101–111.

BUELL, J., STODDARD, P., HARRIS, F., & BAER, D. (1968). Collateral social development accompanying reinforcement of outdoor play in a preschool child. *Journal of Applied Behavior Analysis, 2*, 167–173.

CANTOR, S. (1982). *The schizophrenic child: A primer for parents and professionals*. St. Albans, VT: Eden Press.

CARR, E., BINKOFF, J., KOLOGINSKY, E., & EDDY, E. (1978). Acquisition of sigh language by autistic children. I. Expressive labeling. *Journal of Applied Behavior Analysis, 11*, 489–501.

CARR, E., NEWSOM, C., & BINKOFF, J. (1976). Stimulus control of self-destructive behavior in a psychotic child. *Journal of Abnormal Child Psychology, 4*, 139–153.

CARR, E., SCHREIBMAN, L., & Lovaas, O. (1975). Control of echolalic speech in psychotic children. *Journal of Abnormal Child Psychology, 3*, 331–351.

CENTER, D. (1984). Reducing nonmeaningful vocalizations. *Remedial and Special Education, 5*, 50–51.

COLE, M., & COLE, J. (1981). *Effective intervention with the language impaired child*. Rockville, MD: Aspen.

CORTE, H., WOLF, M., & LOCKE, B. (1971). A comparison of procedures for eliminating self-injurious behavior of retarded adolescents. *Journal of applied behavior analysis, 4*, 201–213.

CREAK, M. (1961). Schizophrenia syndrome in childhood: Progress report of a working party. *Cerebral Palsy Bulletin, 3*, 501–504.

FOXX, R., & AZRIN, N. (1973). The elimination of autistic self-stimulatory behavior by overcorrection. *Journal of Applied Behavior Analysis, 6*, 1–14.

GAYLORD-ROSS, R., HARING, T., BREEN, C., & PITTS-CONWAY, V. (1982). The training and generalization of social interaction skills with autistic youth. In R. Gaylord-Ross, T. Haring, C. Breen, & V. Pitts-Conway (Eds.), *The Social Integration of Autistic and Severely Handicapped Students*. San Francisco: San Francisco State University.

GAYLORD-ROSS, R., & PITTS-CONWAY, V. (1982). Social behavior development in integrated secondary autistic programs. In R. Gaylord-Ross, T. Haring, C. Breen, & V. Pitts-Conway (Eds.), *The social integration of autistic and severely handicapped students*. San Francisco: San Francisco State

University.

GOLDENSON, R. (1970). *The encyclopedia of human behavior* (Vol. 2). New York: Doubleday.

HALL, R., & BRODEN, M. (1967). Behavior changes in brain-injured children through social reinforcement. *Journal of Experimental Psychology, 5*, 463–479.

HANSON, D., & GOTTESMAN, I. (1976). The genetics, if any, of infantile autism and childhood schizophrenia. *Journal of Autism and Childhood Schizophrenia, 6*, 209–234.

HARRIS, F., JOHNSTON, M., KELLEY, C., & WOLF, M. (1964). Effects of positive social reinforcement on regressed crawling of a nursery school child. *Journal of Educational Psychology, 55*, 35–41.

HERMELIN, B., & FRITH, U. (1971). Psychological studies of childhood autism: Can autistic children make sense of what they see and hear? *Journal of special education, 5*, 107–117.

HERMELIN, B., & O'CONNOR, N. (1970). *Psychological experiments with autistic children*. London: Pergamon.

HEWETT, F. (1965). Teaching speech to autistic children through operant conditioning. *American Journal of Orthopsychiatry, 34*, 927–936.

HINGTGEN, J., & BRYSON, C. (1972). Recent developments in the study of early childhood psychoses: Infantile autism, childhood schizophrenia, and related disorders. *Schizophrenia Bulletin, 5*, 8–54.

JOHNSTON, M., KELLEY, C., HARRIS, F., & WOLF, M. (1966). An application of reinforcement principles to development of motor skills in a young child. *Child Development, 3*, 379–387.

KANNER, L. (1943). Autistic disturbances of affective contact. *Nervous Child, 2*, 217–250.

KAUFFMAN, J. (1985). *Characteristics of children's behavior disorders* (3rd ed.). Columbus, OH: Merrill.

KOEGEL, R., & COVERT, A. (1972). The relationship of self-stimulation to learning in autistic children. *Journal of Applied Behavior Analysis, 5*, 381–387.

KOEGEL, R., RINCOVER, A., & EGEL, A. (1982). *Educating and understanding autistic children*. San Diego, CA: College-Hill Press.

KOEGEL, R., RUSSO, D., & RINCOVER, A. (1977). Assessing and training teachers in the generalized use of behavior modification with autistic children. *Journal of Applies Behavior Analysis, 10*, 197–205.

KOEGEL, R., & SCHREIBMAN, L. (1977). Teaching autistic children to respond to simultaneous multiple cues. *Journal of Experimental Child Psychology, 24*, 299–311.

KOLVIN, I. (1971). Psychoses in childhood: A comparative study. In M. Rutter (Ed.), *Infantile autism: Concepts, characteristics, and treatment*. Edinburgh: Churchill-Livingstone.

KOZLOFF, M. (1974). *Educating children with learning and behavior problems*. New York: Wiley.

KOZLOFF, M. (1979). *A Program for Families of Children with Learning and Behavior Programs.* New York: Wiley.

KRUG, D., ARICK, J., & ALMOND, P. (1979). Autism screening instrument for educational planning: Background and development. In J. Gilliam (Ed.), *Autism: Diagnosis, instruction, management, and research.* Austin, TX: University of Texas Press.

LAHEY, M., & BLOOM, L. (1977). Planning a first lexicon: Which words to teach first. *Journal of Speech and Hearing Disorders, 42,* 340–350.

LOVAAS, O. (1977). *The autistic child: Language development through behavior modification.* New York: Irvington.

LOVAAS, O., ACKERMAN, A., & TAUBMAN, M. (1983). An overview of behavioral treatment of autistic persons. In M. Rosenbaum, C. Franks, & Y. Jaffe (Eds.), *Perspectives on behavior therapy in the eighties.* New York: Springer.

LOVAAS, O., BERBERICH, J., PERLOFF, B., & SCHAEFFER, B. (1966). Acquisition of imitative speech by schizophrenic children. *Science, 151,* 705–707.

LOVAAS, O., FREITAG, G., GOLD, V., & KASSORLA, I. (1965). Recording apparatus and procedure for observation of behavior of children in free play settings. *Journal of Experimental Child Psychology, 2,* 108–120.

LOVAAS, O., FREITAG, G., KINDER, M., RUBENSTEIN, B., SCHAEFFER, B., & SIMMONS, J. (1966). Establishment of social reinforcers in two schizophrenic children on the basis of food. *Journal of Experimental Child Psychology, 4,* 109–125.

LOVAAS, O., KOEGEL, R., SIMMONS, J., & LONG, J. (1973). Some generalization and follow-up measures on autistic children in behavior therapy. *Journal of Applied Behavior Analysis, 6,* 131–165.

LOVAAS, O., & NEWSOM, C. (1976). Behavior modification with psychotic children. In H. Leitenberg (Ed.), *Handbook of behavior modification and behavior therapy.* Englewood Cliffs, NJ: Prentice-Hall.

LOVAAS, O., SCHREIBMAN, L., KOEGEL, R., & REHM, R. (1971). Selective responding by autistic children to multiple sensory input. *Journal of Abnormal Psychology, 77,* 211–222.

LOVAAS, O., & SIMMONS, J. (1969). Manipulation of self-destruction in three retarded children. *Journal of Applied Behavior Analysis, 2,* 143–157.

LOWRY, C., QUINN, K., & STEWART, M. (n. d.). *Serving autistic children within a large rural area: A resource manual.* Iowa City, IA: University of Iowa Press.

PECK, C., APPOLLONI, T., COOKE, T., & RAVER, S. (1978). Teaching retarded preschoolers to imitate the free-play behavior of nonretarded classmates: Training and generalized effects. *Journal of Special Education, 12,* 195–207.

POTTER, H. (1933). Schizophrenia in children. *American Journal of Psychiatry, 12,* 1253.

QUAY, H. (1983). A dimensional approach to behavior disorder: The revised behavior problem checklist. *School Psychology Review, 12,* 244–249.

REPP, A., & DEITZ, S. (1974). Reducing aggressive and self-injurious behavior of institutionalized retarded children through reinforcement of other behaviors. *Journal of Applied Behavior Analysis, 7,* 313–325.

RIMLAND, B. (1964). *Infantile autism.* New York: Appleton-Century-Crofts.

RINCOVER, A. (1978). Sensory extinction: A procedure for eliminating self-stimulatory behavior in autistic children. *Journal of Abnormal Child Psychology, 6,* 299–310.

RINCOVER, A., & KOEGEL, R. (1978). Research on the education of autistic children: Recent advances and future directions. In B. Lahey and A. Kazdin (Eds.) *Advances in Clinical Child Psychology,* Vol. I. New York: Plenum Press.

ROMANCZYK, R., DIAMENT, C., GOREN, E., TRUNELL, G., & HARRIS, S. (1975). Increasing isolate and social play in severely disturbed children: Intervention and postintervention effectiveness. *Journal of Autism and Childhood Schizophrenia, 5,* 57–70.

ROSS, A. (1976). *Psychological aspects of learning disabilities and reading disorders.* New York: McGraw-Hill.

ROSS, A. (1981). *Child behavior therapy.* New York: Wiley.

RUTT, C., & OXFORD, D. (1971). Prenatal and perinatal complications in childhood schizophrenics and their siblings. *Journal of Nervous and Mental Disorders, 152,* 324–331.

SCHOPLER, E., LANSING, M., & WATERS, L. (1983). *Individualized assessment and treatment for autistic and developmentally disabled children* (Vol. 3). Baltimore: University Park Press.

SCHOPLER, E., & REICHLER, R. (1979). *Individualized assessment and treatment for autistic and developmentally disabled children: Psychoeducational profile* (Vol. 1). Baltimore: University Park Press.

SCHOPLER, E., REICHLER, R., & LANSING, M. (1980). *Individualized assessment and treatment for autistic and developmentally disabled children: Teaching strategies for parents and professionals* (Vol. 2). Baltimore, MD: University Park Press.

SCHOVER, L., & NEWSOM, C. (1976). Overselectivity, developmental level, and overtraining in autistic and normal children. *Journal of Abnormal Psychology, 4,* 289–298.

SCHREIBMAN, L., KOEGEL, R., & CRAIG, M. (1977). Reducing stimulus overselectivity in autistic children. *Journal of Abnormal Child Psychology, 5,* 425–436.

SHEPP, B., & SWARTZ, K. (1976). Selective attention and the processing of integral and nonintegral dimensions: A developmental study. *Journal of Experimental Child Psychology, 22*, 73–85.

SILVERMAN, F. (1980). *Communication for the speechless*. Englewood Cliffs, NJ: Prentice-Hall.

STREMEL, K., & WARYAS, C. (1974). A behavioral-psycholinguistic approach to language training. In L. McReynolds (Ed.), *Developing systematic procedures for training children's language*. Washington, D.C.: American Speech and Hearing Association.

TALKINGTON, L., HALL, S., & ALTMAN, R. (1973). Use of a peer modelling procedure with severely retarded subjects on a basic communication response skill. *Training School Bulletin, 69*, 145–149.

TREFFERT, D. (1970). Epidemiology of infantile autism. *Archives of General Psychiatry, 22*, 431–438.

TWARDOSZ, S., SCHWARTZ, S., FOX, J., & CUNNINGHAM, J. (1979). Development and evaluation of a system to measure affectionate behavior. *Behavioral Assessment, 1*, 177–190.

WILHELM, H., & LOVAAS, O. (1976). Stimulus overselectivity: A common feature in autism and mental retardation. *American Journal of Mental Deficiency, 81*, 26–31.

WING, L., & GOULD, J. (1979). Severe impairments of social interaction and associated abnormalities in children: Epidemiology and classification. *Journal of Autism and Developmental Disorders, 9*, 11–29.

# 10

# CAREER EDUCATION AND TRANSITION SERVICES

by

Michael Peterson, Ph.D.

with

David B. Center, Ph.D.

**INTRODUCTION**

A major objective of school services for behavior-disordered students should be to prepare them for adult life. This requires systematic training for entry into work and for living in the home and community.

Follow-up studies suggest that the unemployment rates for the behaviorally disordered are much higher than those of the normal population. They also experience more problems in home and community living. Gill (1984) surveyed 500 special education graduates in Washington and found an unemployment rate of 48%. Another study in Washington (Maddox, Edgar, & Levine, 1984) found an unemployment rate of 36% for learning-disabled and behavior-disordered students. In Vermont, Hasazi, Gordon, and Roe (1985) found that 24% of the special education students were unemployed. Linden and Forness (1986) conducted a follow-up study of the adult adjustment of mentally retarded and emotionally disturbed students. They found that only 30% had a favorable adult outcome.

Studies of mentally ill youth and adults find critical problems in unemployment and community involvement. Dion and Anthony (1987) summarized several studies on the status of persons with psychiatric problems. They concluded that "no accurate estimates exist as to the typical degree of independent living status of persons with severe psychiatric disabilities" (p. 182). They also found that 52 to 92% were high school graduates and 15 to 60% of the high school graduates had attended college. Unemployment, however, may be as high as 64% for this population.

Hippolitus (1984) reported that 70% of disabled students ages 16 to 21 were getting no career training in their school programs. Halpern and Benz (1984) surveyed parents in Oregon about career education. They found that only 50% of disabled students received instruction in vocational skills, functional academics, and home and community living skills. Disabled students need specific training for vocational and functional living. These students are more likely to make a successful transition to employment when this is provided (Hasazi et al., 1985).

Transition from school to work has recently become a priority at the federal level. Public Law 98-199, the 1983 amendments to P.L. 94-142, reflects this new emphasis. This law includes Section 626, Secondary Education and Transitional Services for Handicapped Youth. Section 626 authorizes research and model projects to improve the following:

1. The transition process to adult education

2. Vocational training

3. Competitive employment

4. Continuing education and adult services

5. Programs for secondary special education

To date, there are about 90 funded projects nationwide. A Transition Institute at the University of Illinois evaluates these projects and provides technical help to transition programs. Leadership for this new initiative comes through the Office of Special Education and Rehabilitation Services (OSERS). Other agencies providing leadership include the Administration on Developmental Disabilities, the National Institute of Mental Health, and the Department of Labor.

Another important and recent law related to the transition initiative is the Carl Perkins Vocational Education Act (P.L. 98-524). This act requires a variety of services to help handicapped students enter and be successful in vocational education. A list of some of the act's provisions follow.

1. Access to the full range of vocational programs

2. To inform students and parents about available vocational education classes no later than the ninth grade

3. Vocational assessment of interests, abilities, and special needs for success in vocational education programs

4. Curriculum adaptations and support services to help students be successful in regular vocational education programs

5. Career counseling

6. Services to aid transition from school to employment or further education

The act provides funds to aid public school vocational education and training for behavior-disordered students. The act emphasizes service through regular vocational education classes. Ten percent of all federal funds received by a state must be used for vocational education of disabled students. These funds are only for extra costs over and above the cost for regular students. Fifty percent of the funds can be federal and 50% state or local matching funds. This funding formula favors use of federal vocational education funds to serve students in regular classes. The funds are for a variety of purposes, including the following:

1. Vocational assessment materials

2. Special vocational counselors

3. Adaptive equipment

4. Curriculum materials

5. Small curriculum adaptation projects

Federal funds may be used to support segregated programs. However, local and state funds must be used to fund the program at the level normally provided for normal students.

## CURRICULUM

There are a variety of approaches to developing curricula for career education and transition skills. One approach used to develop curriculum is environmental analysis. Environmental analysis is applied to highly specific environments or to general environments. In either case, the objective is to determine the skills and behaviors needed to be successful in the target environment. Once the analysis is complete, the identified skills and behaviors become the basis for the curriculum. The more specific the environment used for the analysis, the more narrow the resulting curriculum. Curricula developed from analysis of very specific environments can be the basis for highly individual programs. This, however, limits the number of students for whom the curriculum is suitable.

When the analysis uses broader and more general environments, the resulting curriculum is suitable for a wider variety of students. The curriculum will not, however, allow you to meet highly individual needs. Probably the best approach is to use a broad general curriculum in the early stages of education. You should use a more narrow and specialized curriculum in the later stages of career programs.

Brolin (1978) and Kokaska and Brolin (1985) have developed a career education curriculum structure. It is based on a general analysis of work, home, and community environments. The analysis resulted in three broad groups of skills or competencies: daily living skills, personal and social skills, and occupational development skills. There are 22 competencies and 102 objectives in the curriculum (See Table 10-1). You can see in the table that competency 21 has no objectives associated with it. These have been omitted because they pertain to developing specific vocational skills such as those needed by a brick mason. Special educators do not usually teach disabled students specific job skills. Such instruction is better left to vocational educators, who are better prepared to provide it. Special educators should, however, provide support services to handicapped students in vocational education programs and to their vocational teachers. All the other skills in the Life Centered model can and should be taught in special education programs. They can also be infused into regular education classes. It is these skills that will enable handicapped students to benefit from vocational education and be successful in the community.

A balance is needed between participation in the academic curriculum and the career education and transition curriculum. Brolin (1978) suggested a curriculum balance for disabled students in grades K through 12 (see Figure 10-1). The figure shows that academic skills should compose a major portion of the total curriculum at the elementary level. This is especially true for mildly im-

**Figure 10-1**    A chart showing the relative emphasis of different curricula for handicapped students across the public school grades. *From Kokaska and Brolin, 1985.*

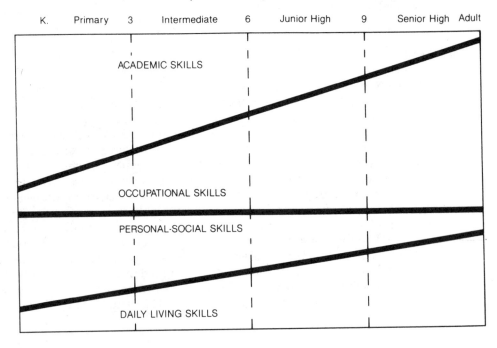

**Table 10–1**  Brolin's (1978) Life Centered Career Education Curriculum competencies and subcompetencies in three domains

| Curriculum Area | Competency | Subcompetencies | | | | | |
|---|---|---|---|---|---|---|---|
| Daily living skills | 1. Managing family finances | 1. Identify money and make correct change | 2. Make wise expenditures | 3. Obtain and use bank and credit facilities | 4. Keep basic financial records | 5. Calculate and pay taxes | |
| | 2. Selecting, managing, and maintaining a home | 6. Select adequate housing | 7. Maintain a home | 8. Use basic appliances and tools | 9. Maintain home exterior | | |
| | 3. Caring for personal needs | 10. Dress appropriately | 11. Exhibit proper grooming and hygiene | 12. Demonstrate knowledge of physical fitness, nutrition, and weight control | 13. Demonstrate knowledge of common illness prevention and treatment | | |
| | 4. Raising children, enriching family living | 14. Prepare for adjustment to marriage | 15. Prepare for raising children (physical care) | 16. Prepare for raising children (psychological care) | 17. Practice family safety in the home | | |
| | 5. Buying and preparing food | 18. Demonstrate appropriate eating skills | 19. Plan balanced meals | 20. Purchase food | 21. Prepare meals | 22. Clean food preparation areas | 23. Store food |
| | 6. Buying and caring for clothing | 24. Wash clothing | 25. Iron and store clothing | 26. Perform simple mending | 27. Purchase clothing | | |
| | 7. Engaging in civic activities | 28. Generally understand local laws and government | 29. Generally understand Federal Government | 30. Understand citizenship rights and responsibilities | 31. Understand registration and voting procedures | 32. Understand Selective Service procedures | 33. Understand civil rights and responsibilities when questioned by the law |
| | 8. Utilizing recreation and leisure | 34. Participate actively in group activities | 35. Know activities and available community resources | 36. Understand recreational values | 37. Use recreational facilities in the community | 38. Plan and choose activities wisely | 39. Plan vacations |
| | 9. Getting around the community (mobility) | 40. Demonstrate knowledge of traffic rules and safety practices | 41. Demonstrate knowledge and use of various means of transportation | 42. Drive a car | | | |
| Personal-social skills | 10. Achieving self awareness | 43. Attain a sense of body | 44. Identify interests and abilities | 45. Identify emotions | 46. Identify needs | 47. Understand the physical self | |
| | 11. Acquiring self confidence | 48. Express feelings of worth | 49. Tell how others see him/her | 50. Accept praise | 51. Accept criticism | 52. Develop confidence in self | |
| | 12. Achieving socially responsible behavior | 53. Know character traits needed for acceptance | 54. Know proper behavior in public places | 55. Develop respect for the rights and properties of others | 56. Recognize authority and follow instructions | 57. Recognize personal roles | |
| | 13. Maintaining good interpersonal skills | 58. Know how to listen and respond | 59. Know how to make and maintain friendships | 60. Establish appropriate heterosexual relationships | 61. Know how to establish close relationships | | |
| | 14. Achieving independence | 62. Understand impact of behaviors upon others | 63. Understand self organization | 64. Develop goal seeking behavior | | 65. Strive toward self actualization | |
| | 15. Achieving problem solving skills | 66. Differentiate bipolar concepts | 67. Understand the need for goals | 68. Look at alternatives | 69. Anticipate consequences | 70. Know where to find good advice | |
| | 16. Communicating adequately with others | 71. Recognize emergency situations | 72. Read at level needed for future goals | 73. Write at the level needed for future goals | 74. Speak adequately for understanding | 75. Understand the subtleties of communication | |

# Table 10 –1 (Continued)

|  | | | | | | |
|---|---|---|---|---|---|---|
| 17. Knowing and exploring occupational possibilities | 76. Identify the personal values met through work | 77. Identify the societal values met through work | 78. Identify the remunerative aspects of work | 79. Understand classification of jobs into different occupational systems | 80. Identify occupational opportunities available locally | 81. Identify sources of occupational information |
| 18. Selecting and planning occupational choices | 82. Identify major occupational needs | 83. Identify major occupational interests | 84. Identify occupational aptitudes | 85. Identify requirements of appropriate and available jobs | 86. Make realistic occupational choices | |
| 19. Exhibiting appropriate work habits and behaviors | 87. Follow directions | 88. Work with others | 89. Work at a satisfactory rate | 90. Accept supervision | 91. Recognize the importance of attendance and punctuality | 92. Meet demands for quality work |
| (Occupational guidance and preparation) | | | | | | 93. Demonstrate occupational safety |
| 20. Exhibiting sufficient physical manual skills | 94. Demonstrate satisfactory balance and coordination | 95. Demonstrate satisfactory manual dexterity | 96. Demonstrate satisfactory stamina and endurance | 97. Demonstrate satisfactory sensory discrimination | | |
| 21. Obtaining a specific occupational skill | | | | | | |
| 22. Seeking, securing, and maintaining employment | 98. Search for a job | 99. Apply for a job | 100. Interview for a job | 101. Adjust to competitive standards | 102. Maintain postschool occupational adjustment | |

Source: A noncopyrighted publication of the Council for Exceptional Children.

paired students. However, as a student moves through the grades, the curriculum emphasis shifts toward career education and transition skills. Besides the change in curriculum emphasis across the grades, there are shifts of emphasis within the Life Centered curriculum. There are three phases within the curriculum: awareness, exploration, and preparation. These three phases correspond roughly to the grades in elementary, middle, and secondary schools. In the Life Centered curriculum, you teach a given competency several times as a student moves through the grades. What changes is the way that instruction is done in different phases for the same competency.

## ASSESSMENT

Career assessment involves the ongoing monitoring of student choice, awareness, values, and skills related to work, home, and community. This process should begin with school entry and continue through transition from school into adult life. Career assessment has several major components.

1. Academic or educational assessment, which focuses on assessment of the student in the regular school curriculum

2. Vocational assessment, which provides assessment and exploration experiences related to work

3. Home and community living assessment, which provides assessment related to success in these two areas

Career assessment can be both formal and informal. *Formal assessment* refers to the use of standardized tests or assessment experiences conducted by assessment specialists. These specialists include vocational evaluators, vocational counselors, and school psychologists who are trained to do complete career assessments. *Informal assessment* is often conducted as part of a student's ongoing activities. Informal assessment can be done by teachers and may involve parents or the student. Career assessment should involve both formal and informal assessment, with an emphasis on informal assessment of ongoing activities.

### Role of Parents and Students

Parents and students must be active partners in the assessment process and involved in planning activities. Parents can often provide data about a student's skills and interests observed at home and in the community. A student can also be a good source of data. However, students with behavioral disorders are not usually good informants about behavior, e.g., social behaviors.

### Career Counseling Interview

There is a direct method of obtaining data about a student's interests and goals—simply ask during a career counseling interview. A structured format for such interviews is often used. The structured interview specifies questions and points for discussion but allows for exploration (Czerlansky & McCray, 1986; Pruitt, 1986). Career counseling interviews can be done individually or in a group. Career counseling interviews are probably most effective when done along with career-related learning experiences.

### Vocational Interest Inventories

When used properly, interest inventories can provide useful data for discussion and decision making. Vocational interest inventories do not tell students what they "ought" to be. They simply show how a student's interests relate to various jobs. For students who have limited reading ability, the Wide Range Interest Option Test (WRIOT) is suggested. It provides a clear, useful interest assessment across a wide range of jobs. The California Occupational Preference System (COPS) is an interest inventory for skilled and technical jobs keyed to the Dictionary of Occupational Titles. A low-reading-skills version of COPS is also available. For professional careers, the Strong-Campbell Vocational Interest Inventory (SVII) is one of the most researched tests available.

### Vocational Exploration and Decision-Making Programs

Several tests are available to aid self-assessment and job exploration. The focus of such programs begins with interests but also includes skills. One useful instrument is the Self-Directed Search (SDS). The SDS helps students select their vocational personality based on career daydreams, interests, activities, and skills. It also encourages and helps structure vocational exploration activities. Several computer programs are available that engage students in similar activities. One such program is the Career Planning System (CPS), which is useful for students with limited reading ability (Peterson, 1986).

### Rating Scales and Checklists

For behavior-disordered students, social behavior in work, home, and community settings is especially important. Marr and Means (1984) identified some of the more important problems. These are problems of behavioral excesses and deficits, including the following:

1. Dependent behavior

2. Aggressive behavior

3. Withdrawn behavior

4. Immature social and verbal behavior

5. False complaints about sickness and physical problems

If problems occur in such areas, it is important that you recognize and deal with them.

Several rating systems are available. Most assess skills in exploratory job tryouts, vocational classroom tryouts, and other settings involving real work. These rating scales are screening measures to identify strengths and weaknesses. Identified problems need more specific assessment using the behavioral assessment techniques described in Chapter 4.

Most measures, however, focus on general skills important across a variety of work, home, and community situations. These include cognitive and basic academic, physical, social, and behavioral skills. The worker trait system developed by the Department of Labor is the most widely used system covering these skills.

Many skill assessment checklists and monitoring forms are available. A checklist is available for the Life Centered Career Education curriculum developed by Brolin (1978). It is based on the 22 competencies in that curriculum (see Figure 10-2). The SCOR curriculum provides assessment forms with objectives and performance criteria for some 900 target skills for home and community living. The Scales of Independent Behavior (SIB) is an overall measure of functional independence in basic academic, social, personal living, and community skills. SIB uses a structured interview to obtain data (Peterson, 1986).

The Work Adjustment Rating Form (Bitter & Bolanovich, 1970) assesses work readiness and includes eight subscales:

1. Amount of supervision required

2. Realism of job goals

3. Teamwork

4. Acceptance of rules and authority

5. Work tolerance

6. Persistence in work

7. Extent of help seeking

8. Importance attached to job training

A simple but useful rating scale is the MDC Behavior Identification Format (Materials Development Center, 1974). It includes rating and narrative comments about 22 work behaviors. These include such behaviors as irritating habits, ability to cope with work problems, personal complaints, and reactions to changes in work tasks.

Another more detailed rating scale is the Vocational Behavior Checklist (Walls, Zane, & Werner, 1978). This scale contains some 339 behavioral skills compiled from 21 previously developed behavior rating forms. There are seven groups:

**LIFE CENTERED CAREER EDUCATION**
Competency Rating Scale
Record Form
Experimental[1]

OCCUPATIONAL GUIDANCE AND PREPARATION

Student Name_____Date of Birth_____ ____Sex _____

School_____City_____State _____

Directions: Please rate the student according to his/her mastery of *each* item using the rating key below. Indicate the ratings in the column below the date for the rating period. Use the NR rating for items which cannot be rated. For subcompetencies rated 0 or 1 at the time of the final rating, place a check (✓) in the appropriate space in the *yes/no* column to indicate his/her ability to perform the subcompetency with assistance from the community. Please refer to the CRS manual for explanation of the rating key, description of the behavioral criteria for each subcompetency, and explanation of the *yes/no* column.

Rating Key:    0 = Not Competent    1 = Partially Competent    2 = Competent    NR = Not Rated

To what extent has the student mastered the following subcompetencies:

| Subcompetencies | Rater(s) | | | | | | | | | Yes | No |
|---|---|---|---|---|---|---|---|---|---|---|---|
| | Grade Level | | | | | | | | | | |
| | Date(s) | | | | | | | | | | |
| *17. Knowing and Exploring Occupational Possibilities* | | | | | | | | | | | |
| 76. Identify the personal values met through work | — | — | — | — | — | — | — | — | — |
| 77. Identify the societal values met through work | — | — | — | — | — | — | — | — | — |
| 78. Identify the remunerative aspects of work | — | — | — | — | — | — | — | — | — |
| 79. Understand the classification of jobs into different occupational systems | — | — | — | — | — | — | — | — | — |
| 80. Identify occupational opportunities available locally | — | — | — | — | — | — | — | — | — |
| 81. Identify sources of occupational information | — | — | — | — | — | — | — | — | — |
| *18. Selecting and Planning Occupational Choices* | | | | | | | | | | | |
| 82. Identify major occupational needs | — | — | — | — | — | — | — | — | — |
| 83. Identify major occupational interests | — | — | — | — | — | — | — | — | — |
| 84. Identify occupational aptitudes | — | — | — | — | — | — | — | — | — |
| 85. Identify requirements of appropriate and available jobs | — | — | — | — | — | — | — | — | — |
| 86. Make realistic occupational choices | — | — | — | — | — | — | — | — | — |
| *19. Exhibiting Appropriate Work Habits and Behaviors* | | | | | | | | | | | |
| 87. Follow directions | — | — | — | — | — | — | — | — | — |
| 88. Work with others | — | — | — | — | — | — | — | — | — |
| 89. Work at a satisfactory rate | — | — | — | — | — | — | — | — | — |
| 90. Accept supervision | — | — | — | — | — | — | — | — | — |
| 91. Recognize the importance of attendance and punctuality | — | — | — | — | — | — | — | — | — |
| 92. Meet demands of quality work | — | — | — | — | — | — | — | — | — |
| 93. Demonstrate occupational safety | — | — | — | — | — | — | — | — | — |

**Figure 10-2** A portion of the Life Centered Career Education Competency Rating Scale. This is a criterion-referenced rating scale covering personal and social, daily living, and occupational guidance and preparation skills. *From Brolin, 1978.*

1. Prevocational skill

2. Job-seeking skill

3. Interview skills

4. Job skills

5. Work skills

6. On-the-job social skills

7. Union and financial security skills

Again, problems identified need more precise behavioral assessment (Marr & Means, 1984; Hall, 1974).  You can use behavioral assessment techniques described in Chapter 4 to assess these behaviors.

### Functional Skill Tests

There are also several formal tests that focus on the assessment of functional work and independent living skills. Many of these tests are for use with the mentally retarded. They could, however, be used with behavior disordered students as well. One example is the Social and Prevocational Information Battery (SPIB). This test uses a paper-and-pencil format and assesses functional skills in nine areas (Peterson, 1986):

1. Hygiene and grooming

2. Functional signs

3. Job-related behaviors

4. Home management

5. Health care

6. Job-seeking skills

7. Budgeting

8. Banking

9. Purchasing habits

### Vocational Aptitude Tests and Work Samples

Vocational aptitudes are basic cognitive, perceptual, and psychomotor traits related to the way that students learn particular tasks. The Department of Labor (1977) defined 11 aptitudes, such as verbal aptitude, numerical aptitude, and spatial perception. Included is the minimal level of various aptitudes required by a variety of jobs. Many vocational aptitude tests are available which attempt to assess student aptitudes matched to job demands. Two of these are the General Aptitude Test Battery and the Differential Aptitude Test. In addition, there are commercial work sample systems available, e.g., JEVS and SAGE, that focus on work traits (Botterbusch, 1985). Such trait assessment measures are useful as screening devices to identify vocation options for exploration. However, such tests are general and cannot precisely assess a student's present skills or potential. You should use these tests with caution (Peterson, 1986).

### Performance and Work Samples

Work samples use the actual tools, materials, and tasks found on jobs and in vocational training programs, or in independent living tasks. In work samples, students do tasks and their efforts are observed and rated. Although work samples are used mostly with job tasks, you can also use them for independent living tasks. For example, you are interested in whether a student has the skills to learn basic auto mechanics. A work sample might have a student change and set the spark plugs in a car. The student might also use a manual to look up the necessary directions. In independent living tasks, a student might do cleaning and cooking tasks to assess skills in these areas. Work samples are different from observational assessment because they have norms and the behavior ratings are to specific criteria. Many commercial work sample systems are available (Botterbusch, 1985). However, most home and community assessment relies on observational techniques in natural settings. Many assessment specialists develop local work and task samples for vocational assessment and home and community assessment. Peterson (1986), Albright (1977) and the Materials Development Center (1974) provide guidelines for developing work samples for vocational assessment adaptable to other areas.

### Observational Rating

Observation of students' skills in real work, home, or community settings will provide the most valid assessment of skills. Depending on the observational instrument used, observations may be used to assess any skill or ability. You can construct your own instrument by analyzing a competency into a list of skills needed to accomplish it. With this instrument you could then assess a student's skills on a real task. You can do this using the task analysis procedures discussed in Chapter 2. For example, use of public buses might include several skills:

1. Purchasing bus tokens

2. Identifying the correct bus to get on

3. Boarding the bus

4. Identification of destination

**Table 10-2** A comprehensive summary of vocational assessment for handicapped students in public school programs

GRADE LEVEL

| | 1-6 | 7-8 | 9-10 | 11-12 |
|---|---|---|---|---|
| Type of vocational assessment | Curriculum-based vocational assessment | Curriculum-based vocational assessment | Curriculum-based and/or vocational evaluation | Curriculum-based and/or vocational evaluation |
| Agencies responsible | Special education Counseling | Special education Counseling | Vocational education (with special education) | Vocational education Vocational rehabilitation (with special education) |
| Sample methods | Teacher/parent observation Career awareness and interest checklists Psychological educational assessment | Vocational interest and career awareness tests Psych/educational assessment Teacher/parent observations and checklists Dexterity tests | Same plus... Vocational aptitude tests Work samples Performance samples Vocational class tryouts Behavior observation Job tryouts | Vocational education Vocational rehabilitation (with special education) |
| Focus of assessment | Vocational interests Career awareness Prevocational skills Physical skills Functional academic skills | Vocational interests Career awareness Prevocational skills Physical skills Work behaviors Functional academics | Vocational interests Work behaviors Physical skills Functional academics Vocational aptitudes Vocational skills | Vocational education Vocational rehabilitation (with special education) |
| Desired Recommendations | Career education and prevocational skills training | Career education; occupational exploration; prevocational skills training (industrial arts, etx.) Work behaviors training | Entrance into vocational education Support services Prevocational skills Entrance into coop program with rehabilitation | Job placement Referral to community agency |
| Personnel potentially involved | Teachers Counselors School psychologist | Teachers Counselors School psychologists Others | Vocational evaluation specialists Teachers: special, general Counselors School psychologist Rehabilitation personnel | Vocational evaluation specialist Vocational teachers Special and general education teachers Counselors School psychologist Rehabilitation personnel |

Source: Peterson, 1986.

5. Signaling for the bus to stop

6. Exiting the bus.

Table 10-2 is a comprehensive summary of vocational assessment for students with behavioral disorders. The table covers all the public school years. You will also find several aspects of vocational assessment addressed for various grade levels.

## INTERVENTION

The goal of career assessment is to develop a plan for services. The services should help behavior-disordered students select and achieve life and community goals. Planning should include four major areas:

1. The regular school curriculum

2. Work

3. Home

4. Community

For each of these areas, you should specify the following:

1. Long- and short-term goals

2. Educational needs

3. Program placement and strategies

4. Teaching approaches and support services

You can take long- and short-term goals for educational needs from curricula in this and several earlier chapters in this book. We also discussed methods for teaching and behavior change in those chapters. Support services are discussed elsewhere in this chapter. Program placement is discussed in this chapter and in Chapter 11. Individualized education plans are also discussed in Chapter 11.

The intent of such planning is for students, parents, and educators to select objectives and strategies together. The focus should be on a student's involvement in the school curriculum and for living in the adult world. As a student comes closer to leaving school, especially in grades 10 to 12, the objectives for community involvement and work must become very specific.

### Program Placement

First, you identify goals and learning objectives. Next, you decide which program(s) will help a student most in reaching the goals. Program placement may include any of the service approaches described below. In addition,

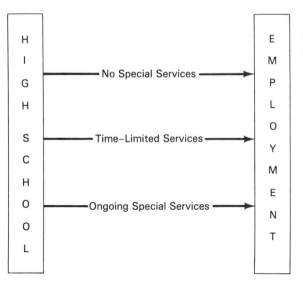

**Figure 10–3**
The major components in the transition process. *From Will, 1984.*

programs may include informal ways to involve parents and community members. Students enter the critical transition years in grades 9 to 12. Program options should be available that aid work, home, and community skills development.

### Instructional Approaches

Specific approaches to teaching and behavior change are discussed in Chapters 2 and 4 through 9. Techniques covered in these chapters should be adequate for most of the objectives in the career and transition curriculum. Thus, we will limit our discussion in this section to other service delivery topics.

### Cooperative Planning for Transition

Will (1984), as Assistant Secretary of OSERS, developed a model of transition from school to work. This model serves as the basis for policy development and the design of transition services. This model includes three major service paths (see Figure 10-3):

1. Students use existing services available to the general public, such as employment services and vocational and technical schools.

2. Time-limited special services, such as vocational rehabilitation, provide special training and aid to disabled students.

3. Ongoing support services, such as various approaches to supported employment, provide help in maintaining a job.

Will's model focuses entirely on employment. Home, community, and leisure skills and interests are important to the extent that they are linked directly to employment outcomes.

Halpern (1985) developed an adaptation of the Will model described as "transition from school to community adjustment." This approach maintains the three service paths described by Will and adds three outcome components:

1. Employment

2. Home living

3. Social networks

For Halpern, the home and residential component includes home living skills, accessing community services, and recreational and leisure pursuits. Social networks include all aspects of human relations, such as daily communication, self-esteem, family support, emotional maturity, and intimate relationships.

The Comprehensive Model of Transition from School to Work (see Figure 10-4) illustrates a complete model for transition from school to work. The

**Figure 10-4**    A comprehensive model for career and transition services for handicapped students. *From Peterson (in press).*

## Comprehensive Model of Career Development and Transition from School to Adult Life

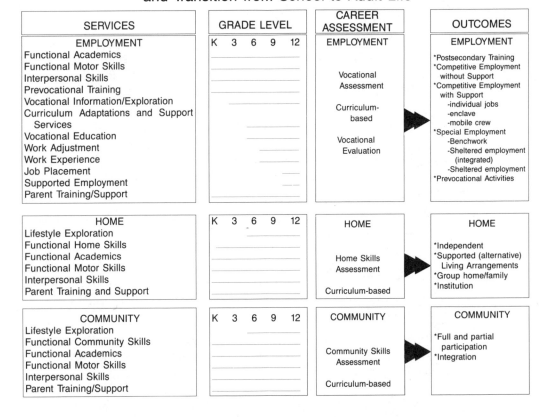

model combines the service programs described above into a total model suitable for behavior-disordered students. The model represents a developmental, inter-agency service delivery system. It includes outcomes and services related to work, home, and community living. The assumption of the model is that students of all ages need Individualized Education Plans with goals for community living. Services begin in elementary school and include use of basic academic, physical, and social skills for community settings. The model is consistent with Halpern's model and Brolin's Life Centered career education approach. Outcomes cover the work, home, and community areas. The model describes time-limited and ongoing support services.

### Career Choice Services

Choice of vocational goals and life-style at home and in the community should begin early. Activities should include those that aid career awareness, career exploration, and self-assessment. Students must engage in experiences that help them to understand opportunities in work, home, and community settings. They must also understand the demands and rewards in those settings. Finally, they should know their own skills and needs, support systems and resources available to them, and how all these fit together.

Although decision making should be systematic and logical, most people make decisions, at least partially, intuitively, based on their experiences. Behavior-disordered students, in particular, need information about work, home, and community options and their own skills and resources. Consequently, you should emphasize experiential techniques. We present next some ideas and resources that may be helpful.

### Career Education

In 1971, the career education movement was formally initiated with a speech by Disney Marland. This speech committed the United States Office of Education to the goal of preparing all students for entry into work or additional education. It was clear at that time that many students were graduating from public school with only minimal skills for obtaining jobs. In the 1980s, there were similar concerns for students with special needs. This resulted in programs related to transition from school to work for "at-risk youth."

Career education programs resulted in much debate about the purpose and definition of career education. This debate led to the testing of several models of career education. Hoyt et al. (1974) defined career education as "the totality of experiences through which one learns about and prepares to engage in work. . . ." According to Herr (1972), career education involves two major components.

1. Focus on training for a specific job

2. A career model focused on broad career patterns focused on home and community involvement and individual life-style

## Models for Career Education

In the early 1970s, four experimental models of career education were developed and tested. These models were school based, employer based, rural and residential based, and home and community based (Calhoun & Finch, 1976). For special educators working with behavior-disordered adolescents, the school- and employer-based models should prove to be the most useful. The school-based model infuses career education into the regular school curriculum.

Career education programs in the public schools are usually based on a career development model with three stages:

1. Career awareness in which students develop an awareness and understanding of themselves and jobs

2. Career exploration in which students actively explore jobs and begin the process of making a career choice

3. Vocational training in which students engage in learning specific skills through vocational education and community colleges.

In recent years, many curriculum materials were developed which attempt to diffuse career education into academic classes. These classes also use special career learning events such as career days. In many schools, there are specific career exploration classes for middle-school students. In these classes students have a chance to explore careers and make career choices.

The employer-based model of career education initially sought to involve employers in the process of career education. This led to the development of the experience-based model of career education (EBCE). EBCE is used in many states to aid students between 13 and 18 years of age to explore careers in work settings.

## Prevocational and Career Exploration Classes

There are specific classes in some states to aid vocational, and sometimes, life-style exploration and decision making. These classes use curricula designed to aid career exploration. Brolin (1978) and his associates reviewed and compiled many curriculum materials useful for this purpose. In addition, job exploration curriculum guides are available from vocational curriculum centers in most states.

## Community Based Activities

Involving students in community activities is also useful. This can be done in several ways.

1. Experience-based career education (EBCE)

2. Work experience and work study programs

3. Community-based special education

In EBCE students enroll in a class and work on a series of community job sites. This provides several weeks of exploration activities and personal skill assessment. A teacher manages the process and provides periodic in-class time when students may discuss their experiences and their job choice. Work experience and community-based special education are similar but focus more on skill development (Calhoun & Finch, 1976).

### Functional, Community-Based Special Education

Experience suggests that disabled students have greater problems than normal students in making the transition from school to adult life. Some special educators have responded by using an approach that is both functional in content and community based in service delivery. In this approach, the curricula in elementary and secondary schools help students learn functional skills for work, home, and community functioning. Rather than just teaching basic academic and social skills, the curricula emphasize specific skills in real-world settings. Thus, behavior-disordered students should not only be taught academic and social skills but also how to apply those skills to life.

The emphasis on functional use of skills is consistent with the Life Centered approach of Brolin (Falvey, 1986; Wilcox & Bellamy, 1987). For example, you can teach a student to control acting-out behavior in a structured classroom. This does not, however, guarantee correct responses to co-workers or supervisors on a job. Behavioral and social learning in actual work situations is an important part of the career education process.

### Vocational Education for Special Students

Vocational education provides education and training for specific jobs for semi-skilled, skilled, and technical jobs requiring less than a college degree. The Smith-Hughes Act was passed in 1917. It made funds available for vocational education in secondary schools and later in adult education. In 1963 a major revision of federal vocational education law increased the focus on students with "special needs." This trend continues in the recently passed Carl Perkins Vocational Education Act (P.L. 98-524).

### Work Adjustment

Work adjustment training programs are designed for people who lack the basic work and social skills needed for employment (Neff, 1968). According to Anthony (1979), the behavior disordered "often lose their jobs, not because of an inability to do job tasks, but because of skill deficits in the personal area of functioning" (p. 129).

Work adjustment programs became part of rehabilitation services in 1965 with the passage of Public Law 89-333. This act authorized work adjustment services, for up to 18 months, for persons with catastrophic disabilities (Field, Gannaway, & Sink, 1978). Since that time work adjustment programs have expanded greatly and serve a variety of disabled people. Such services are especially important for persons with behavioral disorders, particularly, if their social and behavioral skills are affected in work settings.

Work adjustment is a training process, using individual and group work or work-related activities. It also helps students understand the meaning, value, and demands of work. It attempts to modify or develop attitudes, personal traits, work behaviors, and functional skills needed for optimal vocational development (Anthony, 1979). Work adjustment uses real work settings to help students develop suitable work and social behaviors needed to obtain employment. The professional organization most directly concerned with work adjustment is the Vocational Evaluation and Work Adjustment Association (VEWAA). The VEWAA is a division of the National Rehabilitation Association.

Work adjustment programs are most often conducted within rehabilitation facilities. Work adjustment programs use almost any setting where real work activities can provide a context for behavior change. Work adjustment techniques can be useful in special education classes, vocational education classes, community-based training, and supported employment. Work adjustment training is a very important component for career development programs for behavior disordered students.

### Supported Employment

Supported employment is a new approach to job placement and follow-up for persons with severe handicaps. In supported employment people work on a real job. They also get special help from "job coaches," who provide follow-up and support services. Support services include such things as aid in solving problems that develop on the job and during retraining. This approach is especially useful for behavior-disordered students, who may have difficulty coping with job demands. The presence of suitable support services helps students to keep jobs. Otherwise, they lose them and go back into the human service delivery system. Since supported employment focuses on community-based training, all such programs include work adjustment training (Moon, Goodall, Barcus, & Brooke, 1986).

In recent years, many model projects have aided the development of the supported employment model. Rehabilitation facilities use variations on this approach in industry and in work training settings in the community. With the passage of the 1986 amendments to the Rehabilitation Act, supported employment was officially added to the vocational rehabilitation service delivery system. Many "systems change" projects are funded throughout the country. They are shifting the focus in rehabilitation from sheltered employment to supported employment in regular work settings.

### Community Support Programs

Community support programs, e.g., Fountain House (Beard, 1976), have for many years provided help for the mentally ill. Such programs usually use both residential and vocational support services. The community support program is a joint effort of rehabilitation and mental health agencies. They try to provide support for the mentally ill in the community (Grantham, 1980). Since behavior-disordered students are often involved with both agencies, such programs can be very helpful when available. The Rehabilitation Research and Training Center at Boston University publishes a newsletter titled *Community Support Network News*. This publication can help you locate resources and ideas related to community support programs.

### Agencies and Personnel Providing Services

A great many agencies and persons provide career and transition services to behavior-disordered youth. Those most involved include special and regular education, vocational rehabilitation, and mental health centers. Coordinated delivery of services among all these agencies is needed. Unfortunately, this occurs less often than is desirable.

Vocational rehabilitation agencies can provide help in a variety of ways:

1. Counseling

2. Vocational training

3. Job placement

4. Tools and equipment needed for employment

5. Work adjustment training

6. Physical and psychological restoration services

Rehabilitation agencies, for example, may pay the tuition for a student to attend a vocational school or college. Rehabilitation agencies are able to provide funds for a variety of other services also, if they lead to employment. The goal of rehabilitation agencies is job placement in competitive, supported, or sheltered work settings. There are three eligibility requirements for services from such agencies:

1. There must be clear physical or mental disability, including psychiatric and behavioral disorders.

2. The disability must represent a substantial handicap for employment.

3. Services must result in a reasonable expectation of benefit and employment.

Since the passage of the rehabilitation amendments of 1986, rehabilitation counselors must also consider supported employment needs in making eligibility decisions.

Rehabilitation facilities in most states are private, nonprofit organizations. They provide a variety of services, including vocational evaluation, work adjustment, personal adjustment, sheltered employment, community-based training, and supported employment. They provide services by contract to state vocational rehabilitation agencies. Many have developed effective programs to provide complete transition services to disabled students.

Community mental health centers, funded through both federal and local money, provide support services to persons with mental illness. Comprehensive mental health centers often offer a wide range of services. These services may include group, individual, and family counseling; group homes and halfway houses; case management; and other support services. Coordinated services with vocational rehabilitation agencies are sometimes available. Such mental health centers require that individuals have diagnosable disabilities based on the Diagnostic and Statistical Manual (DSM III). They do not use the rule requiring reasonable expectation of benefit from services.

Behavior-disordered students have a greater potential for successful involvement in adult life than they now exhibit. However, for this to occur, they need special services throughout their school careers. Special education must help these students develop the work, home, and community skills they need for a successful transition to adult life.

## RESOURCES

An excellent source of papers discussing career education for students with behavior disorders is a volume edited by Fink and Kokaska (1983). There is a special issue of Exceptional Children edited by Clark and Knowlton (1987). This issue contains a detailed discussion of transition from school to adulthood. Peterson (1986) is a guide to vocational assessment for disabled students that contains much useful information. A volume edited by Brolin (1978) presents a detailed outline of the Life Centered career education model. This volume covers several areas:

1. Curriculum objectives

2. An assessment instrument keyed to the objectives

3. Teaching ideas

4. A list of teaching materials keyed to the objectives

5. A model for IEP development.

Miller, Glascoe, and Kokaska (1986) have developed two activity books for the Life Centered career education curriculum. One of these activity books is for elementary and the other for secondary students. There is also a trainer's guide available for the Life Centered curriculum (Brolin, McKay, & West, 1978). Finally, there are several valuable appendices in a book by Kokaska and Brolin (1985). For example, Appendix B contains a school district plan for Life Centered Career Education. Appendix C contains a list of Life Centered curriculum objectives referenced to the Brigance Essential Skills Test.

# REFERENCES

ALBRIGHT, L. (1977). *Strategies for Assessing the Student's Present Level(s) of Performance*. Champaign, IL: University of Illinois.

ANTHONY, W. A. (1979). *The Principles of Psychiatric Rehabilitation*. Amherst, MA: Human Resource Development Press.

BEARD, J. (1976). Psychiatric rehabilitation at Fountain House. In J. Meislin (Ed.), *Rehabilitation Medicine and Psychiatry*. Springfield, IL: Charles C Thomas.

BITTER, J., & BOLANOVICH, D. (1970). WARF: A scale for measuring job-readiness behaviors. *American Journal of Mental Deficiency, 74*, 616–621.

BOTTERBUSCH, K. (1985). *Comparison of Commercial Vocational Evaluation Systems*. Menomonie, WI: University of Wisconsin-Stout, Materials Development Center.

BROLIN, D. (1978). *Life Centered Career Education: A Competency Based Approach*. Reston, VA: Council for Exceptional Children.

BROLIN, D., McKAY, D., & WEST, L. (1978). *Trainer's Guide to Life Centered Career Education*. Reston, VA: Council for Exceptional Children.

CALHOUN, C., & FINCH, A. (1976). *Vocational and Career Education: Concepts and Operations*. Belmont, CA: Wadsworth.

CLARK, G., & KNOWLTON, E. (1987). Transition from school to adult life [Special issue]. *Exceptional Children, 53* (6).

CZERLINSKY, T., & McCRAY, P. (1986). *Vocational Decision-Making Interview: Administration Manual*. Menomonie, WI: University of Wisconsin-Stout, Research and Training Center.

DEPARTMENT OF LABOR (1977). *Dictionary of Occupational Titles*. Washington, D C: U.S. Government Printing Office.

DION, G. L., & ANTHONY, W. A. (1987). Research in psychiatric rehabilitation: A review of experimental and quasi-experimental studies. *Rehabilitation Counseling Bulletin, 30* (1), 177–203.

FALVEY, M. (1986). *Community-Based Curriculum*. Baltimore: Paul H. Brookes.

FIELD, T., GANNAWAY, T., & SINK, J. (1978). History and scope of adjustment services. *Journal of Rehabilitation, 44* (1), 16–20.

FINK, A., & KOKASKA, C. (1983). *Career Education for Behaviorly Disordered Students*. Reston, VA: Council for Exceptional Children.

GILL, D. H. (1984). *An Employment Related Follow-up of Former Special Education Students in Pierce County, Washington (1983–84)*. Tacoma, WA: ESD 121 Pierce Co, Vocational Special Education Cooperative.

GRANTHAM, R. (1980). What constitutes rehabilitation of the mentally ill in the 1980's? In L. Perlman (Ed.), *The Rehabilitation of the Mentally Ill in the 1980's*. Washington, DC: National Rehabilitation Association.

HALL, R. V. (1974). *Managing Behavior*. Lawrence, KS: H & H Enterprises.

HALPERN, A. (1985). Transition: A look at the foundations. *Exceptional Children, 51* (6), 479–486.

HALPERN, A., & BENZ, M. (1984). *Toward Excellence in Secondary Special Education: A Statewide Study of Oregon's High School Programs for Students With Mild Disabilities*. Eugene, OR: University of Oregon, Rehabilitation Research and Training Center and Western Regional Resource Center.

HASAZI, S. B., GORDON, L. R., & ROE, C. A. (1985). Factors associated with the employment status of handicapped youth exiting high school from 1979 to 1983. *Exceptional Children, 51*, 455–469.

HERR, E. (1972). Unifying an entire system of education around a career development theme. In K. Goldhammer & R. Taylor (Eds.), *Career Education Perspective and Promise*. Columbus, OH: Charles E. Merrill.

HIPPOLITUS, P. (1984, May 17). President's committee says disabled need better preparation for work. *Vocational Training News*, pp. 9–10.

HOYT, K., EVANS, R., MACKIN, E., & MANGAM, G. (1974). *Career Education: What It Is and How To Do It*. Salt Lake City, UT: Olympus Publishing Company.

KOKASKA, C., & BROLIN, D. (1985). *Career Education for Handicapped Individuals* (2nd ed.). Columbus, OH: Merrill.

LINDEN, B., & FORNESS, S. (1986). Post-school adjustment of mentally retarded persons with psychiatric disorders: A ten-year follow-up. *Education and Training of the Mentally Retarded, 20* (7), 157–186.

MADDOX, M, EDGAR, E., & LEVINE, P. (1984). Post school status of graduates of special education (Working paper). Seattle, WA: University of Washington, Experimental Education Unit.

MARR, J. N., & MEANS, B. L. (1984). *Behavior management manual: Procedures for psychological problems in rehabilitation.* Little Rock, AR: University of Arkansas, Arkansas Rehabilitation Services, Arkansas Rehabilitation Research & Training Center.

MATERIALS DEVELOPMENT CENTER (1974). *MDC Behavior Identification Format.* Menomonie, WI: Author, University of Wisconsin-Stout.

MILLER, L., GLASCOE, L., & KOKASKA, C. (1986). *Life Centered Career Education: Activity Books I* (elementary) and *II* (secondary). Reston, VA: Council for Exceptional Children.

MOON, S., GOODALL, P., BARCUS, M., & BROOKE, V. (1986). *The Supported Work Model of Competitive Employment for Citizens with Severe Handicaps: A Guide for Job Trainers.* Richmond, VA: Virginia Commonwealth University Rehabilitation Research and Training Center.

NEFF, W. (1968). *Work and Human Behavior.* New York: Atherton Press.

PETERSON, M. (In press). *Career Assessment and Planning for Special Persons.* Boston: Allyn and Bacon.

PETERSON, M. (1986). *Vocational Assessment of Special Students: A Procedural Manual.* (Available from VOC-AIM; 27475 Golden Gate West; Lathrup Village, MI 40876).

PRUITT, W. (1986). *Vocational Evaluation.* Menomonie, WI: Walt Pruitt Associates.

WALLS, R., ZANE, R., & WERNER, T. (1978). *The Vocational Behavior Checklist.* Morgantown, WV: West Virginia Rehabilitation Research and Training Center.

WILCOX, B., & BELLAMY, G. T. (1987). *The Activities Catalog: An Alternative Curriculum for Youth and Adults with Severe Disabilities.* Baltimore, MD: Paul H. Brookes.

WILL, M. (1984). *Bridges from School to Working Life.* Washington, D. C.: Office of Special Education and Rehabilitation Services.

# 11

# PROVIDING EDUCATIONAL SERVICES

## INDIVIDUALIZED EDUCATION PROGRAMS (IEP)

Public Law 94-142 requires that all handicapped students receiving special education services have an IEP. The recognition that handicapped students need individualized education goes back at least to the hand training movement in the 1860s. There was a child-centered period in American education during the earlier part of this century. During this period, individualization was the objective for all students. It was not until World War II and the baby boom that followed that the child-centered orientation ended. Since the 1960s, the need for individualized education for handicapped students has been widely accepted. One rationale for the smaller classes characteristic of special education is the greater need for individualized instruction for handicapped students. This recognition was formally endorsed and legally required with the passage of P.L. 94-142 in 1975.

### Purposes of the IEP

The IEP serves several purposes. First, it is a management plan. This means that an IEP is intended to aid planning and delivery of appropriate services. It should present in broad outline the student's needs and how they will be met. That is, it is a guide to follow in planning instruction. It is not, however, a detailed prescription for daily instruction. Second, it helps to ensure that appropriate services are provided. It does this by requiring instruction based on appropriate assessment data and by involving specific individuals in the process, e.g., teachers, parents, support personnel, and administrators. Third, the IEP requires a formal commitment of resources. It must specify what type of services are going to be provided, how much service will be provided, and who will provide the services. Fourth, it is an evaluation document. It provides a vehicle by which the delivery of services can be monitored and progress can be evaluated. Fifth, the IEP is a communication device. It provides a focal point for communication between the school and parents about a student's education. The IEP also represents a focus for resolving differences between the school and a student's parents.

### Components of the IEP

Each IEP must include specific components (see Box 11–1) to meet the legal requirement in P.L. 94-142. We will now take a brief look at each of these components.

**Box 11–1**    A sample IEP for a self-contained BD student in the middle grades[a]

---

**INDIVIDUALIZED EDUCATION PROGRAM**

STUDENT: Bill Blunder                  D.O.B.: June 6, 1974

DISTRICT: Proper Valley             SCHOOL: Prim Middle School

GRADE: Seventh                          TEACHER: Mrs. Righteous

IEP MEETING: May 25, 1988

PLACEMENT: Behavior Disorder

PARTICIPANTS:    Mrs. Overseer, Principal
Dr. Norms, School Psychologist
Ms. Hawkeyes, BD Teacher
Mrs. Blunder, Parent

CURRENT LEVEL OF FUNTIONING: (See attached report)

INTELLIGENCE: WISC-R Full Scale 93.

VISION and HEARING: Normal.

SPEECH: Adequate.

PERCEPTUAL INTEGRATION: Normal.

ACADEMIC SKILLS: Reading 4.5, Math 4.0, English 5.0, & Science 5.5.

STUDY SKILLS: Inadequate.

VOCATIONAL SKILLS: Inadequate pre-vocational skills.

SOCIAL BEHAVIOR: Excessive interpersonal aggression, deficits in age-appropriate

**Box 11–1    Continued**

social skills, and immature social reasoning.

EMOTIONAL BEHAVIOR: Inappropriate anger and excessive irrational thinking.

**Long-Term Goals**

1. To improve decoding and comprehension skills by one grade level.
2. To improve math computation skills by one grade level.
3. To improve writing skills by one grade level.
4. To demonstrate a knowledge of basic concepts in earth science.
5. To develop specialized reading skills and study skills.
6. To exhibit appropriate pre-vocational work behaviors.
7. To reduce inappropriate, interpersonal aggression.
8. To develop prosocial alternatives to aggression.
9. To advance one stage in social reasoning about friendship and peer relations.
10. To develop self-control of anger responses.
11. To develop rational-emotive problem-solving skills.

**Short-Term Objectives**

1a. To pronounce correctly new words containing consonant blends and digraphs.
    Evaluation: CRT     Criterion: 95% accuracy.
1b. To pronounce correctly new words containing vowel digraphs.
    Evaluation: CRT     Criterion: 95% accuracy.
1c. To pronounce correctly new words containing vowel dipthongs.
    Evaluation: CRT     Criterion: 95% accuracy.
1d. To answer correctly factual questions in material at instructional reading level.
    Evaluation: CRT     Criterion: 95% accuracy.
1e. To answer correctly inference questions in material at independent reading level.
    Evaluation: CRT     Criterion: 95% accuracy.
2a. To multiply correctly two-digit numerals by two-digit multipliers.
    Evaluation: CRT     Criterion: 95% accuracy.
2b. To divide correctly multiple-digit numerals by two-digit dividers.
    Evaluation: CRT     Criterion: 95% accuracy.
2c. To demonstrate an understanding of basic concept of fractional parts through ninths.
    Evaluation: CRT     Criterion: 95% accuracy.
3a. To use correctly the comma, semicolon, and colon within sentences.
    Evaluation: CRT     Criterion: 90% accuracy.
3b. To demonstrate a knowledge of basic contractions and be able to use them in written sentences.
    Evaluation: CRT     Criterion: 90% accuracy.
3c. To use correctly common adjectives and adverbs in written sentences.
    Evaluation: CRT     Criterion: 90% accuracy.
3d. To write correctly a paragraph with a topic sentence and at least three sentences that support the topic sentence.

**Box 11–1**   Continued

    Evaluation: CRT     Criterion: 90% accuracy.

3e. To write correctly a short report following an outline.

    Evaluation: CRT     Criterion: 90% accuracy.

4a. To demonstrate a knowledge of the earth's structure and composition.

    Evaluation: CRT     Criterion: 80% accuracy.

4b. To demonstrate a knowledge of the basic mechanisms of geological processes.

    Evaluation: CRT     Criterion: 80% accuracy.

4c. To demonstrate a knowledge of the oceans and their processes.

    Evaluation: CRT     Criterion: 80% accuracy.

4d. To demonstrate a knowledge of the atmosphere and weather.

    Evaluation: CRT     Criterion: 80% accuracy.

5a. To demonstrate the ability to preview reading assignments correctly.

    Evaluation: CRT     Criterion: 90% accuracy.

5b. To demonstrate the ability to use skimming and scanning techniques correctly in reading.

    Evaluation: CRT     Criterion: 90% accuracy.

5c. To demonstrate the ability to use correctly the POINT system for studying.

    Evaluation:    Teacher checklist of steps.
    Criterion:     Teacher judgment of satisfactory on all checklist items for three consecutive assignments.

6a. To demonstrate the ability to be punctual.

    Evaluation:    Event recording.
    Criterion:     Tardiness no more than once per nine weeks.

6b. To work cooperatively with others.

    Evaluation:    Duration recording.
    Criterion:     Five consecutive group assignments requiring no less than 30 minutes.

6c. To accept supervision appropriately.

    Evaluation:    Teacher checklist of components.
    Criterion:     Teacher judgment of satisfactory on all checklist items for three consecutive weeks with supervision occurring at least three times per week.

7a. To reduce verbal threats and insults directed at other students.

    Evaluation:    Event recording.
    Criterion:     80% reduction from baseline for three consecutive weeks.

7b. To reduce hitting and pushing other students.

    Evaluation:    Event recording.
    Criterion:     95% reduction from baseline for three consecutive weeks.

8a. To make complaints to others appropriately.

    Evaluation:    Teacher checklist of components.
    Criterion:     Teacher judgment of satisfactory on all checklist items for five consecutive opportunities to observe use of the skill.

8b. To ask permission of others appropriately.

    Evaluation:    Teacher checklist of components.
    Criterion:     Teacher judgment of satisfactory on all checklist items for five consecutive opportunities to observe use of the skill.

8c. To use negotiation appropriately.

**Box 11–1**   Continued

    Evaluation:    Teacher checklist of components.
    Criterion:      Teacher judgment of satisfactory on all checklist items for five consecutive opportunities to observe use of the skill.

9a. To demonstrate age-appropriate reasoning in discussion groups about friendship dilemmas.

    Evaluation:    Event recording.
    Criterion:      Minimum of 60% of arguments in discussion groups over a three-month period are, by teacher judgment, at Selman's stage two reasoning.

9b. To demonstrate age-appropriate reasoning in discussion groups about peer group dilemmas.

    Evaluation:    Event recording.
    Criterion:      Minimum of 60% of arguments in discussion groups over a three-month period are, by teacher judgment, at Selman's stage two reasoning.

10a. To develop self-statements appropriate for neutralizing feelings of anger.

    Evaluation:    Self-report rating scale.
    Criterion:      Reduction of 80% in the intensity of feelings of anger for three consecutive months.

10b. To inhibit any overt signs of anger in provocative situations.

    Evaluation:    Latency recording.
    Criterion:      Absence of any overt sign of anger for at least 5 minutes in 9 out of 10 observed situations known to elicit anger in the past, for three consecutive months.

11a. To demonstrate an understanding of the relationship between thoughts, feelings, and behavior.

    Evaluation:    Anecdotal record of REE groups.
    Criterion:      Appropriate analysis, by teacher judgment, of majority of discussion problems for three consecutive months.

11b. To demonstrate an ability to use self-disputation.

    Evaluation:    Anecdotal record of REE groups.
    Criterion:      Appropriate challenge and restucturing of beliefs, by teacher judgment, for three consecutive and different problems brought up in REE groups.

INITIATION OF SERVICES: August 27, 1988.

DURATION OF SERVICES: One year.

PLACEMENT: BD self-contained class.

PARTICIPATION IN REGULAR EDUCATION: Social Studies.

RELATED SERVICES: None.

REEVALUATION DATE: April 15, 1991.

COMMITTEE SIGNATURES:

    Olivia Overseer

    Nelson Norms

    Helen Hawkeyes

    Beula Blunder

[a]The IEP shows examples of objectives from most of the curriculum areas discussed in the text. Subsequent illustrations related to pretests, lesson plans, and record keeping will draw on items from this IEP.

***The Student's Present Level of Performance.*** This means that the IEP must be based on current assessment data that is both reliable and valid. It also means that the data must be educationally relevant. The assessment data must provide specific information about the educational needs of the student. The best way to obtain specific data on educational needs, in most areas, is through informal, criterion-referenced assessment. To provide appropriate data the criterion-referenced assessment must closely reflect the curriculum in the student's educational program. Norm-referenced assessment is valuable for making comparisons between a student and peers. Norm-referenced assessment provides data useful for deciding whether or not a student needs special programming. It is not too useful for identifying a student's specific needs. The educational needs of a student, particularly behavior-disordered students, is not limited to traditional academic needs. As we have seen in previous chapters, behavior-disordered students have educational needs in the academic, social, and emotional domains.

***Annual Goals.*** This means that the IEP must include appropriate annual goals for the student. These goals should represent your best judgment about what can be accomplished with the student during a school year. There should be goals in all areas in which the student has recognized needs. This may include any of the major problem areas discussed in previous chapters. It certainly should include academic goals, but clearly should not be limited to academic goals for behavior-disordered students. Annual goals are best expressed in broad terms. The following are a few examples.

1. The student will master word decoding skills covered in the fifth-grade curriculum.

2. The student will master both the behavioral and cognitive skills necessary for age-appropriate social functioning.

3. The student's inappropriate conduct behaviors will be reduced to within the range typical of nonhandicapped age peers.

4. The student will master the cognitive skills needed to monitor and control emotional responses to a level that is age appropriate.

5. The student's inappropriate emotional reactions will be reduced to within the range typical of nonhandicapped age peers.

6. The student will demonstrate a knowledge of occupations represented in the local community.

***Short-Term Objectives.*** The IEP should include short-term objectives matched to the annual goals. Each annual goal should have several associated short-term objectives. These objectives represent intermediate steps that must be taken to reach the associated annual goal. Short-term objectives are stated more narrowly than annual goals. They should, however, still be stated somewhat broadly. They are not intended to be highly specific objectives that would be appropriate for daily lesson plans. Each short-term objective represents a goal for a briefer period of time than a year but not as brief as a day or week. Usually, these objectives represent goals appropriate for a month or more of instruction. The teacher uses the short-term objectives as a guide when planning the daily instruction needed to meet the objective and ultimately the associated annual goals. It is the teacher's responsibility to break the short-term objectives down into more specific objectives that can be used as the focus for daily lesson plans. We will discuss lesson plans in more detail following this discussion of the IEP. Each short-term objective may be broken down into many instructional objectives. Our earlier discussion of content and task analysis applies to this process. The following are a few examples.

1. The student will master the structural analysis skills covered in the fifth-grade curriculum.

2. The student will master conversational skills.

3. The student will develop an age-appropriate conception of friendship.

4. The student will reduce antisocial behaviors to within the range typical of age peers.

5. The student will demonstrate a knowledge of common emotions.

6. The student will reduce anxiety in evaluation situations to within the range typical of age peers.

7. The student will demonstrate a knowledge of the work roles of employees in occupations in the local community.

*Services.*    The IEP must specify the special education and related services to be provided. This would include the type of program the student will be in, which in our case would be behavioral disorders. It should also indicate the type of service delivery model under which the services will be provided. The choice of service delivery model is related to the requirement for placement in the least restrictive environment and depends on the seriousness of the the student's handicap. A brief discussion of service delivery models will follow the discussion of lesson plans later in this chapter. This component would also specify any related services the student will receive, e.g., counseling services.

*Regular Class Participation.*    In this component of the IEP, the extent of the students' participation in the regular educational program must be specified. The degree of participation in the regular educational program will depend on the the type of service delivery model through which the student is served. Handicapped students should only participate in regular educational programs to the extent that they can be successful in those programs. This means being successful with support services from special education, not successful entirely independent of special education services.

***Initiation of Services.***    The IEP should specify the date on which special education service will begin. This date should not be any later than 30 days from the date the student was ruled eligible for special education services.

***Duration of Services.***    The IEP should specify the period of time during which special education services will be provided. Every student must be reevaluated within three years of being ruled eligible for special education services. Thus, in no case should the duration specified for services exceed three years.

***Evaluation.***    The IEP must provide for at least annual evaluation of the annual goals and short-term objectives. The method of evaluation and the criteria for the evaluation should be specified. Evaluation of student progress toward meeting the goals and objectives on the IEP should be an ongoing process, but must be done no less frequently than once a year.

***Responsible Parties.***    The IEP must specify who the responsible parties are for implementing the IEP. In general, this means the persons who must sign the IEP. The special education teacher and an administrative representative of the special education program are the minimum for the school system. If other school personnel have specific responsibilities on the IEP, they too must sign the IEP, e.g., speech therapist. In addition to school personnel, the signature of at least one of the student's parents is required. There are some special circumstances where this may be omitted. We will briefly discuss the involvement of parents in the educational process following the discussion of service delivery models later in this chapter.

## LESSON PLANS

The short-term objectives on the IEP represent beginning points for developing lesson plans. The first step is to select a short-term objective and determine what must be taught to meet the objective. This is where the process of task analysis we discussed earlier in Chapter 2 becomes important. Let's take a possible short-term objective from Table 2-2. The objective on the IEP might read, "The student will master the multiplication of two-digit numbers by two-digit multipliers." We must answer two questions before doing our first lesson plan. First, what are the individual skills needed to meet this objective? Second, has our student already mastered any of these skills?

The answer to the first question is obtained using task analysis. Assuming that the student has already mastered multiplying two-digit numbers by one-digit multipliers, we might identify a sequence similar to the following:

1. Order of multiplication operations

2. Placement and alignment of products

3. Addition of products

4. Multiplication by two-digit multipliers, ending in zero, without carrying

5. Multiplication of two digit numbers by two digit multipliers without carrying

6. Multiplication of two digit numbers by two digit multipliers with carrying

Our analysis suggests there are at least six skills involved in meeting the short-term objective. We may have to do lessons on each of the six, or only some of them, for any given student. Before proceeding with lesson planning, we need to know if any student who has this IEP objective can do any of the subskills. To determine this, we need to develop a criterion-referenced pretest. In Chapter 2, we discussed criterion-referenced tests for evaluating the effect of instruction. We will now see how to apply this technique to pretests or posttests.

There are two differences between the use of the technique for pretesting and for evaluating instruction. First, we will be testing more than one subskill on the same test. Second, we need to meet our consistency criterion without doing multiple administrations of the test. Looking at the analysis of the objective, we can omit items designed to specifically test for subskills 1, 2, and 3. These can be omitted because the data we need on these subskills can be obtained from an error analysis of computations on problems for the other subskills. We need test items for the last three subskills.

Let's set a performance criterion of 80 percent accuracy and a consistency criterion of three consecutive demonstrations at 80% accuracy. This means that we will need 15 problems for each subskill or a total of 45 problems on the pretest. We must have multiples of five in order to obtain an 80% criterion. Since the consistency criterion requires three demonstrations, we must have three sets of five problems for each subskill on the pretest. We also need three separate demonstrations, so we can't present the 15 problems on one subskill consecutively. Thus, our three sets of five problems for each subskill must be intermingled with sets of problems for the other subskills being tested. That is, we can get separate demonstrations by either separating the demonstrations by time or by some different intervening activity. On the pretest, we will get separation by an intervening activity. The intervening activity will be work on problems for a different subskill.

We can lay out the organization of the pretest using symbols before actually writing it. We need items for subskills 4, 5, and 6. We need three sets of items for each subskill. We will designate these sets A, B, and C. We also need five problems in each set and will designate this numerically (5). Now we can lay out the organization of the pretest.

| Page 1: | 4A(5) | 5A(5) | 6A(5) |
| Page 2: | 4B(5) | 5B(5) | 6B(5) |
| Page 3: | 4C(5) | 5C(5) | 6C(5) |

The first page of the pretest is shown in Box 11–2. Each student will have an opportunity to attempt problems related to each subskill three separate times on the pretest. To meet the performance criterion, a student must get four problems correct out of the five in a set. To meet the consistency criterion, a student must get four out of five correct in each set of the three sets for any given subskill. A student meeting the performance and consistency criteria for a given subskill would show, by our criteria, mastery of that subskill. No instruction would be needed on that subskill by the student. Periodic review might still be needed to maintain the skill. You could also set criteria on the pretest to help you decide who needs remedial instruction and who needs initial instruction. In the former, the pretest would suggest that a student has had some previous instruction on a subskill but hasn't mastered it (intermediate accuracy). In the latter, the pretest would suggest that a student has probably never had any instruction on the subskill (little or no accuracy).

After you know what you need to teach, you can begin developing lesson plans. A lesson plan has five parts (see Boxes 11–3 and 11–4). First, you

**Box 11–2**    The first page of a pretest on two-digit by two-digit multiplication illustrating one set (A) of five problems for each of three subskills (4, 5, and 6) being tested

---

Name_____        Date_____


Do all of the following problems and show your work. You may not know how to do some or even all of the problems. Please try each problem and do the best you can. Thank you.

$$
\begin{array}{lllll}
(1)\ \ 14 & (2)\ \ 31 & (3)\ \ 22 & (4)\ \ 11 & (5)\ \ 33 \\
\times\ 20 & \times\ 10 & \times\ 40 & \times\ 50 & \times\ 30
\end{array}
$$

$$
\begin{array}{lllll}
(6)\ \ 36 & (7)\ \ 24 & (8)\ \ 12 & (9)\ \ 31 & (10)\ \ 22 \\
\times\ 11 & \times\ 22 & \times\ 33 & \times\ 31 & \times\ 42
\end{array}
$$

$$
\begin{array}{lllll}
(11)\ \ 27 & (12)\ \ 19 & (13)\ \ 33 & (14)\ \ 43 & (15)\ \ 18 \\
\times\ 14 & \times\ 26 & \times\ 35 & \times\ 26 & \times\ 16
\end{array}
$$

**SCORES**

Subskill (4) Set A _____ Set B _____ Set C _____
Subskill (5) Set A _____ Set B _____ Set C _____
Subskill (6) Set A _____ Set B _____ Set C _____

**Box 11–3**   A detailed illustration of an academic lesson plan using an instructional objective derived form an IEP short-term objective[a]

**Objective**

The student will correctly compute two-digit by two-digit multiplication problems without carrying.

**Teaching strategy**

Direct instruction using modeling will be used for initial acquisition and accurate performance of the skill. The computation process will be demonstrated for students on the chalkboard accompanied by verbal explanation. Both correct and incorrect examples will be used, with an explanation of why the incorrect operations are wrong. The modeling will illustrate and explain the order of operations, placement of products, and addition of products. The modeling illustrations will include prompts. Students will be reinforced through the classroom checkmark system and praise during planned activities. Reinforcement will begin on a continuous schedule and stretched to a 1:10 schedule by the time that mastery of the objective is achieved.

**Activities**

During the modeling presentation students will be asked probe questions to check their understanding of what is being presented.

Students will be given a prompted model to keep in front of them while they do application activities. The prompted model will be in the following form:

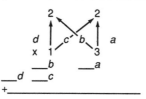

Students will be given one problem at a time to do initially with five problems per session. As the reinforcement schedule is stretched the number of problems given at one time will increase to five and then to ten at a time. The reinforcement schedule will stretch first to 5:1 and then to 10:1. The criteria for stretching the schedule will be the evaluation criteria. As the schedule is stretched, if accuracy under a new schedule drops to 60% or less, more practice under the former schedule will be given.

When a student can do 10 problems at a time to the evaluation criteria, prompts will be systematically faded from the student's model problem. Prompts will be faded in the following order.

1. Addition sign
2. Product placement labels, i.e., a, b, etc.
3. Alignment markers, i.e., _____
4. Operation prompts c and d
5. Operation prompts a and b

The evaluation criteria must be met at each step before the next prompt is faded.

**Materials**

1. A set of problem examples

**Box 11-3**   Continued

2. A set of five sequenced, prompted problem models

3. A pool of two-digit by two-digit multiplication problems that don't require carrying

### Evaluation

The performance criterion will be a minimum of 80% accuracy. The consistency criterion will be three consecutive sessions. Mastery will require meeting these criteria without any prompts and working under a 1:10 fixed-ratio reinforcement schedule. Graphing will be used to monitor and make decisions about the progress of instruction.

[a]A written lesson plan would not typically include this much detail, although all the major components would need to have been planned and noted in summary form.

**Box 11-4**   An illustration of a social reasoning lesson plan using an instructional objective derived from an IEP short-term objective[a]

### Objective

The student will demonstrate age-appropriate reasoning about the motives involved in forming and maintaining friendships.

### Teaching Strategy

Cognitive-developmental discussion groups will be used as the teaching approach for this objective. The group size will be limited to five. The range of stages in the group will be limited to two adjacent stages. Students will be seated in a circular arrangement. The discussions will employ dilemmas focused on the issue of motives in friendships. The dilemma for each session will be presented and them followed by questions to promote:

1. Understanding of the issue

2. Contribution of related personal experiences

3. Expression of opinions about the dilemma

4. Examination of the underlying basis for opinions

5. Taking the perspective of characters in the dilemma

6. Interaction of students at adjacent stages

7. Clarification of the reasoning at different stages represented in the discussion

### Activities

After a brief presentation of the situation and nature of the dilemma, selected students will be assigned characters and provided a script for their character. A brief role-play of the dilemma will precede the discussion.

Following the role-play, the critical decision to be made by the central character will be put to each student. After each student has stated an opinion about what the central character should do, questions will be used to stimulate discussion and interaction. Questions directed at complicating and extending the issue will be asked of any sudent in the highest stage represented in the group.

If there is too much agreement among the members of the group to produce a good discussion, the group will be divided and assigned a position to defend.

### Materials

1. A set of dilemmas focused on motives in friendships

**Box 11–4**   Continued

> 2. Scripts for the dilemmas for use in role plays
> 3. A set of questions for each dilemma to aid in promoting discussion
> 4. A stuctured anecdotal record sheet
>
> **Evaluation**
>
> An anecdotal record will be kept on each discussion group. The notes will summarize the reasoning behind each student's position. Stage estimates for each student's reasoning will also be noted. The anecdotal record will be based mostly on responses to questions from category seven in the teaching strategy.

[a]A written lesson plan would not typically include this much detail, although all the major components would need to have been planned and noted in summary form.

need an instructional objective for a subskill that needs instruction. The objective should be stated as a measurable student outcome. For example, the student will correctly multiply two-digit numbers by two-digit multipliers, ending in zero, without carrying. Second, you need to plan your teaching strategy. This is the planning instruction component in the direct instruction model for the sample instructional objective above. It could also be a teaching strategy of the other chapters if the objective was in one of those areas. In short, this specifies what you are going to do. Third, you need to plan student activities. Student activities are of two types. One type of student activity is called *participatory*. These are activities students are called on to do during the actual instruction, e.g., answer probe questions or give examples. The other type of student activity is called *application*. These are activities that follow instruction and give students tasks to practice what has been taught and receive feedback on their effort to apply the instruction. Participatory activities are not always necessary. All skill-based lessons must include application activities. Fourth, you need to specify the teaching materials that you will need for the lesson. This may include media equipment, examples, application tasks, and so on. Finally, you need to plan for evaluation. The evaluation plan should usually specify the components of a criterion-referenced test that will be used to evaluate the lesson. You should also specify any performance conditions that will apply to the test, for example, if the students will be allowed to use any aids, e.g., a number line, or have a time limit, e.g., 40 minutes for the test.

Good instructional data and record keeping are critical for effective instruction. Good data will be obtained if you plan your assessments properly using the procedures already discussed. Once you have begun collecting data, you need to record it in usable form. In addition to the traditional recording of numeric data in a grade book, there are two other record keeping techniques that can be useful.

First, you can keep performance graphs for each student on each objective you are working on. Performance graphs were discussed in Chapter 2 and again in Chapter 4. The baseline on an academic performance graph can be obtained from your pretest data. In our example of a pretest above, you would use the performance score on each of the three sets of problems, for a given subskill, as separate data points in the baseline phase on your graph. Scores on application activities and evaluation activities would be used as data points in the intervention phase on your graph. If you do a post-test at the end of a grading period, you can put in a follow-up phase on your graph. Record the performance scores on each of the problem sets for a given objective on the post-test as separate data points on the graph. These graphs can serve several purposes. They can help you monitor the effect of your instruction and aid you in making instructional decisions. They can help you communicate with others, e.g., parents or a supervisor about a student's performance. They can also be used to provide students with feedback about their progress on an objective.

Second, you can use curriculum arrays (see Box 11–5) for all the objectives in a content area that you teach in your program. You should keep a curriculum array in each subject area for each student. The array for a student in a given content area can be limited to the instructional objectives that lead to meeting the student's IEP, short-term objectives in that content area. Mastery of any objective demonstrated by a pretest can be marked off with an X immediately. Other objectives should be marked off with a / if they are currently being taught and with an X when they have been mastered. Objectives that haven't been mastered and aren't currently being taught should be left blank. These arrays can also help you in several ways. They can help you monitor a student's progress toward meeting IEP objectives and making instructional decisions. They can help you communicate with others. They can be used to provide feedback to a student about progress. They can also be useful when you are writing a new IEP for a student, e.g., for the next school year.

**Box 11–5**    A curriculum array of selected short-term objectives and their associated instructional objectives[a]

| | | Status | Start | Finish |
|---|---|---|---|---|
| 2a(1) | Two-digit multipliers ending in zero | | | |
| 2a(2) | Two-digit multiplication without carrying | | | |
| 2a(3) | Two-digit multiplication with carrying | | | |
| 5c(1) | Developing questions for studying | | | |
| 5c(2) | Identifying key ideas and facts | | | |
| 5c(3) | Relating detail to major ideas | | | |

Name_____

**Box 11-5**    Continued

| | Status | Start | Finish |
|---|---|---|---|
| 5c(4)  Developing notes on the study material | | | |
| 5c(5)  Self-testing with the study questions | | | |
| 7b(1)  Reduction of hitting | | | |
| 7b(2)  Reduction of shoving | | | |
| 7b(3)  Reduction of tripping | | | |
| 7b(4)  Reduction of throwing | | | |
| 9b(1)  Motives for peer groups | | | |
| 9b(2)  Unity in peer groups | | | |
| 9b(3)  Conformity in peer groups | | | |
| 9b(4)  Rules in peer groups | | | |
| 9b(5)  Conflict in peer groups | | | |
| 9b(6)  Leadership in peer groups | | | |
| 9b(7)  Exclusion by peer groups | | | |
| 11b(1)  Identifying self-talk | | | |
| 11b(2)  Identifying beliefs in self-talk | | | |
| 11b(3)  Evaluating beliefs against common irrational beliefs | | | |
| 11b(4)  Testing beliefs against objective evidence | | | |
| 11b(5)  Restating an irrational belief rationally | | | |
| 11b(6)  Developing alternatives to irrational beliefs | | | |
| 11b(7)  Practice in using a new belief | | | |

[a]This array would be used for record keeping. A / would be entered beside an objective in the "status" box when instruction begins. The begining date would be entered in the "start" box. When the objective is mastered, the / would be changed to an X and the date entered in the "finish" box.

## SERVICE DELIVERY

As we mentioned earlier, the type of service delivery model used is related to the concept of least restrictive environment (LRE) or in educational terminology, mainstreaming. It should be recognized that the term *mainstreaming* is an educational concept, not a legal concept; it is not used in P.L. 94-142. The term used in the law is *least restrictive environment*. The law requires that handicapped students be placed in the least restrictive environment appropriate. The rationale for LRE is that a student should not be deprived of contact with the normal environment and the learning opportunities in that environment to any greater extent than is clearly necessary. A student in a residential placement is in the LRE if that is the closest approximation to a normal educational environment that is appropriate for the student, that is, if that is the only environment in which a student's needs can be appropriately met. A more complete discussion of mainstreaming students with behavioral disorders is available and suggested for supplemental reading (Pappanikou & Paul, 1977). There are several service delivery models available. Each represents progressively less exact approximations to a normal educational environment. We will begin our discussion with the closest special education approximation to the normal environment.

### Consulting Teacher

This is an indirect service model, which means that a student is provided service through teacher consultation. The consulting teacher does not work directly with a student but rather, with a student's regular class teacher or teachers. This is a model appropriate for the most mildly handicapped students eligible for special education services.

A consulting teacher should have several characteristics. First, a consulting teacher should be familiar with the regular classroom program. This includes the regular class curriculum, materials, teaching methods, practices, and expectations. The consulting teacher should also be be competent in special education techniques for mild problems, adapting materials, and data collection techniques. In addition, the consulting teacher should be skillful at working as member of a team and have good interpersonal skills.

The consulting teacher's role is primarily educational. The consultant attempts to teach regular classroom teachers to use special techniques and to adapt regular class materials and practices to make them suitable for mildly handicapped students. The consultant provides regular class teachers with assistance in planning for mildly handicapped students. The objective, however, is to help the regular class teacher become as independent of this assistance as possible. At times the consultant may work directly with a mildly handicapped student in the regular classroom for demonstration purposes.

The consulting teacher usually begins by conducting an interview with the regular classroom teacher. This interview will attempt to gain as much information as possible about the student's problems as they are perceived by the regular classroom teacher. Some of the questions that will be explored in this interview are listed in Box 11–6. After the interview data is collected, the consulting teacher may do some informal assessments of the student, behavioral observations, or both. Behavioral observations will usually begin with narrative recording. This recording is usually done using a recording form similar to the one in Box 11–7. After doing narrative recording and analyzing this data, the consulting teacher may do behavioral recording for specific, operationally defined behaviors using techniques described in Chapter 4. A matched nonhandicapped student may be observed at the same time to collect comparative data as an aid in determining the seriousness of the problem and to determine appropriate criteria for any subsequent intervention. Finally, the consulting teacher will begin assisting the regular class teacher with planning for the hand-

**Box 11–6**    A set of questions to help guide an interview of a classroom teacher by a consulting or resource room teacher about a problem student with whom the classroom teacher needs help

---

**CONSULTATION QUESTIONS**

**Academic Problems**

1. What subject(s) is the problem in?
2. What is the student's strong point(s) in the subject(s)?
3. What is the student's specific deficit(s) in the subject(s)?
4. What teaching method(s) is being used with the student?
5. What instructional material(s) is being used in the subject(s)?
6. What do you think is causing the student's problem(s)?
7. What would you like for me to do for you, e.g., modify objectives for the student, suggest alternative teaching strategies, adapt present teaching materials, or provide alternative teaching materials?
8. What would you like for me to do for the student, e.g., remediation, tutoring, teach the student learning skills?

**Behavior Problems**

1. Specifically, what is the nature of the behavior problem(s)?
2. How often does the behavior(s) occur, and how long does it last?
3. When and where does the behavior(s) occur?
4. Is there an activity or event that seens to be associated with the behavior(s)? If so, what?
5. What is your response to the behavior(s)?
6. What is the reponse of the class to the behavior(s)?
7. What seems to be associated with the behavior(s) ending?
8. What do you think is causing the problem behavior(s)?
9. What would you like for me to do for you, e.g., observe and collect data, suggest behavior change strategies, help you plan an intervention?
10. What would you like for me to do for the student, e.g., counsel the student, conduct a behavior change intervention, include the student in an affective education group?

**Box 11–7**    A narrative recording form with a sample entry[a]

```
NARRATIVE RECORDING FORM

   Name_____          Date_____
```

| DURATION | ANTECEDENTS | BEHAVIOR | CONSEQUENCES |
|----------|-------------|----------|--------------|
| 9:10:05 | Bill whispers something in John's ear. | John spits on Bill. | Bill yells at John and hits him. Everyone laughs. Teacher takes John to the office. |
| 9:10:20 | | | |

[a]The form is arranged to make sequence analysis easy to do after the recording is complete.

icapped student. Techniques from various areas discussed in previous chapters will usually be appropriate.

### Resource Teacher

This is both a direct and an indirect service model. This means that a student is provided service both directly through working in a special education classroom and indirectly through regular class teacher consultation. The special education class is called a *resource room*. In practice, this model often functions primarily as a direct service model, although this was not the original intent. This is a model appropriate for mild to moderately handicapped students. Students served under this model should be able to stay in a regular classroom for over half of their educational program. This means that they should be able to be successful in the regular classroom, with support services, for over half their program. Typically, a student being served through a resource program will spend from one to three hours per day in the resource room. It is unfortunate that many school systems use this model as if it were solely a direct service model. It is the indirect component that should be primarily responsible for providing the support services needed by many mild to moderately handicapped students in order to be successful in the regular class program.

A resource teacher should have all of the characteristics described above for a consulting teacher. A resource teacher should also be more thoroughly familiar with the specialized curriculum and teaching techniques that we have discussed in this book. This greater familiarity is necessary because the resource teacher will be working directly with more seriously handicapped students on a daily basis.

The role of the resource teacher is similar to that of the consulting teacher, where support services are involved. The resource teacher is also responsible for planning and implementing intervention programs for academic, social, and emotional problems. In addition, the resource teacher may be responsible for career development activities for some students. This is most likely to arise in secondary programs. Besides performing activities similar to those described in the consulting process, the resource teacher must actually conduct the intervention programs planned for the direct service component. Resource teachers also have to concern themselves with scheduling students for direct services. If the resource teacher is solely responsible for a subject area for a student, the student should be scheduled for the resource room during the time that subject is taught in the regular class program. If there is joint responsibility between the resource and regular programs for the subject, the student should be scheduled for the resource program at a time other than the time the subject is taught in the regular class program. In the latter situation, it is necessary to develop a cooperative relationship between the two programs. The responsibility for doing this is largely that of the resource teacher.

There are three areas that may require a cooperative relationship with the regular class. Two of these are particularly important when there is joint responsibility for a subject area. First, there is a need for coordination between the programs in the area of instructional planning. This can be done with a parallel planning form like the one in Box 11–8. This form should be completed weekly and show the subject area, objective, and materials for each of the programs for each day of the week. This can be done either in a joint conference between the teachers involved, or completed independently by each and then a meeting held if there are any points needing discussion. Second, there is a need for coordination when both programs are responsible for determining a student's grade in a subject. This can be done by a negotiation process involving the regular teacher and the resource teacher. In this negotiation, specific requirements for various possible grades should be decided and agreed on in advance. It is best if these are written down and signed by both teachers. The student and the student's parents should also be made aware of what the criteria are. The student and parents can be informed through a personal or telephone conference or by letter. In all cases, a written copy of the criteria should be given to the parents. A form for grade criteria is illustrated in Box 11–9.

Third, with behavior-disordered students you may need to coordinate behavior management procedures between the regular and resource programs. One way of doing this is through the classroom token economy described in Chapter 4. You can give the regular classroom teacher a rating scale for behavior in the regular class (see Figure 11–1). You should set this rating scale up so that the rating received during a regular class period or for the day in the regular

**Box 11–8**   A form to aid coordinating objectives, teaching methods, and materials between the regular class and special class for a handicapped student

**PARALLEL PLANNING FORM**

Name_____          Date_____

Objective(s) _____

_____

_____

| Day | TEACHER:<br>Regular Classroom | TEACHER:<br>Special Classroom |
|-----|------------------------------|------------------------------|
| MON |                              |                              |
| TUE |                              |                              |
| WED |                              |                              |
| THU |                              |                              |
| FRI |                              |                              |

class can be applied to the token system in the resource room. In Figure 11–1 the rating scale is a five-point bipolar scale. Let's assign a label to each rating.

1 = much worse than typical behavior

2 = worse than typical behavior

3 = typical behavior

4 = better than typical behavior

5 = much better than typical behavior

**Box 11–9**    A form to aid agreement between two teachers jointly responsible for assigning a grade for a handicapped student

---

**JOINT GRADE AGREEMENT**

Name_____    Date_____

Subject_____    Term_____

    The following are the agreed-upon criteria to be met by the students named above in order to receive a grade of A, B, or C.

_____

**GRADE OF A:**

    Classwork:

    Homework:

    Projects:

    Tests:

_____

**GRADE OF B:**

    Classwork:

    Homework:

    Projects:

    Tests:

_____

**GRADE OF C:**

    Classwork:

    Homework:

    Projects:

    Tests:

_____

    Regular Teacher:    _____

    Special Teacher:    _____

---

    Now let's set a point relationship between the ratings and the token economy. The following ratings might result in fines or rewards on this schedule.

    1 = a fine of 10 points

    2 = a fine of 5 points

```
┌─────────────────────────────────┐
│       Student Rating Card       │
│                                 │
│ Behavior: _____ │
│                                 │
│ Much                       Much │
│ Worse    1  2  3  4  5   Better │
│                                 │
│ Teacher's                       │
│ Initials: _____  Date:____ │
│                                 │
└─────────────────────────────────┘
```

**Figure 11–1**
A student rating scale for use by a regular class teacher to provide feedback on student behavior to a special class teacher

3 = no change

4 = a reward of 15 bonus points

5 = a reward of 30 bonus points

The actual number of points you should use depends on the length of time covered by the rating scale and the size of fines and rewards in the token economy in the resource room.

When you have several students involved in the program, particularly if they get into competition with one another. You could set this up as a feedback chart in your resource room (see Figure 11-2). You can put it on a bulletin board or on poster board and tape it to the wall. The board should be set up to look like a race. The race track is divided into increments that can be used to measure progress along the track. In the race track illustrated in Figure 11–2, there are three students involved. They are each interfaced with one regular class. They can get up to 5 points per day with the rating scale. The objective is to have them get 80% of the possible points for the week. Thus, the finish line is placed 20 intervals from the starting line. Each student is represented in the race by a different color-map pin. A student's map pin is moved each day the number of intervals corresponding to the rating received on the rating scale. There is also an extension of the track labeled "tie breaker." This helps decide a winner of the race when more than one student has reached the finish line. You place an empty brown sandwich bag at the end of the track and label it "Mystery Bag." The winner gets the contents of the bag. You should vary the

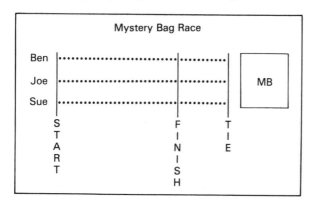

**Figure 11–2**
An illustration of a weekly feedback race used to establish a behavioral interface between a special class and a regular class using a behavior rating scale.

contents each week but keep the value of the contents the same from week to week. You can also have a consolation prize for any student who reaches the finish line but isn't in the lead. If you have two or more students go the maximum distance, you can declare an "All-Star Finish" and either split the contents of the bag between them or give duplicate prizes.

The curriculum for the resource room program will be determined by the needs of the students served and their IEPs. The various curriculum areas discussed in the text should cover most of the curriculum needs for a behavioral disorder program. Your interventions for decreasing inappropriate social behavior directly with behavioral techniques should be ongoing. You should provide academic interventions daily or at least three times a week. You should plan at least two hours per week for other curriculum areas, such as social skills, social reasoning groups, rational emotive groups, reduction of inappropriate emotional behaviors, and career development. You might try to schedule academic interventions daily. You might then schedule students for an additional 1/2 to 1 hour per day two days a week for nonacademic education programs. Alternatively, you could schedule academic intervention programs three days a week and nonacademic education programs the other two days each week. If you are addressing more than two nonacademic areas, you can alternate two programs from week to week for the same day and time. For example, if you are doing both social skills and social reasoning and have a 1-hour period on Tuesday available, you could do social skills one Tuesday, social reasoning the next Tuesday, and then go back to social skills the next Tuesday. When you are alternating programs this way, you should coordinate them if possible. If you are alternating social skills and social reasoning, try to develop dilemmas that are related to the social skills you are teaching. For example, if you are working on the social skill of saying "No!" to an unacceptable suggestion, you might use a dilemma the preceding or following week that involves a values conflict over dealing with an unacceptable request, e.g., to smoke pot or steal something. If you are alternating counterconditioning with rational-emotive counseling, you should focus on the same problem in both sessions.

### Self-Contained Teacher

This is a direct service model. It is used for full-time placements, although students may go out to regular class programs once or twice a day in some cases. The teacher has complete or nearly complete responsibility for the educational program. This is a model appropriate for moderately to severely handicapped students. Because of the seriousness of the problems in students served by a self-contained behavioral disorders program, the self-contained class often has a para-professional teacher's aide as well as a teacher. Self-contained classes are used in public school programs, in special day schools operated either by public schools or privately, and in residential programs operated either publicly or privately.

A self-contained teacher has to have the same characteristics as those described earlier for consulting and resource teachers. The self-contained teacher must be well trained to deal with the most serious academic and non-academic problems. This teacher must have a very thorough knowledge of the various curriculum areas and intervention strategies that we have discussed in the text. The self-contained teacher must also have supervisory skills.

The role of the self-contained class teacher is to plan and implement interventions for all areas of the behavioral disorder curriculum. The teacher may also have to plan for and coordinate the activities of a teacher's aide. The self-contained teacher may have to do some consulting and program coordination with other teachers but not as much as the resource room teacher. Some of the same procedures as those described for the consulting and resource teachers can be used by the self-contained teacher when coordinating with regular class teachers. The self-contained teacher is more likely to have to coordinate with support personnel such as counselors, psychologists, and consulting psychiatrists. The self-contained teacher is also more likely to become involved in home programming, that is, advising parents about problems they are having to deal with at home, extending educational interventions into the home, and training parents in techniques to use at home. We will have more to say about working with parents and other professionals in a section to follow. This teacher may also have to provide training for the teacher's aide.

In many ways, curriculum planning for this model is easier than in the resource model. Since the teacher has complete responsibility for the educational program and often has an aide, it is much easier to work out a schedule. At least 60% of the program should be devoted to academic instruction. The balance of the program should be directed at nonacademic education programs. It is best to schedule some of both types of programming on a daily basis. It is often best to reserve nonacademic education programs for the afternoons and devote mornings to academic programming. It is possible to do both types of programs at the same time through the use of a teacher's aide. The aide can be assigned monitoring duties for academic application or review activities, with some students, while the teacher conducts a nonacademic education program with one or more students. This same type of rotation plan can also be used solely for academic instruction. Hewett and Taylor (1980) first described this type of rotation plan. The Hewett and Taylor system divides the classwork and students into three groups. Classwork is divided into instruction, application activities, and review activities. Students are placed into three relatively homogeneous groups. The teacher does all of the instruction. The teacher begins with instruction for group A, while the aide monitors and assists groups B and C with application and review activities. Next, the groups rotate so that group C rotates into instruction, A into application activities, and B into review activities, and so on.

When you arrange your classroom, regardless of whether it is a resource or self-contained class, you should arrange your furnishings to avoid having congested areas. You should also be certain that you can visually monitor all the students from anywhere in the room. It is important to use an arrangement that will ensure that all students can see and hear you. If it is important to control movement in and out of the room, try to arrange your room so that you spend most of your time near the door. That is, place your primary instructional area near the door. You may also want to consider having more than one type of seating arrangement in your class. Axelrod, Hall, and Tams (1972) found that behavior problems were reduced when students were seated in rows rather than around tables. This may be the best seating arrangement when you are doing group instruction or students are engaged in independent tasks. Highly distractible students will probably do independent work better if placed in a study carrel or otherwise isolated. On the other hand, when you are doing activities such as discussion in groups, use a seating arrangement that puts students face to face. Heron and Harris (1982) found that face-to-face arrangements promote interaction. You should also plan space for time-out or social isolation of misbehaving students. You should plan space for recreational activities, too, if they will be part of your program, e.g., as rewards in a behavior management system. Finally, be sure that each student has some space of his or her own, even if it is only an assigned space on a shelf.

### Model Programs

There have been a number of model programs developed for serving behavior-disordered students. We will briefly look at four of these models. All four can be excellent sources of ideas for planning an effective program. You should go to the referenced sources for more detailed discussion of these models.

*The Psychodynamic Approach.*    Redl and Wattenburg (1959) and Redl (1966) report on one of the earliest models for serving behavior-disordered students. This model takes the position that group dynamics is of major importance when working with disturbed students in an educational setting. Group dynamics is seen as important because the model assumes that children behave differently in groups, groups create their own psychology, and group behavior is influenced by students' perception of their teacher. The model emphasizes understanding the group life of students particularly through the influence of various roles played in the group by students. These roles include the leader, clown, fall guy, and instigator. Interventions under this model are divided into four categories. First, there are interventions that support self-control, e.g., ignoring. Second, there is situational assistance for behavior control, e.g., routines. Third, there is reality and values appraisal. This area uses a specialized counseling approach called *life-space interviewing.* Finally, there is the use of the pleasure-pain principle or reward and punishment.

*The Structured Approach.*    Haring and Phillips (1962) discuss their model for serving students with behavior disorders. The emphasis of their approach is on a structured approach to academic instruction and management of behavior. They emphasize structuring the classroom to reduce distracting stimuli, to reduce activity in the classroom, and to minimize requirements for group functioning. They also focus on reduction in the level of academic task demand, concrete presentation of academics, carefully sequenced instruction, clear expectations, and immediate feedback and recognition. Their approach to behavior management emphasizes the use of natural consequences rather than punishment. The teacher in this model must be fair but firm. Problems should be handled in an unemotional and matter-of-fact manner. Blaming and scolding is viewed as ineffective and to be avoided.

***The Technological Approach.***   Hewett and Taylor (1980) discuss their model, which is called the *engineered classroom*. This model is based on the principles of behavior modification. The model is organized around a learning triangle. The triangle includes their three key ingredients. First, you must select appropriate educational tasks for your students. Second, you must provide meaningful reward following task success. Third, you must keep the classroom under your control through the effective use of rewards and punishments. This is accomplished through a token economy based on checkmarks. Educational tasks are selected from a developmental hierarchy covering the following seven areas: attention tasks, response tasks, order tasks, exploration tasks, social tasks, mastery tasks, and achievement tasks. Their classroom is divided into three educational centers. The division is based on the hierarchy of tasks. Each child works in all three centers each day but spends the most time in the center dealing with the area of greatest need. Maladaptive behavior is handled through curriculum adjustment, checkmark system, and social isolation.

***The Ecological Approach.***   Hobbs (1966) and Lewis (1967) describe this approach to educating behavior disordered students, which is called *Re-Education*. The basic premise of this approach is that only part of the problem belongs to the child. The broader environment is also viewed as important. This includes the home, school, and community. Treatment is focused not only on the child but also agents within the broader environment who appear to be part of the problem. The intervention with the child emphasizes several components.

1. Meaningful involvement in living

2. Normal growth and development

3. Development of trust, especially of adults

4. Development of competence, particularly academic competence

5. Control of symptoms

6. Development of cognitively based self-control

7. Appropriate group functioning

8. Order in daily affairs

9. Recognition of self-potential and limitations

10. Understanding and expressing feelings

11. Involvement with and understanding of the community

12. Anticipation and experience of joy

### Working with Parents

From personal experience, I would say that the most important relationship builder for working with parents is an effective program. Nothing will gain credibility for you as quickly with parents as having a significant impact on their child's problems. Other things that will aid building relationship with parents include communications phrased such that parents can understand them, regular reports on progress, and invitations to visit the classroom to observe. Things that need to be communicated to parents include their child's needs, the kinds of demands there are on their child, and things they can do to help their child succeed at school. One critical aspect of good parent communication is a well-organized conference conducted in a relaxed and friendly manner. Kroth and Otteni (1983) developed a checklist for planning parent conferences which you may find helpful (see Box 11–10). Progress reports should not be limited to report cards. You will find that brief written progress reports focusing on IEP objectives will be more informative and be appreciated by many parents. In any written communication with parents, be very careful about your spelling and grammar. Poorly constructed written communications from a teacher can give a negative impression to parents, regardless of content.

Invite parents to visit the classroom and observe regularly. Try to use the observation to show parents effective ways you have found to deal with some of their child's problems. Try to arrange pre- and post-observation briefings for parents. In the pre-observation briefing, give them some advance organizers to help them structure their observation. During the post-observation briefing go back over what has taken place during the observation in terms of the advance organizers you have given them. Be sure that you give them opportunities to ask questions and make comments. Don't give the impression that you have all the answers. Solicit input from the parents. After all, they probably know the child better than anyone else. Parents can often make useful suggestions or observations.

Parent training can be a useful way to both build a relationship with parents and to help them with problems they must deal with at home. Training parents can help you make more progress with their child at school, too. With only a brief investment of time you can teach parents how to use simple behavior management strategies like contingency contracts. You can also teach them to do some types of tutoring tasks at home. You should plan these tasks carefully so that they are clear, well structured, and include all necessary materials. You should keep the objective for tutoring tasks uncomplicated and short-term. Avoid complex and long-term tutoring tasks unless you have enough experience with the parents to know that they can handle the task. It is often useful to have the parents come in and receive instruction on the tutoring task, at least initially. A teacher aide can be very useful in your work with parents because the aide

**Box 11–10**    A parent conference checklist developed by the Parent Center, Albuquerque
Public Schools

**CONFERENCE CHECKLIST**

**Pre-conference**

___1. Notify

___purpose, place, time, length

___2. Prepare

___review student's folder

___gather examples of work

___prepare materials

___3. Plan agenda

___4. Arrange environment

___comfortable seating

___eliminate distractions

**Conference**

___1. Welcome

___establish rapport

___2. State

___purpose

___time limitations

___note taking

___options for follow-up

___3. Encourage

___information sharing

___comments

___questions

___4. Listen

___pause once in awhile

___look for verbal and nonverbal cues

___questions

___5. Summarize

___6. End on a positive note

**Post-conference**

___1. Review conference with student if appropriate

___2. Share information with other school personnel

___3. Mark calendar for planned follow-up

Source: Kroth and Otteni, 1983.

can often relate better to the parents' perspective and communicate more easily with the parents in nontechnical language. Observation sessions can also be useful for demonstrating to parents how to conduct various procedures with their child.

Another good way to help parents is to encourage them to join parent support groups for parents with children who have problems similar to their child's problems. If no such group exists, you can promote the idea with parents and help them set up such a group. Once such a group is formed and operating, it can become a valuable aid to parent education. It can also help reduce unfounded parental anxieties and concerns more easily than you can.

More formal parent training programs are sometimes done by special education personnel. These are too involved to go into in this brief discussion. Kroth and Otteni (1983) discuss parent education programs in more detail. If you are interested in starting a more formal program, you should examine their discussion of parent education. Another useful resource is a workshop manual (Kelker, 1987) developed for use with parents of behavior-disordered students. You will also find useful the proceedings of a recent conference on parents as allies, which focused on ways of developing working relationships with parents of students with behavioral disorders (McManus & Friesen, 1986).

### Working with Other Professionals

As a special education teacher you are a member of a professional team. The composition of this team will always include other teachers and administrative personnel. The team will at times include various support personnel. This may include social workers, counselors, school psychologists, curriculum specialists, speech and language therapists, clinical psychologists, and psychiatrists. You should consider it your responsibility to open lines of communication with these professionals, particularly when they are school personnel. It is important for you to know what their role is and to understand their function. It is also important for you to be familiar enough with their area of expertise to be able to communicate with them on a professional level. This means that you need to be able to talk their language. You don't have to be an expert in their areas, but you must know enough to be able to communicate with them and to benefit from their knowledge and skills.

You should jointly review objectives and coordinate services with support personnel with whom you have a student in common. Invite support personnel to visit your program and observe students of common concern, examine materials you use, and discuss procedures used with the students. Seek input from these personnel and try to use their suggestions whenever appropriate. Keep support personnel informed about progress of students on a regular basis. Whenever you plan a meeting, e.g., a parent conference, invite support personnel to attend and participate. Always try to keep interaction with other professionals on a friendly but business-like basis. Do not criticize them or make personal remarks to others about them or their practices.

### Teachers and Student Medication

It is not uncommon that behavior-disordered students are on medication or being treated nutritionally through diet or supplements. If a student is on medication, it is important for you to know what that medication is. You also need to know the expected effects of this medication, both positive and negative. If you know the name of the drug and want to learn more about it and its effects, you can find it in the *Physician's Desk Reference*. This reference book can be found in any good library. Another useful resource is a two-volume work (Gadow, 1986) designed to give teachers and other nonmedical persons information about children on medication.

Most drugs that students will be on are classified as psychoactive and will usually be either a stimulant or a tranquilizer. Some common psychoactive drugs and descriptive information are listed in Table 11–1. When you have a student on medication, you should observe the student for possible adverse side effects. If you believe a student is having an adverse side effect, you should report it to the parents. It is their responsibility to report or not report your observations to the student's physician.

**Table 11–1**    A summary of the major categories of psychoactive drugs sometimes used to treat behavioral disorders, their uses, brand names, and side effects

| | |
|---|---|
| *Antipsychotic Agents* | Major use: to reduce agitation, panic, severe anxiety, and psychomotor excitement<br>Common brand names: Thorazine, Mellaril, Trilafon, Stelazine, Prolixin, Haldol, and Navane<br>Common side effects: sedation, rigid shuffling walk, lack of facial expression, hand tremor or repetive hand motions, restlessness, rocking, fidgeting, dizziness, dry mouth, nasal congestion, and constipation |
| *Antianxiety Agents* | Major uses: to reduce situational stress or anxiety associated with an emotional condition<br>Common brand names: Valium, Librium, Serax, Tranxene, Vistaril, Atarax, Equanil, and Miltown<br>Common side effects: tolerance, physical dependence, drowsiness, uncoordinated movement, impaired emotional and intellectual functioning, and lethargy |
| *Antidepressants* | Major uses: to reduce depressive mood, restore activity, reduce negative expectations, and reduce self-blame<br>Common brand names: Tofranil, Norpramin, Pertofrane, Elavil, Aventyl, Sinequan, Vivactil, Triavil, Etrafon, Marplan, Nardil, and Parnate<br>Common side effects: dry mouth, nasal congestion, constipation, dizziness, sedation, fine motor tremor, and muscular jerkiness |
| *Antimanic Agents* | Major uses: to reduce the occurrence and the frequency and intensity of manic and depressive episodes<br>Common brand names: Eskalith, Lithane, and Lithonate<br>Common side effects: slight nausea, vomiting, sleepiness, thirst, dazed feeling, weakness, tiredness, muscular tremors, muscular rigidity, loss of appetite, and diarrhea. |
| *Sedative-Hypnotics* | Major uses: sedation, insomnia, reduction of inhibitions, and mood elevation<br>Common brand names: Amytal, Seconal, Tuinal, Nembutal, Pentothal, Luminal, Placidyl, Doriden, Noludar, Noctec, Dalmane, Quaalude, Sopor, and Parest<br>Common side effects: slurred speech, impaired intellectual functioning, impaired motor performance, passivity, tolerance, and physical dependence |

**Table 11–1**   Continued

| | |
|---|---|
| *Stimulants* | Major uses: suppression of appetite, narcolepsy, increased alertness, decreased sense of fatigue, elevated mood, improved motor performance, and reduction of hyperactivity in some children |
| | Common brand names: Benzedrine, Dexedrine, Methedrine, Desoxyn, Dexamyl, Ritalin, and Perludin |
| | Common side effects: loss of appetite, nervousness, restlessness, insomnia, tolerance, and psychological dependence |

At times you may be asked to become involved in administering medication to a student. You should check your school system's policy about such activity by teachers before becoming involved. Many school systems will not allow teachers to administer medication or even have it in the classroom. Often, school systems require that medication be kept in the school office and may even require that it be administered by a school nurse. You will find additional discussion of teachers and medication in Chapter 12.

# REFERENCES

AXELROD, S., HALL, R., & TAMS, A. (1972). A comparison of common seating arrangements in the classroom. Paper presented at the meeting of the Kansas Symposium of Behavior Analysis in Education, Lawrence, KS.

GADOW, K. (1986). *Children on Medication* (Vols. 1 & 2). Reston, VA: Council for Exceptional Children.

HARING, N., & PHILLIPS, E. (1962). *Educating Emotionally Disturbed Children.* New York: McGraw-Hill.

HERON, T., & HARRIS, K. (1982). *The Educational Consultant: Helping Professionals, Parents and Mainstreamed Students.* Boston: Allyn and Bacon.

HEWETT, F., & TAYLOR, F. (1980). *The Emotionally Disturbed Child in the Classroom* (2nd ed.). Boston: Allyn and Bacon.

HOBBS, N. (1966). Helping disturbed children: Psychological and ecological strategies. *American Psychologist, 21,* 1105–1115.

KELKER, K. (1987). *Working Together: The Parent/Professional Partnership.* Portland, OR: Families as Allies; Research and Training Center to Improve Services for Seriously Emotionally Handicapped Children and Their Families; Regional Research Institute for Human Services; Portland State University.

KROTH, R., & OTTENI, H. (1983). Parent education programs that work: A model. *Focus on Exceptional Children, 15*(8), 1–16.

LEWIS, W. (1967). Project Re-ED: Educational intervention in discordant child rearing systems. In E. Cowen, E. Gardner, & M. Zax (Eds.), *Emergent Approaches to Mental Health Problems.* New York: Appleton-Century-Crofts.

MCMANUS, M., & FRIESEN, B. (1986). *Families as Allies: Conference Proceedings.* Portland, OR: Families as Allies; Research and Training Center to Improve Services for Seriously Emotionally Handicapped Children and Their Families; Regional Research Institute for Human Services; Portland State University.

PAPPANIKOU, A., & PAUL, J. (1977). *Mainstreaming Emotionally Disturbed Children.* Syracuse, NY: Syracuse University Press.

REDL, F. (1966). Designing a therapeutic classroom environment for disturbed children: The milieu approach. In M. Knoblock (Ed.), *Intervention Approaches in Educating Emotionally Disturbed Children.* Syracuse, NY: Syracuse University Press.

REDL, F., & WATTENBURG, W. (1959). *Mental Hygiene in Teaching* (2nd ed.). New York: Harcourt.

# 12

# LEGAL ASPECTS OF WORKING WITH BEHAVIOR-DISORDERED STUDENTS

by
James K. McAfee, Ph.D.
with
David B. Center, Ph.D.

## INTRODUCTION

### The Need for Legal Knowledge

All teachers need some knowledge of education law. Teachers of behavior-disordered students need a more thorough knowledge of the legal aspects of teaching for several reasons.

1.  The traits of some behavior disordered students make them especially vulnerable to injury (e.g., self-abuse, aggression, impulsivity).

2.  Some of the treatments used with behavior-disordered students are potentially abusive (e.g., punishment, aversive stimulation, time-out). Courts have become involved in reviewing these treatments.

3.  Service to many behavior-disordered students is in residential programs that are primarily psychiatric rather than educational. Courts apply stricter standards to the care of students in such programs. Teachers working in residential programs may not enjoy the same degree of immunity from civil suits as do teachers in educational settings.

4. Because their students usually are disruptive, teachers of behavior-disordered students are subject to pressure for isolation and removal of the students from mainstream settings.

5. P.L. 94-142 and Section 504 of the Rehabilitation Act of 1973 provide for a strong federal role in the education and treatment of handicapped students. Because of this, the federal courts become involved in questions related to civil and constitutional rights.

## The Changing Nature of Legal Practices

Since the 1954 Brown v. Board of Education decision, the courts have scrutinized educational practices more closely. Educators who work with handicapped students should realize that legal standards can change overnight by legislative act (e.g., P.L. 94-142), court decision, or regulation.

There have been many major changes in legally acceptable educational practices that affect the education of behavior-disordered students.

1. It is no longer permissible routinely to segregate behavior-disordered students.

2. Some states now prohibit corporal punishment of handicapped students.

3. Immunity of teachers to personal injury lawsuits has eroded.

4. Recent court rulings limit expulsion and suspension of handicapped students (McAfee, 1985b; McAfee, 1987).

We will discuss these and other changes in greater detail later in this chapter.

### Concepts and Definitions

Anyone reading the transcript of a court decision, a legislative act, or an education law text will be struck by the strange language. Therefore, to understand the law, you must understand certain key ideas. Definitions and explanations of these legal ideas and terms follows.

*Tort.*    A civil action based on the legal obligations that one individual has toward another (Thurston, 1982). A precise definition of tort is difficult because courts are constantly adding or considering new causes for tort action.

*Negligence.*    A failure to behave in an acceptable manner. To prove negligence, the failure to act acceptably must result in an injury. A teacher who leaves behavior-disordered students unsupervised could be negligent. This is most likely to occur if an injury occurs while the teacher is absent.

*Standard of Care.*    A standard to which people should adhere during interaction with others. Sometimes standards are formal. For example, a state regulation may require continuous supervision for students in time-out. Or, they may be informal but traditional. For example, shop teachers should not give aggressive students sharp tools to use without close supervision (Mc-Afee, 1985b).

>   ***Defamation of Character.***    An untrue or subjective statement in written (libel) or oral (slander) form. The statement must be intentional and result in damage to the subject of the statement (Connors, 1981).

>   ***The Rule of Seven.***    A legal standard that states that children under 7 are not legally responsible. Adult standards may apply to youth over 14. Courts use the Rule of Seven to determine how much supervision students need. That is, students under 7 need continuous supervision. Courts also use the rule to determine whether an injury is one's own fault or someone else's fault (McAfee, 1985b).

>   ***In Loco Parentis.***    An idea that dates back several hundred years, it means that teachers may act in the place of parents when students are in their charge (McAfee, 1987).

## LEGAL ASPECTS OF BEHAVIOR MANAGEMENT

Behavior-disordered students present many challenges to teachers. Reduction of acting-out, aggressive, and self-injurious behaviors often requires techniques that involve unpleasant consequences. Many state education and regulatory agencies have restrictions on or guidelines for suspension, expulsion, physical punishment, time-out, behavior modification, drug therapy, and aversive conditioning. Teachers of behavior-disordered students should be aware of the guidelines. Failure to know or observe the guidelines may result in costly litigation.

### Expulsion

Expulsion may occur when students engage in behaviors that are highly disruptive or dangerous. Federal courts have ruled that any disciplinary removal from school for more than 10 days is expulsion. Case law that supports the rule includes *Blue v. New Haven Board of Education* (1981), *Board of Education of the City of Peoria v. Illinois State Board of Education* (1982), and *Goss v. Lopez* (1975). Some states define expulsion as any disciplinary removal of more than 5 days (McAfee, 1985a).

Courts and state education agencies (SEA) place many restrictions on expulsion, especially expulsion of handicapped students. The basis for court decisions on expulsion lies in the Fifth and Fourteenth Amendments of the U.S. Constitution. These amendments protect a citizen's property from seizure without due process of law. The courts view education as a property right because it has value to the student. Therefore, you cannot deny students access to education without a hearing (*Goss v. Lopez*, 1975).

According to the U.S. Supreme Court (*Goss v. Lopez*, 1975), a student who faces expulsion has certain minimal rights.

1. Notification of the pending expulsion

2. A hearing

3. A list of charges

4. The opportunity to tell his or her side of the event

For expulsion of handicapped students, the courts have special rules.

1. Expulsion of handicapped students is a change in placement (*Honig v. Doe*, 1988). In such cases, the due process requirements of P.L. 94-142 apply. For example, parent notification and an opportunity for a hearing (*Kaelin v. Grubbs*, 1982; *S - 1 v. Turlington*, 1981; *School Board of Prince City v. Maline*, 1985; *Stuart v. Nappi*, 1978).

2. If the student's behavior is directly related to the handicap, expulsion may not occur (*S - 1 v. Turlington*, 1981; *School Board of Prince City v. Maline*, 1985).

3. A group of professionals and not a school board must determine if there is a relationship between the handicap and the behavior (*S - 1 v. Turlington*, 1981).

4. Expelled handicapped students must receive an alternative education (*Lopez v. Salida School District*, 1978; *Stuart v. Nappi*, 1978).

5. If a behavior is a clear danger to self or others, immediate removal for up to 10 days is permissible (*Honig v. Doe*, 1988; *Jackson v. Franklin County School board*, 1985).

We can draw two conclusions from the discussion above.

1. You cannot expel handicapped students without first having a change in placement hearing.

2. You can remove a dangerous student for up to 10 days even if the behavior is linked to the handicap, while seeking a change in placement. You must, of course, follow due process any time that you make a change in placement. If the parents do not agree with the proposed change, you cannot change the student's placement unless you have a court order permitting you to make the change (*Honig v. Doe*, 1988). Under the Honig ruling, however, you do not have to exhaust all administrative remedies before going to court.

### Suspension

By definition, suspension is removal from school for 10 days or less (Hindman, 1986). In some states, courts view suspension of handicapped students as the same as suspension of normal students (McAfee, 1985a). Suspensions do not require full due process hearings. The following are guidelines for suspension of behavior-disordered students based on court decisions.

1. Suspension can be a disciplinary measure for handicapped students (*Board of Education of the City of Peoria v. Illinois State Board of Education*, 1982).

2. Suspension (for less than 10 days) is not a change in placement. It requires neither parent notification nor an opportunity for a hearing (*Board of Education of the City of Peoria v. Illinois State Board of Education*, 1982).

3. Short-term consecutive suspensions cannot be for more than a total of 10 days (15 days in Minnesota) (*Blue v. New Haven Board of Education*, 1981; *Mrs. A. J. v. Special School District 1*, 1979).

4. Suspension of handicapped students requires an IEP review. The IEP team must develop a disciplinary plan that may include suspension (*Philip Pratt v. Board of Education of Frederick County*, 1980).

Teachers should recognize that procedures for discipline (including suspension) vary from state to state. Barnette and Parker (1982) surveyed SEAs. They found that only nine states had specific discipline policies and procedures for emotionally disturbed students. Illinois, for example, allows suspension or expulsion of handicapped students only when the student's behavior is dangerous. Missouri requires an offer of alternative education to suspended handicapped students. We can't, however, go into a state-by-state discussion in this chapter. You should make sure that you know and understand the procedures in your state.

### In School Suspension

In school suspension (ISS) is removal from the usual class assignment to a disciplinary class for no more than 10 days (Center, 1986; Center & McKittrick, 1987). There appear to be no court cases involving in school suspension. The rules for its use with handicapped students are logically the same as those for out-of-school suspension. According to Noblit and Short (1985), ISS has become increasingly popular. These researchers found that there was a wide difference between what ISS should be and what is actually done. Often, students in ISS do no academic work and fall further behind. The effect on handicapped students could be significant. Teachers and schools that use ISS should ensure the following.

1. Students should receive adequate assignments.

2. The teacher assigned to ISS should supervise students' work.

3. A student's regular teacher and the ISS teacher should discuss the student's work and needs on a regular basis.

4. When used, ISS should be part of the student's IEP.

### Change of Placement

Often, students who are behavior disordered engage in behaviors that require a change in placement. Changes in placement should provide a student with a more appropriate environment, not serve as punishment. There have been many accounts of declining discipline in schools (Bauer, 1985; Campbell, Dobson, & Bost, 1985). Several writers have noted an increase in demands for isolation (in special classes or special schools) of all students with behavior problems (Huntze, 1985).

Courts have consistently ruled that movement to more restrictive placements for behavior-disordered students is permissible. However, this is true only if the placements are appropriate and necessary to provide service (*Jackson v. Franklin County School Board*, 1985; *Stuart v. Nappi*, 1978). You cannot place a behavior-disordered student in homebound services or in a residential school merely for convenience or without due process (*Blue v. New Haven Board of Education*, 1981).

### Aversive Techniques

Aversive techniques include punishment, corporal punishment, time-out, isolation, electric shock, noxious stimulants, social punishment, e.g., scolding and ridicule and after-school detention. Each of these techniques involves application of consequences that are usually painful or unpleasant. Because teachers act *in loco parentis*, they can use aversive techniques such as punishment. Court decisions restrict the use of some of the foregoing techniques. Some are also restricted by state regulation or legislation.

***After-School Detention.***    Keeping students after school as punishment for undesirable behavior is a long-existing and widely used practice. Within this author's knowledge, there have been no court rulings placing restrictions on the use of detention. However, detention does provide a potential source for tort liability. When detained after school, there is a disruption of a student's normal sequence of activity. For example, the student may miss a bus and have to walk home. Or, if the student usually walks home, crossing guards may be absent by the time the student leaves school. The school and the detaining teacher may be legally responsible for injuries that occur as a result of the detention (Connors, 1981). Connors states that elementary school students should not walk home after detention if they normally ride a bus. Students who live a long way from school or who have to travel dangerous roads should have bus transportation if detained. In addition, behavior-disordered students who are impulsive may lack the skills necessary to walk home by themselves. They are at a higher risk for injury, and teachers of such students should adhere to a strict standard of care.

***Time-out.***    Time-out is one of the behavioral techniques frequently used with behavior-disordered students. There are different guidelines for time-out depending on the type of the service provider. Courts are usually reluctant to intervene in educational matters. Thus, schools have a wide latitude in determining what is acceptable educational practice (*Gordon v. Oak Park School District*, 1974). When there are restrictions, they are usually prescribed by the SEA or LEA rather than the court. Kerr and Nelson (1983) noted that some states provide guidelines for the use of time-out in public schools.

Court rulings restrict the use of time-out when the intervention is in public or private institutions. Courts take the position that in institutions closed to the public, there is more potential for abuse. Therefore, court review of aversive procedures in institutions occurs with some regularity.

Courts discriminate between the use of time-out in public schools and in residential programs. Even so, some professional organizations, e.g., the Council for Exceptional Children and the American Psychological Association and some SEAs, endorse court guidelines. The guidelines are both reasonable and ethical and ensure that time-out is not abused. Therefore, all teachers including public schools would be wise to adhere to the following.

1. Time-out should be for brief periods of no more than 50 minutes (*Morales v. Thurman*, 1974).

2. Students in time-out should not be in locked rooms (*Wyatt v. Stickney*, 1972).

3. Students should have constant supervision while in time-out (*Rogers v. Okin*, 1986; *Wyatt v. Stickney*, 1972).

4. Time-out is appropriate for behavior not controllable by less intrusive means. It is also acceptable when a behavior is likely to cause injury (*Wyatt v. Stickney*, 1972; *Morales v. Turman*, 1974).

5. The effect of time-out needs monitoring. If it isn't effective in reducing disruptive behavior, after a reasonable trial, discontinue it (Gast & Nelson, 1977).

Teachers should recognize that there is a big difference between time-out and long-term isolation. Time-out is systematic. Data on its effects are also necessary. Students placed in time-out should be there for specific preset periods. Long-term isolation or isolation without supervision are indefensible practices.

***Social Punishment.***    Teachers use various forms of social punishment. These include scolding, public embarrassment, and ridicule. Only one court case appears to exist in which the charge was psychological abuse. This case was brought for excessive and unfair social punishment. In the case, a student charged that consistent public embarrassment (including imitating the student's lisp) was psychological abuse (*Gordon v. Oak Park School District*, 1974). The idea of *in loco parentis* resulted in the dismissal of the suit. The court reasoned that parents had the right to punish students in any way that didn't result in significant physical harm. Therefore, teachers acting in place of the parents had the right to punish students in any way that didn't result in significant physical harm.

Obviously, embarrassment, mimicking, and other forms of punishment are not sound educational practices. They may lead to aggression or withdrawal. You should remember that the court did not condone the use of these procedures. It simply ruled that it was a matter for educators, not courts, to decide. Teachers should recognize that most professional codes of ethics specifically prohibit psychological abuse.

***Corporal Punishment.***    According to Wood and Lakin (1982), 45 states allow corporal punishment in their public schools. Court rulings (*New York Association for Retarded Children v. Carey*, 1975; *Davis v. Watkins*, 1974) prohibit its use in institutions. The U.S. Supreme Court (*Ingraham v. Wright*, 1977) ruled that corporal punishment was an acceptable part of discipline in schools.

Corporal punishment for handicapped students requires special considerations. First, severe corporal punishment for small, fragile, or health impaired students is dangerous. Serious injury may occur. Second, some students with severe disabilities may not understand why they are being punished. This is especially true when there is a delay in administering it. In North Carolina, a state court ruled that corporal punishment isn't permissible with retarded students. The only exception allowed is if it is in the student's IEP (*Haats v. McEachern*, 1985). West Virginia law prohibits corporal punishment of handicapped students. One teacher in Louisiana was put in jail for child abuse after striking a handicapped student (*Louisiana v. Spencer*, 1986).

Rose (1983) found that corporal punishment is widely used with behavior-disordered students. Behavior-disordered students are more likely to receive corporal punishment because of their high rates of disruptive behavior. Yet there is much research showing that corporal punishment has many undesirable side effects. Conversely, some mild forms of corporal punishment are effective for severely disabled students who engage in self-abusive behavior.

Although this author does not condone corporal punishment, there may be situations that warrant mild forms of punishment. Furthermore, in some states corporal punishment is routine and widespread. The following are guidelines for the use of punishment.

1. Use corporal punishment only as a last resort.

2. Take into consideration the age and condition of the student before using it.

3. Discontinue ineffective punishment.

4. Keep records on the use of corporal punishment.

5. Continuously monitor its effect.

*Noxious Stimulation.* Corporal punishment is usually not a systematic, preplanned, and predictable response to behavioral problems. Instead, it occurs when school authorities lose their patience with a student. It may follow a disruptive behavior one day and not the next. Under such conditions, it isn't possible to use corporal punishment as a sound scientific intervention for behavior-disordered students. Noxious stimulation, however, involves the systematic, consistent application of unpleasant stimuli, e.g., offensive odors or tastes. There has been much debate in the professional literature about the success and ethics of such procedures. These techniques have not been subject to court review until recently. A Massachusetts court ruled that a private agency serving students with severe behavioral disorders could resume the use of noxious stimuli. In this case, there was a state agency ban on using noxious stimuli. The court considered testimony by parents and professionals. They testified that the use of the procedures was a last resort and that other means were ineffective (*Behavior Research Institute, Inc. v. Leonard*, 1986).

Educators who work with the behavior disordered may encounter students, e.g., the self-abusive, who do not respond to techniques except those with unpleasant effects. When this occurs, an IEP or treatment team can consider using noxious stimuli. The team should follow these guidelines.

1. Make sure that there are no other alternatives.

2. Check state regulations about the use of aversive conditioning.

3. Develop a written procedure for the use of noxious stimuli.

4. Monitor the student's responses and stop the treatment if it is ineffective.

### Behavior Modification and Token Systems

A behavior modification system involving primary and secondary reinforcers is the most commonly employed intervention for students with behavioral disorders. At first glance, behavior modification systems and token economies may appear to be rather benign methods of intervention. There is potential for abuse, however. Again, token economies in institutions come under stricter scrutiny than those in public schools. Perhaps this is because the potential for abuse is greater in residential settings. Institutions provide residents with all basic necessities. There are many cases where residents of institutions lost access to food, clothing, a bed, recreation, therapy, or education in token economies (Defense Department, 1974; *Morales v. Turman*, 1974; *Wyatt v. Stickney*, 1972). Furthermore, in institutions, many of the staff have not been adequately trained to use token programs effectively and ethically (*Morales v. Turman*, 1974).

Based on many court decisions, state regulations, and research findings, the following are some guidelines for legal and ethical token systems.

1. Token economies should stress goals that foster individual development rather than group or institutional convenience (Martin, 1975).

2. Limit the range reinforcers. Students in schools and residents in institutions should not have to earn basic necessities. In institutions, necessities are food, clothing, shelter, and treatment. In educational settings, students have a right to the prescribed educational program. Access to classes that are part of the program should not be contingent upon performance in the token program. This would violate the Fourteenth Amendment.

3. People who administer token programs must have thorough training in behavior modification procedures, record keeping, and analysis. Token programs also need regular review from professionals and human rights committees (*Wyatt v. Stickney*, 1972).

4. Keep thorough records.

5. Stress positive reinforcement over punishment. Use punishment only when positive methods have failed repeatedly.

6. Teachers should ensure that all token and behavior modification programs are free of racial and sexual bias.

7. It appears that teachers have a right, acting *in loco parentis*, to prescribe a behavior modification program without the permission of the student or the parents. There has, however, never been a challenge of this in court. For ethical reasons, you should describe behavior management programs and include them in your IEPs.

8. Don't use behavior modification programs to reduce or eliminate behaviors that are legally protected, e.g., freedom of speech (Martin, 1975).

9. Behavior modification programs must not require students or residents to do work for which they are not paid, e.g., cleaning a school, tending to younger students. Such work is peonage and violates the Thirteenth Amendment, which prohibits involuntary servitude (*Souder v. Brennan*, 1973). This does not mean that students are not responsible for maintaining their work areas or helping their classmates. Intent is the primary factor in determining if work assigned to students is peonage. If the work is assigned primarily to benefit the school or institution, it is peonage. If assigned to teach the student or to correct a behavior, it is not peonage.

### Medical Interventions

Medical techniques include drug therapy and psychosurgery. Teachers can't prescribe medical treatment. However, in both educational and residential settings teachers influence the prescription of drugs. They also provide information about the success of drug treatment. There is a large body of conflicting literature about the efficacy of psychopharmacology. Most problems arise from using medication for punishment, as the sole means for therapy, or in large amounts for the purpose of excessive sedation (*Wyatt v. Stickney*, 1972).

When teachers work with medicated students, they should follow these guidelines:

1. Be aware of the expected effects of the drugs.

2. Watch for undesirable side effects.

3. Use objective measures when attempting to determine if the drugs are having the desired effect.

4. Refrain from making suggestions to place students on drugs.

## TORT LIABILITY

Teachers are responsible for students placed in their care. Their obligations include several things:

1. Supervision adequate for the activity at hand

2. Safety instruction

3. A set of rules for behavior

4. Systematic enforcement of rules.

Any breach of these obligations may lead to a tort action against the teacher. Students limited in intellect or physical abilities and those whose behavior is not predictable require special supervision. Below is a discussion of some of the common areas of tort liability and the implications for teachers of behavior-disordered students.

### Teacher Absence

Many court cases involve injury to students that occurred when a teacher was not present where students were working. Courts take the position that if the teacher's presence would have prevented the injury, then the teacher's absence is negligence. Several cases highlight the reasoning of the courts. In *Ohman v. Board of Education of the City of New York* (1949), a student was struck in the eye by a pencil thrown by another student. The court ruled the action of the student, i.e., throwing the pencil, was not predictable and could occur even with the teacher present. Therefore, the teacher was not negligent. Conversely, in *Schnell v. Travelers Insurance Company* (1972), a teacher placed a sixth-grade student in charge of a group of first-grade students. An injury to one of the students occurred during the teacher's absence. The court ruled that the teacher was negligent because first-grade students are likely to misbehave without proper supervision. Thus, the age of the students is critical in determining negligence. In the Ohman case the students were in junior high school; in the Schnell case they were in elementary school. The Rule of Seven suggests that young students are not responsible for their actions. Thus, adult supervision must be close and continuous.

Teachers in public and private schools enjoy a greater degree of immunity from negligence suits than do employees of psychiatric facilities. In *Evans v. New York* (1986), a psychiatric patient received an award for damages after an attacked by another patient. The court ruled that psychiatric hospitals must provide greater supervision than schools and are not immune to lawsuits under the doctrine of sovereign immunity. Sovereign immunity is an idea that exists to varying degrees in all states. It provides protection from lawsuits to public employees who are operating within the scope of their employment.

Teachers who work with behavior-disordered students should adhere to the following guidelines for supervision.

1. Always supervise young students or students who have a history of disruptive or aggressive behavior.

2. Dangerous activities, e.g., field trips, industrial arts, and playground, should be closely supervised.

3. Older students (above 16) may usually be left unsupervised for brief periods. This is true, however, only if there is no history of dangerous behavior, and the current activity is not inherently dangerous. Still, all teachers should provide supervision at all times except when it isn't possible.

4. When you are training students for independence, e.g., transition and community living programs supervision should gradually be reduced. Observe and record the responses of the students and reintroduce stricter supervision if the student's behavior deteriorates (*Hunter v. Evergreen Presbyterian Vocational School*, 1976).

### Aggressive Students

Courts have ruled that teachers and other professionals may be liable for the injuries suffered by a student assaulted by another student. This is especially true when the assaulting student has a history of aggression. It is also true when some tension was apparent between the students (*Evans v. New York*, 1986; *Lauricella v. Board of Education of the City of Buffalo*, 1976; *Raleigh v. Independent School District*, 1978).

When professionals work with psychiatric patients, they are responsible for their safety. In two cases (*Evans v. New York*, 1986; *Gobel v. New York*, 1986) professionals were liable for injuries suffered by psychiatric residents at the hands of other residents. The extent of liability for educators in schools may be less than in psychiatric facilities. However, a recent decision (*Phyllis P. v. Superior Court*, 1986) awarded damages when a principal and a teacher covered up a sexual assault.

Clearly, students with behavioral disorders are likely to engage in assaultive behaviors. Therefore, You should take the following precautions:

1. Always supervise students with a history of assaultive behavior.

2. Take steps to ensure supervision in hallways and rest rooms whenever students are present or whenever tension exists between two or more students.

3. Report all assaults to school officials and parents.

### Defamation

Teachers control much information about the students in their classes. Legislative (*Family Educational Rights and Privacy Act*, 1974) and litigation (*Blair v. Union Free School District Number 6, Hauppauge*, 1971; *Vigil v. Rice*, 1964) require teachers to protect the confidentiality of information. They must also ensure that information is accurate, objective, and free of malice. Teachers who divulge information about students to neighbors or friends are guilty of a breach of confidentiality. Teachers who make subjective, malicious comments about students are guilty of slander or libel.

The following three guidelines should protect you from charges of breach of confidentiality or defamation:

1. Maintain all educational records in a secure place.

2. Do not share information about students with anyone outside the school or institution. Limit access to information in the school or institution to those people who are working with the student.

3. When entering information in educational records, make it factual and objective. For example, say "Johnny struck Melinda twice," not "Johnny is a bully."

### Child Abuse

Every state has a law requiring teachers to report child abuse. Failure to report abuse can result in both civil and criminal charges (*Doe v. Special School District of St. Louis County*, 1986; *Louisiana v. Spencer*, 1986).

Laws protect teachers who report child abuse against charges of defamation from the suspected abuser. You have this protection as long as your report was made in good faith. You should only make reports based on observations of the child's condition and concern for the child's welfare. You should never file a report with malicious intent, i.e., with an intent to harm the accused.

## CONCLUSION

Teachers of behavior-disordered students are especially vulnerable to lawsuits. This is because behavior-disordered students are especially vulnerable to injury and abuse. Knowledge of the law is a good way to protect yourself from suits. The best protection, however, is to abide by a good professional code of ethics and standards of practice (see Appendix A). Most courts are unwilling to challenge educational practices supported by research and professional organizations. Most of the sections presented in this chapter conclude with a discussion of guidelines for professional conduct. These are guidelines based on court rulings, state and federal regulations, codes of ethics, and research. They are not exhaustive. Every professional must operate within the rules and procedures of the employing organization. When critical rules or procedures do not exist, the wise professional lobbies for their creation. The absence of a procedure places the burden on the individual to decide what is prudent conduct.

Many of the cases discussed in this chapter have occurred during the last 10 to 15 years. The development of new techniques will result in new cases. As treatments for students with behavior disorders becomes more effective and complex, professionals will have to adhere to new standards. The wise professional will maintain a current knowledge base in his or her specialty area. This should include both practices and legal requirements.

## REFERENCES

BARNETTE, S. M., & PARKER, L. G. (1982). Suspension and expulsion of the emotionally handicapped: Issues and practices. *Behavioral Disorders, 7*(3), 173-179.

BAUER, G. L. (1985). Restoring order to the public schools. *Phi Delta Kappan, 66*(7), 488-491.

BEHAVIOR RESEARCH INSTITUTE, INC. v. LEONARD, No. 86E 0018-G 1 (Massachusetts Probation & Family Court, Bristol City, June 4, 1986).

BLAIR V. UNION FREE SCHOOL DISTRICT NUMBER 6, Hauppauge, 324 NYS 2d. 222 (1971).

BLUE V. NEW HAVEN BOARD OF EDUCATION, No 81-41 (D. Conn, Mar. 23, 1981).

BOARD OF EDUCATION OF THE CITY OF PEORIA V. ILLINOIS STATE BOARD OF EDUCATION, No 81-1125 (C.D. Il, Feb. 4, 1982).

BROWN V. BOARD OF EDUCATION, 347 U.S. 483 (1954).

CAMPBELL, N., DOBSON, J., & BOST, J. 1985). Educator perceptions of behavior problems of mainstreamed students. *Exceptional Children, 51*(4), 298-303

CENTER, D. B. (1986). *Expulsion and suspension of handicapped students.* Reston, VA: Educational Document Retrieval Service. (ED 274 069)

CENTER, D., & McKITTRICK, S. (1987). Disciplinary removal of special education students. *Focus on Exceptional Children, 20*(2), 1-10.

CONNORS, E. T. (1981). *Educational Tort Liability and Malpractice.* Bloomington, IN: Phi Delta Kappa.

DAVIS V. WATKINS, 384 F. Supp. 1196 (1974).

DEFENSE DEPARTMENT CHAMPUS PROGRAMS (1974). Permanent Subcommittee on Investigations,

Committee on Government Operations, United States Senate, Ninety-Third Congress, Second Session, July, 23-26.

DOE V. SPECIAL SCHOOL DISTRICT OF ST. LOUIS COUNTY, 637 F. Supp. 1138 (E.D. M. 1986).

EVANS V. NEW YORK, 497 NYS 2d. 949 (1986).

THE FAMILY EDUCATIONAL RIGHTS AND PRIVACY ACT (Buckley Amendment) 20 U.S.C. 1232 (1974).

GAST, D. L., & NELSON, C. M. (1977). Legal and ethical considerations for the use of timeout in special education settings. *Journal of Special Education, 11*, 457-467.

GOBEL V. NEW YORK, 507 NYS2d. 35 (N.Y. App. Div., 1986).

GORDON V. OAK PARK SCHOOL DISTRICT #97, 320 N.E.2d. 389 (1974).

GOSS V. LOPEZ, 95 S.Ct. 729 (1975).

GUYTEN V. RHODES, 29 N.E.2d 444 (1940).

HAATS V. McEACHERN, No. 85-106-Civ. 3 (E.D. N.C. Oct. 29, 1985).

HINDMAN, S. E. (1986). The law, the courts, and the education of behaviorally disordered students. *Behavioral Disorders, 11*(4), 280-289.

HONIG V. DOE, U.S. Supreme Court, January, 1988.

HUNTER V. EVERGREEN PRESBYTERIAN VOCATIONAL School, 338 S.2d. 164 (1976).

HUNTZE, S. L. (1985). A position paper of the Council for Children with Behavioral Disorders. *Behavioral Disorders, 10*(3), 167-173.

INGRAHAM V. WRIGHT, 430 U. S. 651 (1977).

JACKSON V. FRANKLIN COUNTY SCHOOL BOARD, 606 F. Supp. 152 (S.D. Miss. 1985).

KAELIN V. GRUBBS 632 F.2d. 595 (6th Cir. 1982).

KERR, M. M., & NELSON, C. M. (1983). *Strategies for Managing Behavior Problems in the Classroom.* Columbus, OH: Merrill.

LAURICELLA V. BOARD OF EDUCATION OF CITY OF BUFFALO, 231 NYS 2d 566 (1976).

LOPEZ V. SALIDA SCHOOL DISTRICT, CA No. C-73078, Dist. County Ct. of Denver (Jan 20, 1978).

LOUISIANA V. SPENCER, 486 S.2d. 870 (La. Ct. App., 1986).

MARTIN, R. (1975). *Legal Challenges to Behavior Modification.* Champaign, IL: Research Press.

McAFEE, J. K. (1985a). Discipline, special education and students rights. *Information Edge, 1*(4), 1, 4.

McAFEE, J. K. (1985b). Liability in early childhood special education. *Topics in Early Childhood Special Education, 5*(1), 39-51.

McAFEE, J. K. (1987). Emerging issues in special education tort liability: Implications for special educators and teacher trainers. *Teacher Education and Special Education, 10*(2), 47-57.

MORALES V. TURMAN, 383 F. Supp. 53 (E.D. Tex. 1974).

MRS. A. J. V. SPECIAL SCHOOL DISTRICT No. 1, 478 F. Supp. 418 (D. Minn. 1979).

NEW YORK ASSOCIATION FOR RETARDED CHILDREN V. CAREY, 393 F. Supp. 715 (E.D. N.Y. 1975).

NOBLIT, G. W., & SHORT, P. M. (1985). Rhetoric and reality in in-school suspension programs. *The High School Journal, 68*(2), 59-64.

OHMAN V. BOARD OF EDUCATION OF THE CITY OF NEW YORK, 90 N.E.2d. 474 (1949).

PHILIP PRATT V. BOARD OF EDUCATION OF FREDERICK COUNTY, 501 F. Supp. 232, (D.D. M. 1980).

PHYLLIS P. V. SUPERIOR COURT, 228 Cal. Rptr. 776 (Cal App. 2 Dist. 1986).

RALEIGH V. INDEPENDENT SCHOOL DISTRICT, 275 N.W. 2d 572 (1978).

ROGERS V. OKIN 638 F. Supp. 934 (D. Mass. 1986).

ROSE, T. L. (1983). A survey of corporal punishment of mildly handicapped students. *Exceptional Education Quarterly,* 3, 9-19. S - 1 v. Turlington, 635 F. 2d 342 (1981).

SCHNELL V. TRAVELERS INSURANCE COMPANY, 264 So. 2d 346 (1972).

SCHOOL BOARD OF PRINCE CITY V. MALINE, 762 F 2d 1210 (4th Cir. 1985).

SOUNDER V. BRENNAN, 367 F. Supp. 808 (D.C. 1973).

STUART V. NAPPI, 443 F. Supp. 1235 (1978).

THURSTON, P. W. (1982). Torts. In P. K. Piele (Ed.) *The Yearbook of School Law* (pp. 182-208). Topeka, KS: National Organization of Legal Problems of Education.

VIGIL V. RICE, 397 P. 2d 719 (1964).

WOOD, F. H., & LAKIN, K. C. (Eds.) (1982). *Punishment and Aversive Stimulation in Special Education: Legal, Theoretical, and Practical Issues in Their Use With Emotionally Disturbed Children and Youth.* Reston, VA: council for Exceptional Children.

WYATT V. STICKNEY, 344 F. Supp. 373, 344 F. Supp. 387 (M.D. Ala. 1972).

# APPENDIX A

## CODE OF ETHICS AND STANDARDS FOR PROFESSIONAL PRACTICE*

Adopted by the CEC Delegate Assembly, April 1983

■ Standards of a profession are formally codified sets of beliefs. As such, they should be based upon universal ethical principles. In the standards that follow, special education professionals charge themselves with obligations to three parties: the exceptional student, the employer, and the profession. Ethical responsibilities in these three areas have been translated into eight principles which form the basis for all professional conduct. These eight principles comprise the *Code of Ethics* for special educators. They, in turn, have been translated into a set of minimum standards of conduct called *Standards for Professional Practice*. Taken together, the code of ethics and standards for practice provide guidelines for professional etiquette, for effective interpersonal behavior, for resolution of ethical issues, and for making professional judgments concerning what constitutes competent practice.

## CEC Code of Ethics

We declare the following principles to be the Code of Ethics for educators of exceptional persons. Members of the special education profession are responsible for upholding and advancing these principles. Members of The Council for Exceptional Children agree to judge by them in accordance with the spirit and provisions of this Code.

I. Special education professionals are committed to developing the highest

*From The Council for Exceptional Children, 1983, *Exceptional Children*, 50(3), 205–209.

educational and quality of life potential of exceptional individuals.

II. Special education professionals promote and maintain a high level of competence and integrity in practicing their profession.

III. Special education professionals engage in professional activities which benefit exceptional individuals, their families, other colleagues, students, or research subjects.

IV. Special education professionals exercise objective professional judgment in the practice of their profession.

V. Special education professionals strive to advance their knowledge and skills

regarding the education of exceptional individuals.

VI. Special education professionals work within the standards and policies of their profession.

VII. Special education professionals seek to uphold and improve where necessary the laws, regulations, and policies governing the delivery of special education and related services and the practice of their profession.

VIII. Special education professionals do not condone or participate in unethical or illegal acts, nor violate professional standards adopted by the Delegate Assembly of CEC.

# CEC Standards for Professional Practice

## 1. PROFESSIONALS IN RELATION TO EXCEPTIONAL PERSONS AND THEIR FAMILIES

### 1.1 Instructional Responsibilities

1.1.1 Special education personnel are committed to the application of professional expertise to ensure the provision of quality education for all exceptional individuals. Professionals strive to:

1.1.1.1 Identify and use instructional methods and curricula that are appropriate to their area of professional practice and effective in meeting the needs of exceptional persons.

1.1.1.2 Participate in the selection of and use appropriate instructional materials, equipment, supplies, and other resources needed in the effective practice of their profession.

1.1.1.3 Create safe and effective learning environments which contribute to fulfillment of needs, stimulation of learning and of self-concept.

der specific conditions of written consent and statutory confidentiality requirements.

### 1.2 Management of Behavior

1.2.1 Special education professionals participate with other professionals and with parents in an interdisciplinary effort in the management of behavior. Professionals:

1.2.1.1 Apply only those disciplinary methods and behavioral procedures which they have been instructed to use and which do not undermine the dignity of the individual or the basic human rights of exceptional persons (such as corporal punishment).

1.2.1.2 Clearly specify the goals and objectives for behavior management practices in the exceptional person's Individualized Education Program.

1.2.1.3 Conform to policies, statutes, and rules established by state/provincial and local agencies relating to judicious application of disciplinary methods and behavioral procedures.

1.1.1.4 Maintain class size and caseloads which are conducive to meeting the individual instructional needs of exceptional persons.

1.1.1.5 Use assessment instruments and procedures that do not discriminate against exceptional persons on the basis of race, color, creed, sex, national origin, age, political practices, family or social background, sexual orientation, or exceptionality.

1.1.1.6 Base grading, promotion, graduation, and/or movement out of the program on the individual goals and objectives for the exceptional individual.

1.1.1.7 Provide accurate program data to administrators, colleagues, and parents, based on efficient and objective record-keeping practices, for the purpose of decision making.

1.1.1.8 Maintain confidentiality of information except where information is released un-

1.2.1.4 Take adequate measures to discourage, prevent, and intervene when a colleague's behavior is perceived as being detrimental to exceptional persons.

1.2.1.5 Refrain from aversive techniques unless repeated trials of other methods have failed and then only after consultation with parents and appropriate agency officials.

## 1.3 Support Procedures

1.3.1 Adequate instruction and supervision shall be provided to professionals before they are required to perform support services for which they have not been previously prepared.

1.3.2 Professionals may administer medication, where state/provincial policies do not preclude such action, if qualified to do so or if written instructions are on file which state the purpose of the medication, the conditions under which it may be administered, possible side effects, the physician's name and phone number, and the professional liability if a mistake is made. The professional will not be required to administer medication.

1.3.3 Professionals note and report to those concerned whenever changes in behavior occur in conjunction with the administration of medication or at any other time.

## 1.4 Parent Relationships

1.4.1 Professionals seek to develop relationships with parents based on mutual respect for their roles in achieving benefits for the exceptional person. Special education professionals:

1.4.1.1 Develop effective communication with parents, avoiding technical terminology, using the primary language of the home, and other modes of communication when appropriate.

1.4.1.2 Seek and use parents' knowledge and expertise in planning, conducting, and evaluating special education and related services for exceptional persons.

1.4.1.3 Maintain communications between parents and professionals with appropriate respect for privacy and confidentiality.

1.4.1.4 Extend opportunities for parent education, utilizing accurate information and professional methods.

1.4.1.5 Inform parents of the educational rights of their children and of any proposed or actual practices which violate those rights.

1.4.1.6 Recognize and respect cultural diversities which exist in some families with exceptional persons.

1.4.1.7 Recognize that the relationship of home and community environmental conditions affects the behavior and outlook of the exceptional person.

## 1.5 Advocacy

1.5.1 Special education professionals serve as advocates for exceptional persons by speaking, writing, and acting in a variety of situations on their behalf. Professionals:

1.5.1.1 Continually seek to improve government provisions for the education of exceptional persons while ensuring that public statements by professionals as individuals are not construed to represent official policy statements of the agency by which they are employed.

1.5.1.2 Work cooperatively with and encourage other professionals to improve the provision of special education and related services to exceptional persons.

1.5.1.3 Document and objectively report to their supervisors or administrators inadequacies in resources and promote appropriate corrective action.

1.5.1.4 Monitor for inappropriate placements in special education and intervene at the appropriate level to correct the condition when such inappropriate placements exist.

1.5.1.5 Follow local, state/provincial, and federal laws and regulations which mandate a free appropriate public education to exceptional students and the protection of the rights of exceptional persons to equal opportunities in our society.

## 2. PROFESSIONAL EMPLOYMENT

### 2.1 Certification and Qualification

2.1.1 Professionals ensure that only persons deemed qualified by having met state/provincial minimal standards are employed as teachers, administrators, and related-service providers for persons with exceptionalities.

### 2.2 Employment

2.2.1 Professionals do not discriminate in hiring on the basis of race, color, creed, sex, national origin, age, political practices, family or social background, sexual orientation, or exceptionality.

2.2.2 Professionals represent themselves in an ethical and legal manner in regard to their training and experience when seeking new employment.

2.2.3 Professionals give notice consistent with local education agency policies when intending to leave employment.

2.2.4 Professionals adhere to the conditions of a contract or terms of an appointment in the setting where they practice.

2.2.5 Professionals released from employment are entitled to a written explanation of the reasons for termination and to fair and impartial due process procedures.

2.2.6 Special education professionals share equitably the opportunities and benefits (salary, working conditions, facilities, and other resources) of other professionals in the school system.

2.2.7 Professionals seek assistance, including the services of other professionals, in instances where personal problems threaten to interfere with their job performance.

2.2.8 Professionals respond objectively when requested to evaluate applicants seeking employment.

2.2.9 Professionals have the right and responsibility to resolve professional problems by utilizing established procedures, including grievance procedures when appropriate.

### 2.3 Assignment and Role

2.3.1 Professionals should receive clear written communication of all duties and responsibilities, including those which are prescribed as conditions of their employment.

2.3.2 Professionals promote educational quality and intra- and interprofessional cooperation through active participation in the planning, policy development, management, and evaluation of the special education program and the education program at large so that programs remain responsive to the changing needs of exceptional persons.

2.3.3 Professionals practice only in areas of exceptionality, at age levels, and in program models for which they are prepared by reason of training and/or experience.

2.3.4 Adequate supervision of and support for special education professionals is provided by other professionals qualified by reason of training and experience in the area of concern.

2.3.5 The administration and supervision of special education professionals provides for clear lines of accountability.

2.3.6 The unavailability of substitute teacher or support personnel, including aides, must not result in the denial of special education services to a greater degree than to that of other educational programs.

## 2.4 Professional Development

2.4.1 Special education professionals systematically advance their knowledge and skills in order to maintain a high level of competence and response to the changing needs of exceptional persons by pursuing a program of continuing education including but not limited to participation in such activities as inservice training, professional conferences/workshops, professional meetings, continuing education courses, and the reading of professional literature.

2.4.2 Professionals participate in the objective and systematic evaluation of themselves, colleagues, services, and programs for the purpose of continuous improvement of professional performance.

2.4.3 Professionals in administrative positions support and facilitate professional development.

## 3. PROFESSIONALS IN RELATION TO THE PROFESSION AND TO OTHER PROFESSIONALS

### 3.1 To the Profession

3.1.1 Special education professionals assume responsibility for participating in professional

organizations and adherence to the standards and codes of ethics of those organizations.

3.1.2 Special education professionals have a responsibility to provide varied and exemplary supervised field experiences for persons in undergraduate and graduate preparation programs.

3.1.3 Special education professionals refrain from using professional relationships with students and parents for personal advantage.

3.1.4 Special education professionals take an active position in the regulation of the profession through use of appropriate procedures for bringing about changes.

3.1.5 Special education professionals initiate support and/or participate in research related to the education of exceptional persons with the aim of improving the quality of educational services, increasing the accountability of programs, and generally benefiting exceptional persons. Professionals:

3.1.5.1 Adopt procedures that protect the rights and welfare of subjects participating in research.

3.1.5.2 Interpret and publish research results with accuracy and a high quality of scholarship.

3.1.5.3 Support a cessation of the use of any research procedure which may result in undesirable consequences for the participant.

3.1.5.4 Exercise all possible precautions to prevent misapplication or misuse of a research effort, by oneself or others.

### 3.2 To Other Professionals

3.2.1 Special education professionals function as members of interdisciplinary teams and the reputation of the profession resides with them. Professionals:

3.2.1.1 Recognize and acknowledge the competencies and expertise of members representing other disciplines as well as those of members in their own disciplines.

3.2.1.2 Strive to develop positive attitudes among other professionals toward exceptional persons, representing them with an objective regard for their possibilities and their limitations as persons in a democratic society.

3.2.1.3 Cooperate with other agencies involved in serving exceptional persons through such activities as the planning and coordination of information exchanges, service delivery, and evaluation and training, so that no duplication or loss in quality of services may occur.

3.2.1.4 Provide consultation and assistance, where appropriate, to both regular and special education as well as other school personnel serving exceptional persons.

3.2.1.5 Provide consultation and assistance, where appropriate, to professionals in non-school settings serving exceptional persons.

3.2.1.6 Maintain effective interpersonal relations with colleagues and other professionals, helping them to develop and maintain positive and accurate perceptions about the special education profession.

# APPENDIX B

# RESOURCE PUBLISHERS' ADDRESSES

Academic Press, Inc.
1250 Sixth Avenue
San Diego, CA 92101

Addison-Wesley Publishing Co., Inc.
Rte. 128
Reading, MA 01867

Allyn and Bacon, Inc.
7 Wells Avenue
Newton, MA 02159

Aspen Systems Corp.
1600 Research Boulevard
Rockville, MD 20850

Brunner/Mazel, Inc.
19 Union Square W
New York, NY 10003

Cascade Press
Book by Gerald Kranzler was
printed by Cascade Press
but distributed by Gerald Kranzler
Division of Developmental Studies
and Services
University of Oregon
Eugene, OR 97401

Cedars Press, Inc.
P.O. Box 351
Columbus, OH 43229

College-Hill Press
4284 41st Street
San Diego, CA 92105

Coronado Publishers
1250 Sixth Avenue
San Diego, CA 92101

Council for Exceptional Children
1920 Association Drive
Reston, VA 22091

Delaware County Public Schools
Secondary Mainstream Program
309 South Middletown Road
Media, PA 19063

Developmental Learning Materials
P.O. Box 4000
One DLM Park
Allen, TX 75002

Dialogue Books
Responsible Action Press
P.O. Box 924
Davis, CA 95616

Encyclopedia Britannica Educational Corp.
Reference Division
425 North Michigan Avenue
Chicago, IL 60611

Greenhaven Press, Inc.
577 Shoreview Park Road
St. Paul, MN 55126

Guidance Associates
Communications Park
Box 3000
Mount Kisco, NY 10549

Guilford Press
72 Spring Street
New York, NY 10012

Holt, Rinehart and Winston, Inc.
Orlando, FL 32887

H & H Enterprises, Inc.
P.O. Box 3342
Lawrence, KS 66044

Human Sciences Press, Inc.
Behavioral Publications, Inc.
72 Fifth Avenue
New York, NY 10011

Institute for the Advancement of
Philosophy for
Children
Montclair State College
Upper Montclair, NJ 07043

Institute for Rational-Emotive
Therapy
45 Cast 65th Street
New York, NY 10021

Irvington Publishers, Inc.
551 5th Ave.
New York, NY 10176

Jossey-Bass, Inc., Publishers
433 California Street
San Francisco, CA 94104

Judge Baker Guidance Center
295 Longwood Avenue
Boston, MA 02115

Longman, Inc.
Longman Building
95 Church Street
White Plains, NY 10601

Love Publishing Company
1777 South Bellaire Street
Denver, CO 80222

Merrill Publishing Company
963 Eastwind Drive
Westerville, OH 43081

Milliken Publishing Company
P.O. Box 21579
1100 Research Boulevard
St. Louis, MO 63132

Moral Education and Research Foun-
dation
Harvard University
Cambridge, MA 02138

Oxford University Press, Inc.
200 Madison Avenue
New York, NY 10016

Pergamon Press, Inc.
Maxwell House, Fairview Park
Elmsford, NY 10523

Plenum Publishing Corp.
233 Spring Street
New York, NY 10013

PRO-ED
5341 Industrial Oak Boulevard
Austin, TX 78735

Project STILE
Lawrence High School
2017 Louisiana Street
Lawrence, KS 66044

Research Press
2612 North Mattis Avenue
Champaign, IL 61821

Science Research Associates, Inc.
155 North Wacker Drive
Chicago, IL 60606

University of Iowa Press
Graphic Services Building
Iowa City, IA 52242

University of Melbourne
Department of Education
Melbourne, Australia

University Park Press
300 North Charles Street
Baltimore, MD 21201

University Press of America, Inc.
4720 Boston Way
Lanham, MD 20706

VOC-AIM
27475 Golden Gate West
Lathrup Village, MI 40876

John Wiley & Sons, Inc.
605 Third Avenue
New York, NY 10158

# INDEX

## NAME

## SUBJECT